MEDIEVAL PANORAMA

VOL. I. FOREGROUND:
SOCIETY AND INSTITUTIONS

Too many of the really important and enduring books in the fields of history, literature, philosophy, science, archæology and art are not obtainable at prices which the reader can easily afford. The aim of the Fontana Library is to make available in a pleasing format at a low price books which are both intelligible to the layman and indispensable to the scholar.

THE FONTANA LIBRARY

WALTER PATER: *The Renaissance*

BERNHARD BERENSON
The Italian Painters of the Renaissance

EMILE MÂLE: *The Gothic Image*

F. W. MAITLAND: *Domesday Book and Beyond*

G. G. COULTON: *Medieval Panorama*
Vol. I: Foreground: Society and Institutions
Vol. II: The Horizons of Thought

LORD ACTON: *Lectures on Modern History*

H. A. L. FISHER: *A History of Europe*
Vol. I: From the Earliest Times to 1713
Vol. II: From the Beginning of the 18th Century to 1935

ARTHUR BRYANT: *Pepys*
Vol. I: The Man in the Making
Vol. II: The Years of Peril
Vol. III: The Saviour of the Navy

EDMUND WILSON: *Axel's Castle*

EDMUND WILSON: *To the Finland Station*

R. H. TAWNEY: *The Acquisitive Society*

MARIO PRAZ: *The Romantic Agony*

L. DUDLEY STAMP: *Britain's Structure and Scenery*

SIR E. JOHN RUSSELL: *The World of the Soil*

JOHN OMAN: *Grace and Personality*

MARTIN BUBER: *Between Man and Man*

WILLIAM JAMES
The Varieties of Religious Experience

RUDOLF BULTMANN: *Primitive Christianity*

G. G. COULTON

MEDIEVAL PANORAMA

VOL. I

Foreground:
Society and Institutions

Collins

THE FONTANA LIBRARY

First published by the Cambridge University Press 1938
First issued in Fontana Library 1961

Printed in Great Britain
Collins Clear-Type Press
London & Glasgow

CONTENTS

Contents (*cont.*)

PREFACE

He that contemneth small things shall fall by little and little
(ECCLESIASTICUS, xiv 1)

Almost three generations ago, Carlyle complained that historians seldom tell us how our forefathers actually lived and thought: " What all want to know is the condition of our fellow-men; and, strange to say, it is the thing of all least understood, or to be understood as matters go." Even in those days, no doubt, the public had Macaulay's classical Third Chapter; and J. R. Green's more recent work is priceless; but much more remains to do. Too rarely does any great archivist, like Siméon Luce, condescend (or, as some might say, rise) to pregnant exercises of imagination. The popularization of the linen shirt in the fourteenth century (argues Luce) marks not only an obvious advance in personal hygiene, but also an impetus presently given to the manufacture of rag-paper, and thus to literature; so that this century of social refinement became " the worthy precursor, or rather the indispensable preparative, of the age of printing ".* Right or wrong, a suggestion like this is certainly stimulating, and deserves our gratitude.

It may be natural and right that universities should spend more time and labour upon the collection and minute criticism of evidence than upon weaving the threads into historical tapestry. But the fact is so; although to-day's public thirsts more than ever, probably, for history that shall be picturesque, yet reasonably accurate. The intelligent reader—professional or business man or artisan, who has some leisure for quiet thoughtful browsing—is too often puzzled to see what it is all about, or is even driven to wonder whether the writer himself sees quite clearly. The Cinema has indeed stepped in to supply the demand, but only in its own garish fashion. The most

* *La Jeunesse de Bertrand du Guesclin* (1882), p. 64.

successful film can present little more than superficialities; moreover, even among these, there is an almost irresistible temptation to falsify the proportions for the sake of spectacular effect. For many years past I felt this very strongly. Then circumstances seemed practically to command "Now, or never": and this volume marks the reaction to that challenge. There is little here which I have not said already before widely different audiences, during the past thirty years. Much, I need hardly say, has been learned from pupils and critics. The book makes no pretence either to exhaustiveness or to finality. It tries to bring some sort of order into a mass of details, each interesting in itself, but resting necessarily, in most cases, upon other men's researches and judgments. It looks forward to correction and amplification by others; but it hopes to supply, for the time being, the sort of scaffolding which the author would have been very glad to find before him fifty years ago.

It is difficult, even at the present day, to find one's way through the medieval jungle without a good deal of direct axe-work; but those controversial matters are relegated as far as possible to the notes. References are given only for points on which the reader might wish to verify the statement for himself from the original record; or, again, where the subject is interesting enough to tempt him farther than I have found possible to go within my limited space.

My debts are too many to acknowledge here in full; but I must specially thank Professor G. R. Potter, Professor R. W. Chambers, Mr H. S. Bennett and Mr J. E. A. Jolliffe, who have read my proofs critically. The officials of the University Press have given me the most ungrudging help and invaluable advice.

G. G. COULTON

August 1938

INTRODUCTION

The true field of Historic Study is the history of those nations and institutions in which the real growth of humanity is to be traced: in which we can follow the developments, the retardations and perturbations, the ebb and flow of human progress, the education of the world, the leading on by the divine light from the simplicity of early forms and ideas where good and evil are distinctly marked, to the complications of modern life, in which light and darkness are mingled so intimately, and truth and falsehood are so hard to distinguish, but in which we believe and trust that the victory of light and truth is drawing nearer every day.

W. STUBBS, *Lectures on Medieval and Modern History* (1886), p. 83.

To many of us, and perhaps especially to those whose daily task is most modern and monotonous, the medieval scene brings all the charm of foreign travel. In both cases we find a change of sights and sounds, buildings and fashions of dress, work and play and gestures and accent, things commonplace to them, but holiday things for us. Thus the merest trivialities bewitch us away from the daily routine of home, revealing our own human nature in a fresh, and therefore refreshing light.

To borrow an almost inevitable simile, the reader may thus stand upon Malvern Hills, in the heart of England, and look down with the medieval dreamer William Langland upon the Field Full of Folk. Looking eastward and westward by turns, he may get a clear and balanced vision of the whole, and mark how the level and populous east shades off into the mountains of the scattered Western folk. Not, of course, that the Westward view is entirely mountainous, or the Eastward unbrokenly flat. Bredon rises almost in the Eastern foreground, and Malvern can listen to those Sunday bells which Housman has immortalized. Next come the Cotswolds, with Edgehill in the far distance; and then, beyond our bodily vision, those Eastern counties which, with their Fenland, were once the wealthiest and most populous of the Kingdom. Westward, again, we know that Snowdonia rises in the background, far overtopping these Black Mountains which close our view. Thus, however East and West may shade off into each other, yet as we stand here facing the rising sun there is a real gulf between the forward and the hindward landscape; a wide difference, in the mass, between Eastern or Western land, Eastern or Western folk. We must not exaggerate this; but we shall go still further astray if we ignore it. Geographically and historically, the division is real.

Again, though in the mass East differs thus from West, and Past from Present, yet each has its own interior differences which cannot be ignored. While insisting that there was once a distinctively medieval civilization, and therefore a medieval mind, a medieval character, we must not forget that this medievalism had its own variations from time to time and from place to place. Especially must we bear in mind that in this far-off world nothing *is* for more than a moment; everything is in process of *becoming*. The England of Edward III differed much from that of William I; and Henry VIII's England differed widely from both. This needs special emphasis in a volume like the present, where the necessary division into subjects rather than into periods renders it almost impossible to remind the reader of change at every turn. It is to be hoped that the constant supply of dates may enable him to trace for himself, if only roughly, both the extent to which medieval society was not static but organic, and also the actual trend of its evolution from 1066 to 1536.* Yet the matter is so important that it may be best to start here explicitly upon this note, and to sum up, in a few pages, the action of that long drama which will occupy my fifty-two formal chapters. What were the Seven Ages of this Medieval Man?

Roughly speaking, the Conquest made William into the

* Where dates are definite, they will be found in round brackets (); where they are only approximate, in square [].

Universal Landlord of England; the Battle of Hastings gave him the right of transferring confiscated Saxon lands to his Norman followers. But the Anglo-Saxon law, on the whole, suffered no violent interruption; though it was necessarily patched and amended and added to as time went on, yet it is still the foundation of English Common Law, upon which, again, the United States of America founded their own. Thus, when Abraham Lincoln saw that, to win the war, he must needs follow the example of the South and conscript all able-bodied men for his armies, this was done in virtue of the obligation which had been part of English Common Law from time immemorial, before the Conquest and afterwards.

With such important basis of law in common, the conquering minority and the conquered majority had practically coalesced within three generations. They were now strong and united enough to resist further invasion, and to work out their own political salvation undisturbed by forcible interference from interested outsiders. King and barons, here as on the Continent, struggled for supremacy: but the balance was nice enough in England to make both parties appeal for popular support; and thus the generally beneficent despotism of the earlier kings—altogether beneficent as compared with the anarchy which was then the only alternative—was gradually modified by those constitutional checks which are at the foundations of modern democracy.

In process of time, the Commons were summoned regularly to the King's council. They came at first merely to approve of what he decreed for them, on the old legal principle that "what concerns all should have the consent of all". Then, from at least 1314 onwards, they permit themselves a certain boldness of initiative, laying their petitions before the King. Presently we find that such petitions are fruitful; that they result in new royal Statutes. Then, we find the Commons bargaining with the Crown; taxes are voted in return for redress of grievances; and this is the thin end of that almost irresistible modern wedge, the Power of the Purse. The growing strength of the Commons is emphasized by the fact that, under a Common Law which made every man his own soldier and his own policeman, the King could never control the whole armed forces of the country with that directness with which they were controlled under hireling professional armies elsewhere. The depositions of Edward II and Richard II were done not only in legal form but with legal reason at their back. Even when medieval society began to disintegrate at the end of the fourteenth century, and a generation of civil wars set in, foreign observers admired the comparatively clean and decent prosecution of those quarrels in England; there was no *tertius gaudens* from the Continent to foment English civil wars for his own profit. When, again, a strong monarchy emerged under Henry VII and his descendants, this was far less despotic, far more considerate of popular opinion, than in any parallel case on the Continent.

Meanwhile the material progress, though slow and sometimes fitful, kept pace with the slow and fitful constitutional development; men felt the growing-pains; theory outran practice, and eager spirits experienced the sickness of hope deferred. But, gradually, forest and fen and fell were subdued to the plough; buildings increased in scale and in elaboration; even where the high-water-mark of taste was past in art, the wealth of ornament still increased. By 1500, the inventories of furniture and plate in our parish churches show double the value of those in 1300; for this, again, was part of the forward movement of the common folk. If one of William's Norman knights or his Saxon tenant could have seen Tudor England, the change in outward aspect would have bewildered him. So was it, again, with the inward organization, quite apart from Parliament and the Court. The growth of the Jury system was a great step: so, again, was the fourteenth-century development of Justices of the Peace, intermediary between the royal judges and the minor magistrates: "an extraordinary experiment in justice which was at once anti-feudal and a reversal of the hitherto universal trend towards centralization."*

So, again, with the rapidly increasing franchises of the

* J. E. A. Joliffe, *Constitutional History of Medieval England* (1937), p. 413.

towns, and their experiences in local self-government which bore rich fruit in the national councils of later generations. Then, as now, men were everywhere struggling to combine personal freedom with collective action and efficiency; and the sum-total was progress, if only that of a man who is pursuing a rainbow. There is a deep pathos for all generations in Dr. Salter's quiet remark about the Oxford citizens of 1199: the city obtained royal licence to elect a mayor, "and there seems to have been a general impression that to have a mayor would bring the millennium".† English trade had expanded by 1500 to a point which would have amazed the Conqueror. Modern capitalism had begun, and society had long since abandoned the original absolute prohibition of taking interest for moneys lent. Edward I had expelled the Jews; but the Christian usurer had not proved more merciful; soon, therefore, the State ceased to interest itself in the lender's soul, and set itself only to limit his rate of interest. As the citizen grew richer, and was proud to enrich his parish church with paintings or carvings or plate, so he became dress-proud for himself. Our later medieval satirists echo in substance, though in other words, Dante's yearning retrospect to the palmy days when great citizens were not ashamed to go girt with leather belts and clasps of bone. More simple and graceful forms of mantle and tunic, which had reigned even in the highest classes down to the latter half of the fourteenth century, gave way to a vulgar extravagance of form and colour; eccentricity often killed good taste. It seems fair to trace here a symptom of greater changes on the horizon: even where the old things were perfect in their own simpler fashion, men must needs have something newer for sheer novelty's sake. Archdeacons, on their visitations, would condemn a church as "too small and too dark": in other words, they would have had the little Norman or Early English building replaced by one in the new-fashioned Perpendicular style.

So much for the building: and the great institution itself, the Roman Church, had gone through a similar evolution. Throughout the period covered by this volume, Eastern and

† *Medieval Oxford* (1937), p. 49.

Western Christianity were eager rivals, and sometimes even bitter enemies; but this must not make us forget how much they always had in common. Though the break between pagan antiquity and medieval Christianity was neither so sudden nor so complete as is often imagined, yet the Middle Age was definitely a Christian era in a sense which cannot be predicated of preceding or of succeeding generations. The belief in one body of Scriptures and (though less uniformly) in one common tradition of Heaven and Hell, one ethical code, one common core of liturgical worship in spite of local variations, had leavened the whole of European thought and practice more deeply and widely than anything else. By William's time, the Western branch of this Church, the *Ecclesia Romana* as it constantly called itself both colloquially and officially, had become one of the completest examples of a Totalitarian State that history records. It claimed to swallow up and standardize all important variations, so that there should be only one Party, that of the State. For this end almost all means were justified; almost all were employed; and, for many generations at least, they were employed with success.

Yet before 1500, for all her greatness, this Church was in many ways out of touch with the "modern" world, to use an adjective which was in men's mouths from the twelfth century at least. In England, however, as compared with the Continent, the Church might claim to have run something of the orderly course which we have traced in our political institutions. Each, of course, acted and reacted on the other. The Conquest brought us strong prelates, some of them equally conspicuous for piety, and therefore a stricter discipline. The impulse for founding monasteries was almost stronger here, for five generations or more, than anywhere else. Even when the abbeys had become overloaded with riches, the English political and social atmosphere tempted less to that unabashed worldliness which disgraced so many Continental prince-bishops, prince-abbots, and monasteries into which none were admitted but scions of noble stock. Our prelates were among the most prominent lawyers, especially under Henry II and Edward I; thus the State reaped the great benefit of their help, in those days when learned laymen were almost non-existent. But the Church herself lost those men's individual services almost altogether; and the system of clerical lawyers, reprobated at first by Popes themselves, brought its final Nemesis. Great Churchmen were among the most prominent statesmen in the earlier fight for liberties, even when they, like the barons, were mainly and most directly concerned with the liberties of their own order. But, as time went on and the richer Church endowments went more and more systematically by royal appointment (apart from papal nominees who were often non-resident aliens), then prelates and archdeacons and rich rectors were increasingly degraded to the position of courtly tools or pettifoggers or clerical drudges. If the Churchman had not become so much of an ordinary politician, that division between clergy and laity would have been avoided of which our ancestors complained with increasing bitterness; and the Church herself, under Henry VIII, would have been far less vulnerable to the slings and arrows of baser political conflict.

Meanwhile, the Church's own beneficent work had raised up rivals against her. Such schools as existed had always been clerical, and the population had slowly begun to grow out of its primitive illiteracy. Before the end of the twelfth century, writing was entirely superseding oral tradition among the lawyers. By the thirteenth, manorial accounts were written everywhere, and manorial customs were frequently committed to parchment. The growing numbers of "copyholders" were peasants whose position at law depended primarily on a written "copy". Then, in the fourteenth century, while some of the countryfolk could see nothing better than to burn all the manorial records in revenge, others of their class, and still more among the citizens, were listening to the subversive doctrines of Wyclif and clamouring for an Open Bible. At the same time there was intensive multiplication of orthodox religious treatises and pious manuals for the people. This movement was enormously hastened on both sides by the invention of printing. Thus, before our period ends, the serious and resolute peasant or artisan is often in a position to form some religious judgment for himself; while the bishop or the University scholar has at his disposal, if he chooses to taste of it, the vast and epoch-making work of Erasmus.

Everything, therefore, is ripe for revolution in English thought by the time we come to 1536; and on the verge of that revolution we stop. The defeat of Roman Catholicism in this country, and the follies or crimes with which the revolutionaries sullied their victory, and the subsequent alternations of success or failure in a war of ideals which is not yet fought out, would belong to quite another story. In this volume, it is enough to attempt a picture of the social drama as it was acted between two crucial events in our early annals—the Norman Conquest and the Reformation.

1. THE CAULDRON OF GOD'S WRATH

We cannot deal with the civilization even of a single country at a definite period without a preliminary glance at the world-culture upon which it was grafted. Thus the Middle Ages can be rightly understood only as a period of convalescence—slow at best, and with continual relapses—from the worst catastrophe recorded in the whole history of the Western World.

The Roman Empire had begun with benevolent despotism, an active and fairly healthy body: it ended as an unwieldy machine. " Augustus, with his genius, succeeded in restoring not only the State but also the prosperity of the people; Diocletian and Constantine, on the other hand, doubtless against their own will, sacrificed the interests of the people to the salvation and security of the State "; such is the summary of the greatest modern authority on this subject.[1] The Empire was defended no longer by its old citizen armies, but by hirelings recruited mainly from the less settled frontier districts. Finances were disorganized; taxation pressed intolerably upon the middle class, and especially the yeoman-farmers, while multitudes lived upon the dole—*Panem et Circenses.* Literature and art showed less and less originality. A period of peace, unexampled in world-history for depth and duration, had not in this case made for higher civilization, by whichever of the current standards we may judge. Crude experience had belied the philosophic ideal. The Higher Pacifism, an active virtue, was too heavily alloyed with that passively defensive mood which claims the same title: War had still her victories, but Peace had not. What wrecked the Empire, as I shall presently try to show, was not such peace as Christ had preached, but, in part at least, the dilettantist patriotism which puts words before deeds. Men followed the line of least resistance, and called it peace. On the other hand, what carried the invading barbarians forward was not their brutality, but the energy and courage which are so often bound up with that vice. We may say of the Roman Empire that, as so often occurs in history, it was more concerned for peace than for justice.

Be that as it may, one thing is certain: the break-up of this vast Empire was followed by scenes of disorder, not only far more intense than what we have seen in the most unhappy districts of modern times, but prolonged for a period exceeding the worst that we can reasonably fear as a result of the present international rivalries and class-conflicts. Even in the comparatively fortunate East, and before the great barbarian invasions, Origen had struck a painfully modern note in his commentary on Matthew xxiv. 7-8. The earth, like the human body, must naturally decay before its final dissolution; and thence "it follows that, through lack of food, men should be stirred to greed and wars against those who suffer no want; and that, through comparison with others who abound in things needful, some men should rise against their fellows, and nation should fight against nation, and kingdom against kingdom. For it is not possible that, together with the lack of other things, there should also be a lack of men who have good sense, so that there should be no quiet and peaceful life among many folk; yet insurrections and quarrels and perturbations come to pass, sometimes through greed, sometimes again through covetousness of leadership, sometimes by reason of mad longing for vainglory, sometimes also through vainglorious greed of princes, who are not content with their own kingdoms but desire to extend their principalities and subdue many nations to themselves." Generations later, when the barbarians had burst in and Alaric the Goth had even taken Rome, men felt as though the sky had fallen. Jerome, who had played so great a part in the civilization of the Eternal City, wrote from his retreat at Bethlehem, in his Preface to Ezekiel: "No doubt all things born are doomed to die. . . . But who would have believed that Rome, victorious so oft over the universe, would at length crumble to pieces? . . . She who made slaves of the East has herself become a slave; and nobles once laden with riches come to little Bethlehem to beg. In vain I try to distract myself from the sight by turning to my books; I cannot fix my thoughts on them." The oppression and the tumult grew worse and worse; and we find St Gregory the Great, five generations later, writing in even deeper despair:[2] "What is there now, I ask, to please us in this world? Everywhere we see mourning and hear groans. Cities are destroyed, strong places are cast down, the fields are depopulated, and the land is become desert. No inhabitants remain on the land, and scarce any in the towns; yet even these scanty relics of humanity are beaten with daily and incessant stripes. Moreover, the scourge of God's justice resteth not, because men's guilty deeds have not been corrected even under this scourge. We see some led into bondage, others mutilated, others slain . . . nay, what is left of that Rome which once seemed mistress of the world? She is ground down with manifold and immeasurable pains by the desolation of her citizens, the pressure of her enemies, and the frequency of ruin; so that we see that fulfilled in her which Ezekiel saith against the city of Samaria: *Set on a pot, set it on, I say, and put water into it; heap together into it the pieces thereof*: and a little further: *The seething thereof is boiling hot, and the bones thereof are thoroughly sodden in the midst thereof*: and again: *Heap together the bones, which I will burn with fire; the flesh shall be consumed and the whole composition shall be sodden and the bones shall be consumed; then set it empty upon burning coals, that it may be hot and the brass thereof may be melted. . . .* For where is now the Senate, and where is the people? The bones have been dissolved and the flesh consumed; all pride of worldly dignity hath been extinguished in her. The whole composition of her is sodden, nevertheless even we, the few who are left, are yet daily oppressed with the sword and with innumerable tribulations. Let us say, therefore: *Set it empty upon burning coals,* for, seeing that the Senate is gone, the people have perished, and yet, among the few that are left, pain and groans are daily multiplied; now Rome stands empty upon the fire. Yet why do we speak thus of the men, when ruins multiply so sore that we see even the buildings destroyed? Wherefore it is aptly added concerning the now deserted city: *Let it be hot and let the brass thereof be melted*: for now the pot itself is being consumed wherein aforetime the flesh and bones were consumed; for since the men have failed the very walls are falling. But where are they who once rejoiced in her glory? . . . Boys and young men of the world and the sons of worldly folk flocked hither from every hand when they wished to profit in this world. No man now hasteneth hither for worldly profit; no mighty and violent man is now left to snatch his prey by oppression. . . . Moreover, whatsoever we say concerning the grinding of Rome to pieces we know to be repeated in all the cities of the world. For some cities are desolated by ruin, others consumed by the sword, others tormented with famine, others swallowed up by earthquakes. Let us, therefore, despise with all our heart this world, present or destroyed. Let us at least end our worldly longings with the end of the world."

Though Jerome's first cry had been one of despair, yet he laboured on as before for ten years longer; and his contemporary Augustine was nerved only to greater efforts by the fall of Rome. Augustine's greatest work, which dominated the whole Middle Ages, expressed the most vehement reaction against what so many others regarded as an irremediable disaster. Paganism was now raising its head again; men cried that this collapse had been due to Christianity, and that the one cure was to recant this modern heresy and go back to a Golden Age. In face of this, Augustine insisted that the true lesson was one of hope in the deepest sense. Rome, after all, had not lasted longer, and was not greater, than other empires which had perished before her; nor had she been so pure that we must look upon her fall as an irremediable loss. The city itself had been founded in fratricide. Its history had been stained by an endless succession of bloody wars, both foreign and civil; and when she had ruled supreme her hands had reeked with the blood of Christian martyrs. The first half of Augustine's *City of God* is thus devoted to destructive criticism; he exposes the Roman Pantheon in all its absurdity and immorality. On the other hand he fully admits all the true greatness that was to be found in her past, and claims Rome as the παιδαγωγός—half-nurse, half-tutor—providentially appointed to prepare the world for Christianity. Thence he passes to his main theme, the indestructibility of spiritual life. Rome had perished, as all earthly things are destined to perish; but the spirit is immortal. All the evils of this life fit together into a divinely-appointed scheme of trial; gradually the evil dies and the good survives. "There remaineth therefore a rest for the people of God"; upon that note, from the Epistle to the Hebrews, he concludes.

The immense and enduring influence of this book was due not only to its great literary merit, but also to the special needs of St Augustine's and many succeeding centuries. In coldest blood we may claim that this *City of God* expounds a true philosophy of history in the main. The dualism of its theme is, at bottom, true for all ages. There always has been this contrast between spirit and matter; between the visible existing institutions which we obey as a matter of present duty, and the future world which we hope for, to be built some day upon the ruins of what now exists. The problem is equally insistent at all periods of the world, though different ages state it in different terms. Augustine commended it with the eloquence of a deep and passionate soul, which had probed every corner of human nature, and with the uncompromising courage of a man ready to die for his opinions, in days when death was the too frequent fate of men who proclaimed the truth as they saw it. And, at that particular time, it is difficult to see how the world could have done better than to follow his lead. For we must try to visualize the void which Augustine strove to fill. In the earlier days of Graeco-Roman civilization, a man's duties were confined, in the main, within the four walls of his own little city. Righteousness meant to be in a right relation towards one's πόλις and its tutelary deities. Then, as city after city was swallowed up by Rome, the outlook widened: the righteous man was he who stood right with the Empire. Here, then, in that Empire, was a society which had often thrust aside all abstract considerations of morality or theology in its reliance upon its own greatness, and upon the comparative peace which that half-divine institution assured to all its citizens. But now Rome was sacked: the Empire was breaking up: sixty years later, it would cease to exist even in name. For the Western World, drifting now without rudder or compass, it was necessary to find some system of thought which not only accepted far wider responsibilities than the old (except, of course, the higher philosophies, which were held only by a few), but which should also be far more independent of outward and visible support from the State. In this, Augustine succeeded. Apart from his extraordinary knowledge of human nature, and his contagious earnestness and eloquence, his philosophy rested in the main upon an impregnable foundation; upon the assertion of the reliability of the spiritual life, and of its indestructibility. To cling to a Crucified Leader, to insist upon the truth of spiritual brotherhood among all mankind—a brotherhood which could not be broken by all the changes or revolutions of states or cities—to insist upon these truths was to steel the soul against all outward enemies; for everything was thus based upon the fundamental fact that outward failures may be turned to inward success; he that loseth his life shall find it. We cannot escape the fact that all real life is a great adventure; we are all either adventurers or sluggards.

Gibbon casts ridicule on Tertullian's boast, early in the third century, that a Christian mechanic will now give a ready answer to questions which have puzzled the wisest heads of antiquity. From one point of view the criticism is justified; such dogmatism often springs from the valour of ignorance. Yet century after century discovers for itself that truth is not a matter of naked intellect; that character is sometimes even more important for the conduct of life than scientific observation or rigid logic; that the world is ruled, and rightly ruled, almost more by the imponderables than by the ponderables. Gibbon's sneer, therefore, ignores a factor as important as that on which he himself rests; the factor admirably expressed in Robert Browning's *Christmas Eve and Easter Day*, where he gives an imaginary epitaph from a martyr's tomb in the Catacombs:

> *I was born sickly, poor and mean,*
> *A slave: no misery could screen*
> *The holders of the pearl of price*
> *From Cæsar's envy; therefore twice*

I fought with beasts, and three times saw
My children suffer by his law.
At last my own release was earned:
I was some time in being burned,
But at the close a Hand came through
The fire above my head, and drew
My soul to Christ, whom now I see.
Sergius, a brother, writes for me
This testimony on the wall—
For me, I have forgot it all.

Thus it was that the faith in a crucified carpenter revolutionized European civilization. It took more men out of themselves, and took them farther out of themselves, than any other recorded event in Western history, and, as most of us would think, in the history of the whole world. By whatever process, it fused into one single wire the main strands of pre-existing thought: Roman State Religion, Philosophy, Judaism, and the Oriental Cults. From the first it took its impressive ceremonial and system of government; from the second, higher speculation; from the Jews their monotheism, and from the Cults their mystic exaltation. Not, doubtless, without some of their weaker qualities also; not without State formalism and philosophic word-splitting and Jewish intolerance, and something of that temperamental licence which, in the Cults, put enthusiasm above morality. Yet these weaknesses came out mainly in the course of time, and with the dilution of the original impulse. Primitive Christianity was democratic, however autocratic the hierarchy may have finally become; it was spiritual at first, however rigid in its later institutionalism. Gibbon's and Tertullian's artisan had in many ways the valour of ignorance; but courage at least he had, and that is always one of the rarest of human virtues. He had a fire of mind and soul which took him out of those decadent dilettante surroundings; which compelled him to regard deeds rather than words, and brought him face to face with the problems of to-day and to-morrow. The first step in all learning is that of interest. Descartes, in that brief *Discours de la Méthode* which is often taken as the primer of modern philosophy, insists that the first and foremost requisite for the discovery of truth is not to be born with a great brain, nor to live in the happiest circumstances, but to have the determination of arriving, by hook or by crook, at such measure of truth as our own capacities can contain. From Socrates onwards, philosophy herself proclaims the superiority of character over what is called pure intellect.

So, at least, it would seem to have been in those days in which the fermentation of good and evil in Europe can be studied on so great a scale. Next to St Augustine's *City of God,* no book is more illuminating here than his *Confessions.* In this, he invented a new literary type: it is the first of formal autobiographies. But its historical value surpasses even the psychological: the story of this man's conversion shows us, incidentally, how Europe was converted. In the 8th book (chs. 2-6) he recounts the story of Victorinus, and that of the two young officers at Trier. The latter is perhaps the more striking tale; but the former teaches the deeper lesson. Here was a man, among the oldest and most learned professors at Rome, who had taught so many noble senators that he had even earned, in his lifetime, the honour of a statue in the Forum. His insatiable love of reading brought him at last to the Christian Scriptures; and he felt their force. He began to say privately to his friends, but quite plainly: "I am now at heart a Christian." But he still shrank from public conformity, and from the breach that this must make with his past. "Why need I do this? Does God ask us for more than our hearts?" Why, indeed, should he leave the marble temples, the accumulated statues and paintings of all the centuries, the stately ceremonial, the white-robed priest and the incense, the grave honourable well-born men and women, thronging the sanctuary? Why leave these people, whose mere conformity with the ancient ritual, however superficial or careless, grouped them round the daily sacrifice into a picture more impressive than any on the walls of the temple itself? for, though modern writers may claim that the Roman Mass-ritual is "art at full tide", yet Pagan worship, under that Southern sun, must have been even more picturesque. How could he leave all this, to go and worship, after the fashion of the Christians of those early days, in a little room bare of statues or pictures, bare even of all the rudest ornaments, where his own tailor's or shoemaker's son might be the celebrant of the new-fangled uncouth mysteries? Could he not accept all that was best of the new, without making so cruel a breach with the old? But Augustine tells us how the working of Victorinus's own thoughts gradually drove him out of all these excuses; how justly he feared to be denied in heaven by a Christ whom he had shrunk from confessing on earth. We read how he left his colleagues, his friends, his equals—left them to go on in their stately way which to them seemed the only part in life's pageant that could possibly be played by scholars and gentlemen—and, himself, made the most public possible profession of faith in the Christian conventicle. He accepted meekly what Clough's fastidious Oxford scholar calls "the horrible pleasure of pleasing inferior people", and suffered the crowd of cobblers and weavers to hail him as a brother in triumphant chorus —Victorinus! Victorinus!—while he made his public profession of faith and bowed his head to the baptizing priest.

Against this new spirit the Pagan reactionaries fought in vain. With all its faults, this Christian enthusiasm roused men from a past which, however dignified at its best, had often been scarcely more than a state of respectable stagnation. The economic historian Rostovzef, who will not be suspected of bias in this direction, writes most emphatically here:[3] "The watchwords of the State were oppression, coercion, and persecution; the maxims of the Church were love, compassion, and consolation. The Church, and she alone among the different religious communities, offered not only spiritual comfort but also practical assistance amidst the miseries of present life, while the State oppressed and persecuted the comforters."

In this Ezekiel-cauldron, seething over the fire of God's indignation, there was no practical contact between the Higher Paganism and the masses. Stoicism and Neoplatonism had lofty thoughts; but here was now a world in which exalted idealisms must stoop to conquer. We see this at its crudest in King Bogoris of Bulgaria [910], converted by the missionary Methodius whose artistic skill enabled him to paint the walls of the royal palace with realistic scenes of hell-fire and the eternal torments of unbelievers. Again it comes out, under a far more sympathetic form, in Bede's story of the conversion of King Edwin of Northumbria. After bishop Paulinus had pleaded Christianity before him, the Pagan high-priest, Coifi, assented approvingly, on the selfish grounds that these gods of his had never fitly rewarded his own merit. Then an old noble took up the word : " O king, I see the present life of man upon earth, in comparison with all that time which is dark to us, as when thou art sitting at supper in wintertide with thy warrior-chieftains and thy ministers, while the fire burns bright in the midst of the hall and spreads its warmth all around, and everywhere outside the furious gusts rage with sleet or snow; then comes a sparrow and flutters hastily through the hall, entering at one door and departing forthwith by another. For that brief space that he passes here within, he is sheltered from the wintry tempest; but that little respite of calm is quickly past; from the winter he came and to winter he returns forthwith, and is lost to thine eyes. Thus doth man's life pass for a while before our eyes; but that which shall come after, or which did come before, is to us altogether unknown. Therefore, if this new doctrine brings us more light upon this matter, it would seem right and just that we should follow it."[4]

In these two cases we see both the strength and the weakness of Christianity. It compelled men to face the future; and prevision is one of the matters in which man differs most from the lower animals, and the civilized man most from the uncivilized. But that picture of the future was distorted, in the Middle Ages and beyond, to an extent which brings its own retribution in modern times. Its strong point was that it gave greater faith in the future; the faith of St Paul and of the Epistle to the Hebrews. Life is a struggle, but that struggle is a trial under just conditions, and " there remaineth a rest for the people of God ". The weak point was that this faith was also bound up with the past, and a past which tended more and more to gain the upper hand. Man's chance of this Saints' Everlasting Rest was now made to depend upon his attitude towards past events and traditions; and the main deciding factor, according to this present creed, was his belief in the past at the moment when his soul quitted his body. This naturally threw an overwhelming weight upon the Church's Sacraments, and especially upon Extreme Unction. Thus sudden death was regarded, in spite of Christ's express words, as a special judgment of God; and burial in consecrated ground was sometimes denied to those who had died intestate. From this naturally followed two extremes of thought: two exaggerations in opposite directions. The thoughtless man, as priests complained, would plead, in defence of his irregular life, "Three words at the last will save me!" Disciplinarians, on the other hand, shocked at this prevailing levity, were driven into the conviction that the large majority of mankind must go to hell; we shall see that there was more unanimity on that point throughout the Middle Ages, and even beyond, than on a large number of the present-day questions at issue between the Roman and other Churches.

Christianity, interpenetrating Paganism, was much modified by Pagan influences, and in no matter more strongly than in this of heaven and hell. The few words of Christ on this subject were now interpreted in a fiercely literal sense in which the Jews of His own day would not have understood them. The infernal pains of Graeco-Roman poetry, which Lucretius so freely satirized, pale before these often-quoted words in which Tertullian, maddened by the savage persecutions of his time, hurls back at the persecutors the prospect of an eternity filled with still more intolerable torments. Yet even those words, which form one of the crudest pages in Lecky's *History of Rationalism*, were outdone by the descriptions of medieval mission-preachers. More significant still, the Schoolmen themselves adopted all this; so that, as we shall see, the measured and conscientious logic of St Thomas Aquinas speaks here with a voice weightier than the most passionate rhetoric.

These matters will occupy us in greater detail as our survey proceeds; but, at this point, it is opportune to emphasize the three considerations which, more than any other, differentiate medieval from modern thought. First, faith became more and more a matter of loyalty to tradition, and that tradition changed imperceptibly but steadily into something very different, in certain important respects, from primitive Christianity. Secondly, faith became more and more definitely bound up with such beliefs about the next world as are no longer held by any religious body in their medieval crudity. Thirdly, the anarchy and distress of the invasions bred in almost all men's minds a passionate longing for unity; unity even at the cost (if so it must be) of tyranny. These will explain many things which are too often ignored or minimized in polite history, but which are perfectly natural if we forget modern British or American ideas and consider the actual circumstances of these distant times. England, from the Conquest to the Reformation, was peopled by men and women who, born at that earlier age of the world, had less political and social and even religious experience than the average reader of to-day. In the sight of God they were doubtless very much as we are. That, however, is a mystery which no man can attempt to penetrate: in every age, to the question: "Lord, what shall this man do?" Christ's answer comes: "What is that to thee? follow thou me!" But, in the things which man is able to judge, and in judging which he shows his superiority over the lower animals—in those things after which ordinary good folk have striven from generation to generation, and are striving still—in those manners and attainments which are the outward and visible signs of civilization—it will be natural to find our ancestors, at the distance of so many centuries, living at a somewhat rudimentary stage. There need be no guilty censoriousness in noting these things narrowly, nor is there any solid virtue in ignoring them as a matter of deference to polite conventions. We should rather hope that succeeding generations may tell equally plain truth about ourselves. Moreover, the recognition of plain truth about the past is an integral part of our own culture. Only thus can we measure the gulf which society has crossed, through the brave efforts of good folk from age to age; only thus can we find solid reasons, as apart from easy and superficial hopes, for future progress. Some of the worst among human errors are rooted in ignorance of the past, whether accidental or slothful or wilfully perverse. European society, during all that welter of invasion, and even while it was struggling out of disorder into a civilization of its own, was as unlike to the world in which we live as trench-life in war is unlike to the normal life of peace. Therefore we cannot understand the Middle Ages unless we are willing to bear constantly in mind two complementary truths : first, the essential similarity of human nature in all ages : and, secondly, the dissimilarity of men's environment—we may sometimes say, the almost incredible dissimilarities—at that distance of time. These will explain on the one hand the remarkable self-devotion and self-discipline of the best characters and, on the other, the carelessness of the multitude, into whom the current theological teaching seldom penetrated beneath the surface.

2. BISHOPS OF ROME

While this Christian Church, little by little, was emerging from the general dissolution of the Roman Empire, there also emerged gradually at its head a new figure, the Pope.

We must face this fully; for it is at the very foundation of our subject. Beyond all questions of our agreement or disagreement with the Papacy lies the fact that this is one of the most remarkable phenomena in social history. The Papacy, even to-day, is one of the strongest forces in European society; it illustrates the value of a positive and definite programme, however imperfect, as against any programme of mere negation. This is a point which needs to be emphasized most strongly by those of us who feel bound most uncompromisingly to combat whatever we judge to be hollow or excessive in the claims of the Roman Church. Whatever may be said of the line of Japanese Emperors, at least in this West of ours there is no succession of sovereigns comparable in length to that of the Popes; and that is all the more remarkable because, even at the most worldly times of the Papacy, the armies which any Pope could directly command have been so insignificant in number. Lamentably as Roman Catholicism (like many other Churches) has often employed physical coercion, it has never relied preponderantly upon brute force. The Pope's dominion has always been, in the main, what it has professed to be—a power exercised rather over men's minds than over their bodies. With this reservation, we can echo the celebrated epigram of Hobbes in the seventeenth century: "If any man will consider the original of that great ecclesiastical dominion, he will easily perceive that the Papacy is none other than the ghost of the deceased Roman Empire, sitting crowned upon the grave thereof." So far as that word "ghost" might imply contempt, it is mainly false; the Roman Church was far more than a mere pallid shade, a mere reflection, of the Roman Empire. If, however, we might take it as laying stress on the comparatively abstract and intangible nature of the papal dominion, then we should need to make no reservations.

The Pope was something very different from anything known to Graeco-Roman civilization. Perhaps the nearest parallel, strange as it may seem at first sight, was the Roman Emperor, who, in his later development, claimed a dominion over religion as complete as that which the later medieval Popes claimed over the sovereigns of Europe. In both cases the mainspring of power was men's passionate desire after unity; after any escape from mere anarchy. The Roman Republic, weary of a civil strife which was followed regularly by proscription and murder of the beaten party, had been finally content to let Augustus assemble all the key-offices in his single person, and thus to rule despotically under time-honoured traditional forms. So the Church, in its turn, became the one constructive thing which emerged from the welter of anarchy; and it gradually commanded the same loyalty to a central idea. The totalitarian State in one form or another, Soviet or Fascist, is a natural, if not inevitable, reaction from excessive social decomposition. Christianity, democratic in its origin, had split during its first hundred years into almost a hundred sects. Thus these centrifugal forces became intolerable, and the large majority of Christians gravitated definitely to that body which, from one point of view, was only the greatest of such sects, owing its unquestionable majority to its combination of tradition with such modifications as appealed to the average man. Representing thus a nucleus of enthusiastic inspiration tempered by natural human instincts, good and indifferent, it made so strong an appeal that in cases of direct conflict it could almost always claim an overwhelming majority over its rival of the moment. Thus, through a series of victories in separate conflicts, it made its own preponderance still more conspicuous; and therefore, in those times of intolerance, more overwhelming both physically and spiritually. Hence it is natural that, almost from the earliest of the Christian records, we should find this dominant majority claiming the title of *Catholic,* i.e. *Universal*; a name which rests upon no more obvious exaggeration than other flattering epithets which other institutions or peoples have arrogated to themselves. When, therefore, we say that the Pope was a unique person in many ways, it would be more correct to say that he was representative of a unique institution. He had grown as the Church grew.

Among the many bishoprics of Christendom, Rome had gradually forged far ahead. This was neither the earliest bishopric, nor the most learned; but many causes had contributed to bring her as definitely to the front as Birmingham now is in the midlands or London in the whole kingdom. She relied mainly upon the literal interpretation of Matthew xvi. 18: "Thou art Peter, and upon this rock I will build my church." True, the majority of the Early Fathers interpreted this text more or less metaphorically: but the letter always appeals to the multitude, and it would be difficult to name any single written sentence in world-history, except perhaps the parallel *Hoc est corpus meum,* which has been more desperately fought over than this. Not only have thousands been ready to die for one or the other interpretation, but thousands have died for it.

Yet, in these days, it is possible to look at it without too much prejudice either way; and the questionable basis of this Petrine claim has been brought out even by the most distinguished among modern Roman Catholic Church historians of our generation, Monsignor Duchesne. Although the Early Fathers had mostly interpreted this text metaphorically, and St Paul had been put side by side with St Peter even at Rome, yet gradually in that city men began to insist that the one Apostle, Peter, had a God-given primacy over all other Christians. Thence they jumped to the conclusion that the primacy thus promised to Peter necessarily descended to his successors. This, again, rested upon the further hypothesis that Peter had been first bishop of Rome. Yet in fact, though historical documents do indeed point to the high probability (we might almost say the practical certainty) that Peter ended his life at Rome, they do not prove, and rather tend to disprove, that he was ever bishop there. His name is absent from the earliest list, and St Paul has a better historical claim to the actual foundership of the

Christian community in Rome. The very base, therefore, is uncertain, and every joint of the superstructure is loose. To the majority of historians it seems one of the most confused theories that ever took real hold of the imagination of so large a proportion of the civilized world : some, indeed, would compare it with that "Nordic" theory on which the present-day German Reich takes its stand. Yet the real cause of power, in both cases, is not the theory itself, but the facts upon which it is based. Not on past historical facts, which they vainly claim in their favour, but on present political facts; upon what men could then see, and can see now, under their eyes. The striking fact of Mahomet's magnetic personality and generally beneficent influence made it possible for whole tribes to believe in his revelations while his own wife disbelieved them. Similarly, it was the fact of the Church's enormous and generally beneficent power which enabled men to believe that Christ had formally conferred the divine sovereignty of the world upon those bishops of Rome who had inherited some of the prestige of the old Empire, who could have relied more and more definitely, as time went on, upon a plebiscite in their own favour, and who possessed hitherto unprecedented opportunity for, and organization of, propaganda. In those days when history in the modern sense was impossible, and when the comparison of conflicting records and their impartial valuation was practically beyond the reach even of the most learned, a movement of this kind was irresistible. Nearly all men whose voices could be heard were echoing identical doctrines, and the few exceptions whispered dissent at their own risk. Then, as in all ages, men mostly believed what they found it convenient to believe; and the system worked, century after century, with sufficient success to bring the Popes at last to a point at which they might truly have anticipated Louis XIV's claim : "L'Église, c'est moi."

In his person itself, the Pope had many striking points reminiscent of antiquity, quite apart from the costume, the ceremonies, and the bureaucratic framework which he inherited quite naturally from Pagan Rome. At a very early date, we find bishops from different parts of the world appealing to him as arbiter; he occupied here an interior angle. These appellants very naturally addressed him in language of high-pitched praise, not to say adulation. True, this never quite rose to that level of flattery to which the Emperors were accustomed; and even those modern writers who claim a quasi-imperial position for the Roman pontiffs have never produced anything approaching the *Maximus pius felix invictus augustus sempiternus* of Constantine I, to omit whole pages which might be quoted of later and more bombastic imperial titles.[1]

Yet, within less than 500 years from the Crucifixion, this Leader of the Christians had reached a point at which his Church began so far to overlap the State that a concordat became necessary. This may be read in a famous letter from Gelasius I to the Emperor Anastasius.[2] In secular matters, it is for the Emperor to make laws, and for the Churchman to obey them. In matters of religious faith, and in the administration of the sacraments, it is the Pope's duty to decide, and to tell the Emperor without reserve what he thinks. And it is the Emperor's duty, not as a sovereign, but as a Christian, to accept the doctrine taught by the Church, and the sacraments as administered by her priests. But hundreds of cases must necessarily occur in which the limits between religious and secular authority are highly disputable; and it is all-important to note here the attitude of one of the greatest and boldest of early Popes; of that St Gregory I who was the second converter of England, just a century after this Gelasian Concordat. Writing to the Emperor Maurice,[3] he confessed himself "sorely affrighted" by an imperial decree which "closed for many men the way to heaven", since it prescribed that no man, once sworn in as a soldier, might enter a monastery until he had served out his time in the army. Here was a question which touched religion very nearly: yet Gregory, even while remonstrating with the Emperor, writes: "What am I but dust and a worm? . . . Being subject to [your] command, I have caused this law to be promulgated throughout all parts of the earth." He showed that same Christian moderation in refusing the title of "Universal Bishop"; and again in his instructions to his missionaries in England. Let them shock no prejudices without necessity: while yielding nothing in essentials, let them do all in their power to ignore minor differences. Let them adapt the existing heathen temples to Christian worship; let them suffer men to keep the old feasts, only slaying their oxen no longer as a sacrifice to devils, but in thanksgiving to God.

It is well to dwell a little more on this Gregory, to whom England owes so much. Not only that his reign marks a definite step in the development of the modern Papacy, but that it comes at a period when the Western Church and its Ruler were still incontestably among the greatest, and probably the very greatest, of civilizing forces in Europe. Gregory, like his contemporaries and predecessors and successors, was haunted by the imminence of Antichrist and Armageddon and the shrivelling of this world like a parched scroll. His overpowering other-worldliness led him into injustice towards the great classical past. He had spent a long time as ambassador in Constantinople, yet had never learned the Greek language. He valued Roman habits of business in politics and in social life, just as he valued the great Roman palace which he had inherited from his ancestors, and which he made into a monastery. But he had no value for Roman literature as such. In one well-known preface he repudiated care for mere moods and tenses; the Oracles of God must not be enslaved to the rules of the grammarian. In another often-quoted letter, he rebuked the bishop of Vienne: "We hear that thou expoundest grammar [that is, classical literature]. . . . Our former good opinion of thee is turned to mourning and sorrow. The same mouth singeth not the praises of Jove and the praises of Christ. . . . [Cast away] the idle vanities of worldly learning." Those who read this too literally do not realize how much religious reason underlies it all; for it was common to give boys Virgil's *Eclogues* to begin upon for their next step after the rudiments, and here they found: "We begin with Jove, O ye Muses; all things are full of Jove." Yet John of Salisbury records the tradition that Gregory burned the great Palatine Library as a hindrance to Bible studies; and, though there is no real evidence for this, the very legend is significant. But the greatest of all his own books is that on *Pastoral Care*, of which our

Alfred gave a translation to his people; a book which starts from the maxim that the art of arts is the rule of souls. He had lived this book before he wrote it; his contemporaries called him *Argus luminosissimus*; his eyes were everywhere: even in remote England. He is the first Pope of whom we know that he kept a thoroughly businesslike register of all his important letters. There were other imperfect registers before him, but this of Gregory's marks an epoch. He supervised the vast papal estates (many as far off as Sicily) as carefully as the hardest business-man could have done, grudging the waste of every farthing that might have been collected and given to the poor. He kept his hand tightly over every bishop in the West. As a ruler, he held his own in diplomacy against the Emperor on the one side, and the half-barbarous Lombards, Visigoths and Franks on the other: and the term *Gregorian Chant* reminds us of his love of sacred music, though it may be doubtful how far he was in fact its active reformer.

In those days, there still remained much of the original democratic spirit—or, at least, egalitarian—in Christianity. At first all Church offices had been elective, just as the State offices had been for centuries before Christianity was born. Priests and bishops were chosen by their flocks, and for many centuries men saw no reason whatever why the bishop of Rome should be chosen differently from any other. They did not even trouble to keep exact record of the names of the first few. St Cornelius (251) was elected Pope (writes St Cyprian) "by the testimony of nearly all the clergy, by the college of aged bishops, and of good men". But, when the Church grew more worldly, this became more and more inconvenient, especially as there was no formal delimitation of the parts to be played by clergy, bishops and "good men" respectively. In 366, the papal election ended in wholesale bloodshed. The adherents of Damasus held the Liberian basilica; those of Ursinus stormed it, and 137 corpses were counted there at the end of the day. The Pagan historian Ammianus Marcellinus remarks that the temptation was overwhelming, since the bishop of Rome, through the munificence of pious ladies, was able to enjoy comfort and pomp, and to give some of the best dinner parties in the metropolis. Thus popular election became increasingly unreal; and Professor C. H. Turner gives the succeeding steps very clearly in the first volume of *The Cambridge Medieval History*. In the sixth and seventh centuries, Popes were often practically appointed by the Emperors. In the eighth century, the part of the laity was reduced to mere acclamation. In 824 Louis the Pious exacted an oath from the Romans that none should be consecrated Pope without the permission and presence of his ambassadors; and in 898, in consequence of very serious election-riots, John IX gave papal sanction to this imperial control. The Emperor Otto I (963) compelled the Romans to swear that they would never elect or ordain a Pope without his or his son's consent: and it was the Emperors who, at one point, rescued the Papacy from the control of unscrupulous local barons, and from the lowest degradation in all its history. Even such bold and organizing Popes as Gregory the Great and Nicholas I had never grasped this nettle; and when, in 1059, Nicholas II attempted so to regularize those elections as to dispense with imperial control and to obviate disputes, he built upon the foundation of a gross and fatal ambiguity. This matter is so important not only in its direct bearing upon religious and social history, but also in its side-lights on medieval mentality, that I must treat it here at some length, following mainly the great legal historian Esmein, in his essay on *l'Unanimité et la Majorité* (*Mélanges H. Fitting* (1917), vol. 1).

The Church "accepted the law of simple and absolute majority only with difficulty, and at a late date, when canonical election had lost its most important applications". After the distant and obscure years of early Christianity, we find that the bishop is elected by the clergy and the community; *a clero et populo*. But, already at that date, the clergy play the principal part; they choose, and the people are called in to accept and confirm the choice. St Ambrose's election by mere popular acclamation at Milan in 374, before he had even been baptized, was a relic of the earlier Christian practice. In principle, the whole population—the males at least—might take part in the election. But, strange as it may seem, their choice was, theoretically, unanimous. We find this in England even as late as Lucius III (1181-4), whose decree, enshrined in Canon Law, bids the clergy "procure the king's assent, and agree unanimously upon an honest, literate and proper person, and elect him consentaneously as pastor and bishop"—*unanimiter conveniatis, eligatis concorditer.*

Here, at least on the face of it, we have the old Germanic principle, common to rudimentary civilizations, of compulsory unanimity. Agreement to differ is one of the latest steps in social evolution. Tacitus describes these Germanic people, still far removed from such political organization as the Roman Empire could boast, where the magistrates had little executive power, and the operative factor was the assembly of the whole tribe or clan, and yet the decisions were unanimous. The hearers showed disapproval by a hollow murmur, or approval by the clashing of shields and spears, and the result was something like the unanimity which reigns in certain countries of to-day. In twelfth-century London the chronicler gives us something like the same picture of a folk-moot, the populace securing decision by their shouts of "Ya, ya!" or "Nay, nay!"[4] This same principle of unanimity survives in our modern jury, not always entirely free from all elements of intimidation or coercion. Yet this principle may be traced in many councils, civil or ecclesiastical, in East and West. At Nicaea, for instance, the minority of twenty out-and-out Arian bishops was gradually reduced to two by imperial and other pressure; and those two, obstinately refusing to sign, were sent into exile. Therefore we need not choose between the great authority of Gierke, who traces the unanimity principle to Germany, and Esmein, who would stamp it as a Christian idea. "In itself", writes Esmein, "the choice [of the populace] for the election of the bishop, God's minister *par excellence*, is not a natural and comprehensible thing. . . . But, so long as this electoral system persisted, the idea crept in that such elections took place in peculiar conditions, under the inspiration of the Holy Ghost, whose invocation was always the first of electoral acts. . . . The election must needs be unanimous, but God provided for that." Yet "this unanimous election was at the same time informal.

Votes were not collected and counted. It is possible that, in the earliest ages, there had been a show of hands; but [in the early Middle Ages] the popular voice was expressed by clamours, by acclamations or by hooting. That was one of the reasons which facilitated unanimity: it was enough that the choice should appear unanimous. It sufficed that there should be no manifest opposition; or, if any such appeared, that it should be silenced. This latter result might be obtained by the exhortations of the [presiding] bishops: it might also be due to other methods, such as the fear of one's opponents." Those were the practical facts underlying this very rudimentary procedure in one of the matters most important for the well-being of Christendom; for the Pope was a bishop, and all that is said here applied to him also. It took many centuries to bring Europe to the idea of a majority-election, whether in the barest sense or in any clear and business-like form. Meanwhile the Church, so meticulously prudent and business-like in some ways, neglected human nature in some of its most obvious impulses and left things to arrange themselves in one of the most vital fields, the election of "Christ upon Earth". She deified Chance under the name of Holy Ghost. Stephen VI (886-9) decreed: "The election pertaineth to the priests, and the consent of the faithful populace must be obtained; for the people must be taught, not followed." Very similar, at this period, was the election of civil magistrates: on the Continent the count proposed the candidate and the people acclaimed him, and things seem to have followed much the same course under the sheriff (*vis-count*) in early England.[5]

St Leo the Great (440-61) had ruled that, where the election was not unanimous, the archbishop should choose the fitter of the two candidates. The fact that this decretal was enshrined in Canon Law and became the foundation of future legislation shows how embryonic the whole system was. Even when the great Lateran Council of 1215 had fixed new and preciser methods for ecclesiastical elections, it still left room for the old idea of unanimous acclamation; the electors need not follow the new forms "if the election had been made by all in common, without fault, as if by inspiration".

Then, as the greater precision of the numerical voting system became evident, the principle of majority decision crept in little by little. At first it was hedged in by a very serious qualification; a bare majority would not suffice; it must be a majority not merely of numbers but of quality; one of the two sides must be able to show not only more, but "sounder", electors: *major et sanior pars.* That principle appears already in St Benedict's Rule (ch. 64); it was taken into Gratian's *Decretum* as a supplementary note, and consecrated by Innocent III at his Ecumenical Council of 1215. Here it is decreed that the candidate is to be counted as bishop elect "upon whom all, or the *major et sanior pars* of the chapter, have agreed".

But here is a gross ambiguity. A child can count the *majority* among fifty votes, but who is to distinguish the *saniority*? No Pope or council, through all the medieval centuries, ever attempted this. Innocent himself can scarcely have been ignorant of the fact that, some eighty years earlier, Europe had been plunged into conflict and bloodshed by a disputed papal election. There, the numerical minority of electors claimed superior *sanioritas* for Innocent II because they had on their side more cardinal bishops; and the numerical majority, because they had more who had been raised to the cardinalate earlier than their opponents. To one side, "soundness" meant rank, and to the other, seniority: hence civil war. When the canon lawyers were confronted with this crucial phrase, and mere evasion under vague generalities was no longer possible, it may almost be said that their professional definition was even more vague than that which they set out to define: *ignotum per ignotius.* This is so important for the estimate of medieval mentality that I must here add another paragraph for the sake of all readers who are interested in the progress of human thought; other readers may prefer to take it as read.

Esmein (p. 375) quotes the definition of one of the greatest medieval canonists, Panormitanus, who died in 1453 and had the collective wisdom of two centuries of predecessors to work upon. It runs thus: "*Sanioritas* consists in *authority, zeal,* and *merit. Authority* may be seen in the dignity of the electors, their greater age, their more ancient appointment, and their higher [ecclesiastical] orders. Those who are superior in these different claims have weighty voices [*ponderosas*]. *Zeal* consists in feeling: that is, in the motives actuating the electors, whether it be kindred or friendship or bribery; whether they have accepted payment or have voted by reason of the elect's merit. And, since zeal consists in feeling, it must be proved by presumption, since feeling admits of no other proof. It is said also that this sort of *sanioritas* consists not only in zeal but in facts and the operation itself. But operation concerns merit; for the party which elects a better candidate appears the sounder party; and that refers to the persons elected, considered from the point of view of morals, life, etc. It may also refer to the electors, if we consider that, being more honest, they have more *merit*, and that this renders their votes all the fatter [*pinguiores*]." What pettifogger could wish for a richer job than a lawsuit in which the crucial question was that of greater age, earlier appointment, and higher orders, in a community in which it might happen that one-third were older and one-third senior by appointment (or, again, one-third bishops, one-third priests, one-third deacons); with no criterion whatever to decide whether age, seniority or rank was to be taken as the weightier consideration in case of conflict? Or, again, consider this system in which comparative morality was supposed to be crucial, and in which lawyers might claim the morality of the elector as reflecting decisive light upon the fitness of the person elected or (to make confusion worse confounded) *vice versa.* Moreover, Panormitanus reveals to us these difficulties not merely in theory but in practice. He writes: "The gloss here . . . concludes that the sounder part, even though numerically less, ought to prevail. But [five of the greatest authorities] hold the contrary opinion here, saying that, since the two qualifications are copulatively required [major *et* sanior], therefore either, taken by itself, is insufficient." As Esmein points out, although Innocent III prescribed a comparison of extreme delicacy (morals, etc.) yet "singularly, he had not prescribed who was to make this comparison, or the authority whose duty it was to proclaim the result of the voting": and the exposition of Hostiensis, one of the earliest and greatest commentators on this decree of 1215, amounts to "mere anarchy". St Bernard, whose piety and zeal and intellect and personal fearlessness and nobility of birth made him for a while the arbiter of Christendom, did indeed solve admirably that election disputed between Innocent II and Anacletus on the dubious point of *sanior*; but he cut the knot with the sword of the Spirit, and in the teeth of statute-law. How many equals had St Bernard, in that combination of qualities, during the whole Middle Ages?

Therefore so little can we wonder at the papal schisms which sometimes rent the Latin Church, or even at the shattering magnitude of that Great Schism in the fourteenth century, that it might rather have been counted a miracle if no such convulsions had occurred. This, to the medieval mind, would of course present far less difficulty than to us; the presumption in those days was as strongly in favour of miraculous intervention as it is against it to-day. St Francis, in the matter of the Portiuncula Indulgence, is said to have refused the proffered papal bull, saying: "The Blessed Virgin Mary shall be the charter and Christ the notary, and the angels shall be the witnesses." The result was that, as soon as the story of this Indulgence was really spread abroad, it was violently contested by the Dominicans, and there have been the gravest historical doubts down to the present day. So was it also with papal elections, as with those of meaner importance; the hierarchy might take refuge in their reliance upon miracles, yet none came in answer to their cries. It is natural therefore to ask whether these disastrous failures might not reasonably have suggested to the ecclesiastical legislator that, by his hugger-mugger treatment of plain business issues, so vital to the health of Christendom, he might be tempting the Lord his God. For it is now admitted on all hands that the Great Schism was one of the prime causes of the Reformation.

Slowly, then, the modern idea crept in of counting by percentages, which do at least give a clear verdict. As early as 1203, Innocent III had decided a disputed election in a monastery on the ground that one candidate had received nearly two-thirds of the votes (24 out of 38), and must therefore be presumed to have been elected "by good zeal", unless he could be proved unfit in other ways.[6] And then, in 1215, Innocent III brought in the percentage rule "in order to avoid discord in the election of the Roman Pontiff", because, in spite of former regulations, the Church hath suffered grievous schism through the audacity of wicked ambition." If two-thirds of the cardinals are on one side, that majority shall be decisive: only in case of lesser majorities shall the question of *sanioritas* come in.[7] And, finally, this rule was extended to all ecclesiastical elections by Gregory X in the second Council of Lyons (1274). Thus, though the old uncertainties of *sanioritas* persisted throughout the Middle Ages in normal cases, yet, when a two-thirds majority could be secured, it was superseded. The Council of Trent, by instituting the secret ballot, finally consecrated the majoritarian principle; for, obviously, where no voter could be identified, no superior *sanioritas* could be pleaded.

The doctrinal history of the Papacy had been almost equally haphazard; a process of gradual consolidation far less through definite foresight than through a series of opportunisms. When the Church was rent with disputes as to the validity of heretical baptism, the salvation of thousands or millions was at stake, since both orthodox and heretics looked upon baptism as the necessary gate to heaven. St Cyprian and his fellow-bishop Firmilian here defied the Pope, who contented himself with condemning them by letter, and made no attempt to beat them down by his authority in open fight. It was no Pope, but St Augustine, after many generations, who settled that question, once for all, against Cyprian. Honorius I, again, was condemned for heresy; that condemnation stood for priests to read yearly in the Breviary until the seventeenth century, when it was silently expunged. Whatever may be thought of fine-drawn modern arguments in defence of this Pope, the fact still remains that, all through our period, his heresy was regarded as notorious and undisputed. Again, Charles the Great has been described by the great Roman Catholic scholar Edmund Bishop as "his own Minister of Public Worship". Once even, with his clergy in full synod, he contradicted a Pope on the crucial question of image-worship, and called upon him by implication to reverse his solemn judgment. By an extraordinary perversion of the facts, it is often asserted that, from 597 onward, all our archbishops had to receive their pallium from Rome, and to take a special oath of obedience. That claim, for the generations down to the eighth century, was exploded by Professor J. P. Whitney in *The Cambridge Historical Journal* for 1932. It does not become fully true until the eleventh century. Moreover, between A.D. 688 and 1050 there were consecrated 376 bishops in England by the action of the Chapters, the King and Witan, but without a trace of papal interference. "I have verified", adds Professor Whitney, "this calculation." These things, and many more for which there is no place here, must be borne in mind when we try to visualize the light in which Popes appeared to far-off England from the Norman Conquest onwards. William had landed at Pevensey with a Papally-blessed banner: Gregory VII reminded him, later, that he himself had incurred no little obloquy from his fellow-cardinals for his own encouragement of this bloodshed. Yet, though William was quite willing to follow the Pope's bidding in the matter of married clergy, he was not equally ready to renounce his traditional right of appointing bishops; and, when Gregory claimed homage from him, he answered bluntly: "I neither would nor will do homage; for I never promised it, nor can I find that my predecessors ever did homage to yours."

3. CONVERSION OF THE WILD MEN

Yet, as we shall see, papal power was very great here in our islands, in spite of its basis in custom rather than in law, and the fitful incidence of its claims. We can best see this if we go back here, for a while, to earlier times.

The original British Church was comparatively independent of Rome. Its origins are lost in the mists of antiquity: but, when it first comes into the light of history, it differs strongly from the Roman upon two points which to us seem trifling, but to which contemporaries attached so much importance that, sometimes, quite good Christians of the opposing parties refused to sit down to table together or to use each other's dishes. One was, the precise shape of the clerical tonsure, and the other, the date of Easter. On this latter point Rome herself had been as inconsistent as in the matter of papal elections. In the earliest times, there were considerable differences in calculation between the Roman and the Eastern Church; the latter calculating Easter on the same principles on which the Jews had calculated for their Passover, while Rome reckoned differently. In 460, however, Rome adopted one of the Eastern principles, though without thus obtaining complete uniformity. In about 530 she made another concession; and this was the state of things when Augustine came to England as missionary from Gregory I. He thus found himself, naturally enough, at variance with the English, Irish and Scottish Churches, which were still calculating by the earlier Roman cycle, and had also introduced a change of their own. The great Celtic missionaries, St Columba, St Columban, St Aidan, and their whole school of Iona, were thus at variance with the Roman use; and Bede notes how, when St Chad was consecrated bishop, "there was but one canonically ordained bishop in the whole of Britain": only one, that is, whose ordination came from those who followed the orthodox Roman use. Thus, at the court of King Oswy, the bishop was of the Celtic Church, while the queen had brought "a priest of Catholic observance" from her native Kent; "whence it is said to have befallen sometimes that Easter was twice celebrated in one year; for, while the king had dissolved his [Lenten] fast and was celebrating Christ's Paschal feast, the queen and her followers persisted in fast and were keeping Palm Sunday." This had been tolerated in Aidan's time, in consideration of his saintly character and the fact that both Celts and Romans, at heart, were celebrating the same essential mysteries. But then came St Wilfrid, tutor to Oswy's son, who had made the pilgrimage to Rome and come back to fight for Unity with all his inborn passionate zeal. The king, therefore, held a synod at Whitby at which Wilfrid confronted Colman, the bishop who now held St Aidan's see. It was Oswy's set purpose now to secure Unity; and therefore he was resolved to decide once for all between these hitherto irreconcilable parties. Colman pleaded that his method was what had been handed down by his predecessors, going back ultimately to St John, the Beloved who had lain at the Last Supper upon the Lord's breast: in other words, his was the Eastern tradition, as opposed to the Roman. Wilfrid confessed the discrepancy, but pleaded that St John was, in the nature of the case, a Judaizing Christian who, like other Apostles, was unable to make a crude breach with Jewish customs. He then pointed out that the Celts did not, in fact, follow St John's observance exactly: thus "ye are in conformity with neither John nor Peter, neither the [Mosaic] Law nor the Gospel". Colman fell back upon the immemorial tradition of his own Church, consecrated by Columba and other saints, through whom so many signs and miracles had been wrought. The reply was crushing: "I might answer that there are many who will plead with the Lord that they have prophesied in His name, and cast out devils and wrought many miracles, yet to whom He will reply that He has never known them. But far be it from me to speak thus of your Fathers." For, behind this, he had the usual appeal to St Matthew. "If that Columba of yours (and, I may say, ours also, if he was Christ's servant) was a holy man and powerful in miracles, yet could he be preferred before the most blessed prince of the Apostles? to whom our Lord said, *Thou art Peter, and upon this Rock I will build my Church, and the gates of hell shall not prevail against it, and to thee I will give the keys of the kingdom of heaven.*" "When Wilfrid had spoken thus, the king said, 'Is it true, Colman, that these words were spoken to Peter by our Lord?' He answered, 'It is true, O king!' Then said he, 'Can you produce any such power given to your Columba?' Colman answered, 'None.' Then added the king, 'Do you both agree, without dispute, that these words were principally directed to Peter, and that the keys of heaven were given to him by our Lord?' They both answered, 'We do.' Then the king concluded. 'And I also say unto you, that this is the door-keeper, whom I will not contradict, but will, as far as I know and am able, in all things obey his decrees; lest perchance, when I come to the gates of the kingdom of heaven, there should be none to open them, he being my adversary who is proved to have the keys.' The king having said this, all present, both great and small, gave their assent."[1]

The victory here was complete, and Wilfrid did much in other ways to strengthen the bond between Rome and England. He brought in books and learning, and especially artists, to whom, as will be seen later on, we may attribute with great probability those magnificent Northumbrian crosses which, at first sight, seem so impossible for England at that early date. Yet in one respect neither he, nor those others who were naturally attracted by the culture of that great capital, ever dreamed of Romanizing to the extent which has sometimes been claimed for them.[2]

Soon after this fateful Synod of Whitby, Roman discipline gained even greater victories on the Continent through the direct agency of another Englishman, St Boniface. Here, as often, it is the most turbulent and difficult stock which produces the most fiery and energetic converts. Gaul and portions of Germany had already been evangelized to a great part by Celtic missionaries, not very ready to render strict obedience to Rome. Now, this distant Anglo-Saxon outsider came forward to do more for Roman Unity than had been done, for some time, by any churchmen of Latin race or of closer geographical proximity to the capital of the West.

Boniface (in Old English, Winfroth) was certainly a Wessex man; and the tradition is very probable which makes him born at Crediton and educated at Exeter. At that time (about 680) Exeter was a city of two tongues, and thus, to a certain extent, of two creeds. The most conspicuous church in the north of the city was dedicated to the British saint Petroc, while in the south there was the Saxon church of St Sidwell. British Christianity had its own customs differing from those which were afterwards brought in by St Augustine and his Roman fellow-missionaries: and, as is common between close neighbours, these minor differences caused quite disproportionate friction; in some cases the clergy of one observance would refuse even to eat with the other. This boy Winfroth cannot but have been impressed by the fact that the two churches differed about the computation of the most important among Christian feasts, so that, every seven years, while the people of St Sidwell were fasting and mourning for the Passion, those of St Petroc were in full rejoicing for the festival of Easter. Such scenes of disunion, so crude and so distressing to any impressionable youth, would go far to account for the later activities of this Devonshire monk who did more than any Italian of his age to bring not only the Germanic tribes, but even Frankish Gaul, under the direct discipline of Rome. He had apparently become an "oblate" monk (i.e. offered at the altar by his parents) before his seventh year; his piety and learning gradually earned him distinction; and, at the age of thirty-eight, he felt the missionary call. Our Saxon kinsmen of Friesland were among the hardiest of European populations, and among the most obstinate pagans. Their king, Ratbod, was reported by later tradition to have refused baptism on the ground that, since his ancestors were in hell, it would be disloyal to desert them. Boniface, refusing an abbacy in England, left for Rome in order to obtain the blessing of Gregory II. This was in 714; two years later he began his preaching in Frisia, where Ratbod had destroyed the Christian Churches erected by the Anglo-Saxon Willibrod, and had reinstated the idols. Ratbod died in 719; Charles

Martel had imposed Christianity upon the Frisians by force of arms, and the mission prospered. In 722, the Pope consecrated Boniface as missionary bishop, compelling him to swear absolute obedience to the Roman Church, and sent him with a commendatory letter to Charles Martel. Henceforward he became the special apostle of Germany, beginning with Hesse and Thuringia. Thence to Bavaria, where, as in England, there were remnants of Celtic Christianity which Boniface subordinated to Rome. Thence, again, to Franconia, and then back westwards to Frankish Gaul, where he held a council in 745 which definitely imposed the Roman organization and discipline. Even this summary and imperfect list of his activities may show how justly Berthelot can write:[3] "The régime of pontifical authority, established already in England and Germany, was thenceforward accepted by the ancient Church of Gaul. It was purified, disciplined, and commanded; and we know very well how great was the place which it held in Gaul." All this had cost Boniface not only much faith and energy, but also much of difficult—we may even say, of bitter—compromise. The clergy at the court of Charles Martel disgusted him; yet (as he wrote to his former bishop in England, Daniel) he cannot break with them entirely: for "without the patronage of the Frankish King I can neither govern the people nor defend priests or deacons, monks or nuns, nor even forbid the pagan rites and idolatrous sacrileges in Germany without the commands and the fear of that man [Charles]."[4] Among those pagan rites were actual human sacrifices. The story told by Boniface's letters to the Holy See and to English bishops is gloomy indeed. The one all-important point is that religious and cultural progress is being made, yet with a slowness disappointing to those who were giving their lives to the work. Anarchy or tyranny in the State reacted upon the Church.[5] The layfolk had invaded ecclesiastical offices and revenues; Charles Martel, recently dead, had been the worst offender here; it was with Church plunder that he had maintained the army which saved Europe from the Saracens. Moreover, the Church herself was struggling but slowly from that quagmire of ignorance which had inevitably followed the barbarian invasions. We see this most plainly, perhaps, in her hesitation about marriage, not yet formally claimed as a Sacrament in those days. In 742, Boniface appealed to Pope Zacharias concerning a great difficulty which had arisen in the person of a layman of great authority who "asserted that he had received licence from Pope Gregory of holy memory to take in marriage the widow of his own uncle, who herself also was the wife of his cousin, and she, during his lifetime, departed from him . . . moreover, she vowed to God the vow of chastity, and took the veil, and then cast it away and was married for the second time. For the man aforesaid asserts that the Holy See hath permitted him such a marriage." Zacharias, who was a saint and a strong Pope, naturally supported Boniface in so glaring a case as this; yet Boniface's question was not so superfluous as it might seem, since he had received from the preceding Pope, Gregory II, a matrimonial decision most embarrassing to many theologians of to-day.[6] It ran: "As to the point you propose, what if a woman, who has been seized by an infirmity, is incapable, what shall her husband do? It would be good if he would so remain, and give himself to abstinence. But, since this is for great souls, he who cannot observe continence should rather marry; but he should not cease to support the woman who is prevented by illness, not cast out by loathsome sin." As to the "priests or bishops, involved in many vices, whose life defileth the priesthood in their persons",[7] Boniface should not refuse to eat or speak with them; by kindly intercourse he might possibly gain some of them over.[8] Some years later, Boniface complains that the synod he held has brought upon him "many injuries and persecutions, especially from false priests and adulterine deacons and fornicating clergy". There is a good deal of social significance, also, in the smaller matters which troubled Boniface and his Popes, behind the great questions of religion and morality. Zacharias is so troubled by pagan customs that he forbids the consumption of "jackdaws [or jays] and rooks and storks, which Christians must by all means avoid eating: moreover beavers and hares and wild horses should be much more strictly avoided". Patients with jaundice are to be segregated, lest others catch the contagion.[9]

Most interesting of all is the Pope's attitude towards the Antipodes. A certain Virgilius or Ferghil, probably the same man of that name who was Bishop of Salzburg, had come into conflict with Boniface, whom he scandalized also by his geographical theory. The Pope's decision ran: "concerning this man's perverse and iniquitous doctrine, which he hath spoken against God and his own soul, if it be clearly proved that he professeth that another world and other men are beneath the earth, or a sun and moon, then do thou take counsel [*or*, hold a council] and expel him from the Church, depriving him of the honour of priesthood."[10]

If Boniface had remained at home in England he would have been confronted with much the same problems, as we may see from his letter to his fellow-archbishop, Cuthbert of Canterbury. Among the Anglo-Saxons there was more than one bishop who cared less to feed his flock than to shear it: "Who doth not tremble at these things, save only those who have no belief in the world to come?" He exhorts Cuthbert: "Let us die, if so God will, for the holy laws of our forefathers, that we may earn with them an everlasting inheritance." "Moreover I do not conceal from you, loving brother, that all God's servants here [in Germany] who seem most approved in Scripture or in the fear of God, are displeased that the good and honour and modesty of your Church are mocked; and it would be some relief from our shame if your synod and your princes would forbid to women and to veiled nuns that frequency of pilgrimages that they make, going to the city of Rome and back; for the greater part of them come to ruin, few remaining intact. For there are very few cities in Lombardy or Franconia or France wherein is no adulteress or harlot of English race; and this is a scandal and a foul blot upon your Church."* He goes on to speak of the extent to which earls or great men, "manslayers of the poor", seized upon the abbeys and appropriated the wealth "which had been bought with the blood of Christ". Finally, he reprobates the extravagant worldly dress of clergy and monks, harbingers of Antichrist, whose cunning it was "to introduce, through his ministers, fornication and

* See below here, Chapter LI.

lechery into the monastic cloisters".[11] This was written probably in 745; and, just ten years earlier, the Venerable Bede had drawn a still gloomier picture in his appeal for reform to Archbishop Egbert of Canterbury. Egbert, he hopes, will not act like so many of his fellow-bishops, and surround himself with men not of religion or continence, but rather buffoons and belly-gods. Every nerve must be strained to teach the so-called Christian folk at least the Apostles' Creed and the Lord's Prayer in their own tongue; it is significant that there is no mention here of the Hail Mary, which in the parallel episcopal injunctions of five centuries later had become a third item inseparable from those two. This teaching is necessary "not only for the layfolk, who are yet living the life of the people, but even for clerics or monks who are ignorant of the Latin tongue . . . wherefore I myself have oftentimes given both these, the Creed and the Prayer, translated into the English tongue, to many unlearned priests". There are many remote villages and hamlets in which a bishop has never been seen for many years past; and thus the folk are never confirmed; for this rite, all through the Middle Ages, was performed normally only by bishops on their travels of visitation. Greed of money is here at fault: bishops grasp, for money's sake, at a greater extent of territory than they can truly administer. Bede complains how, in this "modern" Church of the eighth century A.D., by contrast with that of the first age, too many Churchmen not only do not sell the possessions they have, but even grasp at such as they have not. The whole of England [together with Southern Scotland] is divided into only twelve bishoprics. The abbeys are rich, and this wealth should be employed in part for the foundation of new sees; for "there are innumerable so-called monasteries, as we all know, who have nothing whatever of monastic conversation: I would that some of these might be transferred, by synodical authority, from lechery to chastity, from vanity to temperance, from intemperance of the belly and gluttony to continence and piety; and they might be taken in aid of an episcopal see which should lately have been founded." On this subject of monastic decay he harps again and again: there are only too many who spread a moral plague around them; and, by a still graver abuse, powerful lay-folk "give the king's money, and buy for themselves, under pretext of founding monasteries, estates wherein they may more freely exercise their lusts", and procure foundation-charters and privileges signed not only by kings but also by bishops, abbots and worldly potentates. "It is thine office to see to it that the Devil should not usurp his reign in places consecrated to God." As to general piety, even "those [of the population] who seem among the most religious do not presume to take the Holy Communion except at Christmas and Epiphany and Easter, although there are innumerable boys and girls, young men and maidens, old men and women, innocent and of chastest conversation, who, without any controversial scruple, are fit to communicate every Sunday, or even on the days of holy apostles or martyrs, as thou thyself hast seen done in the Holy Roman and Apostolic Church." Here, again, we may compare this with the thirteenth century, by which time the laity, all over the Latin Church, very seldom communicated more than once a year, at Easter. But to return to Bede. It may too often be said now as Christ said to the Pharisees: "wherefore do ye transgress the commandments of God through your tradition?" Men think to redeem their sins by "the alms which, amid their daily concupiscence and delights, they seem to give to the poor", but alms, to weigh in God's balance, must be brought by clean hands. "Let these things be said briefly against the poisonous love of money. But if I would treat in the same way concerning drunkenness and surfeiting and lechery and other such contagions, the length of my letter would extend to immensity."

Even if those words stood alone, and were not supported by evidence from other angles, they would suffice to warn us against over-estimating the power of the Church during the so-called Dark Ages, while we freely admit that she was the greatest existing power for good in those half-civilized societies. For Bede is the last man to be dismissed as a mere rhetorician or purblind carping critic. True, he had the monastic mentality; he had fled from Vanity Fair to save his soul; but, among all those who looked down from that cloister-refuge upon the follies and crimes of the world, there was none more understanding and temperate and reasonable than he.

To return to Boniface. His letter of 745 may very reasonably be connected with the fact that, two years later, a synod was held at Cloveshoe which stands out as a landmark in English Church legislation. The assembled Fathers grappled there with many of the abuses he describes and (*inter alia*) made the first attempt, not very effective, as we shall see, to set up something like a school system throughout the land. Boniface's work cannot be summarized better than it has been by a Devonshire educationalist, Mr F. H. Colson, before a Devonshire audience. "He stands, in fact, for efficiency, for hard work, for firmness of principle, tempered, however, with that opportunism which springs from good sense and reasonableness; for organization, for discipline. And, indeed, we may regard him not only as the father of English missionary work, but as the first-fruits of the colonial and imperial instinct of Englishmen, as the spiritual father of Raleigh and Drake, of the Pilgrims, who sailed from Plymouth in the *Mayflower*. . . . Except, of course, in one matter. That Boniface was a loyal adherent of the Pope is obvious, and it may well be argued that he did more than any one in history to make the Papacy what it was during the next few centuries. Personally, I hold that he was right, and this I think is an opinion in which both halves of Western Christendom may well acquiesce. Those who feel most thankful that the North of Europe threw off in the sixteenth century the authority of the Bishop of Rome, may still quite logically believe that that authority was necessary for the world's development in the earlier centuries."

Thus, though the wild men who had conquered Rome were being gradually Romanized again, the extent of this victory was limited. St Vitus (for instance) christianized the island of Rügen in the Baltic; but, a few generations after his death, the inhabitants were found to be worshipping a great idol which they named Santovit, and to which, by preference, they offered sacrifice of Christian blood. The Monk of St Gall tells how the Danish ambassador would seek baptism at each of his yearly visits, for the sake of the new clothes and accoutrements that were given when he rose from the purifying waters. Charles the Great converted the Northern Saxons by fire and sword and banishment; with the result that these exiles cast in their lot with the sea-rovers, and he lived to see them sailing up his own rivers. The monasteries founded by Boniface and his fellows became a sort of papal blockhouses. In North Italy, for example, though Columban's Celtic foundations were originally very independent in their attitude towards the Pope, the essential similarity of aim soon produced close alliance, and it was precisely these Celtic Continental abbeys whose influence was decisive in favour of Rome when the Lombard princes leaned rather eastwards, and seemed likely to found a rival Patriarchate at Milan. But this mixture of politics with religion, however natural and inevitable, had its weaker side. The converted Germans or Slavs received their commands in terms which distinguished imperfectly between the moral and the legal sanctions. "Thou shalt pay thy tithes to the priests" was decreed in the same tones as "Thou shalt do no murder"; and in each case transgression was punished both by Church and by State. This, however convenient in many ways for the Church, did in later days render her far more vulnerable on the spiritual side; for she thus gave heavy hostages to fortune.

Such, then, was the Papacy at the beginning of our period: incomparably the strongest spiritual power in Europe, and rapidly extending that power by encroachment upon the civil sphere. There was as yet no theory of Papal Infallibility in the modern sense; and, when the question definitely emerges in the fifteenth century, it will be decided almost unanimously against the Pope. Yet already in the eleventh century there is a general agreement that what Rome thinks to-day is pretty nearly that which the Western World will think to-morrow. On the strength of this, it has become comparatively easy for the Pope to condemn a sovereign so definitely in the religious or moral sphere that there can be but one consequence in the civil sphere: this man is unfit to reign. The story of Gregory VII and Canossa is known everywhere; but there is perhaps even greater significance in Gregory's letter to Sweyn, King of Denmark, offering to his son, to conquer and take for himself, "a certain most opulent province hard by us, which is held by vile and grovelling heretics"—*quam viles et ignavi tenent haeretici.*[12] Here is the assertion of a principle big with consequences for the future. For by this, and by their utilization of those False Decretals which had been forged neither by themselves nor for this immediate purpose, the Popes constructed a bridge which enabled them now to trespass upon the sphere reserved for the civil powers by the Gelasian concordat; but a bridge which lent itself, when the world had developed still further, to devastating counter-attacks. We shall see later on how this Gregorian doctrine of the Omnicompetence of the Church gave occasion, by reaction and by a reversal of weapons, to a harshly contradictory doctrine, that of the Omnicompetence of the State.

4. FEUDALISM EMERGES

We have seen how the Church emerged from this welter of barbarism. Let us now trace the emergence of feudalism. This system is proverbially difficult to define; and many writers escape from the difficulty by denying that there is any system at all. Yet at least feudalism is a collection of customs which, however much they may differ from time to time and from place to place, have certain main characteristics in common; and to that extent we may certainly speak of it as a system. We must therefore consider it fully, detail by detail. First, let us glance briefly at its growth from a mingling of Roman and Germanic ideas. Then we can come to a rough definition; and thence we can pass to a fuller view of its development step by step.

As a general description of its growth we may say that it sprang from composite Romano-Germanic society: let us therefore look at these two elements separately. We cannot say that it is only necessary to take Germanism and Romanism and shake them together, and that the mixture will produce feudalism; but at least feudalism did grow naturally out of those two separate roots.

The *German*, as described by Tacitus, was an individualist. He was a peasant, herdsman or agriculturist or hunter, and inclined to say, as the Mongols said: "We are all kings in our own country." He was dimly conscious of duties to his village: more vaguely of certain duties to his tribe. The idea of a nation he grasped, in so far as he ever grasped it at all, only in such great crises as those of war; very much as it needed the Great War of 1914 to make Europe think seriously of a League of Nations.

The *Roman* of the Empire at its full development was, on the contrary, brought up to strict collectivism: he was forced to feel that the State was infinitely more than the individual. He lived under a most complicated bureaucratic machinery, in which he knew himself to be only one of a hundred million cogwheels, and he knew that the Emperor was the mainspring of it all. He passed his life, therefore, under the most perfect and comprehensive system of laws devised up to that time by the genius of man. He was met at every step by " the State commands this ", " the State forbids that "; and at every step he found a State official to enforce these commands and these prohibitions, until he scarcely felt that he had a will of his own.

Such, it may be said almost without exaggeration, was the civilized Roman mentality, although we must remember that there was much evasion or violation of the laws whenever the subject thought he could find a chance. Feudalism, then, is a step forward in collectivism for the German, a step backward for the Roman. Yet the germs of it are clearly traceable in both systems. Roman society, in its decay, tended to feudalism; German society, in its forward growth, tended the same way. We associate it mainly with the most Romanized Germans—the Franks—among whom it had its fullest development. Yet in England also a real rudimentary feudal system existed already before the Norman Conquest, among that mixed population of Celts, Anglo-Saxons and Scandinavians who had practically forgotten the Roman element that in earlier times had worked in British civilization. We may consider this Romano-Germanic development under two heads; first from the social and next from the political point of view.

Socially, feudalism grew up through the loss of the ordinary man's independence; or, shall we say, of such small measure of independence as he could enjoy under the imperial bureaucracy. When the barbarian invasion came, there was a more or less sudden dissolution of those laws which, while they restrained him in a hundred little details of life, did nevertheless protect him within the network of those details. Life became so definitely a struggle for survival that the smaller man had no chance, either financially or physically, without the protection of some bigger man. Thus many little peasant-proprietorships gravitated together into a single great estate, resembling what in medieval times would be called the *manor*: here alone was a financial unit strong enough to survive, the only change being that the lord was now one of these military conquerors instead of the old hereditary possessor. Thus the yeomen proprietors became vassals to the lord of the manor; and this gave them not only some sort of protection from physical violence, but might also supply the financial support which enabled the small man to outlive a bad harvest.

Politically, the change may be traced mainly to financial causes. Civilization was now almost altogether agricultural. On the one hand the great arts and commerce of the Roman Empire had almost entirely perished; on the other, those arts which were destined to raise our Gothic cathedrals, and that trade which carried Marco Polo all over Asia, will not come for many centuries yet. Thus the main, and almost the only, financial reality is land and the produce of land. Even money is extremely scarce. This we can see very plainly in the ordinances of Charles the Great. That great Emperor had no means of spending a considerable part of his income but by eating and drinking it, he and his servants, straight from the farm. We see him, as we see sovereigns and great nobles all through the Middle Ages, travelling from one estate to another with his ministers and his train: eating up the year's produce in a week or a few days, and then passing on to eat up a fresh estate. Under those primitive conditions tenants naturally paid their rent in kind or in service, more especially in the latter. The peasant held his little plot on condition of three days' work for his lord and three for himself; and, since fighting was a very prominent part of the world's work, therefore the peasant must march under his lord's banner. Again, since the royal law-courts are distant and probably weak, perhaps in some cases almost non-existent, therefore the lord naturally asserts jurisdiction over the tenant; especially since medieval jurisdiction is a very profitable job, resting mainly upon a tariff of fines for each offence. Hence the medieval maxim, *magnum est emolumentum iustitia.* Not only was it thus the landlord's interest to judge, but the tenant would rather be judged by the petty tyrant of his own fields than have no judgment at all.

Therefore he accepted the system of manorial courts which grew up, with such rights of appeal to royal courts as good luck might enable him to preserve.

Thus then we have already a rudimentary political system, in so far as we can give the name of *system* to that which grew up mainly through custom, and which differed so widely in details at different places and times, and which never arrived at so high a point of definition but that it left great room for disputes. It is difficult to make a modern reader realize how far custom and verbal agreement took the place of written law, not only in the Dark Ages, but even to the end of the Middle Ages; yet, on the other hand we must beware of a tendency to exaggeration on this point which has shown itself, especially in the last thirty years or so. The men of those times were themselves under no illusions as to the inferior preciseness of tradition when compared with the written word. In the eleventh and twelfth centuries, when written charters become frequent, it is almost common form for the contracting parties to explain that they commit this to writing for the sake of superior durability of parchment, or (to quote the exact words of one monastic charter): "Man is a forgetful animal." In the later Middle Ages, therefore, we find the earlier customs constantly committed to writing. Thus, at least in the modified sense here indicated, feudalism was not only a system, but a political system. Groups of peasants were bound to a lord in three senses alike—financial, legal and military. The lord himself, with many of his fellows, was probably similarly bound to a greater noble; the greater noble again to his count or his duke; and the count or duke still owed service and obedience, if only nominal, to the sovereign.

In this way, apart from those who depended directly upon the sovereign as immediate tenants (*tenants-in-chief*, as they were called), the shadow, at least, of central authority was kept up by this network of responsibilities all converging upon the prince. The legal theory which accounted for both aspects of the system, social and political, crystallized finally into this: that the whole land of the State belonged in fact to the prince; that he was the one Universal Landlord; that he let out large districts to the counts and dukes under certain conditions of service; they in their turn to smaller lords; and so on down to the peasant. In other words, you could measure a man's status in the Middle Ages by his land, possession always implying a corresponding proportion of service. Moreover, although under this fully developed feudalism tenure had become hereditary, the lands passing by immemorial custom from father to son, yet the theory which distinguished such mere occupation from ownership in the strictest sense was maintained, among other ways, by the system of wardship and marriage. When a man died leaving children under age, the over-lord took over his lands and administered them until the heir came to his majority. If it was a girl-heiress, the overlord had similar rights. In France, indeed, he had only a veto on the girl's marriage: he could prevent her taking a hostile, or in any way inconvenient, husband. But in England the guardian might himself dispose of her in marriage; and our nobles may be found openly making large sums in this way; trading in marriages—to use the brutal word—practically as men trade in shares and investments to-day.

Thus (to take a last look at the system from this point of view of development from Romano-Germanic origins), in theory it kept up collectivism. It was highly centralized; it was an elaborate network leading inevitably upwards towards the sovereign. In practice, however, it was Germanic individualism in larger groups. The unit was no longer the family, but the manor or group of manors; and these larger groups had become practically independent of the sovereign. In its most developed form—that is in eleventh-century France—the national system had become obliterated. The central authority was nominal; nearly all the sovereign's power had passed into the hands of his greater tenants, each of whom was a petty sovereign on his own lands, enjoying practically every one of those rights which the sovereign enjoyed only in theory throughout the whole State.

There, then, is a rough-and-ready description of the development of feudalism, as a practical necessity under the circumstances of that time. The German conqueror knew too much now to go on living that primitive life of forest-clearings as described by Tacitus. But he did not yet know enough to organize a great bureaucratic state such as Constantine's Empire had been. Some dim resemblance to Constantine's state was possible for a moment under Charles the Great; but under his successors the centrifugal forces became too great for the rudimentary coherence of this vast mass. The Empire, therefore, from being one great planet rolling in the heavens, split up into a planetary system, a multitude of stars revolving more or less regularly round the Emperor or some other sovereign.

From this rough sketch of the stages of development we can now proceed to a definition. Feudum, or fee, or fief, is land (or office, or revenue) held in dependence upon any person. In its most definitely crystallized form, all landholders thus depend upon the sovereign. All are his dependants, either directly *in capite* or indirectly through some other lord. Then, as a complement to this, every man owes homage and service, especially military service, to the man from whom he holds land. Thus, he stands to that man not only as tenant to landlord, but as vassal to over-lord. So that, as Maitland says,[1] "Feudalism" is an unfortunate word; it expresses only half the thing; the full word should be "feudo-vassalism"; for under real feudalism the two ideas were inseparable—the ideas of financial dependence and personal dependence. We must therefore bear in mind Maitland's further warning that "the difficulty is not one that could be solved by any merely verbal devices. The impossible task that has been set before the word *feudalism* is that of making a single idea represent a very large piece of the world's history, represent the France, Italy, Germany, England, of every century from the eighth or ninth to the fourteenth or fifteenth."

Having followed the growth of feudalism just sufficiently to make that brief definition comprehensible, let us now try to form a clearer conception of it by tracing its growth in closer detail. We will trace it first in the Roman State; secondly, in the Germanic; and thirdly in the medieval State, developed from those composite Romano-Germanic origins. Moreover, we will take notice of its double character, personal and financial.

(1) ROMAN.

(*a*) The personal relation is here the oldest; that relation of the client to his patron which we find from almost the earliest times in Roman civilization. In later times, under the Empire, this system by which the small man formally placed himself in dependence upon a great man is called *patrocinium*.

(*b*) The financial relation of dependence grew up under the Empire, and was called *precarium*. This originally signified a tenancy by friendship or favour, from *precare*; *X* prays *Y*, as a favour, to let him have the use of a plot of land. "It is a flea-bite to you," he says, "but it would be a godsend to me"; and the other answers: "Yes, you shall have it on a precarial tenancy, giving you no legal claim upon it. I may alter the terms at will, or resume the whole grant at will; and at my death my heir is not in any way bound to continue this agreement." Hence, at Roman law, a *precarial* tenant has no rights as against his landlord, though he has such against other people. When, in times of trouble, a poor man besought a great man to protect his farm, the great man would naturally reply: "I can protect my own property, but not yours; make the land mine, and you shall have it back as a *precarium*." Thus the bargain would be struck. After the tenant's death, his children would make the best terms they could. The great man's interest was not to be too harsh, and custom consecrated increasingly the idea that these precarial tenancies should be allowed to continue so long as the tenant did his duty.

There can be little doubt that the enormous financial burdens of the later Roman Empire, which laid all the stress of taxation on the middle-class proprietors, ended by reducing thousands of those men to absolute poverty. They thus found themselves compelled to abandon all, responsibilities and ownership alike, to some other landholder who was ready to bear them. Therefore, just as some of these bankrupts would protect themselves personally by *patrocinium*, others would protect themselves financially by *precarium*, and many would take advantage of both customs. Thus we have already a rudimentary feudo-vassalage system.

(2) GERMAN.

(*a*) Personal. Here again the " client " system meets us from the earliest times. Tacitus describes how distinguished warriors would gather around them a whole following of satellites, in proportion to their own reputation and influence; he calls this companionship *comitatus*. He describes this fellowship-tie as stronger than that which bound the man to his State. It was a lifelong dishonour for the companion to come back alive from a battle in which his lord had fallen.

(*b*) Financial. There was no early German analogy here. They had nothing resembling a *precarium*; probably because early German society was as yet too undeveloped to admit of such financial relations.

(3) THE ROMANO-GERMAN.

(*a*) When invasions and conquests came, then these barbarian conquerors found themselves face to face with Roman institutions, to which they had frequently the wisdom to adapt themselves. Their *comitatus* and the Roman *patrocinium* shook hands at once; it is difficult to say that either needed to undergo much modification; except perhaps a numerical increase. The times were more turbulent, the poor man stood in greater need of protection; *patrocinium* therefore was more frequent and systematic than under the Roman Empire.

(*b*) For the same reasons the *precarium*, though new to the conquerors, was rapidly adopted by them. With the Germans, as with the Romans, the great man was glad to add to his estate; the poor man needed help even more; and therefore the *precarium* developed as rapidly among the Franks as the *patrocinium*, only changing its name to *beneficium*. Moreover, under the Merovingian kings two steps were taken which were most important for the development of feudalism. First, even great men adopted the *precarium* tenure: and, secondly, *precarium* and *patrocinium* were fused into one single system.

Here, as so often in the Middle Ages, the Church led the way even in matters of worldly business. Her estates soon became very great, tempting the spoiler; therefore the obvious policy was: "Let us enlist the spoiler on our side." Moreover, the bishop or abbot had official public functions as a great landowner; and it was convenient to shift those upon the shoulders of fighting men. Therefore they often let considerable estates on *precarium* tenure to great men, who were glad to get them on such terms. Gradually, therefore, precarial tenure increased in dignity; in the first place it was founded on written contract; secondly, the tenant held it for life; and thirdly, the landlord, for his part, received some sort of rent, though not the full value.

While the Church was protecting herself by thus enlisting great lords on her side through precarial tenures, small cultivators were using the same device to secure this powerful spiritual protection. Vinogradoff points out that "the monastery of Fulda, the famous foundation of St Boniface, gathered 15,000 *mansi* in a short time from pious donors.*. . . A considerable part of this property came from small people, who tried in this way not only to propitiate God, but also to win protectors in the persons of powerful lords." That is these peasants granted to the monastery the *lordship* of the land, and received it back as a *precarium*.[2]

Then, under the Mayors of the Palace, *precarium* and *patrocinium* coalesced, and became full-fledged feudo-vassalism.

(*c*) Merovingian kings had secured fighting men by grants of royal land; indeed, one reason of the impotence into which they lapsed was that they had thus squandered their lands so recklessly as nearly to exhaust their own power. But their successors, the Mayors of the Palace, lacking a legitimate hereditary title, were under still stronger necessity of buying the support of fighting men. To this we must add the fact that the average warrior, by this time, had become a much more

* *Mansus* is very nearly equal to the *caput* of Constantine's taxation —i.e. enough land for one man to till in a year.

expensive person. The formidable Arab invasions from Spain had shown the value of the mounted man. The long warfare in Southern Gaul, by which the Franks held these Arabs in check, necessitated a large body of cavalry; and this broke down the prehistoric principle that the soldier is not only recruited by compulsion, but must serve at his own expense. Hitherto it had only been necessary to pay the greater men who led the armies; the rank and file, in so far as they were paid at all, were rewarded from the booty. But the ordinary peasant cannot buy and keep horses at his own expense. On both sides, therefore, the question of payment for military service became vital and highly perplexing. The obvious temptation was to fall back here upon the Church, which by this time had become immensely rich; it is often estimated that her lands amounted to one-third of the whole soil of Gaul. The problem was solved in this sense by the conqueror of the Arabs, Charles Martel, who argued: "the army lacks money, the Church abounds; let us therefore pay the army out of Church lands, and by the methods which the Church has already invented." Thus these Church lands were granted on precarial tenure, the rent being paid in military service. In this way *precarium* (*feudum, beneficium*) coalesced with *patrocinium* (vassalage), and we have a real system of feudo-vassalism. This is why Charles Martel, in spite of the fact that he had saved Christendom by his battle at Poitiers and by other successes against the Arabs, was seen after his death by a pious visionary writhing in the lowest depths of hell.

Charles the Great seems to have seen clearly the centrifugal tendency of this system, and for a time he combated it; though at last the necessities of his vast Empire reduced him to compliance. The first necessity was this, that he had organized his dominions on the county system; this meant that the count had exceptional advantages for increasing his own body of vassals. He could take care, at least, that all who did not thus seek his protection should get rather more than less than their full share of military and other public duties; and in many cases he applied the screw more tightly still. We therefore find Charles legislating firmly against this, and trying to make it easier for the poor man to fulfil his military duties directly to the State. But the task was too great; Charles had to give it up, and we find him finally facing the facts. Then he simply compels the count or great lord to appear in the field with so many men, and leaves it to him to raise them, thus lightening the central government of a great burden, but sowing the seeds of future troubles. The great vassals, being thus allowed to surround themselves with an army of smaller vassals, became more and more independent. They reverted more and more to the old Germanic custom noted by Tacitus, where the *comitatus*, the personal tie between a great fighting man and his dependents, was far stronger than the ordinary citizen's loyalty to the State. He was no longer the Emperor's man, so much as the count's (or other lord's) man. Feudal loyalty overshadowed State loyalty. This, which seems so strange to us, that even formal legislation should treat loyalty to the immediate lord as a matter of such supreme importance, comes out very strongly in the Laws of Alfred. The testimony is all the more important, because it is not that of an extremist; England at this time was not more feudalized, but distinctly less, than most European countries. Yet, under Alfred, murder may be compounded for by a fine, a fine will atone for almost any other offence; but not treason against the lord—whether king or minor lord. And this is put on Christian grounds: the traitor's crime is the crime of Judas. When the law treated disloyalty to small and great lords alike as capital crimes, the subject naturally obeyed not that distant abstraction, the king, but rather the near and tangible authority, the immediate over-lord.*

It will be seen, then, that we can call this a "system", and speak of it as "logical", only in the sense that it had the logic of natural growth. Indeed, the comparatively homogeneous character of Anglo-Norman feudalism is one of the most exceptional phenomena in this whole sphere. In other words,

* Compare similar evidence from the Laws of Edmund Ironside and Henry I in Pollock and Maitland, 1,300. In the former, the vassal's loyalty to the smaller lord is actually taken as the model of his loyalty to the king: "He shall swear fealty to King Edmund as a man ought to be faithful to his lord."

here, even more than elsewhere in the Middle Ages, to be regular is itself an irregularity. In A.D. 800 Charles the Great was still casting all his weight against it: yet, scarcely more than a century later, it reigned everywhere as the alternative to anarchy. The small Latin kingdom of Jerusalem did indeed draw up deliberately a feudal constitution, though it is very doubtful how far this ever worked. But, among great States, feudalism was most regular and logical in England after the Conquest, for the simple reason that it was introduced as a fairly well-grown plant from Normandy, by a sovereign who intended, and was able, to keep his new kingdom in a firm grasp. The extent to which pre-Conquest England had already become feudalized by a natural process of growth is still disputed; but it is generally admitted that, until that date, we and the Scandinavians were the least feudalized of nations. William, by his Oath of Salisbury, initiated the policy of assuming that all his vassals should swear allegiance to the Crown, whatever other allegiance they might owe to each other. Thus, and by Edward I's statute *quia Emptores* (1290), England never suffered from anything approaching to the complexity of feudal relations which developed in France (for instance) through changes and divisions of ownership. The Count of Champagne was one of the greatest lords in France, yet for only a small fraction of his princely territories did he own the king as over-lord. The rest he held from a foreign sovereign (the Holy Roman Emperor); from the Duke of Burgundy, who owned small allegiance to France; from two archbishops, four bishops and an abbot. Seignobos quotes a case where he has found one man holding "the third part of the half of two-thirds of the tithe" of such-and-such an estate:

$$1/3 \times 1/2 \times 2/3 \times 1/10 = 1/90.$$

Cases could be quoted of nine different men holding the same piece of land, in gradation, above the tenant who tilled it.[3] Pollock and Maitland quote instances for England; but far less complicated than this. Even here, however, a man might hold his lands from a dozen lords, and in those cases personal service necessarily broke down; whether *military* service, which was the commonest form of tenure, or *socage*, as most forms of non-military service were called. This is admirably exemplified in the case of copyholds, which by the conservatism of English law survived until a few years ago. In the later Middle Ages, even great men thought it no degradation to hold lands in socage tenure from others far below themselves in the social scale; and sometimes they even held copyholds, which rendered them liable to the pecuniary burdens of villein tenants. I have heard that, in the later nineteenth century, Lord Rothschild bought an estate of which part was copyhold under New College, Oxford. The Warden and Fellows, therefore, were in that respect his lords, and he had to redeem the freehold in all haste lest, at his death, these over-lords should claim as a heriot his " best beast " which, in the case of so distinguished a racing man, might have been worth £20,000 or more. Whether the facts were exactly thus or not, the case was certainly quite possible. Therefore, already in the twelfth century, lawyers had begun to distinguish between " liege-homage ", which was unlimited, and simple " homage ". In the latter case, the tenant swore: " I do you homage, saving the fealty that I owe to my liege lord." Thus, finally, by far the greatest number of tenures became practically confined to financial and judicial relations. First came the tenant's rent, either in produce, labour, or money. Then, for all cases of dispute resting upon his tenure, he was bound to plead in the lord's court.

In England, therefore, with our comparatively regular feudal arrangements from the Conquest onwards, we may look upon it as normal (amid many exceptions) that all land belongs in theory to the sovereign; others are his tenants, whether directly or indirectly. All tenancies involve homage and service. The tenant must sue in his own lord's court for all cases except murder or " mayhem " (maiming), for which even the bondman may go for redress to the king's courts. Finally, these conditions are hereditary; the lord has no option but to admit the heir to his predecessor's tenancy, so long as he is ready to do homage and render the attendant services.

It will be seen how all this consecrated the division of classes; in eleventh-century Christendom it was almost as in Islam; we had a fighting caste supported by a working caste. Liberty was but half-developed: as Lord Acton says, it depended upon property; or, as Maitland puts it, *libertas* in legal language meant freedom to oppress others. Even in the towns with their gilds, "democracy, as they understood it, was nothing but the democracy of the privileged".[4] The Church did indeed help a little; yet, as we shall see, no orthodox Churchman protested against the principle of serfdom; that was left to the heretic Wyclif. As we shall see again, even the democratic author of *Piers Plowman* felt it perverse that a bondman's son should be made a bishop, rare as such an occurrence might be. Outside the clergy, barriers were far more severe. It was difficult, within our period, for a man to break through these class distinctions even by the greatest services in war. There was then no parallel to that which might happen under the Pagan Empire, when (for instance) the Asiatic peasant Justin fought his way up from a common soldier's pay to the imperial throne. Du Guesclin himself, the ablest commander on either side in the Hundred Years' War, was long kept in the background by the disadvantage of birth: he was noble, indeed, but only of the lesser nobility.

5. LAND AND FOLK

Having now taken a brief constitutional survey of the rulers, both civil and ecclesiastical, we may cease for a while to consider them in their daily action, and look at the land and the people upon whom they were to act. English Common Law is in its foundation a collection of folk customs; and, again, it might perhaps be as true to say that the folk made medieval religion, as that the religion made the folk. The story of development here will help to illustrate a truth too often neglected in our present natural reaction against the Great War: that nationalism is a necessary and healthy step towards internationalism.

Anglo-Saxon England clearly showed a want of national coherence. It needed the Conquest to bring the people to that point of civilization at which they should be conscious of nationality all over the country. For instance, a year after Hastings, the South-West was still unsubdued, openly defying William; so again was the North—Yorkshire and Northumberland. Yet there was no attempt at concerted action. The two risings were not even timed to be simultaneous; so that William was easily able to beat each in detail. He had the immense military advantage of a more despotic government. This Saxon incoherence was remedied by the Conquest. Here was a strong man, able to hold the country when once he had taken it, and supported by companions in arms whose interests coincided with his own; so that the Norman rule, continuing unbroken for nearly a century, welded England together by its heavy irresistible presssure. It was well for us that the victory at Hastings lay with such a race as the Normans, men whose coming into France marks an epoch in the history of that nation, and even more definitely of our own. The Norman was certainly a very remarkable social element, which asserted itself wherever it went; an element so important that we must consider it in closer detail. Let us first regard the Norman characteristics in themselves, and thence proceed to enquire how far they were strictly racial, or how far they were due to other than hereditary causes.

The Norman characteristics have never been better described than by the eleventh-century Italian chronicler, Geoffrey Malaterra, who had observed these people closely during their conquest of Sicily and Southern Italy. He writes: "They are a most cunning and revengeful race. They leave their native fields for the hope of richer booty; greedy of gain, greedy of dominion; prone to imitate whatsoever they see; evenly balanced between lavishness and greediness [i.e. you never know whether you will find them spendthrifts or robbers]. Their princes are most generous where they hope to earn fame by their generosity. These Normans can flatter when they choose, and are so eager to become accomplished speakers that even the boys argue like trained rhetoricians. They are headstrong to excess unless they be curbed by the stern hand of justice. They are patient of cold if need be, patient of hunger, patient of hard work; they are passionately fond of hawking, of riding, of warlike armour, and of splendid garments." Freeman (whose article in the 11th edition of *The Encyclopaedia Britannica* is most valuable and illuminating) notes this curious combination of the masterfulness of the man of action with the pettifogging lawyer's mind. He points out how this comes out not only in William the Conqueror, but in several of his descendants, down to Edward I at least; and he adds: "If the Norman was a born soldier, he was also a born lawyer." Very remarkable also was the similar combination of strength with pliancy. No people have ever shown themselves more adaptable to changing circumstances. When they settled in North-Western France, Neustria, they became rapidly more French than the French: in twelfth-century Ireland it was noted of these Norman invaders that when once they had settled down they became *Hibernis ipsis Hiberniores*. These Normans—or Northmen, as at first they had been called—were the last and most terrible of the heathen invaders who broke into the Roman Empire. Yet they soon took their place among the most loyal sons of the Christian Church. They were, as Freeman says: "The most lavish in gifts to holy places at home, and the most unwearied in pilgrimages to holy places abroad. . . . The Norman was a crusader before the crusades." Their restless energy is emphasized by two early English historians, William of Malmesbury and Henry of Huntingdon; and these characteristics were doubtless to a great extent racial, shared by the modern Norwegian, Swede and Dane. The country of Nansen, Ibsen, and so many fruitful democratic experiments in our own day, still keeps much of the rough energy, yet ready adaptability, which a race naturally acquires in a long struggle against a rigorous climate and a dangerous sea. But we must not imagine complete racial homogeneity among those Northmen of the Dark Ages, who, when they settled down, came to be called Normans. Hastings, one of the most celebrated "Northmen" pirates of the ninth century, is said by the chronicler Ralph Glaber to have been a French peasant from the district of Troyes. It is most probable, indeed, that many of the so-called Normans who began pillaging the Empire during the last years of Charles the Great were really heathen Saxons who had been driven out by his conquests, refusing to reconcile themselves on any terms with Christianity. We may take it as practically certain that, though the large majority would come from one northern land or another, yet the bond of union was community rather of circumstances than of race. Something had turned them all into sea-robbers: they were a horde of pirates which welcomed recruits from all quarters indiscriminately. And the circumstances may be roughly enumerated as follows.

First, the struggle for life, naturally fierce in those simple times under so inclement a sky and over so niggardly a soil as are usual in the North. In Jutland, for instance, there was a formal law that, every five years, the population should be reduced by sending younger sons into exile; and even without such a regular law the fight for existence would naturally reduce many either to slavery at home, or to exile. In those circumstances the bolder spirits would unquestionably choose exile. Then again, a man might flee or be banished for some crime; the thief, the manslayer, would naturally take refuge with these outlaws. Thirdly, we must reckon with the sheer love of adventure, such as that which drove so many before the Great War to turn their back on the deadly dullness of village existence and "see life" in the army. In all these cases the Northman who left his native land would be a rougher, more resourceful man than the average of those who stayed at home. And, as they were thus picked men to begin with, so also their mode of life would sift them into a sort of uniformity. Seafaring is a rough job at best. Dr Johnson was accustomed to wonder how any man went to sea who had the alternative of going to prison; and in the tiny open boats of those days the hardships must have been incomparably worse. These sea-rovers lived in continual conflict, in which the weakest would go to the wall. They suffered terrible hardships of storm and hunger and thirst: and, what perhaps would be still more trying to nature, the wild excesses at moments when they had successfully plundered a ship or a town. All these conditions would give the Northern pirate a particular stamp, quite as marked as any racial character. The only men who could survive this kind of life would be precisely of the kind which Malaterra describes—uniting violence with cunning; restless energy with the most pliant adaptability. The Anglo-Saxons, of course, had once been a people of this kind. But they were a numerical minority in England; these conquering races have always been minorities. By long intermarriage with the conquered, by long devotion to agriculture and forgetfulness of his past seafaring habits, the Anglo-Saxon of 1066 had become a very different person from his ancestors who first came over. The people of England, and English civilization, needed a fresh stimulus and a strain of new blood.

Before the Conquest, then, these original Northmen had settled in Italy, and had adapted themselves to that Southern civilization; in France, again, they had picked up all they could learn from their more cultured neighbours. The insular Saxons, on the other hand, in their comparative backwater, were at a distinctly lower stage of civilization. Ordericus Vitalis, who was of mixed parentage and knew both nations well, writes:

" The Normans found the English a rustic and almost illiterate folk." William of Malmesbury, who again was of mixed blood, tells us how in process of time the desire after literature and religion had decayed, for several years before the arrival of the Normans.[1] " The clergy, contented with a very slight degree of learning, could scarcely stammer out the words of the sacraments; and a person who understood grammar was an object of wonder and astonishment. The monks mocked the rule of their Order by fine vestments, and the use of every kind of food. The nobility, given up to luxury and wantonness, went not to church in the morning after the manner of Christians, but merely, in a careless manner, heard Matins and Mass from a hurrying priest in their chambers, amid the blandishments of their wives. The commonalty, left unprotected, became a prey to the most powerful, who amassed fortunes, either by seizing on their property, or by selling their persons into foreign countries; although it be an innate quality of this people, to be more inclined to revelling than to the accumulation of wealth. There was one custom, repugnant to nature, which they adopted; namely, to sell their female servants, when pregnant by them and after they had satisfied their lust, either to public prostitution, or to foreign slavery. Drinking in parties was a universal practice, in which occupation they passed entire nights as well as days. They consumed their whole substance in mean and despicable houses; unlike the Normans and French, who, in noble and splendid mansions, lived with frugality. The vices attendant on drunkenness which enervate the human mind, followed." We must make that allowance for these picturesque descriptions which is nearly always necessary when we use medieval literary sources for social life. Authors wrote then with more impulse and less restraint; and these two quotations must be discounted by the studies of Professor Chambers (for instance) in pre-Conquest social history.

There, then, are the two different races. Now let us consider their interaction after the Conquest. The political change was the most obvious. To describe it roughly, something like 20,000 foreigners replaced 20,000 Englishmen, and naturally took the highest places. The king was a Norman; so were the earls, the bishops, the abbots, and nearly all the owners of great estates. Again, the greatest among the townsfolk were generally displaced by these conquerors. In a few cases the invader married the widow or daughter of the man he displaced, but such cases were naturally exceptional. The men who thus took the pick of the country to themselves were better educated, better managers, hardier and thriftier, and in far closer touch with Continental civilization. The spirit of adventure was fresher in them than in those Anglo-Saxons who were so many generations removed from the old conquering days. Again, these adventurers had not yet settled down into the content natural to a saturated population. They were quicker to seize upon new ideas, and had the unscrupulousness which is the natural effect of such qualities. They introduced far better organization into the country; and their adaptability and sense of reality saved them from any attempt to suppress the native language. The bulk of the conquered nation retained this as obstinately as Alsace kept German under the French Governments from Louis XIV to Napoleon III. It has often been remarked that, whereas our flesh foods are all French in name, christened as they came to the Norman table, yet this "beef" and "pork" and "mutton" were still called "ox" and "swine" and "sheep" by the Saxons who tended them.

Giraldus Cambrensis, whose descent from Welsh kings gave added force to his natural scorn of a rival nationality, rejoices to think that "the English are servants to the Normans—and basest of servants". Yet within an extraordinarily short space these two nations were practically fused. The Danish conqueror had soon become almost indistinguishable from those whom he had conquered; and, if something like the same result took place with the Normans, it was to a great extent because they also came originally from a northern stock or civilization. To begin with, William showed a sense of justice (or, if you will, of enlightened prudence) such as was shown by few medieval conquerors. He retained the old English laws as much as possible; fortunately for us, the Norman laws had not been committed to writing, so that it was only a case of conflict between the unwritten custom of a small minority and the partly written customs of a great majority; the concordat was therefore comparatively easy. We are told also that he even tried to learn English for the sake of dealing justice himself. Again, the two great Norman archbishops, Lanfranc and Anselm, did very much to soften the rigours of conquest; and, in spite of natural exceptions, it may truly be said that the Church in general contributed much to this process of fusion. The cases of St Elphege and St Wulstan of Worcester will explain this. Elphege, the Saxon, would have been expunged by Lanfranc from the calendar but for St Anselm's defence; and Wulstan's story is so picturesque that it may well find a place here in the racy English of Caxton's *Golden Legend.* Whether the details given by the biographer be historically true or false, they are none the less significant for the spirit of Norman and Saxon at that moment. "When William Conqueror had gotten all England, and had it under his power, then he began to meddle with the Church, and by the advice of Lanfranc, the holy bishop St Wulstan was challenged that he was not able of letters, ne of conning for to occupy the realm and office of a bishop, and was called tofore Lanfranc, and willed him to resign by the consent of the king to the said Lanfranc, archbishop, that a man of greater conning might occupy the dignity. To whom Wulstan said: 'Forsooth father, I know well that I am not worthy to have this dignity, ne am not sufficient to occupy so great a charge, for I knew well mine unconning at such time when I was elect thereto, but I was compelled by our holy father the pope, and by good king Edward, and sith it pleaseth the council that I shall resign, I shall gladly resign, but not to you, but to him that compelled me to take it.' And he departed incontinent from the archbishop Lanfranc, and went straight to the tomb of S. Edward [the Confessor] with his cross in his hand, and he said to S. Edward, as he had then been alive: 'O thou holy and blessed king, thou knowest well that I took this charge on me against my will, but by constraint of the pope and thee I obeyed to take it, and it now so is that we have a new king, new laws, and giveth new sentences, in reproving thee of thine error for so much as thou gavest it to me, simple and unconning man, and me, for the presumption that I would consent to take it. That time thou mightest well have been beguiled, for thou wert a frail man, but now thou art joined to God, whereas thou mayst not be deceived. Thou gavest to me the charge, and to thee I here resign it again.' And with that he fixed his staff into the hard stone of his tomb, saying: 'Take this and give it to whom it pleaseth thee.' And the hard stone that lay upon his tomb resolved by miracle, and received his cross or pastoral staff, and held it so fast that it might not be taken out by man's hand. And anon he did off the habit of a bishop, and did on a cowl, and stood among the monks in such degree as he did tofore ere he was bishop. And when word came, and was reported to them that had consented to his resignation, they marvelled greatly and were all abashed, and some of them went to the tomb and would have pulled out the staff, but they could not move it. And when the archbishop Lanfranc heard thereof he commanded to Gundulf, bishop of Rochester, to go and fetch to him the pastoral staff, but when he came he set hand on it and pulled at it, but the stone held it so fast that he might not move it, wherefore he was sore abashed, and came to Lanfranc, and told him of this miracle. Then the king and Lanfranc were abashed and came both in their persons to see this thing, and there made their prayers. And after, with great reverence, Lanfranc assayed and set hand on the staff for to have pulled it out, but it would not move. Then the king and the archbishop were sore afraid, and repented them, and sent for to seek Wulstan, whom they found among the monks and brought him tofore the king and the archbishop, who anon kneeled down and asked forgiveness. And Wulstan meekly kneeled down and prayed them not so to do to him, and humbly and meekly pardoned them and prayed the archbishop humbly to bless him." Yet, although the influence of the clergy here and always was internationalistic to a certain degree, that was far from sufficient to bridge the gulf completely. Becket was the first English-born Archbishop of Canterbury, and even he was not English by race: his father was a Norman who had become an English citizen. Some of our sees, again, had no English bishop until even later dates.

Another cause which made for fusion between the two nations was Anselm's resistance for conscience sake to William Rufus, and afterwards to Henry I. This tended to bring together all who were inspired by the spirit of freedom in their resistance to royal despotism. Another step was marked by that Charter of Henry I which definitely fixed the "Laws of King Edward" as English Common Law, and by his marriage to the Saxon Princess Matilda. These were definite statesman-like concessions in favour of the English. Moreover, for several generations common sufferings and common dangers bound the two races together. When the barons revolted under Rufus, he used the Saxon term in appealing to all his subjects; he would brand as *nithing* every man who refused to march with him against these undisciplined depredators. So, again, the feudal anarchy under Stephen created in all orderly people a common interest to support the Crown; and, lastly, when the Scots invaded England, the two races vied with each other in bravery at Northallerton (1138). But perhaps the most important cause of all was one which has run throughout our post-Conquest history like a consecutive thread. Since 1066 we have had no real invasion. No foreigner has ever succeeded in interfering in our politics, and hindering us from working out our own salvation. Thus the problem of English politics has always been essentially simple: just the eternal difference between the conservative and the progressive mind. We have never had, in England proper, those other national factors which complicate the problem indefinitely, since each fresh party in a contest increases the difficulty not in arithmetical but in geometrical progression. Nor, again, have we had that foreign invading element which would find its natural interest in fomenting the quarrel between the other two. We have only to think how Ireland has suffered in that way, and how the worst difficulties of the French and the Russian Revolutions came from the interest which powerful neighbours found in fomenting discord. Thus faced only with the simple problem, England acquired a feeling of real nationality within a surprisingly short time after the Conquest. Henry of Huntingdon, writing before 1150, coined that phrase which has become proverbial—" Merry England "—*Anglia plena jocis.* In the face of the random use of this phrase in our own day, it is necessary to point out that the England of which Henry was writing was the England mainly of his own upper class, from whose standpoint he writes. We shall see presently how little the words were strictly applicable to the vast majority of the population. But the phrase was borrowed, a century later, by the encyclopaedist Friar Bartholomew, whose description is worth quoting in its fourteenth-century translation: " England is a strong land and a sturdy, and the plenteousest corner of the world; so rich a land that unneth [scarcely] it needeth help of any land, and every other land needeth help of England. England is full of mirth and of game, and men oft-times able to mirth and game; free men of heart and with tongue, but the hand is more better and more free than the tongue." Moreover, Henry incorporates in his Latin Chronicle a great deal of Old English literature: the *Battle of Brunanburh* and a number of other poetical fragments. So also does his contemporary, William of Malmesbury, himself of mixed Norman and Saxon race. But the plainest of all testimonies to the mingling of the races comes to us from a law-book of about 1180, the so-called *Dialogue of the Exchequer.* By the Conqueror's disposition, whenever a Norman was found dead, and the slayer could not be discovered, it was presumed that he must have been slain by a Saxon; the utility of this provision is obvious for the protection of a small foreign garrison. In virtue of that presumption, a heavy fine was imposed upon the Hundred; i.e. that section of the community in which the corpse was discovered, unless indeed they could clear themselves by producing the murderer and giving him up to vengeance. " Then ", asks the pupil in this Dialogue, " why is there no such disposition when an Englishman is found slain?" To which the master replies: " There was no such disposition at the first institution of this law, as thou hast heard; but now that English and Normans have lived so long together, and have intermarried, the nations have become so intermingled (I speak of freemen only) that we can scarce distinguish in these days betwixt Englishman and Norman; excepting of course those serfs bound to the land whom we call *villeins*, and who cannot quit their condition without leave of their masters. Wherefore, in these days, almost every secret manslaughter is punished as *murdrum*, except those of whom (as I have said) it is certain that they are of servile condition."[2] Yet, although that law had practically fallen into desuetude by 1180, it was not formally abolished until 1399.

Moreover, we must remember that, though this fusion may be spoken of as practically complete, there would be a good many exceptions: numerous survivals, for many centuries, of the ancient divisions. In the first place nearly all the serfs, as we have seen, were of Saxon origin. Then, again, "Norman" on the one side, and "English" on the other, become fairly common surnames. It is true also that the French tongue long remained that of the upper classes. We find allusions to this, as late as the end of the fourteenth century, in *Piers Plowman*; and again, in episcopal visitations to nunneries at the same time, when Latin was not used the language was French. Moreover, the diversity of English dialects did a good deal to maintain Norman-French in this superior position. Yet the sense of practical fusion between race and race was so strong that Higden, at the beginning of the fourteenth century, describes this mingled people in very much the same terms as those which Malaterra had used for the Normans alone. He writes:[3] "The Englishmen that were in England, that have been mingled with other peoples . . . are so uneasy, also unpatient of peace, enemy of business and loving of sloth. . . . These men be speedful both on horse and on foot, able and ready to all manner deeds of arms . . . and curious, and can well enough tell deeds and wonders that they have seen. Also they go to divers lands. . . . They can better win and get new than keep their own heritage. Therefore it is that they be y-spread so wide, and consider that every other land is their own heritage." He adds: "The men be able to all manner sleight and wit, but before the deed blundering and hasty, and more wise after the deed; and they leave often lightly what they have begun. . . . These men despise their own and praise other men's, and be scarcely pleased with their own estate." At the same time he is strongly conscious of the distinction between North and South. "Scots be light of heart, strong and wild enough, but by mixing with Englishmen they be much amended. They be cruel upon their enemies, and hate bondage most of anything, and they hold it a foul sloth if any man dieth in his bed, and great worship if he die in the field. They be little of meat and may fast long, and eateth well seldom while the sun is up, and eateth flesh, fish, milk and fruit more than bread, and though they be fair of shape they be defouled and made unseemly enough with their own clothing. They praise fast the usage of their own fathers, and despise other men's doing." It is a thousand pities that no contemporary Scottish chronicler has left us his own judgment on these and similar points.

6. THE VILLAGE (I)

Now that we are in a position to deal with ordinary life in greater detail, there can be little doubt as to the class with which we must begin. In the England of our period, at least 90 per cent. of the population were villagers; and the main features differentiating life in those days from life in ours were the ordinary differences between urban and rural civilization. Moreover, it is precisely these village communities to which modern reactionaries look back most fondly, and, on the whole, with most justice; since it must be the concern of all men that we should not lose anything that was of permanent value in that simple and patriarchal state of society. It would be well to take the evidence here mainly from about 1280 to 1380, as the century in which the manorial system is fully developed and for which trustworthy written business documents are abundant to check the literary evidence.

The general population at that time was probably about three and a half to four or four and a half millions, that is little more than one-tenth of what we have to-day. The villages were very small; the average for Western Europe would run from two hundred to 400 or 450 souls : that is, from forty to eighty adult males. Let us travel from Cambridge to Trumpington one day in mid-August. Sir Giles de Trumpington, the lord of the manor, who is now about thirty-three, if we had an introduction to him, might show us with some pride what is still one of the sights of the district; the monumental brass, under its sculptured canopy, which commemorates his lately deceased father. He might also offer us wine from the Trumpington vineyard, for which documentary evidence has survived. We should not drink lavishly of this. After that courtesy, he might well charge his steward to show us round the village. The cottages are small; here for instance is the specification of one which a new tenant is bound to build in order to house a predecessor.

"He is to build her a competent dwelling for her to inhabit, containing thirty feet in length within the walls, and fourteen feet in breadth, with corner-posts and three new and competent doors and two windows."* Another specification of 1325 describes a cottage 24 ft. by 11, built "to the use of Geoffrey Whitring and Mabel his wife and John their son." The dilapidation of an ordinary village is described, perhaps with some rhetoric, on p. 69 of the *Magna Vita S. Hugonis*: "decrepit hovels, with rotten beams and half-ruined walls." The same source, among many others, shows how easily the ordinary cottage could be dismantled and removed. We have similar evidence from Halesowen and from Kirkstall Abbey farms; even more vivid, again, from Italy at about the same time. For the Friar Salimbene, describing the civil wars of 1287, names six villages in his neighbourhood where "the men carried away their houses and rebuilt them" on hill-tops, for security against marauders. Again, speaking of the bonfires lighted that year by exultant victors, he says, "even as the country-folk do at carnival-times, when they burn down their cottages and hovels". Here, again, is an extract from a manorial record: "Richard, son of Thos. Sibil, granted to Thomas his elder brother a parcel of land; and, if it so befall that the said Richard wishes to move his house, the said parcel of land where it now stands shall remain in possession of the said Thomas, and he shall pay 2*d.* rent per annum." Even at the end of the fifteenth century, when St Catharine's College was founded at Cambridge, the three original Fellows seem to have lived, for a time at least, in a timber house set up first at the neighbouring village of Coton, bought and transported later some six miles across the river to Horningsey, and brought back in the third instance to Cambridge.[2] Nearly all of these Trumpington cottages and farms we shall find clustered together in the village, each with its little garden or toft. A few may possibly be scattered outside; but in most cases it was too dangerous to live far from the hue and cry of one's neighbours. As for the peasants' tools, here is a chance inven-

* Most of the details in this and the next two chapters have been printed, with full references, in my *Medieval Village*.

tory. The man had a hoe, a spade, an axe, a bill-hook, two yokes for buckets, and a barrel. The total value was estimated at 10*d.*; about 30*s.* in modern values. As we pass through the village into the open field, we see the peasants and their wives reaping, with an overseer holding a long stick over them. This is "Walter son of Alger, who holds three hundred acres for which he doth homage to Sir Giles; and he will come personally to all the extra workdays, holding his rod over the workers; and on those days he shall have his dinner in Sir Giles's kitchen." If we ourselves were Cambridge University men of that day, we might very well recognize several undergraduates among the harvesters; the Long Vacation, such as it was, would include both hay and corn harvest, and some students, like their brethren of America to-day, must have been able to do manual work in part payment of their expenses. It is similarly significant that university account and audit days were in early October. Even so solemn an assembly as the Convocation of the Clergy, if the session were unduly prolonged, might adjourn for harvest. The arable land is divided into three distinct "fields", entirely without hedges, but often separated into strips by narrow "balks" of unploughed turf. This "three-field system" is on the whole the commonest, though there is sometimes a "two-field system", and sometimes again there is scarcely any general system at all. Where the fields are three, the crops are alternately wheat and barley, with a third year of fallow. In 1300, for instance, we will suppose that all plough and sow wheat in October and reap it in the following autumn, 1301. In 1302, ploughing will be done in March and barley will be sown. After the autumn harvest of 1302 the land is untouched until June 1303, when it is ploughed twice and left to rest until October; then it is sown with wheat, and the round begins again. By the "two-field system" the treatment seems to have been alternately wheat or barley one year and fallow the next. Under both systems the crop was necessarily prescribed by the lord; only under such compulsory uniformity could the tillage work. There must also have been—and of this we have occasional documentary proof—a good deal of communal tillage, as there is still communal cheese-making in the Alps. Where the strips were much intermingled, it was obviously advantageous for all parties to treat the most intricate parts as one block, the different owners ploughing in common, sowing in common, reaping together and dividing the proceeds in proportion to the area that each held. At Martham in Norfolk, where the details have been worked out by the late W. Hudson, an extraordinarily laborious and accurate antiquary, we may see that many tenants had more ploughs than land, while others had more land than ploughs. He concludes: "The whole was sown with one crop and reaped in common."[2] This explains why (in the Durham Halmote Rolls, for instance) it is a punishable offence for the peasant to sell his crops separately. After harvest, the cattle and fowls were allowed to wander free over this wide unhedged communal field: hence the gastronomic reputation of a stubble-goose, or Michaelmas-goose, that is, a bird killed at the exact point when there was no more left to gather from the grains scattered by the harvesters or buried at the roots of the stubble.

For the question of subdivision of holdings we may take this same manor of Martham as typical. The peasant's original holding was somewhere about ten or twelve acres; in other districts something like thirty seems to have been typical. At Martham, the pre-Conquest population had been mainly Danish and, by Danish custom, freemen. But when, in 1101, its lord the Bishop of Norwich granted the village to the monks of his cathedral priory, the thirty-six freemen were gradually turned into villeinage tenants, and the twenty-seven socmen into customary tenants. Mr Hudson succeeded in ascertaining, with mathematical exactness, the subdivisions in 1292 of two tofts—i.e. a block of six acres—which had once been held by Ivor Blackman, and was now divided among ten different tenants. Only one tenant now bears the original name; this is William Blackman, and he holds only three perches. It seems plain that this was just a garden round his cottage; that he was by this time superannuated, and that the main arable land had gone to the younger generation. Clement Rediere, again, is in an exactly similar position. A third, Thomas Elsey, has likewise his cottage and three perches, while around him are other

Elseys, probably his children, and also some Longs, between whom and the Elseys Mr Hudson traces a connection by marriage. Of the remaining seven tenants, four hold an acre and a half to just short of an acre, and three about a quarter of an acre each. And, although this Blackmanstoft is the only holding which the documents have allowed Mr Hudson to map out with absolute certainty, yet all are similarly broken up. Between Domesday and 1292, the Martham tenants had naturally increased in numbers; from 63 to 107. But the subdivision had gone on at an enormously greater rate of increase; there were now 935 holdings, in more than 2000 separate strips. Each tenant, that is, had on an average nearly twenty separate strips, and these might be scattered about anywhere on the manor: in some cases, perhaps, no two were actually contiguous. We possess no contemporary map of any manor until after the Reformation, when the process of consolidation of holdings had already been powerfully at work; yet even those Elizabethan and Jacobean maps always show a bewildering maze of tenements.

The self-sufficiency of the medieval village has often been exaggerated; but it was still very great. The number of adults, even in the larger villages, was no greater than could be contained in two London omnibuses; and of these at least one-tenth might never have strayed outside in their lives. On the busier roads there would be coming and going; but these were comparatively rare; and, outside, the ways or tracks were not designed for continuous travel; they made only for the nearest village, without any more distant horizon in thought. The nearest market might well be too distant to be worth while: *à fortiori* the nearest annual fair. One or two of the most prominent villagers would be called away occasionally on business, to the Hundred or Shire Moot, or as bailiff from manor to manor, or as sidesman to an archidiaconal or ruridecanal visitation. The pedlar would bring a little news: better still, the wandering friar. If the church were to be built or rebuilt, that would bring a whole group of wandering masons, with the ideas of travelled men. But, when every allowance has been made, the average medieval villager was more cut off from the world than can easily be imagined in our own day. There must have been very many who, like the Veronese peasant of Claudian's poem, had spent childhood to old age in one and the same cottage:

Felix, qui propriis aevum transegit in arvis.
Ipsa domus puerum quem videt, ipsa senem.

Normally, the village supplied everything: home-grown food, clothes of home-spun and home-woven wool or linen, home-made tools shod with iron at the village smithy, cottages and carts built by the village carpenter or wheelwright. The satiric theme of the rustic staring wildly about him in the town had something of the same actuality in those days as it has in ours.

Domesday Book is a record of unique value for English village life. We have seen already how William of Malmesbury stigmatizes the prevalence of slavery in Anglo-Saxon times; and this is borne out by a Statute of the Council of Eynsham in 1005.[3] "The Wise Men decree that innocent Christians be not sold beyond the bounds of this land, or at least not unto heathen folk; but let men beware diligently lest that soul be lost which Christ bought with His own life." Domesday records a good many slaves, in this strictest sense of the word. The real freemen form a definite minority of the whole population. For the unfree, apart from those actual slaves, there is more than one medieval name: *serf, villein, bondman*; terms between which it is impossible to distinguish with exactitude, even when they were not interchanged at random. For these unfree there was one general rule, as definite as anything could be in those ages of unwritten custom, so variable at different times and places as to preclude absolutely correct generalizations at any point. That principle was, that the serf possessed nothing of his own; yet he might enjoy his land so long as he rendered three days' work in the week to his lord in lieu of rent. Before those days of the later thirteenth century, when the multiplication of records enables us to get a far clearer view of the details, it is evident that a so-called "day's work" had often been reduced to a half-day of real honest labour. At Great Chesterford, in 1270, each villein owed 714 week-works, each of which occupied a quarter of his day. In addition, at ploughing time he had to plough 16¼ acres. This totals at nearly three days a week. Some of these customary burdens are very complicated; here, for instance, are the requirements on a Glastonbury manor. Between Michaelmas and November 11th the serf had to plough one acre; another half-acre later when called upon. He must harrow every Monday in the year; three times a year he must carry a load for my lord; he must mow three days, and go to the vineyard. All this he must do anyhow; then comes a rather more complicated list of works for which he may compound, if he chooses, by a payment of 3*s.* 4*d.* a year. Beyond this also he must pay certain parish contributions in money to the Church.

It is obviously advantageous both for lord and for tenant to simplify such a tangle; therefore, even before 1300, the tide was setting definitely towards commutation of these services for money payments. At Chesterford the week-work was valued at ½*d.*; this would mean that, if the lord allowed the bargain, the tenant could redeem that whole burden for £1. 9*s.* 9*d.* a year, a figure which might represent about £59 nowadays. Moreover, it is obvious that the old complicated customs left far more room for quarrel than modern money transactions. Walter Algerson with his stick, for instance, has disappeared from our English havest field. He is four whole centuries out of date; whatever friction there may be in a modern lock-out, that is less than under any system of corporal chastisement. But the medieval lord, personally or through his officials, had always the legal right of chastising his serf, provided that neither death nor mutilation ensued. In those two extreme cases the king's court would intervene; otherwise nearly all disputes between the lord and his unfree tenants were heard in the manor court, presided over by the lord's bailiff or steward. It is true that another village official, the reeve, was elected by the peasants, nominally at least, to act as their representative in the court; and, again, the judgments, the "dooms", were pronounced by the peasants themselves, with reference to ancient custom, oral or written. But, as a matter of fact, we constantly find the reeve appointed from above and not from below; and, though the manor court probably achieved about the same proportion of abstract justice as the other courts of those days, yet it must be obvious that the lord was able to load the dice even more than any plutocrat can load them to-day. We shall see this more fully in Chapter XXX. In *Piers Plowman*, there is bitter complaint against the perjured jurors; and, as we shall see later, contemporary medieval descriptions of justice stigmatize, almost without exception, the venality even of the king's and the Pope's judges. It was one of St Thomas More's most definite claims to sanctity that he never took "gifts" on the bench.

The single matter of measures may give us some idea of these medieval difficulties. In my *Medieval Village* I have devoted a chapter to the subject (No. V); and a few examples may suffice here. On one manor of the Abbot of Ramsey, the serf had, among other labours, to do one day's work in the abbot's wood, collecting "one hose of reasonable size, full of nuts well cleaned of their husks". Hosen, by this time, commonly came up well above the knee, and were on their way to that further growth which, with junction at the hips, has now created the modern trousers. It must be evident how much compromise was needed in the interpretation of that simple phrase "of reasonable size"; how much tyranny the steward might exercise, or how dishonestly the man might shirk. Again, after reaping, the serf sometimes had permission to carry off as much as he could bear on the handle of his scythe; if in his greed he overloaded it to the breaking-point, then he lost all that he had tried to carry off, and must compound with the abbot as best he could for a fine. Again, a reeve, after his year of office, may take for his perquisite as much of the bottom of a haystack as he can pierce with one stroke of his pitchfork. In Germany, where the manorial customs are more detailed and have survived in greater numbers, such "natural measures" are even more frequent and peculiar. A new settler in the village may take for his fowl-run as far as his wife, sitting on the roof ridge, can throw an egg wrapped in her scarf. One of the most regular dues was one or more "Easter hens". The tenant obviously would not offer his best; what then is to be the test of fitness in face of his lord? The hen is placed in front of a fence or a gate; if, when frightened, she has strength enough to fly or scramble over, the bailiff must accept her; she is fit. A gosling, again, must be accepted if it is mature enough to pluck grass without losing its balance and sitting down ignominiously. The tenant, again, has sometimes the right of carrying as much wood from the forest as he can manage without getting caught. Even in England, and in cases where measures were more definite and more or less protected by royal or provincial or urban proclamations, they often differed considerably. Many lords were obliged to suffer half a dozen different measures on their different manors, each having grown up separately by local custom. The almost incredible variations of measures in France, where these medieval conditions lasted until the Revolution, are notorious.

Another great difficulty was that of accidental interruption to labour. If for any cause a day is lost, is the lord to accept the loss, or shall he cast it upon his tenant? At some of the Ramsey manors, " if any holy-day come upon the day when the serfs should work [for the abbot] it shall not be allowed to them, but they shall work on another day instead ". On others, again, the division is equitable. " Of all the holy-days which come on work days, one shall be accounted to the lord abbot, and the next to the workers." If bad weather stops the work, the peasant must do it some other day. If the serf be too ill to leave his house, he may be excused from all work except the ploughing and half the harvest (the other half, no doubt, he must pay for in some way) until a year and a day. After this respite, he must begin to satisfy the lord again; the only alternative, no doubt, would be to give up his holding. Some customs gave him only a fortnight or three weeks. At Barton, under the Abbot of Ramsey, " if he be so ill as to take the Holy Communion, then he shall be quit of all work for the next fortnight following ".

Again, where so many payments on either side were rendered in kind, there was far more chance of disagreement than with money. A labourer may have a right at harvest time to three herrings and a loaf; much will here depend upon the age and condition of the herrings. No doubt all these little bickerings would affect our medieval peasant far less than ourselves; we must always bear in mind that, for good or for evil, his mind was in many ways simpler and less sensitive. In Southern Italy, to the present day, bickering over trifles in the market is not only part of the housewife's daily work but often one of her daily interests in life. This, however, has its limits; and therefore, as we have already seen, money compositions had become fairly common even before 1300. The Black Death naturally hastened this evolution; although, as modern researchers have proved, it had far less influence here than students assumed thirty years ago.

There was always a proportion of peasants who had never been unfree; moreover, modern research is tending to show that the free labourer, living as best he could by casual work, was much commoner in our period than historians have often assumed. At Borley, in 1301, little more than half the work on the lord's demesne was done by villein labour; the rest was performed by free labourers, partly paid by the money contributions of villeins who had compounded for their services. The compounding villein was called a "copyholder"; since the conditions of his composition had been written upon a slip of parchment of which he had one copy and the lord another. This copy secured both sides from quarrel on almost all questions of mere rent; but rent was far from exhausting the hold which the lord had over him. Originally all the serf's earnings belonged to his lord; so that, even in the thirteenth century, when the Abbot of Burton quarrelled with those on his manor, we find him boasting against them that in law they possessed "nothing but their own bellies". In practice, that was long out of date, yet it was still the strict legal theory: and that is only one of many similarly significant touches. Again, in England the serf had no right of migration. In France and elsewhere he could often abjure the whole contract and go out into the world, on condition of leaving not only the land but all his possessions behind him. In England, however, he was bound to the land, with the only counterbalancing advantage that the land, little as it might be, was bound in turn to him, so long as he succeeded in fulfilling the customary duties. As he was riveted to the land, so he and his children could be sold with it. His progeny were not called *familia* in legal documents, but *sequela*—"brood" or "litter". Again, since this little holding was not legally his own, and he was only a life tenant, therefore the lord took a fine to himself at every change of tenancy. At the serf's death (or at that of the copyholder, who lived under many servile disabilities) the lord could claim his best beast under the name of "heriot"; and in many cases the priest took the second best as a "mortuary". If he died with less than three beasts, the best domestic possession could be claimed; a brass pot, for instance, or a cloak. Thus, when the man left only three beasts, the death duty would amount to at least 50 per cent., i.e. the proportion of super-tax paid nowadays as death duty on an estate of £2,000,000. Again, just as the serf was not permitted to leave the land, so neither was his offspring. If a girl married without leave, the father was fined; and in some cases a fine was taken even for marriage by permission. Still more odious and upopular than the heriot was the "merchet", or fine taken for a girl's marriage off the manor. By such marriages the lord lost the hope of her brood, and must therefore be indemnified in money. Originally such marriages had been treated as null and void in manorial law; the Church, however, defended their legality, and the only question became one of pecuniary compensation. Sometimes, especially on the Continent, the matter was settled by a division of the brood among the two competing manors, without regard for the serf's family feelings. For the bondman's whole position was such as to put economic questions in the foreground; therefore widows, like unmarried girls, were often treated as chattels. They were fined for marrying without the lord's leave; or, again, they might be compelled to marry at his will, when he felt that the holding was being neglected for the lack of a strong labourer's arm. It may be that this did not happen very often; but certainly it was frequent enough everywhere to mark a strong distinction between medieval and modern society. Here are examples from the monastery of Halesowen in 1274.

"John of Romsley and Nicholas Serval is given until next court meeeting to decide as to the widows offered to them." Three weeks later, "Nicholas Serval is given until next Sunday [we are now at Tuesday] to decide as to the widow offered to him in the Cellarer's presence." [The abbey Cellarer, in this case, represents the abbot and brethren, lords of the manor.] Then (December 11th, 1279), "Thomas Robins of Oldbury came on summons, and was commanded to take Agatha Halesowen to wife; he said he would rather be fined; and, because he could find no guarantees, it was ordered that he should be distrained. Thomas Bird of Ridgacre and Richard of Ridgacre were summoned also because they would neither pay the fine nor take the wife, and were distrained." Then (January 7th, 1280) only Robins and Richard of Ridgacre are "distrained to take the wives as ordered in last court". On January 22nd Robins at last paid his fine, three shillings; Richard was still under distraint. On February 12th Richard is still holding out under distraint; his heroic resistance was apparently rewarded, for there is no record in the rolls of his fine or of his further molestation. On the manor of Liestal, near Basel, in 1411, it was prescribed that "every year before Shrove Tuesday, when folk are wont to think of holy matrimony, the bailiff shall bethink him what boys and girls are of such age that they may reasonably take wife or husband, so that he may then allot to each his mate, as husband or wife". That would doubtless be exceptional at so late a date; but as late as the tenth century such forced marriages were general among the German peasantry. In the thirteenth century, when Richard of Cornwall, King of the Romans, gave a charter to the inhabitants of Wetzlar, one clause ran: "we grant as a special indulgence that we will never force any citizen to give his daughter, niece, or cousin in marriage to any man without the full consent of the man [or of the lady?]."

In our English court-rolls, the commonest presentments are for very ordinary and natural things: trespasses of cattle, disrepair of hedges, shirking of common works, neglect of land or of buildings, defiling the common springs, or digging clay pits (after the medieval fashion) in the public highway.

Cognizance was very justly taken of tenants who harboured undesirable lodgers. "Common thieves of poultry" are presented; and quite a number of tenants who made a practice of stealing firewood from the hedges. Others moved boundary-stones, or appropriated such waifs and strays as a stranded porpoise, a find of wild honey, etc., etc. The ducking-stools for scolds were indispensable village institutions; villages are repeatedly fined, or threatened, for neglecting to provide them.

Among the peasant's minor disabilities came the compulsory common mill or common oven. The former especially had begun as an advantage to the village, since nobody but the lord was rich enough to build a mill and this on the whole was beneficial. Even then, however, there were some who preferred to grind more cheaply at home in their own hand-mills and who resented the lord's monopoly; this was one of the main causes of the bondsmen's revolt under St Albans Abbey in the fourteenth century. The common oven had much the same origin. It was comparatively exceptional in England, but regular in France, where it was called *four banal,* community-oven. The bread there baked was naturally inferior to the best that could be made in other ways; hence the French adjective "banal" subsists to our own day in the signification of "commonplace", and has found its way into modern journalism. The lord, again, had the right of keeping a dove-cote, and his pigeons preyed terribly upon the crops; we have a similar complaint from the Bishop of Chichester's tenants against the waste committed by his lordship's rabbits. Lastly, the peasant paid a fine for getting his son promoted to clerical orders or even sending him to a grammar school or university; for there the scholars were tonsured, and enjoyed clerical privileges, and thus, by such promotion, the manor lost a labourer and the landlord must be compensated.

7. THE VILLAGE (2)

It may be asked : How did the peasant bear all this? We must not forget that, under the simpler and rougher conditions then prevailing everywhere, men did not feel the contrasts as they would be felt in our own day. Again, the medieval labourer did in some ways grapple more directly with nature, and at his actual work (as apart from his leisure) was less tempted to look upon himself as a mere cogwheel than the modern operative. This, however, is often exaggerated beyond all reason by modern writers; and, even so far as it is true, we must counterbalance it by the consideration that the modern wage-earner, when not at work, has the run of a far wider world, both physically and intellectually, that was closed to his fore-fathers. The sociologist Durkheim has pointed out that, in spite of many things which still remain to be remedied in the modern worker's lot, he has more originality of mind than the noble savage. If we take a hundred of these latter at random, we shall find great uniformity of taste; what one likes, all like, what one dislikes, all dislike. A hundred operatives, on the other hand, liberated from their eight hours of mechanical drudgery in the workshop, scatter to a multitude of various occupations until the work hours come again. At any rate, we have the plainest evidence that the medieval peasant was not content with his lot, quite apart from the bare fact of those bloody revolts which are recorded in almost all countries. In Germany the earliest written laws, the *Sachenspiegel* and *Schwabenspiegel*, show a clear yearning for earlier conditions of comparative freedom. In England, chroniclers describe the bitter resentment of men who felt themselves formed in Christ's image and treated like beasts. The great Froissart, for all his aristocratic tastes and his personal dependence upon the rich of this world, is never more eloquent than when he reports the preaching of John Ball, the socialist priest of Chaucer's day.

"Ah, ye good people, the matters goeth not well to pass in England, nor shall not do till everything be common, and that there be no villeins nor gentlemen, but that we may be all united together, and that the lords be no greater masters than we be. What have we deserved, or why should we be kept thus in servage? We be all come from one father and mother, Adam and Eve: whereby can they say or shew that they be greater lords than we be? saving by that they cause us to win and labour for that they dispend. . . . Let us go to the king, he is young, and shew him in what servage we be in, and shew him how we will have it otherwise, or else we will provide us of some remedy; and, if we go together, all manner of people that be now in any bondage will follow us to the intent to be made free; and when the king seeth us we shall have some remedy either by fairness or otherwise." "Thus", continues Froissart, "John Ball said on Sundays when the people issued out of the churches in the villages; wherefore many of the mean people loved him and such as intended to no goodness said how he said truth."[1] A century later, when the peasant's lot was already bettered, and he was probably in greater material comfort than ever again until quite modern times, we find a bondman under the Abbot of Malmesbury, who had been able to amass a little competence, writing: "If I might bring [my freedom] about, it would be more joyful to me than any worldly good."

These things are too much neglected by those who stress the comparative material comfort of the labourer in the fifteenth century, when his position was at its best, and who exaggerate the monotony of the modern workshop as compared with the daily struggle against earth and the elements. The dead-weight of modern capitalism must not be ignored; we must not forget that there is less freedom in the contract between employer and employed than appears on the surface, and that a man free before the law may yet be a slave to circumstances. But this has been true, to a great extent, in all ages and must remain true so long as nature works for inequality. The weaker in mind or in body must always stand towards the stronger in a position which, in their discontent, they may feel and describe as slavery. Even where, in the modern factory, the worker is merely a "hand", at least the overseer bears no rod, and the "hand's" offspring are no longer just "litter". Circumstances may still make it impossible for a man to rise from class to class—though such facilities have multiplied enormously within the memory of many folk still living—but at least the law no longer consecrates and reinforces the division of classes, or (it may almost be said) of castes. In 1388, a royal statute ran: "Item. It is ordained & assented, That he or she which used to labour at the Plough and Cart, or other Labour or Service of Husbandry till they be of the Age of Twelve Years, that from thenceforth they shall abide at the same Labour, without being put to any Mystery or Handicraft; and if any Covenant or Bond of Apprentice be from henceforth made to the Contrary, the same shall be holden for none."[2] The House of Commons even petitioned against the sending of villeins' sons to school; but that was too odious to be accepted; the man might still give the boy education, so long as he could find or pay a teacher, and afford the fine claimed by his lord.

The extent to which the medieval peasant might look to the Church for help will be dealt with later on. But here is the chance to confute the too-frequent misstatement that Poor Laws came in with the Reformation. True, the Dissolution was, for a time, one cause of a serious economic crisis in the sixteenth century. But England before that event had long been in trouble with her poor: and, afterwards, those of our heretical country had no cause to envy their orthodox brethren on the Continent, until the French Revolution brought in a new spirit everywhere. We may see this clearly enough by turning back from William Cobbett to Arthur Young's *Travels in France,* and onwards again to J. P. Cobbett's *Ride through France* (1826), where we see clearly the immense improvements in the peasant's condition since the Revolution.

The statutes passed by Parliament after the Black Death aimed at preventing any rise either in wages or in prices of commodities. That of 1349 not only fixed a maximum wage, but strictly forbade the migration of labourers in search of a better livelihood. Beggars strong enough to work were to be imprisoned; and strictly speaking, it was punishable to give them alms. The statute of 1360 enacted that "labourers and artificers that absent themselves out of their services, in another township or another county", might be recovered by their employers as runaways and, at the discretion of the justices, branded on the forehead. In 1376 the Commons petitioned that vagrant beggars should be imprisoned till they promised to return home to work, and that it should be forbidden to give alms to persons able to labour. It was proclaimed in 1388 that artificers employed in crafts whereof "a man hath no great need in harvest time" (e.g. the village weaver or carpenter) "shall be compelled to serve in harvest, to cut, gather, and bring in corn". Beggars able to work were to be treated like wandering labourers, and put in the stocks. "But in this act of 1388 we find the recognition of an additional element in the problem. What was to be done with 'impotent beggars', beggars really unable to work? The legislators fell back on the idea of local responsibility: impotent beggars were to remain where they were at the passing of the act, and if the inhabitants of those places were neither willing nor able to maintain them they were to be taken to other towns within the hundred, or to the place of their birth, and there they were to abide for the rest of their lives. The provision was vaguely stated, and no machinery was provided for carrying it out; but it may fairly be looked upon as expressing the hope of the legislators that the charity of the parish clergy, of the monasteries, the hospitals, and private persons would provide in their own neighbourhood for the destitute who were really unable to labour. . . . The law as it had thus grown up in the years following the Black Death remained unchanged for a century and a half."[3]

We get very significant glimpses of village manners from records of manor courts such as the Halmote Rolls of Durham. In disputes between the lord and his tenants we have seen that the dice were loaded somewhat in the former's favour. But in matters of village discipline the lord's authority was mainly beneficent. In 1366 it was enjoined to all the householders that they should "chastise their servants who had been accustomed to play at dice", even as the householders themselves did. Football, too, was strictly forbidden; and this was not altogether undeserved. The fact is that at those mass-matches between village and village, in which the whole male population took part, bloodshed and vendettas were frequent. Extraordinarily interesting, here, is the attitude of the monastic chronicler of King Henry VI's miracles. In one case the witness tells "how William Bartram, being struck in his most sensitive parts by the foot of one who played with him, sustained long and intolerable pains; but, having seen in a dream the glorious King Henry, suddenly received the benefit of health".[4] This was at Caunton in Nottinghamshire, and the monk adds his own reflections: "The game at which they had met for common recreation is called by some the foot-ball-game. It is one in which young men, in country sport, propel a huge ball not by throwing it into the air but by striking and rolling it along the ground and that not with their hands but with their feet. A game, I say, abominable enough, and, in my judgment at least, more common, undignified, and worthless than any other kind of game, rarely ending but with some loss, accident, or disadvantage to the players themselves. What then? The boundaries had been marked and the game had started; and, when they were striving manfully, kicking in opposite directions, and our hero had thrown himself into the midst of the fray, one of his fellows, whose name I know not, came up against him from in front and kicked him by misadventure, missing his aim at the ball."

Moreover, as the sports might lead to a general affray, so also might the women's tongues. The Durham roll records: "From Agnes of Ingleby—for transgression against William Sparrow and Gillian his wife, calling the said Gillian a harlot, to the damage of £2 whence they will take at their will 13*s*. 4*d*.; as was found by the jury—by way of penalty and fine 3*s*. 4*d*.; reduced in mercy to 6*d*. It is ordained by common assent that all the women of the township control their tongues without any sort of defamation." Sometimes, again, we find such general proclamations as this: "It is enjoined upon all tenants of the township of Wolveston that they should procure the arrest of all such as revile their neighbours, or who draw knives or swords against the peace; and if these will not be arrested, let hue and cry be raised, and let every man come to aid." Nor are these complaints mere fancies in the air. There are frequent items such as: "John Smith, for drawing a knife to smite the curate, fined 3*s.* 4*d.*"; "Thomas Milner, for shooting arrows by night, and Lawrence Hunter, 3*s.* 4*d.*", probably a poaching affray. Again we may see how one single act of violence could lead to a general tragedy. In the village of Rowsley, in 1271: "on the feast of the exaltation of the Holy Cross, towards vespertide, Hawise came home from the alehouse—*de cervisia*—with her two daughters, and shut her door, shutting out her eldest daughter, who was followed by her husband. He, wishing to enter as usual, was unable; and therefore he entered through a certain window, breaking into the house and smiting Hawise his wife's mother; whence the hue and cry was raised and the neighbours ran thither. Walter came and assaulted Nicholas and Henry Hall with drawn knife, and the said Walter was wounded, but it is not known by which of the two aforesaid; but it is thought that Nicholas smote him."

Yet these Halmote Rolls are far from presenting a mere catalogue of crimes and petty offences; and for any reader who loves village life and regrets the frequent careless and unjustifiable inroads of modern civilization there is an old-world charm in the very names: John Jentilman, Ralph Jolibody, William Littlefair, John Cherryman, John Merriman, Gilbert Uncouth, Roger Mouse, Roger Litilannotson, John Stoutlook; and most medieval of all, Robert Benedicite. Then, among the ladies, Agnes Redhead, Cicely Wikinsdoughter, Maud Malkynsmaydin, Diote Jaksdoughter, Evote Wheelspinner, Agnes Gibbesdoughter, Alice Robinsdoughter, Emma Androwsmaydin, Margaret Merry; and Watsdoughter, so homely to the manor that the steward feels she needs no second name.

It will be noted that the majority of facts quoted in this present chapter are from monastic estates; this is because so many more records have survived for these than for lay manors.

In the Dark Ages these ecclesiastical estates were unquestionably better managed than those of the average baron or knight or squire. In the period with which we are mostly concerned, I think the balance was still in favour of the ecclesiastic, though not by very much; the natural kindliness of his profession and the altruistic aims of his institution were often counterbalanced by his conservatism (both personal and collective) and by the fact that the average monk was naturally tempted to put his own well-being as the first charge upon the abbey's revenues. Peter the Venerable [1120] might justly claim that his own model abbey of Cluny contrasted sharply with the outside world in its kindly treatment of the serf. But, a century and a half later, the Dominican Cardinal Hugh of St-Cher stigmatized his fellow Religious as more unfeeling in this respect than the ordinary layman. Again on the very verge of the Reformation, Bishop Longland of Lincoln, who was a stern enemy of the Lollards, wrote a plain-spoken letter to the Abbot of Oseney. In this he wrote of avarice as having attacked " the foundations and columns of the Church, viz. abbots and priors ". He continued: " They are intent only upon money and not upon the increase of religious life; and, outside [their monasteries], they flay their tenants worse than the secular clergy or the laity do "—*plus quam seculares aut laici suos firmarios excoriant.*[5] We must not take these indignant words too literally; even in the highest medieval society there was more licence of speech and less cool reflection than we expect from similar classes in our own day. But there are masses of undeniable facts in the background which go far to support these criticisms. To begin with, the Church never fought against the *principle* of serfdom, any more than she had done against the principle of slavery under the Roman Empire. Again, Church laws actually forbade the churchman to free his serf, in all cases where such liberation meant loss of ecclesiastical funds. We find the Bishops of Ely and Norwich, for instance, seeking papal dispensation to free even a single serf; and the Bishop of Exeter, in a deed of manumission, excuses himself on the plea that the man had served long and well and is now past work. Otherwise, the " giving away " of this " chattel " would have been a violation of the oath imposed upon prelates-elect, to alienate none of the possessions of their Church. Hence, although the clergy did good work in recommending manumission to lay lords as an act of charity, yet they themselves liberated very few in comparison; and, wherever we have detailed evidence, it nearly always proves that they sold, not gave, this freedom: sold it for cash, and at market-price. It was on Church estates in England that serfdom lingered longest; and in France the great Abbey of St-Claude, for instance, clung to the system until the Revolution swept it away by force. No passage of Barbour's *Bruce* is so well known as that which begins:

> *Ah, Freedom is a noble thing!*
> *Who freedom hath, hath great liking.*

Yet Barbour himself, as Archdeacon of Aberdeen, was in part a serf-owner and a dealer in serfs. He and his fellow-canons farmed out one of their estates; the lease, which is still extant, runs to the effect that they let the land " with its hawkings, huntings and fishings; with its serfs and their brood ". The conservatism of the Bury monks in this matter, as recorded by Jocelin of Brakelond, has often been noted; and, though the serf's condition did steadily improve on the whole during the later medieval centuries, yet, even then we sometimes find clerical reaction and the recrudescence of the earlier brutal disabilities. It was an Abbot of Burton, as we have seen, who told his serfs that they possessed nothing but their bellies; and the Cistercians of Vale Royal are to be found adopting something of the same attitude. One of the cruellest and bloodiest revolts of our whole period was the Bauernkrieg, the Peasants' War in Germany. This was partly brought about by the policy of the great Abbey of Kempten, which had deliberately set itself to force its serfs back into the cruel conditions of the Dark Ages. Thus the Peasants' Revolt of 1381 in England was marked by great bitterness against the higher clergy, and the monasteries in particular. On the other hand it is on monastic estates that we sometimes find definitely charitable manor customs, such as permission in cases of childbirth for a man to poach on the abbey fish-ponds or to take extra wood from the forests. In

Scotland, again, an enquiry into the estates of the Abbey of Dunfermline [1320] suggests that the monks acted upon the principle of a sort of clan-solidarity with their tenants. I quote the document in full on p. 185 of my *Medieval Village*.

But, when we weigh both sides, we shall easily understand why the medieval peasant would have found it hard to understand the halo of glory which regretful modern writers sometimes see round his head. Chaucer's and Langland's Ploughman are indeed noble figures; but in each case the emphasis is on its exceptional character. Langland paints his opposite more than once.[6] One of his liveliest pictures is where Piers Plowman has set himself to mend society with his gospel of hard work; but the enthusiasm rapidly wanes; and those who were busy in the morning prefer to sit and sing in the afternoon, so that Piers can only warn them how idleness must lead to want. In another passage, the Dreamer sees a typical labourer of the looser sort, careless of real work, and driving through the long day with a light song in his mouth: *Deu vous save, Dam Emme!* At harvest time, idlers flock in who hope "no deed to do but drink and to sleep"; and the ale-house causes great waste of time.

After all, the man is naturally shaped by society's treatment of him; and, quite apart from the purely business questions, the serf was inevitably humiliated by many of the Ghetto-regulations which fenced him in. On the manors of the monks of Durham fines were decreed against those who taunted their fellow-villagers with the despised name of Serf. Everywhere we find similar evidence; and two of the most striking examples may be taken from France. A chronicler writes concerning Queen Blanche, the mother of St Louis: "Since she had pity on the folk who were serfs, she ordained in many places that they should be freed and pay some other due. And this she did partly for the pity she had on girls of that condition, for that men would not take them to marriage, and many of them were deflowered." Again: "In 1472, a poor servant-girl of Champagne, convicted of child murder, excused her misconduct by pleading that she had not been able to marry after her own heart; her father had refused to unite her to 'the man she would gladly have taken' because he was a serf."

It was natural, therefore, that Wat Tyler and his fellow-rebels in 1381 should demand the complete abolition of serfdom, with leases of all lands at a flat yearly rate of 4*d.* an acre. The flatness of rent was doubtless unworkable; but the rate, as an average, was certainly reasonable; for in practice we commonly find land let on those terms after the revolt. In spite of its immediate failure, this movement cannot have failed to affect the landlords in the long run. After a few generations we find servile conditions steadily giving place to more modern arrangements. First came the stock-and-land lease; and then, little by little, the ordinary plain money rent of to-day which made room for the growth of a yeoman class. Latimer's description of his father is not so hackneyed but that it may be repeated here. "My father was a yoman, and had no landes of hys owne; onely he had a farme of iij or iiij pound by yeare at the uttermost, and hereupon he tilled so muche as kept halfe a dosson men. He had walke for an hundred sheepe, and my mother milked xxx kyne. He was able, and did finde the king a harnesse [soldier's arms], with him selfe and his horse, while he came to the place that he should receyve the kinges wages. I can remember, that I buckled his harnesse, when he went unto Blacke heath fielde. He kept me to schole, or els I had not bene able to have preached before the kinges majestie now. He maryed my sisters with five pound, or xx nobles apiece, so that he brought them up in godlinesse, and feare of God. He kept hospitality for his poore neighboures. And some almes he gave to the poore, and all thys did he of the sayde farme."[7] That class, Latimer feared, was dying out; yet when we settled down under Elizabeth a whole mass of yeomen-farmers grew up from the unthrifty dispersion of many estates that had fallen into the hands of the robbers of Church property.[8] The old system had been too wasteful to hold its own against the necessities of change. In Flanders, for instance, much of the land had been reclaimed by pioneers who received each a solid block, and had therefore an independence in methods of cultivation which contrasted with our own mechanical uniformity under the scattered strip-system. There, consequently, there was progress; the modern rotation of crops, by alternating roots with corn, was common in Flanders as early as the beginning of the fourteenth century; with us it became general only four hundred years later.

As to the comparison in prosperity between the pre-Reformation and post-Reformation peasant, we have one indication, fairly precise within its limits, from the increase of population. There is pretty general agreement that England and Wales had about 2½ millions at the Conquest and about 5 under Henry VIII; in other words, that the average increase, in those 450 years, was at most about 0.147 per cent. per annum. Thus, taking a village of average size, with 300 souls or 60 families, it would take nearly seven years before this could rise to 301 souls; and a man of 60 could boast no more than that it had grown to 308 in his lifetime. Such was the increase during those 4½ medieval centuries. But when we look onwards from 1536, we find that the then population more than doubled itself in 275 years: it was 10,160,000 at the census of 1811. Thus the post-Reformation rate of increase was, from the first, far more rapid than the earlier, even before we come to the enormous rise in recent standards of living. If, again, we count the whole period, down to the present day, then we find the population multiplied eightfold in the last 300 years, as against only twofold in the preceding 450. When all allowances are made for the predominantly urban character of modern times, and for the fact that longevity is not, by itself, a conclusive proof of prosperity or happiness, these figures must yet retain a significance which demands serious and scientific answer.

Pirenne, whose exceptional learning and moderation are everywhere recognized, writes of the fourteenth century: "The lord had ceased to consider himself the protector of the men on his estate. His position in relation to his tenants was no longer that of a hereditary chieftain whose authority was accepted by reason of its patriarchal character, it had become that of a landlord and recipient of dues. . . . The large farms established [by the monks] on the demesne lands were a crushing weight upon the villagers." We need no more than this to explain Wat Tyler's revolt in 1381. But why was not that rising more successful, and why was there even less result from similar peasant revolts on the Continent? A great Franciscan mission preacher, Berthold of Regensburg, had already given his explanation of this problem in mid-thirteenth century. In one of his sermons, comparing different social classes with animals, he says:[9] "The fish is a very poor and naked beast; it is ever cold, and liveth ever in the water, and is naked and cold and bare of all graces. So also are poor folk; they, too, are helpless. . . . Because the fishes are poor and naked, therefore they devour one another in the water; so also do the poor folk; because they are helpless, therefore they have divers wiles and invent many deceits. . . . None are so false as the country-folk among each other; for these are so untrue that for envy and hatred they can scarce look upon one another. One will drive another's cattle to his harm and damage, and another will buy his fellow-peasant out of his farm; all from untruth." Then, as now, side by side with the endless little charities that we may find in the dealings of poor with poor, we find no less multitude of petty jealousies and thwartings. If the mills of God grind slowly here, it is because the poor can become politically and socially effective only in so far as they have learned things which cannot be got except through a certain reasonable modicum of physical well-being distributed among the whole population, with freedom from social and political experiments. Here is a vicious circle which meets us constantly in human life; and it would be strange if any single and simple device could get us out of it. Yet here, as in so many other fields, the naked facts of social history should go far to render us, if not optimists, at any rate meliorists. For, when we have faced the worst that can be truly said against our modern world, and made all due allowance for the rhetoric of two great preachers in far-off times, we may congratulate ourselves that the modern villager can no longer be described in the words which St Bernardino of Siena applied to the fifteenth-century peasant in Tuscany, one of the most civilized districts of Europe, and nearest to the fountain-head at Rome.

Yet nobody will doubt that, in all lands, there were many village heroes, and even some village saints, though Berthold of Regensburg feels bound to remark how few were the villagers who had ever been canonized by his Church. Rural life has never lent itself to glaring colours; the true glory of our countryside has always been its meadow-green and its ripening corn and the deep shade of its woods; the thatched roof and the quiet stream; all in harmony with William Morris's picture of the harvester's meal in the noonday shade; bread and cheese and strong onions, with a jug of corny ale. Within that framework, we may well look back upon the old English village with full appreciation of Virgil's *o fortunatos nimium, sua si bona norint*. The bare facts of our forefathers' village life lend themselves neither to easy optimism nor to cheap pessimism.

It is difficult to express identical thoughts in two sets of words; and I can only sum up here in a briefer repetition of what I wrote ten years ago in my *Medieval Village* (p. 392).

The medieval peasant was, essentially, the kind of man who still meets us by the thousand in outlying districts of the Continent, and by handfuls even in Great Britain. He lacked some very important things which his descendants now enjoy even in the remotest corners of Europe; yet, in the main, his existence was what may still be found here and there. Looking closely at him and his village, we see the rough life of labouring folk hardened by their constant fight against land and weather; we see taskmasters whose interests necessarily conflicted with the needs of those elementary breadwinners; yet who, to their credit be it said, did not always enforce every advantage that the strict law might have given them. Our general impression will be that of a society very engaging in its old-world simplicity, but with much to learn before it can struggle through into modern civilization. The old-world villagers show us mankind in the making; human nature in its elementary aspects. If we try to reckon up the things which they most truly enjoyed, we shall find that all, or nearly all, are common to every country and age. That the life of the medieval village had a true dignity at its best, and even a true glory in the highest sense of that word, no man can doubt who reads Chaucer's brief description of the Ploughman. The land is eternally healthy, and we suffer when we feel the least divorce or estrangement from it. But, so long as urban life and village life exist, the peasant will always be a child compared with the city dweller. We should find even Chaucer's Ploughman a child in his serene unconscious conservatism and dead-weight of inattention, concentrated on his own things in his own little corner, while we vainly dangle a crown of more complicated civilization over his head—yet childlike, again, in his divine receptivity at sudden moments, and in his resolve to take the kingdom of glory by force. We should find in him the child's April moods of sunshine and shower; a nature sometimes hide-bound and selfish and narrow to the last degree, and sometimes generously impulsive; with the child's pathetic trust at one moment, and unreasonable distrust at another; and, above all, with a child's fear of the dark.

8. VILLAGE DANCE AND SONG

The depopulation emphasized in my preceding chapter was, of course, often due to infectious diseases; but war and famine were possibly even more operative on the whole, when we reckon not only national conflicts, but civil war between province and province, town and town, village and village. Famine was not only a frequent concomitant of plague, but sometimes, apparently, its actual begetter by reducing the frame to defenceless exhaustion: "*Fames* and *mortalitas*, for the medieval annalist, are almost inseparable conceptions."[1] And, happy as the more well-to-do medieval peasant might be in the possession of his own little holding, the majority lived always on the edge of an abyss into which a single bad harvest might, and a succession must, precipitate them. Even in England, where frosts are never so terrible as on the Continent, the primitive plough never scratched deep enough to protect the grain from any very exceptional winter. Nothing in our own annals equals the Belgian winters recorded in the twelfth century, twelve years of bad weather in one case and thirteen in another: but there was a terrible succession of crop failures with us in the early fourteenth century. The Liége chronicler notes minutely the weather from 1195 to 1198: it is a heart-rending story. More than once, at different times, corn went up to ten times its normal price. In England, apart from the frequent formal records of famine in the annals, we sometimes get sidelights which are still more significant. The barons complained to Henry III in 1258 "that many men come from divers parts of the realm by reason of times of famine; and, passing through divers provinces, they die of hunger and starvation", and then the coroners treat this as a case of murder, in order to get a fine from the township because it had not raised the hue and cry. Here, in famine, was something worse than any pestilence; for this meant death by slow torture: stark foodlessness from day to day, until death came as a friend. "Men ate all kinds of herbs, and even the bark of trees", says one chronicler; and another: "they devoured meadow-grass uncooked, like oxen." A twelfth-century Bishop of Trier, beset on his journey by a famishing crowd, would have given them money: but that was useless to them then and there; they demanded his fat palfrey, which they tore in pieces and devoured under his eyes. Occasionally the chroniclers even tell of cannibalism: the folk-story of Hansel and Gretel is founded, if not on facts, certainly on possibilities. In those days of difficult communication, there was hope of finding a little more in some other province; here, therefore, we find the story of Joseph and his brethren: every famine drove thousands of peasants away from their land, while others were glad to give it up and work for a bare subsistence as hinds. The great Bavarian Abbey of Benediktbeuren, in the famine of 1005, records some 150 tenants who thus deserted in the hope of bettering themselves. And, side by side with the charity, sometimes heroic, shown by clergy and laity, we find contrary records of men who usuriously exploited the misery of their weaker brethren. "The chronicler of the Abbey of Andres records, with a certain naïve pride, how Abbot Iterius, during his whole reign in the great famine-years at the turn of the twelfth century, never sold a bushel of corn for less than 10 *solidi* and often much higher, even to 40: and thus [in his own words] the penury of his neighbours brought him abundance"—*sicque vicinorum penuria ei habundantiam ministravit.*

All these things may truly be said of the medieval peasant, as truly as Ruskin presses upon us similar reflections, and darker still, in his chapter on *The Mountain Gloom* (*Modern Painters,* col. IV, ch. XIX). But those peasants of the Valais, of whom Ruskin writes, suffered more than the average share of work and anxiety; and we miss the true balance if we leave the medieval serf at this point. We have had our temperate English skies and our fertile plains and undulating uplands ever since the beginning of historical time; and, though man's heart is, strictly speaking, insatiable, yet a very little will often satisfy him:

I said it in the meadow-path,
I said it on the mountain stairs—
The best things any mortal hath
Are those which every mortal shares.

"Hope springs eternal in the human breast"; and, while the best of these men had the steady confidence, even the majority of them had some flickering hope, of a happy world beyond the grave. The preacher, as we shall presently see, often did his best to inculcate what is now called puritanism, and to warn them of the predominant chances of eternal torment; yet it was with the peasant as with Dr. Johnson and his old friend Edwards. Though the parishioner, at moments, might "'try to be a philosopher", yet "I don't know how, cheerfulness was always breaking in".

For we must bear in mind the elasticity of human nature, as displayed for instance, within living memory, among the peasants of unreformed Tsarist Russia. Nature, the homely nurse, does all she can; she has her own ways of comforting those who hang directly at her bosom. We need not doubt that medieval famine, like plague, was borne with a stoicism unfamiliar to us of this happier century. With many folk, this was doubtless a sort of fatalism; not merely that reasoned and philosophic determinism against which orthodox medieval writers and preachers had to contend as with one of their greatest spiritual enemies, but the half-dumb fatalism of a suffering animal. The land labourer is so nearly the same in all ages that it may be allowable to quote here from the authentic experience of a modern Norfolk parson. "One of [the new vicar's] earliest pastoral visits was to a small farmer who had lost his wife and been left desolate and alone. The good vicar spoke such comfort as he could, and more than once insisted on the obvious truth that the ordering of 'Divine Providence' must not be murmured at, and that 'Providence' must needs be submitted to with resignation. The sorrowing farmer listened patiently and silently for a few minutes. At last he could refrain no longer, but opened his mouth and spoke, saying 'That's right enef, that es! There ain't no use a gainsayin on it; but somehow that there *Old Providence* hev

been agin me all along, he hev! Whoi! last year he mos' spailt my taters, and the year afore that he kinder did for my tunnips, and now he's been and got hold o' my missus! But ', he added with a burst of heroic faith and devout assurance, 'I reckon there's *One abev* as'll put a stopper on ha if 'a go too fur!' "
Though the food and the general household conditions of the lower peasantry and artisans were such as would arouse strong and just protest from the modern unemployed, and though we find constant signs of dissatisfaction, yet it may well be doubted whether the benumbed souls of those days felt the injustice so clearly and so bitterly. It was only on rare occasions that the pent-up fury burst fully forth. That, again, is another characteristic of those centuries which, as compared with ours, were marked by their own violent contrasts.

Thus the poor man who was not yet far advanced upon the road of " large and liberal discontent ", and who had so little of our own social and religious and political freedom, created minor liberties for himself in those corners where Church and State either left him alone or were unable completely to control him. Here again comes in the parallel with Russia; and, for the matter of that, with the old North American slave-states. When time and opportunity came for merriment, it was loud and boisterous; medieval disciplinarians are never tired of preaching against the paradox that Sundays and holy-days were marked by more drunkenness and crime than all the rest of the week. The most orthodox theologians had begun to plead for restriction, or even abolition, of some of those holy-days long before Henry VIII's parliament put such suggestions into actual practice. But, little as this orthodox puritanism, inherited from the earliest ages of the Church, allowed for mirth and dance and song, we may be glad that the people took it for themselves and let the preacher go his own way. To that extent—and to very little more—we may claim for our country that advantage which, in the form of " Merrie England ", has become a cliché dear to the journalist, though historical students appeal in vain for any but the rarest use of the phrase in pre-Reformation times. This chapter of Dance and Song is so pertinent to the whole true picture of medieval peasant and artisan life, that it deserves a few more pages here. Chaucer's contemporaries, as compared with us their more sophisticated descendants, had much of that picturesqueness which the wild animal in wood or field shows as compared with his cousin in the farmyard.

We shall come later on in the poem of *Piers Plowman* to a great literary work which had a beggar for its father; of the medieval ballad we may almost say that it knew not its own father or mother. We must not accept in its literal exaggeration Jacob Grimm's epigram "The Folk is the Poet" [*das Volk dichtet*]. He himself did not so intend it; but the majority of modern scholars do tend, on the whole, in that particular direction. G. L. Kittredge, in his essay on "The Ballad", points out how in the Faroë Islands, a few generations ago, the whole crowd would stand round an unlucky fisherman and satirize him in verse, each extemporizing a stanza in turn.[1] The same kind of thing was done also in the Russian cigarette-factories; and I myself, in the Wales of fifty years ago, have driven twenty miles home from a football match in a drag full of men who chanted nearly all the way at the traditional satirical song of "Crawshay Bailey", with its perpetually recurring refrain, and stanzas supplied by each in turn, mainly from memory but sometimes topical and extempore. There we have one of the strands in the complex of causes which produced the medieval ballad. The very name betrays its intimate connection with dance, for which the Italian verb was, and still is, *ballare,* surviving with us in *ballet* and *ball.* Another name for this in Middle English was *carole.* It was a round dance, the performers joining hand to hand in a ring. The thirteenth-century poem on St Hugh of Lincoln uses that word *carole* to describe the polished marble columns which still may be seen grouped round the great stone pillars of the cathedral; "those slender columns which stand round the great piers, even as a bevy of maidens stand marshalled for a dance."[2]

The medieval dance was in its origin pre-historic and therefore pagan. Among churchmen it met with almost universal reprobation. Scholastic philosophers, like Albert the Great and St Thomas Aquinas, could not rule it out altogether, since they found it mentioned without reprobation in Scripture, as in the cases of Miriam and Deborah and David; they therefore allow the dance on very exceptional occasions, such as one's country's victory over the enemy, or the homecoming of a friend from a distant land or even sometimes at weddings. St Thomas, again, points out that such bodily exercises were in themselves, quite apart from moral considerations, healthy. Moreover, one popular writer at least, the author of *Dives and Pauper*, who was probably a Franciscan of about Chaucer's time, takes the same comparatively liberal view. Men (he says) may lawfully make mirth on holy-days, "God forbid else". True, St Augustine seems definitely to forbid the dance; but that was "when Christian people was much mingled with heathen people". Dances (except where they lead to fleshly transgressions and to idleness "and to other vices, as it is right likely they do now in our days") are lawful even on holy-days.[3] This, however, is very exceptional liberalism. Among the rest of the numerous moralists and preachers who touch upon the subject, not only is the village dance reprobated in language as strong as that of any later puritan, but one French preacher of about 1500, Pepin, actually stigmatizes the Sunday dance as a mortal sin. For such intolerance as this there was a certain amount of justification in fact. The medieval dance was not only pre-Christian in origin but often un-Christian in practice. Preachers reminded their people that the first biblical account of it comes in the story of the Golden Calf; and how, when Aaron had made that idol in the absence of Moses, "the people sat down to eat and to drink, and rose up to play". Not only history but fact often compelled the priest to regard this riotous and unbridled sport much as the modern missionary regards many native African customs. Canon Law explicitly forbade the participation of any cleric under any excuse soever; yet the priest himself would sometimes "go fanti" with his parishioners.[4] Cardinal Jacques de Vitry [1210] expresses the general clerical disapproval most picturesquely. There was always one leader of the dance (generally a woman, and the same in each village) who marked the time with a little bell. Vitry writes, in one of his anecdotes for preachers: "When a man wishes not to lose his cow, he binds a bell to her neck, that he may hear the sound and be sure that she is still there. Even as the cow that leadeth the rest hath a bell to her neck, so may the woman who leadeth the dance be said to have the devil's bell on hers. For the Devil, hearing the sound, is easy in his mind and saith 'I have not lost my cow; [she is safely mine]'."[5] His younger contemporary Étienne de Bourbon tells us how the country folk often danced on the eves of saints' days in the churchyards or even in the churches, as their forefathers had done with their heathen temples. In one French village "certain young folk were wont to come and ride upon a wooden horse and to dance masked and disguised in the church and through the churchyard on the eve of the dedication-day". A missionary persuaded the majority to desist; but one youth harnessed himself, with curses upon all who should obey this crabbed shaveling. "When, therefore, the aforesaid youth pranced upon his wooden horse into the church, while the congregation were keeping their vigils in peace and prayer, then on the very threshold of the sanctuary, a fire caught him by the feet and utterly consumed him, horse and man . . . from whose body rose so fierce a flame that it seemed to issue forth from the windows of the spire."[6] But the stock example is quoted first from Colbigk in a German chronicle under the year 1013, and thence by the English chronicler William of Malmesbury and by the moralist Robert of Bourne. It tells how, "Upon a Christmas night, Twelvë fools a carole dight". Their refrain was in the shape of an incitement to renew the dance whenever it flagged: "Why standë we, why go we not?" He thus proceeds:

The priestë's daughter they tempted out
With them to carole the church about . . .
The priest put on his robes for Mass
They kept their carolling nevertheless . . .
From the altar down he bent
And to the churchë porch he went
And said " on God's half I forbid
That ye no longer do such deed,

But come ye in in fair mannere
Godes service for to hear."
For all his bidding left they not,
But dancëd forth, even as they thought.
The priest therefore was sore agrieved,
He prayed God, that he on believed, . . .
That they might ever right so wend,
Until that time twelve moneth end.

The curse was effective; their hands became inseparably interlocked. The priest's son rushed forward to bear his sister away: her arm broke off in his hands like a dry bough.

Then he unto his father went
And broughte him a sorry present . . .
" Look, father," he said, " and have it here
The armë of thy daughter dear . . .
Fell was thy curse, and over-soon
Thou askedst vengeance; thou hast thy boon."
These folk that went so carolland
All that yearë, hand in hand . . .
Night or day, they wist of none,
When it was come, when it was gone;
Frost nor snow, hailë nor rain
Of cold nor heat felt they no pain . . .
Thunder nor lightning had none effect,
So did God's mercy them protect,
But ever sang they the song they wrought
" Why standë we, why go we not? . . ."
Their time of grace came, by God's might
At the year's end, on Yulë night.
That same hour that the priest them banned
In that same hour God loosed their hand,
And, in the twinkling of an eye
Into the churchë gan they fly,
And on the pavement fell they down,
As they were dead or fallen in swoon.

For such dances, then, verses were composed, and nearly always in lines of four beats, convenient to mark the time.

There was commonly, as in this Colbigk story, a refrain which had the advantage of lengthening the poem and the dance. As to the authorship of these poems, no doubt in the main they had as personal a composer as any other; but there are several senses in which we must modify this in accordance with Grimm's dictum " the people poetizes ". In one sense the community may be said to have found the subject; for in most cases this is either some well-known legend, or a notorious local tragedy or comedy, such as *The Two Sisters of Binnorie.* Again, the people would not only take up the refrain but sometimes dictate some traditional burden. Many phrases, again, or even whole verses were common property; traditional literary clichés. Moreover, all the earliest ballads were circulated orally. The earliest English that has survived in writing is of the thirteenth century: then come a few in the middle of the fifteenth, but, when we have counted all, only eleven are existent in MSS. older than the seventeenth. Therefore not only did the author compose under communal influence, but he committed it to the communal keeping; and many parallel versions survive to show how the people remodelled it, whether consciously or unconsciously, for better or for worse. Lastly, these ballads show us, even though we had no other indication, the strong survival of pre-Christian traditions among the people. There are, it is true, a few ballads of definite Christian religious character; the finest of these is " The Falcon hath stolen my Make away ". But in most of them, the supernatural is pure magic and witchcraft, with fairies and elves and metamorphoses into wild beasts. If, again, heaven is mentioned, the tone is mainly pagan. The Wife of Usher's Well is able to conjure her sons back again by laying a curse on the winds and the sea until their return. When they have come for that brief moment to comfort her, they must needs return before the dawn:

> *The cock doth crow, the day doth daw,*
> *The channerin' worm doth chide;*
> *Gin we be miss'd out o' our place,*
> *A sair pain we maun bide.*

Again, in the paradise from which they have come, there grows the birk, the familiar tree of their own native valley, the earliest to come out in real splendour of spring green and therefore a tree mystical in its significance. Lastly, even to paradise they cannot return without regrets for the old home comforts:

Fare ye weel, my mother dear!
Fareweel to barn and byre!
And fare ye weel, the bonny lass
That kindles my mother's fire!

In "Clerk Saunders", again, the murdered man comes from heaven to see his love and regrets the things of earth; even celestial psalmody is envisaged as his task to which he must return:

O cocks are crowing on merry middlerd,
I wot the wild fowl boded day,
The psalms of heaven will be sung
And ere now I'll be missed away.

A very large proportion of the best ballads tell of love and death together; yet there the most impressive theme is that of union not in heaven, but in the grave. In the story of Tristram and Yseult, it is a vine and a rose that sprout in token of that past love; so, also, in "The Douglas Tragedy":

Lord William was buried in Mary's Kirk,
Lady Margaret in Mary's quire,
And out of her grave grew a bonny red rose,
And out of the knight's a briar.

Pre-Christian also are these survivals of simple uncivilized conceptions, as of gold and silver and ivory and silk used for the commonest objects; for instance the "web of silken cloth" with which the leak is to be staunched in *Sir Patrick Spens*. Many, again, make the birds and beasts talk, according to the rooted belief among savages. And, finally, their extreme antiquity is suggested by their remarkably wide distribution. W. P. Ker instances the theme of the boy playing roughly at ball and told in taunt to enquire how his father was killed; a theme which appears as wide apart as Scandinavia, Arabia and New Guinea.

Thus far, then, we may maintain that "das Volk dichtet". We may truly call these "folk-songs", so long as we bear in mind that "folk" means the whole population, not only the masses. As the Scottish Bishop Lesley wrote in the late sixteenth century: "Our border men delight in their own music and in the songs that they themselves compose concerning the deeds of their ancestors or their cunning tricks in border frays." The knight would sometimes sing of his own deeds; the lady, some plaintive ballad of "old unhappy far-off things and battles long ago"; the peasant of his own love and labour!

O I'm wat, wat,
Aye wat and wearie!
Fain would I get up and rin
If I could be with my dearie.

Upon which verse a Scottish critic has noted the expressive force of the native dialect: *wat* is as much wetter than *wet* as a Scotch mist is wetter than the English one.

The priest indeed might proclaim not only his personal prohibition but the curse of the Church; we have abundant evidence that he warned them beforehand in his sermons, and those stories tell us how naturally he might come out to defend his own church and yard. But, despite such tales of heavenly vengeance, little impression was made; there might be a few minutes' pause and hesitation, but tradition and impulse were too strong: one dancer, at least, would strike up the well-known refrain "Why standë we, why go we not?" and all protests would be swept away:

On with the dance; let joy be unconfined!
No rest till morn, when youth and pleasure meet
To chase the glowing hours with flying feet.

Ballads, then, were composed by all sorts, even by professional minstrels or by wandering scholars of the Langland type. Alphonse Daudet tells us how his first great editor worked with complete success upon the theory that every man had *dans le ventre* one good article for his paper. We are told that there is enough latent force in a bronze penny to carry a liner to New York and back, if only it can be rightly liberated; and there is more latent poetry in a stockbroker or a soap-boiler than all that is expressed in Shakespeare's plays. Ballads were composed by all sorts, for all sorts; and that is why the best of them live so wonderfully to-day. This was a People's Literature, answering to the People's Art of the Middle Ages; limited, but never falling below a certain standard because the ballads had been sifted through the sieve of memory, generation after generation, before they came down to us. "Oral transmission and its concomitants are not the accidents of the ballad, they are essential to it. . . . Without them the ballad would not be the ballad"[7] Many of the best are those which have been most recently discovered and printed. That is, such as have passed through the longest selective trial; such as had enough life in them to survive centuries of transmission from mouth to mouth. They illustrate, in short, Goethe's dictum that the unsophisticated man is more the master of direct, effective expression in a few words than he who has received a regular literary education.

9. NATURE AND SUPERSTITION

Nearly all superstitions—perhaps we may briefly say, all—are different forms of nature worship. When the Hebrew teacher warned his people not to look up at the stars and worship them he was dealing with a strong temptation of his age; for indeed, of all inanimate creatures, none could be more worthy of man's worship, and none, in fact, did attract it more. Let us look upon Old England now from this point of view—man and nature. The surface of the country, as we have seen, was far wilder than it is now. There was far more forest and fen; and, although a great deal had been done by pioneers in the past, plenty of clearing still remained to be done. We see this, for instance, in some of the enormous parishes in the North or in the Fenland. On the Yorkshire moors, at first, there were villages only at the very edge. Then, as in the cases of Blackburn and Whalley, the hinterland of moor was gradually exploited, and the priest found himself parson no longer to a handful of parishioners, but of several hamlets also, with their attendant chapels. So again at Doddington, on the edge of the Cambridgeshire Fens. That parish, by gradual draining, became so large and so rich that within the last century the tithes of the rectory were worth £10,000 a year. Everywhere, then, the population was thinly scattered in the Middle Ages, and yet in one way less scattered than it is now. There were next to no outlying farms. Nearly all the habitations were grouped in villages, as we see now on the Rhine plain or in many parts of Normandy and Northern France. The village and the town, again, were each mostly self-supporting. One of the best descriptions of this is to be found in Ruskin's *Praeterita*, where he writes on Abbeville as he first remembered it (ch. IX).

There is a great social lesson in that picture from *Punch*

of the London suburban boy who was boarded out for a fortnight in the country, and reported well of it when he came home, with one exception. " Here, we get our milk from clean brass cans; and there they get it from a nasty dirty cow." Four-fifths, at least, of the medieval population had grown their food in their own fields; had spun and woven wool from their own sheep or linen from their toft; and very often it was they themselves who made it into clothes. Nature, therefore, was their immediate friend and benefactor. She fulfilled Wordsworth's lines:

The homely Nurse doth all she can
To make her Foster-child, her Inmate man,
Forget the glories he hath known,
And that imperial palace whence he came.

Nature, then, was man's immediate friend; but she was his enemy also; his God, but his Devil. The wild and picturesque is romantic to us, but it was repugnant to the average man of the Middle Ages. Even nowadays a farmer in North Wales, who goes down to Shrewsbury or Oswestry Fair for the first time, will come back and say that England is a beautiful land, " as flat as a penny ". In Dante himself we find little enjoyment of mountain or forest as such; nor again in sunset or moonlight. Chaucer's Dorigen walks by the sea as a natural place for gentle exercise; but the rocks shock her with a wifely shudder of danger. Again, in the Man of Law's Tale, Ruskin notes his indifference to the poetry of the ocean. Constance voyages for five years long: " yet all this while Chaucer does not let fall a single word descriptive of the sea, or express any emotion whatever about it or about the ship. . . . Neither he nor his audience appear to be capable of receiving any sensation, but one of simple aversion, from waves, ships, or sands." When St Bernard said that he himself had learned most from the trees, this was not in Wordsworth's sense:

The clouds that gather round the setting sun
Do take a sober colouring from an eye
That hath kept watch o'er man's mortality.

St Bernard spoke only of the solitude, the remoteness from human interference. He was capable, another time, of journeying a whole day long beside the Lake of Geneva, without even realizing its existence. As in literature, so in art: there is no medieval painting in which landscape is treated for its own sake. The exhibition at Burlington House in 1936 showed us Chinese artists of Chaucer's age dealing as earnestly and successfully with landscape art, in the modern sense, as no Englishman did until the eighteenth century. In the medieval miniature, and even as late as Giotto, nature comes in only as a background to man; and, we may almost say, studiously and deliberately unnatural even then: carefully bent to something different from its direct purpose. Professor Herford has noted truly the extent to which Chaucer's landscapes are conventional, in spite of that deep sensibility for such simple everyday things as come out in his Nun's Priest's Tale. "Everyone now recognizes that we owe his multitude of May mornings and daisied lawns to no such spontaneous, untaught delight in these things as gave us Wordsworth's celandines or daffodils. But we need not ignore his delight in Nature because it is enriched and directed by his evident delight in the far-off reflection of Nature caught in the verse of Lorris or Boccaccio. . . . There is in any case no doubt of Chaucer's general preference, as an artist, for the trim and ordered landscape. But we should say that in this, as in other respects, the genial freedom of Nature won a securer hold upon his sympathies as his mind and taste matured; and that the man who sent forth his pilgrims in admirable disarray to tell their tales, not in symmetrical decades, or in a closed garden, as in the *Decameron,* but as 'aventure, or cas', or the whim of Harry Bailey might decree, along the Kentish highway, was also by this time no longer quite the poet who had described that severely uniform 'grove' of the *Boke of the Duchesse,* where 'every tree stood by hymselve, Fro other wel ten foot or twelve'. The Athenian forest where Theseus breaks in upon Palamon and Arcite is no such magnified quincunx as this. But, when all is said, it is clear that Chaucer was no fanatical lover of the green wood, like the singers of Robin Hood and of Gawain."[1] For that poem of *Sir Gawayne and the Green Knight*, with its companion *Pearl,* are in this respect exceptional in English literature. The Scottish poets do indeed show something approaching to the modern sense of the picturesqueness of wild country or bad weather, but we find this very seldom elsewhere in the Middle Ages. It is true that the monks chose "romantic" sites; but that was because part of their business was to fight with the fiend. Forest and wilderness were haunted by devils: and the monks had come to molest their ancient solitary reign. At Novalese, under Mont Cenis, the monastic chronicler tells us how he himself had often seen devils in the woods, in the form of serpents or toads. Again, when St Guthlac came to Croyland in the Fens, he constantly heard devils booming like bitterns in the dark, as well he might. Moreover, he heard them sometimes speaking in the Celtic tongue, which he himself had known when he lived in the West. Devils rode in the storm that unroofed the monks' cloister, or in the fire that fell from heaven upon their steeple and burned the church. When St Edmund Rich was a young man he saw at sunset a flight of black crows: these he recognized at once as a swarm of devils come to fetch the soul of a local usurer at Abingdon; and sure enough, when he came to Abingdon, the man was dead. In order to look upon nature as purely beneficent we need to be town-dwellers, taking our milk from brass milk-cans; or, by the latest refinement, from bottles.

This dualism, this constant fight between God and the Devil, was frequently manifested in the grossest forms. In the ninth century St Agobard, Archbishop of Lyons, wrote: "The wretched world lies now under the tyranny of foolishness: things are believed by Christians of such absurdity as no one ever could aforetime induce the heathen to believe, who knew not the Creator of all." He had to contend against weather-wizards who took toll of the peasants' credulity: "We have seen and heard many who are overwhelmed by such madness, carried away by such folly, that they believe and assert that there is a certain region called Magonia [the Magic Land], whence ships come in the clouds: the which bear away the fruits of the earth, felled by hail and destroyed by storms, to that same country; and these sailors of the air, forsooth, give rewards to the weather-wizards, and receive in return the crops or other fruits. Certain folk have we seen, blinded by so dark a folly, who brought into an assembly of men four persons, three men and a woman, as having fallen from the said ships; whom they held in bonds for certain days and then presented them before an assembled body of men, in our presence, as aforesaid, in order that they should be stoned. Howbeit the truth prevailed, after much reasoning, and they who brought them forward were confounded."[2] Elsewhere he complains of the image worship which, under official encouragement, was flourishing among these newly converted pagan tribes. "Perchance a man will say that he does not imagine anything divine inherent in the image which he worships [*adorat*], but that he pays it such veneration only in honour of him whose image it is. Such a man can easily be answered; for, if the image which he worships is not God, it ought by no means to be venerated, as though it were for the honour of the saints, who are far from arrogating to themselves divine honours. . . . If those who had left the worship [*cultum*] of devils were bidden to venerate the images of saints, methinks they would seem to themselves not so much to have quitted their idols as to have changed the outward form thereof." So also his contemporary Claudius, Bishop of Turin: many folk "worship images of saints after the fashion of devils . . . they have not left idols, but changed their names. For if thou dost draw or paint on the wall the images of Peter and Paul, of Jove and Saturn or Mercury, the former are no more truly apostles than the latter are gods; again, neither the former nor the latter are men; and thus it is a [mere] change of name [*ac per hoc nomen mutatur*]. Yet, in both cases, then and now, the error itself remains the same." He continues in almost the same words as St Agobard. Dr R. L. Poole comments upon both: "It was an age of materialism; and there was no possibility that the images should remain in churches without the people worshipping them, or that if they worshipped them they would understand the nice distinction between this worship and that of

God laid down by the second Nicene Council."[3] The cult of images and relics, it may almost be said, was implicit in the religious spirit of the Middle Ages: it often comes out strongest in the light of religious revivals. The Cluniac chronicler Glaber tells us much of struggles for reform in his own age, and of the "white robe of churches", and of the heresies which grew with this growing movement of Catholic revival, and therefore of the beginnings of bloody repression on a great scale: but he complains also of the false relics and false saints which were coming to veneration in those times. He gives concrete examples, and adds: "We, however, have recorded these things in order that men may beware of the manifold errors of demons or of men which abound everywhere in the world; more especially in the matter of springs or of trees incautiously venerated by sick folk."[4] Three centuries later, the chronicler Gervase of Tilbury [ch. XIII] tells of folk who came out of Mass one morning and saw an anchor let down from such a cloud-ship and grappled to a tomb. They heard the cries of the embarrassed cloud-sailors in the fog, until one came down the rope hand by hand and released the anchor. "When, however, he had torn the anchor from the tomb, he was caught by those that stood around, in whose arms he gave up the ghost, stifled by the breath of our gross air even as a shipwrecked mariner is stifled in the sea. Moreover his fellows above, judging him to be wrecked, after an hour's delay, cut the cable, left their anchor, and sailed away." Again he tells us: "It befel upon a time that a native of Bristol sailed to Ireland, leaving his wife and children at home. Then, after a long sea-voyage, as he sailed on a far-off ocean, he chanced to sit banqueting with the mariners about the hour of tierce; and, after eating, as he washed his knife over the ship's side, it slipped suddenly from his hands. At that same hour, at Bristol, the knife fell in through that same citizen's roof-window (which men in the English tongue call *dormer*) and stuck in the table that was set before his wife. The woman, marvelling at so strange a thing, was dumb-founded; and, laying aside this well-known knife, she learned long afterwards, on her husband's return, that his misfortune had befallen on the very day whereon she had found it. Who, then, will now doubt, after the publication of this testimony, that a sea lieth over this earth of ours, whether in the air or above the air?"

This dualism, again, was encouraged by very many Roman Catholic ceremonies. The priest came out and rang church bells to drive off an approaching storm, or sprinkled holy water to exorcize it. Holy water was in constant use in church and in the house. One of the earliest prayers in the Mass is one for exorcism of the house, borrowed from a Frankish liturgy. In this matter, one of the most curious chapters is that of the Excommunication of Animals, which I treat more fully in *The Medieval Village*. Concrete instances of this are numerous; and the practice was formally defended in 1531 by Chassenée, a celebrated legist, in his book *De Excommunicatione Animalium Insectorum*. All beasts (he argues) are subject to man (Genesis i. 26); therefore all are subject to Church Law. We know (he continues) that such excommunications are in fact effective. We know that they can destroy eels in a lake, or the sparrows that infest a church; it is well known how a priest at Toulouse turned a white loaf black by excommunication, and white again by absolution, and how the miracle was repeated by a bishop at Troyes. Since, therefore, caterpillars and other rural pests would simply laugh at a condemnatory sentence from the ordinary civil courts, let us use the weapon of Canon Law; let us strike them "with the pain of anathema, for which they have greater fear, as creatures obedient to the God who made them". A solemn monastic formulary of 1526-31 proclaims that "caterpillars, palmer-worms, or by whatsoever name they be called" are banished from the diocese of Troyes, and all the faithful are summoned, as a requisite preliminary, "to join together in good works and pious prayers, and to pay their tithes without fraud and according to the custom of the district". This due payment of tithes is emphasized as a *sine quâ non*: at these times of common danger, tithe-payer and tithe-taker, parson and peasant, were united against the pests. It was natural, therefore, that the practice should long survive. In the three years 1831-3 the grasshoppers were regularly combated in parts of Champagne by the weapon of ecclesiastical processions and exorcisms.* On this point, Abbé Bergier's religious encyclopaedia of a century ago is most instructive. In defence of those parish priests of his own day who still "exorcise and adjure storms, rural pests, etc." he writes: "Priests have several times got into trouble for refusing to give way to their parishioners' requests. . . . It would be excellent to teach the people natural science, if they were capable of understanding it and incapable of misusing it; but they are neither one nor the other. When people learn that all natural phenomena are the natural effect of physical laws, they will draw the unbeliever's conclusion, that the world made itself and governs itself. Will the people gain much by this? If those who criticize the priests knew the people better, they would be less ready to condemn the priests."

Thus, in most minds, Satan bulked almost as large as God: in some, even larger. The regions of cold and bad weather were his especially; the Devil lived in the north, as we see from Chaucer's Friar's Tale (*Canterbury Tales*, D, 1413). This superstition was doubtless reinforced by such Bible texts as Jeremiah i. 14 and iv. 6: "Out of the north an evil shall break forth", "I will bring evil from the north, and a great destruction". We may thus almost say that the Devil was the God of winter and Jehovah God only of summer and spring. For we must remember the privations men suffered in those ill-built and draughty houses—their food of salt meat killed and preserved in the autumn, since there was no fodder to keep the cattle through the winter; scarcely any vegetables available in the cold months. Even in castles, accommodation was very scanty: the ladies sat all day long over their embroidery or gossip or parlour games, longing for the summer to come again. At last spring comes, and that is the outburst that greets us everywhere

* We may compare with this the medieval custom of condemning and executing criminal beasts—the sow which has devoured a child, or the ox which has gored a man.

in medieval poetry. The Minnesinger records the thrill of delight when the linden shows its emerald green in the castle court:

Ich bin worden gewahr
Neues Laubes an der Linde!

Already among the Anglo-Saxons the gods were mainly nature-gods; their worship was connected with the holy well, the holy glade in the forest, the great holy tree. St Augustine of Canterbury, by the advice of Pope Gregory who sent him, took care not to shock this belief too much. Bede has recorded St Gregory's message to the first missionaries in England (Book I, ch. 30). This ran that the pagan temples in that country should not be pulled down; it being sufficient that the idols in them be destroyed. "Therefore let these places of heathen worship be sprinkled with holy water: let altars be built and relics placed under them: for if these temples are well built, it is fit the property of them should be altered; that the worship of devils be abolished, and the solemnity changed to the service of the true God: that when the natives perceive those religious structures remain standing, they may keep to the place without retaining the error; and be less shocked at their first entrance upon Christianity, by frequenting the temples they have been used to esteem. And since it has been their custom to sacrifice oxen to the devils they adored, this usage ought to be refined on, and altered to an innocent practice." He advises, therefore, that "upon the anniversary of the saints, whose relics are lodged there, or upon the return of the day the Church was consecrated, the people should make them booths about those churches lately rescued from idolatry, provide an entertainment, and keep a Christian holy-day; not sacrificing their cattle to the devil, but killing them for their own refreshment, and praising God for the blessing; that thus, by allowing them some satisfactions of sense, they may relish Christianity the better, and be raised by degrees to the more noble pleasures of the mind: for unpolished ignorant people are not to be cured all at once. He that intends to reach the top of an eminence must rise by gradual advances, and not think to mount at a single leap: thus God, when he discovered himself to the Israelites in Egypt, did not forbid them the customary rites of sacrificing, but transferred their worship from the devil to himself."

This accounts for the so-called "Church Houses", of which a good many remain in western England: a house generally recognizable by its age and its proximity to the church; evidently something more important than the ordinary cottage. It was in such buildings that the "Church Ales" were celebrated; a custom directly continuous from these early pagan rejoicings. On stated occasions food and ale were collected by voluntary contributions; and all who would might come and pay their scot and eat and drink their fill for the benefit of the church funds. It was found convenient in later times to build small houses for this and similar church functions, and records show us that these were sometimes let also to strolling players.

The village dance also was, as we have seen, a direct inheritance from pre-Christian times. It is absolutely necessary to realize that nobody whatever doubted the actual existence of these old pagan gods. They existed as truly as the great God; but, whereas the pagans had taken them for gods, the Christians knew them to be devils. Such gods can be driven out only by the power of a greater God; and, though worsted for a moment, they still linger in the background, ready to snap up everything that the greater God does not definitely protect. Hence, since the Church took a very one-sided view of human life in many ways, whatsoever the ecclesiastic in his narrowness or intolerance cast out, that became the natural domain of the Devil. We must not be pharisaical here. Nowadays not only very good Churchfolk, but very excellent agnostics, may be found fidgety about the spilling of salt, the walking under ladders, or the omission of touching wood. Superstition is, after all, only faith based on ignorance, and we are all very ignorant: ignorance is only a relative matter. But, relatively with our own day, superstition was certainly then enormously prominent. Many of the medieval devils have been driven out more effectually by Pasteur and his fellow-scientists than they were by the ringing of bells or the sprinkling of water. We must remember the unavoidable ignorance of natural phenomena in those days. St Thomas Aquinas, for instance, argues that "to the ignorant it seemeth miraculous that the magnet draweth iron, or that a little fish holdeth back a ship". The first part of this statement is as definitely accepted to-day as in the thirteenth century, but the second part rests upon the ancient superstition of the *remora*, an imaginary fish scarcely a foot long, through which the sailors explained to themselves otherwise unaccountable hindrances or disturbances of their navigation. Take again, for mixture of fact and fancy, the description of the crocodile by Bartholomew the Englishman, one of the stock encyclopaedists of the thirteenth century: "His teeth ben horyble and strongly shape, as a comb or a sawe and as a bores tuske . . . and is a beaste nouryshed in greate glotenye, and eateth ryghte moche: And soo whan he is ful, he lyeth by the brynke or by the clyffe and bloweth for fulnes. If the cocodril findeth a man by the brim of the water or by the cliffe, he sleeth hym if he may, and then he wepeth upon hym and swoloweth hym at the laste."

Not only was scientific observation enormously difficult in those days, but it was not even sufficiently esteemed in itself. In very many cases not only men could not observe patiently, but they did not care to do so. We cannot accept the plea that this fantastic zoology of the medieval mind was due not to lack of intelligence but only to lack of observation; for the unobservant habit is one of the unintelligent habits. We must remember, again, that the Church deliberately inculcated further ignorance of great portions of human life: for instance, we shall see that anatomy was forbidden. Moreover, in those ages when nearly every educated man was a cleric, in Minor if not in Major Orders, the clergy were strictly forbidden to shed blood with their own hands, even in a beneficent cause; so that a priest attempting to relieve a sufferer and inadvertently causing a breach of the skin or bloodshed was suspended from his sacerdotal functions until he had confessed and been absolved by a bishop or some other high ecclesiastic entitled to deal with "reserved" cases.

The Church often suspected nature. We have seen how

St Edmund interpreted the flock of crows. St Dominic, again, when his studies were disturbed by a sparrow fluttering about his lamp, recognized at once the Devil, caught the bird, and, plucking it alive, triumphed in its screams and his own victory over the powers of darkness.[5] It is true that we find love of nature recorded in a small minority of medieval saints' lives. St Francis, St Hugh of Lincoln, St Anselm, and perhaps a dozen others, were notable for their love of, and control over, animals. These, however, are exceptional; and a recent French writer, compiling a book on *The Church and Pity for Animals,* has not been able to swell the medieval testimony beyond about a hundred pages.[6]

The child, nature's work, is impure, tainted with original sin —*massa perditionis.* Nothing but baptism can redeem it from hell, even though St Thomas might persuade himself, and try to persuade his readers, that hell without actual physical torture might be a place of relative happiness. The Church cast nature away, and the Devil took nature for his own. So again with laughter and the dance. Of St Francis and St Bernard their intimate biographers assure us that, though they spent their lives in holy joy, they seldom or never allowed themselves actual laughter. They acted on what had been a tradition in orthodox Christianity, from the time of St John Chrysostom: "Christ is crucified, and dost thou laugh?" Yet laughter, as we all know, is an essential function of human nature. Here we have the testimony of the Franciscan Salimbene. To him, as to Dante, the Emperor Frederick was a man of heroic proportions in his very sins: he made linguistic experiments on the vile bodies of hapless infants, "bidding foster-mothers and nurses to suckle and bathe and wash the children, but in no wise to prattle or speak with them; for he would fain have learnt whether they would speak the Hebrew language (which had been the first), or Greek, or Latin, or Arabic, or perchance the tongue of their parents of whom they had been born. But he laboured in vain; for the children could not live without clappings of the hands; and gestures, and gladness of countenance, and blandishments." As for the dance, we have seen its almost universal discouragement or prohibition by the Church. So, again, in the matter of clerical celibacy, with these thousands of priests and deacons and sub-deacons and monks and friars and nuns. To each of those, half humanity was in many senses professionally non-existent. The practical result we have already seen; a great many very honest and self-denying ascetics, whose religious enthusiasm was, however, sometimes very Utopian and unpractical. Against these we may set many law-breakers and a certain number of downright rascals; and, in between, a middle mass who, on the whole, would have been rather better for leading more natural lives. The practical upshot was that, in spite of attempts to avoid this Manichaean conclusion, family life was put on a lower plane; it was not the choicest offering to God, and therefore it was comparatively favourable to the Devil. It is of the earth, earthly; St Jerome's words were famous: "marriage fills the earth, virginity fills heaven"—*Matrimonium replet terram, virginitas coelum.* Too often, again, the Church suspected human reason. In a sense, no doubt, all her philosophers rested mainly upon it; from their own premises they reasoned with rigorous logic, and Newman could contend in that sense that the scholastic age was pre-eminently an age of reason. But their premises, as we shall see, were commonly derived from tradition, and popular tradition at that; yet traditions of which the Church forbade denial, or even serious doubt, at the risk of death, thus taking away with one hand the rational processes which she had encouraged with the other. There, again, the Devil was too often able to claim reason for his own province.

Moreover, the Church not only left room for many superstitions, but too often deliberately encouraged them. The sceptic on the one side, and the superstitious man on the other, took strength to themselves from the reckless way in which the clergy introduced the miraculous into ordinary life. Not only did they sometimes teach that sovereign virtues were inherent in mere attendance at their services, attentively or unattentively, and in the mere sight of such images as that of St Christopher, but they endowed relics and pious gestures and exclamations with the same miraculous powers. We have a tale first told by a thirteenth-century Cistercian and copied again and again into handbooks of anecdotes for preachers: here it is in fifteenth-century English. "Som tyme ther was a burd that was lernyd to speke. So on a tyme she flow away in the feldis, and the Goshalk [pur]sweid after hur and wold hafe kyllid hur. And whan she saw hym com, as she was lernyd at home, she began to cry, and sayd: '*Sancte Thoma! adiuua me!*' A! Saynt Thomas, helpe me!' And onone this goshalk fell down dead, and this burd esskapid and had none harm. Lo, surs, what vertue it is to call on Saynt Thomas, martir of Cantyrbery, in any tribulacion!"[7] Nor were the clergy always above practising deliberate fraud and boasting of it. From that same Book of Tales for preachers comes the story of the rustic who, having received a bad penny in the course of the year, kept it to offer at Easter as his compulsory Mass-penny. The priest, noting the fraud, slipped that same penny into his mouth instead of the consecrated wafer, to the amazement and repentance of the sinning peasant, who in his simplicity accepted this legerdemain as a miracle from on high. The Mass was naturally the main centre of popular superstitions. One of the most often-repeated stories from all ages and centuries is that of the worshipper who could not believe in Transubstantiation, until one day he saw a wafer turn into a living child in the priest's hand as he blessed it. Again, almost equally frequent is the story of the consecrated wafer, which, if broken or pricked with a dagger, sheds blood. That story was found particularly convenient for anti-Semitic propaganda, as an excuse for massacre and plunder.[8]

The natural result was that such popular superstitions were utilized for the purposes of definite witchcraft, as in the case of the old woman who crumbled the consecrated Hosts over her cabbages to destroy the caterpillars, and of the priest who used one as a love-philtre.[9] The water in the font, having once been consecrated, tempted folk to superstitious uses. In the same way, the people kept up (and the Church often contended against) pagan ceremonies at Christmas and at Eastertide, and especially the mid-summer bonfire. Pagan holy wells, again, the Church often baptized to her own purpose; it is admitted by historians of all religious creeds that the majority of medieval saints' wells were inheritors of a worship from the time of the older gods. We may take, for instance, Tarter's or Tawder's Well, which existed at Grantchester, near Cambridge, until coprolite-digging in the Great War destroyed the flow of water. That well was rebaptized in the Middle Ages to the greatest of local saints—St Etheldreda of Ely. The name Etheldreda was gradually corrupted to Audrey; the great annual fair at Ely was St Audrey's Fair, and the attractive little articles which formed its speciality were first called *St Audrey* articles, then *tawdry*, and have thus given their name to an uncomplimentary modern adjective. Thus St Etheldreda's Well became Tawder's and then Tarter's. It was natural that, whether for love or for fear, the medieval population should still haunt the ancient fountain or glade or tree. At St Joan's trial she admitted that she and her fellows had danced round a particular sacred tree. The mission preacher Herolt, and the medieval witch-finder Sprenger, both agreed that more women will be found in hell than men; because, although the women lead in other respects more regular lives, it is they who are specially given to witchcraft. Berthold of Regensburg [1250] says in one of his sermons: "Many of the village folk would come to heaven, were it not for their witchcrafts. . . . The woman has spells for getting a husband, spells for her marriage; spells on this side and on that; spells before the child is born, before the christening, after the christening; and all she gains with her spells is that her child fares the worse all its life long. . . . Ye men, it is much marvel that ye lose not your wits for the monstrous witchcrafts that women practise on you!" The Camden Society volume of proceedings against Dame Alice Kyteler is most instructive on this subject. Michelet was probably right; women's minds are more conservative and compassionate; therefore many of them could never tear from their hearts the deep pity for these last survivals from the Twilight of the Gods. Constantly we catch, in the Middle Ages, hints of an undercurrent, of a yearning after the pagan past which was in many ways as temperamental as the regret expressed by a modern Huysmans or De Gourmont for the vanished thirteenth century; or, if it comes to that, by the utterly unconverted Heine:

Das Herz ist mir beklemmt, und sehnlich
Gedenke ich der alten Zeit:
Die Welt war damals noch so wöhnlich,
Und ruhig lebten hin die Leut':
Und jetzt ist Alles wie verschoben,
Es gibt ein Drängen, eine Not;
Gestorben ist der Herrgott oben,
Und unten ist der Teufel tot.

Or by Victor Hugo in *Notre-Dame de Paris*; and again in his cry in the poem of much later years:

O! reprends ton néant
Gouffre, et rends-nous Satan!

The superstition of the Evil Eye was specially prevalent and strong. Old women, once suspected of this or of other occult powers, would naturally sometimes encourage the suspicion, for the sake of money or influence. Among the Records of Depositions in the Durham Court, witchcraft plays a prominent part in parochial visitations; and, no less naturally, it is the love-charm that comes to the fore.[10] In 1435 three men accuse Margaret Lyndysay of having cast a spell which renders them impotent; she purges herself with the oath of five women neighbours, and is restored to her good fame, and the three are forbidden to repeat the slander under pain of excommunication. In 1446, two women were accused of "using the art of witchcraft, and saying to spinsters desirous of marriage that they would make them to have the men whom they affect and desire to have". One or two others are accused of witchcraft in general, and are usually submitted to compurgation by the oaths of five or six neighbours. A report was spread that another had so bewitched the curate of the parish to sin and to spend money on her, that he had found his way to prison. At Bromyard "the parishioners say that Alison Brown holdeth such doings that, when she hath cursed any body, in virtue of her curse God shall take vengeance upon him without delay; and this she hath oftentimes done by her [power], which is against the Catholic faith and would tempt God". We find this treated seriously even in the highest places: there are four cases in vol. I of the *Calendar of Chancery Petitions.* At the end of the fifteenth century, for instance, John Dunn of York complained to the Lord Chancellor of England how "Thomas Mell of the County of York, husbandman, through divers erroneous acts, and contrary to the Catholic faith, to wit through sorcery, and in evil example to all folk in the aforesaid country, as is openly known to many folk, hath withdrawn water from a certain pond" on the complainant's land. Another suit is against "Richard Kirkeby, late a Scholar of Cambridge, and said to use necromancies to make himself go invisible".[11] Such a reputation, however, was not without serious dangers. We may see this in a Northumberland Assize Roll for the thirteenth century, where a man is accused of having run an old woman through with a pitchfork, and excuses himself on the ground that she had cast a spell over him. The jury decided that he had killed her in self-defence against the Devil—*quasi se defendendo contra diabolum.*[12] Witch-hunting, however, although it grew in the later Middle Ages, never attained the same proportions in medieval England as in Scotland and on the Continent, among both Protestants and Roman Catholics, in the sixteenth and early seventeenth centuries. The conflict between Sorcery and the Church is told in detail by H. C. Lea in the third volume of his *History of the Inquisition in the Middle Ages.*[13] In the tenth century the Church almost tolerated it; partly no doubt because it was too strong for her to venture upon a life-and-death struggle, but partly also because a few great Churchmen, as we have seen, were enlightened enough to believe that these pagan survivals were groundless superstitions. The real conflict came after the founding of the Inquisition; and, even then, not at first. It is in the first half of the fourteenth century that inquisitors begin to treat witchcraft no less seriously than heresy. But the beliefs were too deep and widespread; and doubtless persecution also gave them the stimulus of advertisement. Thus, in 1398, the University of Paris adopted a series of twenty-eight articles against demonology, declaring at the same time that it is a theological error to doubt the reality of sorcery and its effects. Any denial of this pronouncement was thenceforward sufficient to justify vehement suspicion of heresy. "The Church lent its overpowering authority to enforce belief on the souls of men. The malignant powers of the witch were repeatedly set forth in the bulls of successive popes for the implicit credence of the faithful; and the University of Cologne, in 1487, when expressing its approval of the *Malleus Maleficarum* of Sprenger, warned every one that to argue against the reality of witchcraft was to incur the guilt of impeding the Inquisition." Here, then, war to the knife is declared. But the worst was that, though Holy Water and the Sign of the Cross and other ecclesiastical safeguards might ward off the danger, yet, when once the spell had been cast, nothing could counteract it but counter-spells. It may be doubted whether Lea is altogether right in his belief that the practice of witchcraft actually grew in volume from the fourteenth century onward. On the contrary, there seems evidence that the difference resided not in any greater prevalence of sorcery, but in the more desperate resolve of the Church to adopt remedies against so inveterate a foe. It was only then, when the general public was becoming more educated, and the Inquisition had armed the Church with such enormous fighting power, that she determined at last to drive her adversary to extremities. The Dominicans Nider and Sprenger in the fifteenth century devoted their main writings and activities to witch-hunting; and it was this spirit which was largely responsible for the condemnation of Joan of Arc. At the end of the fifteenth century Sprenger and his colleague boasted that they had burned forty-eight sorcerers in five years. In the sixteenth century "Protestant and Catholic rivalled each other in the madness of the hour. Witches were burned no longer in ones and twos, but in scores and hundreds. A bishop of Geneva is said to have burned five hundred within three months; a bishop of Bamberg six hundred, a bishop of Würzburg nine hundred. Eight hundred were condemned, apparently in one body, by the Senate of Savoy. . . . Paramo [in his history of the Inquisition] boasts that in a century and a half from the commencement of the sect, in 1404, the Holy Office had burned at least thirty thousand witches who, if they had been left unpunished, would easily have brought the whole world to destruction."

10. POPES AND PRELATES

Conventional historiography duly emphasizes the Church's work in shaping medieval Society; but we must not stop there. It is equally important—some might say, even more important—to mark how Society shaped the Church. Roughly speaking, theirs was a peasant world, with peasant mentality. The village was one of its greatest formative sources, operative even in its passivity. Social conditions were the outcome not only of what the peasant actively desired, but also of that which his conservatism could not suffer to be removed or altered. It is only a half-truth to point out that medieval theologians were able to impose a long-disputed dogma upon the official Church. The complement of this is, that the populace could do much the same, almost without enlisting the theologians' services. Image worship, a question so contentious that it led to actual civil war, was finally decided not as the great early Fathers had thought, but as the populace required. In the long catalogue of recognized saints, those who have been canonized by popular acclamation will be found far more numerous than those who have received their credentials directly from Rome, after such examination as the present generation has seen in the cases of Fisher and More. The strength of the winning cause in the Transubstantiation dispute was in its direct and commanding appeal to the people, while scientific theologians could justify it only by the invention of logical devices hitherto unknown to any philosophy. Even the Feast of Corpus Christi, which consecrated that victory, was forced at first upon unwilling theologians by a village girl and a young village priest. The doctrine of the Immaculate Conception, which for centuries no Pope dared to decide, was one which had been rejected by St Bernard and by the whole of the Dominican order, that is, by the most learned theologians; but the people demanded it, and so did the Franciscans, as representatives of the people, and their guides in the sense of "I am your leader; therefore I follow you". Thus, to understand medieval society, we must follow closely not only Church history proper, but also this interaction of village and Church. The upper hierarchy had, of course, great importance; but that consideration is more obvious and needs less emphasis here. We may glance at those great folk; and, at certain moments, we must mark the special influence of one prelate or another. But we must look with far closer attention, and in more minute detail, at this obscure multitude, lay and clerical, out of whose thoughts and wishes the prelate's action normally grew. It is natural, therefore, that from the village flock we should pass on to the spiritual shepherd.

We must begin by getting rid of modern ideas. There is much truth (though we shall have to qualify this later on) in the contention that the Western Church was only one form of the State; that State and Church were different sides of the same institution. The Church included nearly the whole of civilized Europe; all baptized folk were its subjects, and it was punishable to neglect baptism for one's children. Therefore the whole population might be reckoned as Churchfolk. This was the legal basis of the treatment of heresy throughout the Middle Ages as a form of treason. The Jew and the Pagan were under heavy disabilities, but in normal times they were not punished for disbelief. The heretic, on the other hand, was reckoned as a traitor and must therefore be treated as such.

Let us look at this from the point of view first of the clergy themselves, and secondly of the congregations. From that first point of view it will appear that nearly all men of culture were clerics—students, authors, journalists, lecturers, even lower university officials, parish clerks, bedesmen, anchorites and pilgrims. From the other point of view, the congregation was the whole population. It included potentially all elements of present denominations. It included the potential sacerdotalist and the potential Puritan—extremes of superstition, of free thought, and even of infidelity. In short, the strength and the weakness of the medieval Church were not only those of an institution, but those of human nature itself. We must never forget how it had come to dominate the Western World; nor again the extent to which religion gave depth and seriousness to ancient Latin and Greek thought. The Church services, again, kept up to a considerable extent the study of the Latin language; and the Church in its organization was an object lesson in social solidarity. Even under papal despotism there remained more remnants of free discussion and election, on the whole, than could generally be found in civil life.

The Papacy, then, was a great bureaucracy, a network of officials from top to bottom. From at least the time of Hildebrand, that Pope Gregory VII whose relations with William the Conqueror we have already seen, it was a despotism. Though William refused homage to Gregory, John was compelled to pay it to Innocent III, and this was not repudiated until 1374. We may, therefore, divide our period into three portions. First, two centuries of growing papal influence; then one century of waning influence, ending with the Statutes of Provisors and Praemunire, and the repudiation of John's tribute; and, thirdly, two more centuries during which the Great Breach was preparing.

At the head of this bureaucracy was the Pope, ruling from Rome, except for the seventy years of "captivity" at Avignon. He commanded an army disciplined not, it is true, in the strictest modern sense, but very strictly disciplined in comparison with medieval society in general; moreover, most ubiquitous. Under him were the Cardinals, who by this time had become a college of electors for the Papacy, and were constantly used by the Pope as legates to override the local prelates in any country in which he chose to interfere. Under these came the Archbishops and Bishops, the Archbishop's jurisdiction covering roughly the Roman imperial province and the Bishop's that of the Roman *civitas*. The *civitas* under the Roman Empire had been about the size of a modern English county or of a French *département*; thus an ecclesiastical map of France before the Revolution would show divisions answering pretty exactly to the Roman *civitates*. For several centuries, after the rule of popular election had died out, these prelates were appointed mainly by kings, and we may say of England as Imbart de la Tour does of France: "We do not find in fact in documents of the ninth century any texts which allow us to suppose that such bishops had to swear fidelity to the Pope."[1] The contrast between medieval and modern discipline, in this particular respect, is enormous. England had many less bishops than old imperial districts like Italy, France and Spain. At the Conquest we had only 14, increased by two under Henry I; and the want was felt so severely that Wolsey, shortly before the Reformation, proposed to create 20 new bishoprics. Our 16 were divided into two provinces—Canterbury and York. The bishops periodically met their clergy and passed by-laws in synods. Less frequently, the clergy of the whole province met for the same purposes in council.

England had thus, like all other countries, a Canon Law of its own; but only as a code of by-laws subordinate to the Pope's Canon Law, which was binding on the whole of Western Christendom. That law was administered in ecclesiastical courts, by the Archbishops, the Bishops and the Archdeacons. In archdeacons also we were comparatively poor at the Conquest; there was only one for each diocese. Sooon, however, multiplication was found necessary, and we presently find about one archdeacon to each county. This official was often called "the bishop's eye". It was his function to exercise, as deputy, the bishop's supervision over the morals of his diocese, as every reader of Chaucer must remember. In this, the archdeacon did very much to supersede our next official in the hierarchy—the Rural Dean. This was a parish priest elected from among the rest of the clergy and unsalaried, answering very nearly to our unsalaried Justices of the Peace of the present day. On the other hand, since medieval justice reposed so greatly on the system of fines, these rural deaneries were to some extent lucrative. They were generally roughly conterminous with the minor divisions of the county, the "hundreds". In Norwich diocese, for instance, there were 45 rural deaneries to 58 hundreds, but in only two cases was the boundary of the rural deanery different from some hundred boundary. As assistants to the bishop in discipline, these rural deans were concerned with matrimonial and testamentary and moral questions; but the first of these matters became more and more complicated; thoroughly trained lawyers were obviously required; and therefore presently we find the archdeacon practically swallowing all these duties and privileges. Rural deans are not even mentioned in Chaucer, though they do occur once in *Piers Plowman* under the title of "sub-deans". John of Ayton, commenting on English Canon Law [1340], mentions the system as nearly dead; but it has been revived in modern times.

We next come to the ordinary Parish Priest. When Augustine first converted England there was no attempt to divide it into parishes. Each bishop was a missionary, having a staff of missionary clergy living with him, grouped round his cathedral and scouring the surrounding districts. Then, with the complete conversion of the different kingdoms, the pagan ecclesiastical system was naturally merged in that of the conquering religion. Under the heathen Anglo-Saxons, landowners had erected temples on their own estates; and the priests had been paid by tithes or contributions from the peasants. That system in England, as elsewhere, passed naturally into a parochial organization. The land-owner still appointed the priest; and the priest claimed his tithes and other offerings in virtue of universal Canon Law. Thus the rural parish was, as a rule, simply the village in its ecclesiastical aspect. The main endowments of the parish clergy came from tithes. In Norwich diocese, for instance, tithes were two-thirds, offerings one-fifth, and glebe one-eighth of the average total income of the incumbent. This average total endowment in that diocese was roughly about £11. But this was a rich district; and the average of some other counties would be distinctly lower. That £11 represents roughly £400 a year in present currency, in addition to which the priest had his house and garden. This income was nominally earmarked into three portions—one for the priest himself; one for the upkeep of the church buildings and services; and one for the poor. That theory, however, as we shall see later, represented only a pious ideal; nobody has ever attempted to produce documentary evidence from any time or country in which it regularly worked.

England had during our period a little less than 9000 parishes, for a population which probably ranged from about two and a half millions at the Conquest to, at most, four and a half or five millions under Henry VII. Thus the average number of souls per parish was at most about 450—that is, about 180 adults. The town parishes were on an average considerably smaller than those of the villages. Although, then, there were less than 9000 parishes, yet before the Black Death there were probably some 20,000 priests; Cardinal Gasquet has calculated 50,000, but it is very difficult to follow the reasoning by which he arrives at so high a number. It may be worth while to point out that at the present day we have some 21,000 Anglican priests to nearly ten times the medieval population; the reason for this large medieval proportion will be seen later on. Beneath the priest came the clergy in lower orders. There are seven Orders in the Roman Church—four "Minor", and three "Major" or "holy". These minor clerics were extremely numerous; even grammar-school boys were often tonsured as clerics, so were all students of the university. These lower clerics frequently worked as attendants on noblemen, as accountants (hence the modern term "clerical work" for writing and similar occupations), or again for performing minor services in the church—the *Dirige* and *Placebo* of *Piers Plowman*. The most important of these minor clerics, to whom we shall come in detail later on, were the Parish Clerks. Taking them all together, and including the "regular" (i.e. cloistered) clergy, there was probably at least one cleric per hundred of population—that is, about one among every thirty adult males.

All these, then, were organized into a system more elaborate than anything analogous in the State. Here was, in theory, a vast disciplined army at the Pope's beck and call; and, theoretically, the fullest and most elaborate provisions on the one hand for the spiritual needs of the population through teaching and public worship, and on the other for the relief of the poor, whether in their own cottages or as destitute travellers; and, thirdly, even to some extent an educational system.

That is the skeleton of the organization. Let us now trace in greater detail its working in England from the Conquest to the Reformation. In Popes we began well; for 1073 saw the advent of Gregory VII, one of the greatest in the whole series; and the two centuries which followed him were distinctly above the average. We have seen how William I definitely repudiated his claim of homage; yet in most matters the two worked harmoniously: this is very clearly brought out by Dr Z. N. Brooke in his recent *English Church and the Papacy*. William was, on the whole, heartily in favour of Gregory's reforming energies: but he "was determined to be master of all his subjects, a dual authority in the kingdom was to him unthinkable". Like all contemporary kings, he appointed the bishops and ensured their obedience to himself. He allowed Lanfranc to go to Rome for his pallium; by this time, that had become customary: but later, when Gregory again demanded Lanfranc's presence, William refused to permit it, and Lanfranc obeyed the king. In other respects also, the great archbishop behaved rather as the king's than as the Pope's man. We may not go quite so far as Dr Brooke, who seems to imply that, if it had come to an open trial of strength between the two, Lanfranc would have sided with William on these issues, and flatly disobeyed the Pope. In the face of the Forged Decretals, which Lanfranc knew and believed in like everybody else of his day, such definite defiance of a Pope's clear commands would seem impossible. But in fact there never came any such demand for a clear-cut decision between Pope and king; and Gregory, for all his conviction of authority and his masterful spirit, was prudent enough to let sleeping dogs lie. This, in fact, was one of the earliest of those compromises in which English history has been so rich. But papal policy was so consistent, in comparison with that of the lay rulers, that the balance of power tended more and more in favour of the Church as time went on. William I had stoutly maintained his right of recognizing, in disputed elections, the Pope of his own choice. William II, under pressure from Anselm at a moment when he was taken at disadvantage, gave up that right. Henry I, again, under pressure of political difficulties at home, finally gave way to Anselm's insistence and admitted the claims of Paschal II in the Investiture quarrel. Henceforward "not merely the old [Canon] Law, but the new decrees passed at Rome were enforced in England. It was the first breach made in the royal barrier, and it was never during the Middle Ages completely closed again". The next step came with the disputed claim of Stephen to the crown. The barons, in Henry's lifetime, had solemnly sworn to recognize Matilda; Stephen appealed to Rome for a general absolution from that oath. John of Salisbury, who hints broadly that Stephen's money won him the victory here, probably voices the general opinion of his day; but Dr Brooke inclines to the milder judgment that the Pope had made up his mind beforehand, "influenced rather by ecclesiastical than by judicial considerations". In any case, here was the papal wedge driven in a great deal further; and, throughout Stephen's reign, his political weakness compelled him to submit to the dictation of the Church. That fatal blunder in Becket's case which brought Henry II to surrender, and John's grovelling at the feet of Innocent III, are too well known to need repetition here. England was thenceforward, politically as well as theologically, vassal to Rome, until Edward III repudiated the homage and tribute, and restricted ecclesiastical encroachments in his Statutes of Provisors. Yet, even then, the only supreme Church Law in England was Roman Canon Law: and this is a point so often falsified or obscured by interested special pleading, that it needs no emphasis here. It was first brought out briefly by Rashdall; and then by F. W. Maitland so conclusively as to leave no further excuse for Bishop Stubbs's theory of a separate English Canon Law, independent in any real sense of Rome. The Statutes of Provisors logically prove this; for they carefully erected a barrier against the chances that the clergy, even when lay resistance to Rome gave them the most solid support, would capitulate and surrender to the Pope their own rights of presentation, often very lucrative. The omnipotence of Canon Law is most explicitly asserted in Archbishop Arundel's notorious decree of 1407/8, in which (*inter alia*) he condemns as heresy, and therefore as a burning matter, any misinterpretation or repudiation of any papal decretal. So far had papal pretensions grown, in spite of growing lay opposition, within our period.

In the memoirs of Schaunard, dealing with Bohemian life at Paris, there is an anecdote which may be used as a parable to illustrate the subtle growth and pressure of papal power. A sculptor had a model so perfect in manly symmetry and strength that he resolved to immortalize him with a plaster cast. He constructed a great box in which the man stood, while the liquid plaster was poured in up to the neck. In half a minute the model was gasping for breath; a few seconds more, and he was purple in the face: only by the utmost promptitude with hammer and chisel was the sculptor able to break his prison and save his life. It was perfectly simple; the liquid plaster had been "wax to receive and marble to retain". At each breath that the man gave, his chest contracted a little; and the quiet insinuating cream crept in thus far. Then he would have expanded his chest to draw air, but found not the slightest concession: the more he gasped and struggled, the more inexorably was he crushed in this velvet-gloved vice. That is why the violence of Henry VIII, in its results though not in its methods, was welcomed by so many men in his own generation, and is approved by so great a majority of later historians. This, however, is a matter which will engage our attention in my last chapter.

But a few words must be added here with regard to the Popes as politicians; a brief sketch, that is, of their dominance, and of lay opposition, in affairs of State. Innocent III worked so preponderantly for ecclesiastical righteousness that his claims over princes were the less resented. But he died in 1216; and a generation later, under Innocent IV, the moral decline is evident. This Pope was learned, and we need not deny him piety; but he was by nature a politician. He gave a distinctly greater impetus to the political strivings which had always been a temptation concomitant with papal power; and under him we already find murmurings of European revolt. The ominous suggestion of appeal to a General Council of Christendom against this centralized despotism began to be heard. Half a century later, however, Boniface VIII raised papal claims to the highest possible point. The Emperor was to be subject to the Pope not only in the religious, but even in the civil sphere; and this was proclaimed in a bull, *Unam Sanctam,* which is universally admitted to have been *ex cathedra* in its last paragraph, although attempts are made to explain away those earlier and more plainspoken paragraphs which are discordant with present-day ideas. In another bull, *Clericis Laicos,* he attempted to exclude the clergy from taxation, with the result that he was met with direct resistance not only in France but from our Edward I, who practically told him that if the clergy would not pay taxes, neither should they have the use of the king's courts, but must be prepared to find themselves treated as outlaws. Thenceforward, although English sovereigns were always loyal in their professions and obedient in the majority of their actions, the feeling steadily grew in this country that the Pope, however theologically necessary, was politically a foreign potentate, mainly noticeable through his habit of fleecing this distant flock.

As our period begins favourably with a great Pope, Gregory VII, so also with our Archbishops Lanfranc and Anselm. These men, both born on ancient Italian soil, and imported through Normandy, were among the greatest European Churchmen of their age. For a long time prelates were thus introduced to us as civilizing foreigners. Becket was our first English-born archbishop; and in some of our sees there was no English-born bishop until later. The bishops, like the archbishops, were barons in the State by reason of their rich possessions; and one (Durham) had a palace and council of his own, as a necessary bulwark against invasions from the North. But even in Durham the bishop did not approach in power or in secular temptations to the prince-bishops of the Continent; and all through our period English bishops were distinctly above the foreign standard, though not generally equal in brilliancy to the very pick of the Continent. Their temptations were not so great, nor their fall so spectacular. Thus, in England, there are very few traces of that feeling so strong during the thirteenth century in France, Germany, and Italy, that a bishopric involved serious risk to the soul, and that any thoroughly religious man was bound to avoid this distinguished, but dangerous, office, since it would necessarily not only implicate him in worldly cares, but also imperil his spiritual life. Often as they preferred the royal court to residence in their own dioceses, perhaps no other bishop could have been described as the Benedictine chronicler Greystanes paints his own diocesan in 1318. "Louis, Bishop of Durham, was an illiterate person, not understanding Latin, and pronouncing it with difficulty. Wherefore, having to make his public profession at his consecration (although he had taken instruction in the matter for many days beforehand), he was unable to read it; and having at last stumbled on, with the help of kindly prompting, as far as the word *metropolitanus*; and, after many gasps, having found himself unable to pronounce it, he said in the French tongue, 'Let us take that word as read.' Similarly also, when he was ordaining candidates for Holy Orders, and found himself unable to read the words *in aenigmate* ['*through a glass darkly*', I Cor. xiii. 12] he said to those who stood by: 'By St Louis, that was no courteous man who wrote this word!'"[2]

This bishop, naturally enough, has left no register; and scanty indeed are the business records of our three canonized bishops of English blood: St Edmund Rich of Canterbury, St Richard Wych of Chichester, and St Thomas Cantelupe of Hereford. From Grosseteste of Lincoln, whom many would count as greater still than these before man and God, we have no really full register, but (apart from his scientific writings) letters and sermons testifying to his struggles against unruly subjects under him in his own diocese, and an increasingly worldly Roman court set above him. For St Anselm, on the other hand, we have a loving and intimate biography from the pen of a true historian, his fellow-monk Eadmer. This great philosopher was also a great administrator, because he brought to each of those tasks the single eye of perfect inward truth. The medieval bishop was also a medieval baron, whose vast estates involved him in heavy political responsibilities and, often, in the most perilous and difficult litigation. It excited little comment when his manner of life, and his bearing towards his inferiors, were frankly baronial, so long as they kept within the bounds of baronial decency. His origin had sometimes been of the humblest; but he was expected to enrich his kinsfolk. Giraldus Cambrensis quotes Alexander III's saying: "When God deprived bishops of sons, the devil gave them nephews." But of Anselm Eadmer tells us how he made good his power not by self-assertion but by honesty and common sense.[3] He would never suffer any of his people to take advantage of legal quibbles, "making a conscience not to do to others what he would not have done to himself. . . . So it happened that, sitting among the contending pleaders while his opponents were taking counsel by what skill or by what trick they might help their own cause or damage his, he, not minding it, was conversing with any one who wished to address him, either about the Gospel or some other divine Scripture, or some point of right conduct. And often, when he had no one to listen of this kind, quietly at peace in the purity of his heart, he would close his eyes and sleep; and often it came to pass that the cunning devices against him, when they came to his hearing, were at once exposed and torn to pieces, not as if he had been asleep all the while, but as if he had been fully awake and keenly watching. For charity, which envieth not, vaunteth not itself, seeketh not her own, was strong in him, whereby he saw at a glance the things that he ought to see; for the truth was his guide."[4] Thus we see in him the indomitable strength of the true ascetic, upon whom worldly authority can get no hold, because there is nothing worldly about him to hold him by; and, in addition to all this, the persuasive and magnetic strength of human love, when the great man is found as gentle to others as he is strict with himself. Therefore he was the one man who had some power over Rufus. "To all others so harsh and terrible, in Anselm's presence he seemed, to the wonder of the bystanders, another man, so gracious and easy of speech. Years after, when King William was on his forlorn death-bed, Anselm was the man whom he most wished to see."[5]

There, of course, was a man in ten millions, a whole horizon removed from poor Louis of Durham; we should be fortunate if, in those days, such English bishops had kept a formal register of the later pattern. But several such registers have come down from those who were betwixt and between those commanding saints and the ignorant or idle prelates. The bulkiest of these, and perhaps most valuable in every way to the historian, is that of John de Grandisson of Exeter. His three stout volumes, running to 1610 pages, give perhaps the fullest extant picture of any medieval bishop in his diocese, except that of Odo Rigaldi for the diocese of Rouen. The record is so precious that I must beg the reader to forgive here, even at the cost of weariness, sufficient details to make him realize that the picture is not mine, but that of the bishop himself. The real dilfficulty, in fact, is to avoid quoting at far greater length than this from Grandisson's own text.

His register is all the more precious because the Black Death came nearly in the middle of his long reign. His predecessor had been Stapeldon, a royal minister almost always absent from the diocese, whom the London populace had murdered in the streets at the fall of his master Edward II. To this crime, the editor of the register attributes some of the difficulties encountered by Grandisson; but in fact there is scarcely any incident in this episcopate which cannot be paralleled from elsewhere.

In theory, bishops were still elected by their cathedral chapters; but in fact the king and Pope, instead of merely confirming such elections, habitually overrode them. Ayermine, though duly elected to Norwich, had to take sanctuary in his own cathedral (1325); Tottinton (1406) was imprisoned by the king for daring to accept the monks' choice of him. On the other hand, in 1333, though Graystanes was not only elected to Durham but actually consecrated by the Archbishop of York, this was set aside by the Pope. Out of 25 English bishops in 10 years, 17 may be counted who held high ministerial offices under the Crown. Every contested choice, whichever way the verdict might finally go, entailed heavy additional law expenses at Rome. Grandisson's appointment, on the other hand, was by papal favour, and this was a worthy choice. He was of a noble Burgundian family, whose castle still stands beside the Lake of Neuchâtel, a stately monument for visitors. Our John was cousin to the poet who was Chaucer's friend, and brother to the beautiful Countess of Salisbury who is the heroine of Froissart's story of the Garter. The Papal Court claimed 12,000 florins in fees for his appointment, and, though this was afterwards reduced to 5000, it compelled him to borrow at heavy interest from the Florentine banking-house of Bardi, and to beg humbly from all his friends and his superior clergy. A little earlier than this, Archbishop Pecham of Canterbury had been plunged into such hopeless debt by the sums due to Rome for his appointment, and therefore necessarily borrowed from the Pope's Italian usurers, that for a while he was under excommunication as a defaulter, and dared not show his face in his own diocese.

Grandisson, from the first, met with very serious difficulties in his own cathedral. His primary visitation, in 1328, disclosed the following facts. Some canons, as hirelings or even robbers of the Church, kept up only the merest pretence of residence, caring more for their hawks and hounds than for the Church. They seldom come to service, and then they come in late and often go out before the end. Some, again, both of the canons and subordinate ministers, "spend their time not in offering to God due sacrifice of praise, but rather in gabbling through the service, with frequent interruptions of vain and unprofitable discourse, and unlawful murmurs to each other". They neglect to give alms to the poor according to the conditions of their office; the service books are defective, and not duly repaired; some canons are not in priest's orders; the vicars choral (minor canons) are given to tavern hunting and other "insolencies"; the service is unduly hurried through; hence decay of divine service, a falling off of devotion on the people's part, and general scandal of all. Though the editor here pleads exceptional disorder after Stapeldon's murder, yet the visitations of Southwell, Ripon, Beverley and Wells are quite worthy to be put beside this. In several Continental cathedrals, one of the statutes prohibited canons from talking to each other, during divine service, "beyond the 4th [or, in some cases, 5th] stall". Moreover, after two years of this strong bishop's rule, we find him again reprimanding the clergy of his cathedral for their "laughing, giggling, and other insolencies during divine service itself"; for the sorry practical joke of casting candle-snuffings from the upper stalls upon the shaven pates of the clergy in the lower; for their custom of exclaiming aloud, in the vulgar tongue, when a bad blunder had been made in singing or reading, "Cursed be the fellow who told that last lie!" and for the haste with which they gabble through the service, or "cry aloud to their officiating brother, bidding and enjoining him to make haste".[6] Three years later, again (1333), there are the old "damnable and irreverent jests, laughters, gigglings and other insolencies" during divine service, under excuse of the Feast of Fools. And in 1360, after thirty-two years of strenuous work, the bishop finds this same abuse flourishing not only in his cathedral but also in the three great collegiate churches of Ottery, Crediton and Glasney.

Grandisson's further difficulties, to the very end, were such as we find in other episcopal records. The precentor of the cathedral was persistently non-resident; so also the chancellor. This latter, in 1337, had been absent for ten years: Grandisson remonstrated and threatened with ever-increasing vigour; yet in 1339 he was still away, and seems to have retained his dignity and revenues till his death in 1345. In 1344 the canons in general were mostly non-resident, in defiance of their statutes confirmed by a papal legate, and of Grandisson's repeated injunctions and warnings: moreover they embezzled the stipends of the vicars choral and compelled these to hire themselves out for duty elsewhere, thus defrauding the cathedral services. At the monastery of St James, Exeter, Grandisson can produce no effect upon the shockingly dissolute prior; so also at Tavistock, with two abbots in succession; so again at Barnstaple, where again two disreputable priors came in succession. To the rebellion of an archdeacon we shall come presently; and there was trouble with false miracles, with pardoners, with a pre-Wycliffite heretic parson, and with Exeter citizens.

But perhaps the most significant of all these contests, and certainly the most piquant, was with a fellow-prelate, the Bishop of Damascus.[7] Readers may well wonder how that apparently distant dignitary can have crossed the Bishop of Exeter's path, except that there is a D in Damascus and a D in Devonshire. This man was a bishop *in partibus*. The recapture of the Holy Land by the infidels had naturally involved the exile of a whole hierarchy: equally naturally, Rome was unwilling to accept this loss as final. Thus there had grown up a whole hierarchy *in partibus infidelium*; prelates who had never seen, nor would ever see, their diocese, but who were utilized as suffragans, or to whom the Pope gave roving commissions. These were nearly always friars; for the ubiquitous organization of those four orders, and the natural conformity of their interests with those of the Roman see, singled them out for this kind of work as naturally as the Jesuit order in post-Reformation times. Such emissaries did not always command respect; Langland is quaintly contemptuous of these bishops "of Bedleem and Babiloigne", "of Neptalym, of Nynue and of Damaske";[8] and certainly our present subject might richly have earned his scorn. In 1347, just before the Black Death, the Austin friars had been building a chapel at Dartmouth, and thus encroaching upon the spiritual and temporal preserves of the Abbot of Torre: Grandisson had forbidden this. The friars appealed to Rome: judgment was given against them. But they got hold of one of their fellow-friars, Hugh, titular Bishop of Damascus, who came treacherously to Dartmouth disguised as a layman "in a short tight buttoned jacket, with a long sword and buckler by his side". At the Austin convent he doffed his lay attire, put on a friar's frock, and then, crozier in hand and mitre on head, he assembled the people of Dartmouth and told them he was the Bishop of Damascus, sent by the Lord Pope and the Lord Cardinals to consecrate this chapel; which he duly did, and gave an indulgence of 100 days to all the congregation present. After that he confirmed children, and absolved certain persons, in virtue of his papal commission, for the excommunication which they had incurred by laying violent hands on clergy. "Thence he went to many taverns in the said town and drank therein, and showed both to men and women his hand with a ring on it, which he said the Lord Pope had given him with his own hand." Asked why he did all this without leave of the bishop of the diocese, "he answered and said that he cared naught for the aforesaid Lord Bishop, and did and said other abusive things, to the scandal and disgrace of our Lord the Pope and the Lord Cardinals and the Apostolic See and the Cathedral church of Exeter; which things, for the honour of religion, I leave untold for the present". So wrote Grandisson, appealing to Canterbury. This brought from the intruder partly a denial, partly a very humble apology. He pleaded that he could not have passed over the lands of the Abbot of Torre without grievous bodily peril, unless he had thus gone in disguise; as for the absolution given for laying violent hands on clergy, a certain mariner beat him, the Bishop of Damascus, on the arm with his bow, thinking he was the Abbot of Torre; and then, finding that he had incurred the greater excommunication by this blow, "the aforesaid mariner, with many other aiders and abettors, followed him with grisly threats that, if he [the bishop] did not give him absolution, he should never leave the town of Dartmouth alive; and the bishop, overcome by fear, which may fall at times even upon the stoutest hearts,* granted the mariner the required letter of absolution". Upon which humble confession the Archbishop of Canterbury absolved the Bishop of Damascus from the excommunication laid upon him by the Bishop of Exeter.

Worse still was Grandisson's trouble in the matter of archdeacons. We may read it in his formal letter to a brother prelate, making allowance for the probably exaggerated language of a legal indictment.[9] In 1344, a certain John Peris

* This is the common legal formula in the Middle Ages for pleading violent compulsion.

claimed the archdeaconry of Totnes. On St Luke's day, Grandisson was celebrating a Mass in thanksgiving for the sixteenth anniversary of his promotion to the see. While he was preaching, "certain sons of perdition, viz. William de Clavile (alias Wyteprest, alias Hamond), John Attewater nephew, and John de Bodevile cousin of John Peris, with many accomplices, armed both with bows and arrows and with divers other sorts of weapons, having (as is asserted and credibly believed) conspired against my life, broke into the aforesaid church without respect for the place, or the holy-day, or my person or sacred office, and interrupted my devotions and those of the people, like infidels, blasphemers, and barbarians. And whereas I thrice solemnly warned them in vain to depart from the sacred edifice, at length I excommunicated them with all due formalities, as the enormity of their offence required. Therefore, most reverend Father in God, lest the aforesaid children of Satan infect your flock also, may it please you to let it be proclaimed publicly throughout your diocese that the aforesaid evildoers have been and are excommunicate."

In this matter of archdeacons, we English can scarcely plead any superiority over Western Christendom in general. They were, in fact, under almost irresistible temptations. They were mostly either of distinguished birth, or men who had risen by their abilities at the courts of great men; and they needed a professional education far more exacting than that of the bishop or archbishop. It was far easier for a comparatively illiterate prelate to do his work decently, than for an uneducated archdeacon. The difficulties which must always attend marriage law were multiplied tenfold by the labyrinthine perplexities of medieval matrimonial jurisdiction. Testamentary cases, again, are always extremely difficult; and therefore the archdeacon needed to be a first-rate trained lawyer if he was to be at all efficient. That meant that the aspirant needed an expensive education; he must study, probably, at a foreign university, of which Bologna was the greatest in this subject, under the ordinary university temptations and with the necessity of making money when he came back to England, in order to recoup himself for this outlay. The Archdeacon of Ely in the fourteenth century, though far from one of the richest, had two benefices amounting to nearly £95 yearly, with £27 in legal fees from the clergy of the diocese; the equivalent of nearly £4000 to-day. To this we must add the fines which, through his summoner, he took for immoralities; thus he was under the greatest temptations to accept bribes. His financial position in fact resembled that of the *Publicanus* in Christ's day; and this explains all that underlies the unvarying satire of his contemporaries. Even those opening fifty lines of Chaucer's Friar's Tale are less plain-spoken than what his friend the Moral Gower has to tell us about archdeacons. Long before Chaucer or Gower, again, Giraldus Cambrensis had accused archdeacons of actually fomenting litigation, and preventing amicable arrangements "unless their hand be greased"—*nisi peruncta manu*. "For this office is so wholly given over to rapacity nowadays, beyond all others in the Church, that the name of *archdeacon* rings in some men's ears with a sound as horrible as that of arch-devil; for the devil steals men's souls, but the archdeacon steals their money."[10] St Thomas Becket did, in fact, call Archdeacon Geoffrey Ridel "archidiabolus noster."[11] If these writers are ruled out as satirists, let us take John of Salisbury, perhaps our greatest publicist of the Middle Ages. He alludes to a question debated in his time: Can an archdeacon come to Heaven? and here is his own serious characterization of them, for which we need no further discount than for ordinary medieval exaggeration of speech. "They love bribes; they are revengeful and prone to injury. They rejoice in calumny, eat and drink the sins of the people, and live on robbery. . . . Their high office makes it their duty to keep God's Law, yet they keep it not."[12] Henry II, though he again must be heavily discounted, complained that the "archdeacons and rural deans of this realm" extort a greater yearly sum than royalty itself receives. Thus, as Professor Hamilton Thompson writes, "the more valuable English archdeaconries, especially in the latter thirteenth and early fourteenth centuries, were frequently perquisites of cardinals and well-born satellites of the papal court; and at all times it was not uncommon for an archdeacon, especially if he were occupied, as was often the case, in the royal chancery or other office at Westminster, to perform his duties exclusively through an official and the official's clerks ".

Hitherto, we have dealt only with the " secular " clergy: those that lived in " The World " (*in saeculo*). The " Regulars ", those who lived by Rule, and were cloistered, are almost equally important, but must be described later on.

11. RECTOR AND VICAR

There is, however, one important region common to both Seculars and Regulars, which must be treated here.[1] The distinction between *rector* and *vicar* is so little clear, even to many well-informed readers of to-day, that it must be explained before we go farther. The rector is what his name implies, the spiritual "ruler" of the parish. His "benefice" is a freehold; he retains it for life, in default of the gravest causes for deprivation. He is the "parson", the person *par excellence*, in his little domain. Originally, the man who did the spiritual work of the parish was always a rector. But in process of time, partly because the lay patrons so often abused their position to rob the presentees of a great portion of their tithes, and reduced them generally to such servile dependence, it was felt to be a pious act for the layman to give "his church" to some monastery. This was an improvement, so long as the monks either did the parish work themselves or chose their assistant priests with conscientious care. But Popes were soon compelled to forbid that first course, as prejudicial to the discipline of the monastery itself; and, under the second alternative, monks yielded increasingly to the temptation of taking just such toll from their presentees as the lay patrons had been wont to take. Soon, in fact, even the theory which had made them into mere trustees of these parochial endowments broke down altogether; then, with increasing frequency, Popes and bishops permitted the monks (or the cathedral canons) to "appropriate" the "church" which the lay patron had "given" to them: to convert it (as the legal phrase went) "to their own uses"—*ad proprios usus*. From that time forward the monastery was the "rector" of the parish, and the work was done by a hired underling under the title of "vicar": *vicarius* being the regular word for a substitute of any kind. At first such vicars were "curates" in the lowest modern sense of the word; that is, hirelings with no security of tenure beyond the will of their employer. This position, however, led to such obvious abuses that energetic bishops stepped in and compelled the appropriators to consent to a definite legal "ordination" which should give the vicar a living wage and security of tenure. The wage aimed at was, in general, one-third of the total parish revenues, the appropriators taking two-thirds. Sometimes the vicar got more than this, when the parish was large and he in turn was compelled to hire one or more assistant priests. More often than this, however, the vicar who did the work received even less than his one-third of the revenues. But at least he now held his office, such as it was, for life; his vicarage was as truly a "benefice" as the rector's. For that was the distinguishing mark of *beneficium*, that it should be a freehold; the *vicarius* of earlier days, the man dismissible at will, had held only an *officium*. We must pursue this question farther when we come to the "regular", or cloistered, clergy; meanwhile the reader will already see the significance of this "appropriation" system for parish life. Before the Reformation came, about one-third of all our rectories had thus been reduced to vicarages, and two-thirds of their revenues had been diverted from parochial purposes to other quite different—indeed, often distant and almost unknown—beneficiaries. Moreover, in the nature of the case, it was generally the richer livings which fell a prey to these appropriators.

This distinction being clearly grasped, we may now look into the method of presentation to English benefices. Our evidence is sufficiently multitudinous and varied to place beyond a doubt that, as we might expect, the richer livings went to kinsfolk or friends of the patrons, while the numerous peasant-born priests had to content themselves with vicarages or such stipendiary work as assistants in the parish, chaplains to great folk, or Mass-priests on some chantry foundation.

Here, our episcopal registers yield the most curious and startling results. It is a testimony to the comparative orderliness of social, political, and religious life in England, that we possess incomparably more of these records than any other country; but it is not to our credit that so little use has yet been made of them for statistical purposes in history. All past attempts to write our ecclesiastical history without these witnesses are comparable to the fashion, perhaps scarcely dead even now, of writing Old Testament history mainly from Bible records, with comparative neglect of the thousand illustrative documents and monuments. These our episcopal registers, which afford evidence of unique value as to clerical mortality during the Black Death, give us also the most lively picture of the effect which that plague had upon the personnel of our parish clergy.

Exeter diocese was ruled from 1308 to 1324 by that Stapeldon who, like so many other bishops, was a royal minister and frequently away from his flock. During those years, he instituted 376 incumbents to livings in lay presentation; and the examination of those men's status gives surprising results. We must confine ourselves to lay presentations; since, where the "patron" was also "rector" (that is, a religious corporation which left the actual parish work to be done by a man who was practically a perpetual curate), it would have been most scandalous to put in anyone who could not even say Mass. We do, indeed, find the thing sometimes done, and the wretched parishioners thus deprived even of the most necessary spiritual aid; but such flagrant abuses were rare enough for us to ignore them here in this calculation. Under lay presentation, the incumbent was normally rector, and received all the parish revenues, and could afford, if he was ordinarily conscientious, to keep an assistant priest who would do such work as the rector could not perform himself. Those lay advowsons, therefore, are the instances which alone left the patron any real freedom of choice as to the status of the presentee. A mere vicar must needs be a priest, since the salary was scarcely ever such as to enable him to pay an assistant priest, and there must be somebody in the parish for daily Mass and deathbed absolution and unction, with other functions reserved for priests alone. How, then, did the lay patrons exercise their choice, and what were the sort of men whom the bishop instituted at the presentation of these layfolk, finding it probably almost impossible to refuse them even though he should wish? Out of those 376 rectors instituted by Stapeldon, only 135 were in priest's orders: scarcely more than one-third! Three years after Stapeldon's death came Grandisson (1327-69), one of the most energetic and conscientious prelates of our whole period. Taking his first five years, we find that he instituted 31 priests, as against 40 non-priests. Again, in the last 5 years before the Black Death, the proportion was similar: 26 to 35. Thus Grandisson's record is far more respectable than his predecessor's; the minority of 28 per cent. on the priestly side has become a minority of only about 14 per cent. But if we now pass on to take the 5 years which included and followed the Black Death, we find the balance suddenly reversed: 115 priests stand here against 63 non-priests: the earlier steady deficit has now swung round to a favourable balance of 29 per cent. Moreover, when we pass again to Grandisson's last 5 years, the balance is still on the right side: 25 to 13; i.e. 31.6 per cent. more priests than non-priests. The evidence is similar from other dioceses. To the evidence of those 16 years under Stapeldon, and the 20 years taken from Grandisson, we may add full statistics from Brantyngham at Exeter, Rigaud de Asserio and Wykeham at Winchester, Drokensford and Ralph of Shrewsbury at Bath and Wells. From those registers we get a total of 675 lay presentations before the pestilence, and 472 after it. In the earlier period the priestly presentees number 249, or nearly 37 per cent.; in the later 342, or 72.5 per cent. No two students, perhaps, would exactly agree to a unit in the calculation of these figures; but I do not think that any two could differ by more than 10 per cent. at most. The sudden change which the statistics mark, and, what is more, the abiding change, are almost unexampled in Church history. It will be seen later how exactly this statistical evidence fits in with the observations of the chroniclers.

What, then, was the previous history of these rectors and vicars? A multitude of small indications enable us to form a fair general idea. The rectories, numbering about 5500 in all, went mostly to men of middle-class or higher extraction; or at least to those who had some sort of social influence. The bishops disposed of valuable preferments: Winchester, one of the richest, had the patronage of 80 parishes, with an average income of £31. 10*s*. [say, £1260 modern];[2] but, as the prelates themselves were often statesmen, so the episcopal presentees were often distinguished rather for business than for strictly ecclesiastical qualifications. Among such presentations, the most honourable were those which enabled prominent university scholars to continue their study or teaching; for there was no regular endowment for any professorship until the last pre-Reformation years; so that Wyclif the reformer was himself for many years an absentee rector. On the other hand, most of the 3000 vicars, with cantarists and chaplains—that is, some 14,000 priests—would come in overwhelming majority from the peasant, artisan, or, at most, lower-middle classes; the villager's spiritual father was very often, as in Chaucer, his blood-brother. It has in all ages been partly the strength, partly the weakness, of the Roman Church that so large a proportion of her priests are drawn from the least leisured classes. In the Middle Ages, as now, it was a source of legitimate pride to parents, and often of considerable advantage, that they saw their son at the altar. At the same time, this gave point to the very frequent complaint that the moral and intellectual difference between spiritual father and son was regrettably narrow. Great churchmen, from quite early days, and thence again through St Bernard, who gave further currency to the words, were accustomed to quote from Isaiah (xxiv. 2): "As with the people, so with the priest", and to add, with the rhetorical exaggeration of despondent idealists, "nay, but our priests are worse than the people".

Let us follow one of these men from the plough-tail to the altar. The question of medieval education in general must come in a later chapter; but here we may anticipate for a moment and consider the narrower question of clerical training.

12. THE MAKING OF A PRIEST

It is impossible nowadays to accept the optimistic estimate of Bishop Stubbs in his *Constitutional History* (ed. 1878, III, 370). He writes: "The existence of a clerical element in every class of society, and in so large proportion, must in some respects have been a great social benefit. Every one admitted even to minor orders must have been able to read and write; and for the subdiaconate and higher grades a knowledge of the New Testament, or, at the very least, of the Gospels and Epistles in the Missal was requisite. This was tested by careful examination in grammar and ritual at every step; even a bishop might be rejected by the archbishop for literary deficiency; and the bishop who willingly ordained an ignorant person was deemed guilty of deadly sin." The fact that so great a man as Stubbs could write thus is, in itself, one of the most painful testimonies to the neglect of our immense stores of ecclesiastical records. Stubbs, no doubt, knew the cases quoted by Giraldus Cambrensis, but felt justified in ignoring them as the mere exaggerations of a satirist. The study of the registers had not advanced far enough to make him realize that even Giraldus's testimony is outdone by the most cold-blooded ecclesiastical documents.

Dr Rashdall, with the advantage of a whole later generation of study, wrote very differently in answer to Newman's rosy and regretful picture. His words run: "So much party capital has at times been made out of the supposed 'religious' character of the medieval Universities that it is necessary to assert emphatically that the 'religious education' of a 'bygone Oxford', in so far as it ever had any existence, was an inheritance not from the Middle Ages but from the Reformation. In Catholic Europe it was the product of the counter-reformation." Elsewhere Rashdall writes of "the very small proportion of students who ever attained even the B.A. degree, in spite of the mildness of medieval examiners"; and he adds: "There is considerable reason to believe that in the Middle Ages a larger proportion than at the present day of the nominal students derived exceedingly little benefit from their University education."[1] If the register of Bishop Stapeldon of Exeter, in the earlier fourteenth century, can be taken as typical (and certainly it ought not to be far below the average), there were only 25 Masters among the whole cathedral and parish clergy of the diocese; only 25 clergy, that is, who had gone through the full university course, let alone proceeded afterwards to a degree in theology. Again, in the specially important Convocation of 1433, which had to decide whether the English clergy should side with the Council of Basel or with Eugenius IV, there was a proviso in the proclammation of summons that the proctors of the clergy should all be *graduati;* all, that is, at least Masters of Arts.* Nor was this paucity of university graduates atoned for in other ways. The Middle Ages knew nothing answering to the modern seminary system. There were indeed episcopal schools, teaching grammar and a certain modicum of divinity and philosophy: but these were small at the best, and probably often dormant; they come very little into our records. They may sometimes have been among the *studia* to which bishops occasionally sent young rectors to qualify for ordination; but such documents refer far more often to universities. It seems evident that the great majority of medieval parish clergy attained to priesthood very much as a gild apprentice obtained his mastership, by practice and rule of thumb. At the present stage of historical research, far more study is required for any scientific and exhaustive account of clerical training; yet a brief sketch must be attempted here.

We may start from a specially interesting concrete example: the author of *Piers Plowman.* The evidence, after all that has

* I do not think we can interpret the term *graduatus* less strictly than this. The B.A. was not then a degree, but only a step towards one; it would be difficult to find it quoted anywhere in the official way in which "master" is prefixed to a man's name after complete graduation.

been written on both sides, seems definitely in favour of the old tradition that this man was William Langland, and that the apparently autobiographical touches in his poem are as truly autobiographical as they profess to be. All that, however, is irrelevant to the present argument, since the most sceptical critics admit, if only tacitly, that those professedly autobiographical touches are coherent and consistent; in other words, that, even if the portrait they compose is not *vero,* at least it is *ben trovato*; if our poem does not record the actual career of this particular author, yet at least it describes the sort of career that was natural for such an independent clerical author as he professes to be. Moreover, the question is all the more topical at this present moment, when attempts are being made to present Langland to us as a full-blown priest, in contradiction to what seem his own explicit assertions. Starting from the fact, noted long ago, that he sometimes quotes Biblical texts not from the Vulgate version but from the Breviary, it is argued that this proves his priestly status. But, quite apart from the gross logical fallacy of arguing "priests, by Canon Law, must read the Breviary, therefore the man who knows the Breviary must be a priest", the theory does violence to notorious medieval conditions, and rests upon a misunderstanding of Canon Law itself.

There was never in England, until the lifetime of many now living, a real general educational system for all, down to the lowest; nor did such exist anywhere else in the Western Church. Charles the Great might strive after something of the kind; so again might Pope Eugenius II shortly afterwards, but no attempt can be found on the part of Pope or prelate to enforce this as a disciplinary matter: nothing (for instance) comparable for one moment to the systematic campaign against clerical marriage. It remained, therefore, only a pious ideal that the priest or his parish clerk should teach gratis any child who wished to learn. We do find, very sporadically, priests who taught gratis; and, more commonly, clerks who taught for small fees. So far I must here anticipate a later chapter dealing with education in general. From some such priest or clerk, then, a peasant's son might receive the rudiments of education; a better born boy might learn from a private tutor or at a grammar school; but these at the Conquest were extremely few, and, even under Henry VIII, offered far less opportunity than to-day. If the boy's father were a serf he would need to pay a fine for sending his son to school or when the boy took orders. Langland seems clearly to imply, in one passage, that he was bondman-born, but freed by his scholarly tonsure.

The youth, then, learns enough, partly at school and partly perhaps by serving the priest at the altar, to receive one or all of the four Minor Orders, which were commonly given in a lump.* Thenceforward he is qualified to act as parish clerk: a person too much neglected in English history and yet second, perhaps, in sociological importance only to the priest. From very early times it had been decreed in Canon Law that the priest should have a deacon or clerk or "scholar" to help him at his daily services. The ordinary function of this assistant was to render the responses; but, in the absence of the priest, law enjoined upon him to read the Matins and Evensong himself. It is evident that this would form a natural stage of apprenticeship towards the priesthood. A man who, year after year, had followed the service enough to read the responses, and was capable at a pinch of reading the whole service himself, had already gone four-fifths of the way; and it is natural, therefore, that at last we should find this officially recognized. Archbishop Boniface, of Canterbury, decreed in 1260: "We have often heard from our elders that the Benefices of Holy Water were originally instituted from a motive of charity, in order that from their revenues poor clerks might be kept in the schools, and so advance in learning that they might be fit for higher preferment." Therefore (he continues), in churches not more than ten miles distant from cities and towns in Canterbury province, the rectors and vicars must all endeavour to find such clerks and appoint them to this "benefice". In 1280 we find Archbishop Pecham ordaining for a parish and its dependent chapels that the two parish clerks there should also keep school.

* These were Door-Keeper, Reader, Exorcist, and Acolyte, generally summed up in the single term *Clericus* or *Acolitus.* The Major Orders were Subdeacon, Deacon, and Priest.

Thus the system provided for a continuity of ecclesiastical education, after a simple fashion. The canonist Lyndwood, commenting in the fifteenth century on this and on one other similar passage, explains that the clerk in lower orders was *beneficiatus* only if he had a *titulus.* He points out that some of these lower clergy performed simply menial offices (bell-ringing, church-sweeping, etc.); and that it was indifferent whether such a man were married or not; he did indeed count as a *clericus* outside the church, but not inside; his place at service was not in the choir but among the layfolk in the nave. If, however, he were parish clerk in the full sense, then his position would be different. As we have seen, he had there a *titulus,* he had been formally appointed by the incumbent or the parishioners; thus he had in the full sense an *ecclesiasticum beneficium*; and therefore his place must be in the choir, " since the cleric had to serve with the priest at the altar, to sing with him and read the epistle ". Therefore he must not, as a general rule, be married; and in fact we find concrete cases of bishops who object to a married parish clerk. But, at a pinch, " in defect of unmarried clerics " a " married cleric " may act as full parish clerk, and therefore (by implication) take his place in the choir. Here again, therefore, was a possibility for Langland even after his marriage. But we, who still believe in him as an autobiographer, must note that he gives no such hint: he describes himself as living in a far more hand-to-mouth fashion than if he had the *beneficium* of a parish clerk. There seems, however, to exist no real reason why he should not, long before he ever met his wife Kitte or begat his daughter Kalote, have picked up all that knowledge which he shows of the Breviary and the Bible and other patristic or moral scraps. For it must not be forgotten how many scrap-books and common-place books of that kind have survived, first made by one man for his own use, then perhaps sold or left to another, and added to from generation to generation. To treat it as a marvel that Langland was able to quote all the Latin we find in *Piers Plowman* is as perverse as the belief that Shakespeare could not have written as he did unless he had really been Francis Bacon.

In the light of this, it will be easier to understand the jolly clerk Absolon of Chaucer's Miller's Tale. To cense the congregation in church was part of his daily duty at Matins, Mass, and Evensong; on other solemn occasions he sprinkled holy water (in his capacity of "exorcist") from house to house, and received a small fee from each, as also at other times. If Matthew Paris does not exaggerate, such "casualties" might come to 20*s*. a year: i.e. at least £40 in modern terms. He was qualified to sing on his own responsibility (and here again for small fees) such services as the funeral Matins and Evensong for departed relatives, which were called *Dirige* and *Placebo* respectively from the opening words of their anthems: hence our "dirge" for any melancholy song. He could earn small fees for teaching; and, if careful and ambitious, get at least some little training at the university, or at the nearest episcopal school, on the strength of these savings; and thence proceed to the three Major Orders.

But at that point came definite crossways, and a call for final choice. The clerk in Minor Orders was not cut off from marriage. Even if he lost his "benefice" of parish clerk thereby, which was no matter of necessity, there were still certain kinds of "clerical" work open to him, as for instance the keeping and enrolment of accounts. Thorold Rogers assumed too hastily that the dog-Latin of manorial rolls showed unexpected education on the part of the bailiffs; a closer study often reveals the actual sum paid to the "clericus" for doing that job. Even in great monasteries, we often find this item at the end of an account-roll: *item, clerico scribenti hunc compotum*, and so on; and the major monastic officials sometimes had each his own clerk in his office. In very large towns the clerks sometimes formed a gild; "Clerkenwell", just outside the ancient walls of London, is where the clerks of that city were accustomed to hold religious theatrical performances; so they did also at another extra-mural spot, "Skinner's Well". Absolon, it will be remembered, could not only "make a charter of land and a quittance", but, on occasion, he "playëd Herod on a scaffold high".

Such, then, were Langland's chances even after his marriage.

A hand-to-mouth existence, unless he were able to retain his benefice as parish clerk; yet with no more chance of actual starvation than that which confronted all casual labourers. The life suited him better, he tells us, than the field-work with which he was familiar enough, but for which he was too long in body (and, we must suppose, too frail) to stoop. Then, as now, the attractions of brain-work had begotten a "learned proletariat". A fortunate few, like the poet Hoccleve, Chaucer's pupil, found permanent employment under the king: a few others, again, under great nobles or prelates, or at abbeys. Professor Tout has published an interesting monograph on the Civil Servants of those days. But, as we shall see in Chapter XLIII, even Hoccleve, in the royal office of the Privy Seal at Westminster, looked upon himself as an ill-paid drudge, and remained long unmarried for fear of cutting himself off from what was the great hope of every "clerk", whether at or outside the universities, namely, a fat rectory. When a rise came for him, it was in the shape of a pension of twenty marks, to be paid until he could secure some benefice, without cure of souls, of £20 a year. That benefice, however, was so slow in coming, that the expectant burned his boats at last, and took a wife. Reading the rest of his frank autobiographical confessions, we shall see that he was well out of that priesthood and that expected benefice of £20 a year, except in so far as he might have put in a better man to do the parish work for small pay, and enjoyed the remainder here in London and Westminster. For if, with no professional education whatever, he had joined that priestly class and worked his own parish, he would have found himself in a village where those who could read anything whatever could probably be counted on the fingers of one hand, and where none even of those had ever read half a dozen volumes from beginning to end. We must not lay too much stress on mere book-learning; but, on the other hand, it is impossible to ignore the social significance of this comparative illiteracy.

The scattered evidence of episcopal examinations tends to show that, though conscientious prelates took this duty seriously, they had seldom time to deal strictly and searchingly with the large number of candidates. In a few cases, we have record of the actual answers of rejected candidates; these imply that the questions were, in the main, upon elementary points of Latin grammar, or upon ability to sing by note. On one other point, however, the references are rather less scanty, and give more opportunity for testing the success of the examiners. This was the question of "title", which, as an integral part of the system, needs a few words of explanation here.

The law prescribed that the ordaining bishop should assure himself, by personal enquiry, of the candidate's fitness in education and in morals. Besides this, he had to ascertain that the man was insured against becoming a burden upon the Church; for the bishop himself, in the last resort, was bound by law to keep from starvation any man whom he or his predecessors had ordained. Therefore a "title" was always demanded. If the candidate could not show, or swear, that he had a sufficient patrimony, then some other responsible person must go surety for him, and accept the responsibility of his maintenance in case of necessity. A large number of these "titles" were given by monasteries. The reason has never been proved by documentary evidence, but it is possibly connected with the undoubted fact that monks became so overburdened with statutory Masses for departed benefactors that they had no alternative but repudiation of contract or the hiring of priests from outside. Be that as it may, the records show clearly that this question of "title" seriously affected the examination system. Mr H. S. Bennett allows me to quote here from an unprinted study, based upon wide reading in the Episcopal Registers and the Calendars of Papal Petitions and Letters. He writes: "The examiners were often extremely pressed for time; for, besides the more spiritual side of their task, they were entrusted with the very important office of ascertaining the candidates' worldly standing and prospects. This enquiry was very important, and no doubt frequently absorbed much ill-spared time. In short, the examiner's judgments must frequently have been hasty and based on a few minutes' observation and enquiry." Thus, although bishops are often found taking their duty of examination seriously, the results were not always satisfactory. Giraldus Cambrensis, writing as an archdeacon of long experience, one of whose main duties was the supervision of clerical education, speaks twice of episcopal examinations as a farce.[2] The Exeter Synod of 1297 complained that "criminous clerics, or clerics of illegitimate birth, or otherwise unfit for Orders" often flee into other dioceses to get ordained by alien bishops, "from whom they not only conceal their defects but, what is more detestable, often lyingly assert that they have already [Minor] Orders, or that they have higher Orders than in fact they possess": therefore for Exeter diocese strangers must produce their letters dimissory, or at least show testimonials and undergo examination before they are allowed to settle in any incumbency.[3] Mr Bennett's evidence corroborates this. He writes: "Examples might be quoted of cases in which one or another of all the essentials enquired into by the examiners was falsely represented. The *Papal Registers* give us a wealth of information on this subject. Thus, dispensations are gained by men who acknowledge receiving Orders (and therefore of withholding essential information from the examiners) although they were under age, or had not received the necessary inferior orders, or were illegitimate.[4] Serfs were able to pass as free men, while many candidates asserted they had a 'title', which was in truth only a fictitious one. St Thomas More, discussing the weaknesses of the clergy, emphasizes this. 'For it is by the laws of the Church provided to the entent that no priest should, unto the slander of priesthood, be driven to live in such lewd manner or worse, there should be none admitted to priesthood, until he had a title of a sufficient yearly living, either of his own patrimony or otherwise. Nor at this day there be any otherwise accepted.' 'Why,' quod he [More's interlocutor], 'therefore go there then so many of them begging?' 'Marry,' quod I, 'for they delude the law and themselves also. For they never have grant of a living that may serve them in sight for that purpose, but they secretly discharge it ere they have it, or else they could not get it. And thus is the Bishop blinded by the sight of the writing, and the priest goeth a-begging.' "[5]

Side by side with this, let us take the evidence of More's intimate friend Erasmus. He tells us how David, Bishop of Utrecht, "had heard that, among so many who took Holy Orders, there were very few who were educated—*paucissimos esse qui literas scirent*". *Literae* doubtless means here, as nearly always in the Middle Ages, Latin as distinguished from the vernacular. Therefore he conducted his own ordination examination himself, and found only 3 candidates out of 300 who were sufficient for their profession. He was at length compelled to pass the rest, because he found that no better could be found at the starvation wages of a sixteenth-century curate.[6] In the bishop's court, there was the same gulf between legal theory and actual practice which we shall trace later on in other courts. Elsewhere, in his Ἰχθυοφαγία (a colloquy between the Butcher and the Fishmonger), the former complains bitterly of the morals and ignorance of too many clergy. He goes on to speak of perjury, which ruins a business man's reputation, and adds: "Yet no perjury is laid to the account of the priest who lives in public lewdness, though he has publicly sworn himself to chastity." To this the Fishmonger replies: "Sing that song to the bishops' vicars-general, who take an oath at the altar that they have found all the candidates whom they bring up for ordination to be of fit age, learning, and morals; whereas sometimes there are scarce two or three tolerable persons in the whole batch, and many are scarce fit for the plough-tail."

"But" (continues Mr Bennett), "after the examination, the candidates returned to their villages and parishes and pursued their everyday lives, and it is there that we see them in their true colours. Hence the real value of the examiner's work is better tested now, as it was then, not by the records of a brief interview in the examination hall, but by the records we have of the behaviour and learning of the clergy from year to year, and even from century to century. It is sufficiently evident from the reiterated exhortations of the Archbishops and Bishops that they were painfully aware that all was not well with the clergy. Throughout these centuries immediately preceding the

Reformation, there was a growing feeling that the condition of the Church would never be improved until the quality of her clergy was improved."

To follow the line of evidence thus suggested, we cannot do better than turn to Chaucer and his two famous contemporaries, Gower and Langland, for a picture of clerical life as seen by educated English folk of that day. These literary sources must be read, of course, with our usual allowance for medieval rhetoric. But a series of other testimonies, many of them from the coldest and most unexceptionable documents, will enable us to judge whether these poets have stepped beyond legitimate satire into caricature.

Gower is by far the most voluminous of the three. In his *Vox Clamantis* and his *Mirour de l'Omme* he devotes nearly 7000 lines to the Church; and the burden of it all is the decay of religion in his own day. True, a very large part of this is "conveyed" wholesale from Anglo-Norman satirists of the twelfth century, especially Neckham and Wireker; but, though this literary theft is of the frankest medieval type, Gower explicitly makes the stolen matter his own. He claims to speak for the man in the street: twice in the *Vox Clamantis* he writes: "It is the voice of the people which dictates these words of mine"; and in the *Mirour*, complaining of the Pope and his Church, he tells us he is writing not his own ideas but those of "all Christian folk".[7] Moreover, he had not the slightest sympathy with Lollardy: his dogmatic orthodoxy was irreproachable. Little as he sympathized with the doctrinal innovations, we could select from him an indictment almost as formidable in substance, though less bitter in language, as from Wyclif himself.

In the *Mirour* he deals specifically with the *Pope*.[8] This great pontiff loves to be called *Your Holiness*; but that is all the holiness about him. Not Christ but Antichrist rules at the papal court. The Cardinals wear red hats, "like a crimson rose opening to the sun; but that red is the colour of guilty pride". The Bishop is often luxurious, and adds to his great income by taking bribes from rich adulterers: so also does the Archdeacon: they actually find their profit in the sins of the people. The Universities are too often given to idleness and riot; in the parishes the priest is frequently absent; often again he sets a bad moral example to his flock; or is so ignorant that he scarcely knows what he is saying when he mumbles his Latin prayers.[9] Worst of all, the clergy always support each other; even the better priests shield their peccant brethren from justice.[10] This accusation was to some extent admitted by St Thomas More in his own day. The Monks again, were originally men of self-denial and penance: but, "nowadays they have everywhere abandoned this observance; for gluttony guards every gate of the monastery, lest hunger and thirst should enter in and bring leanness into their fat paunches".[11] The old sort of monks have been ousted from the abbeys by a new sort; Dan Charity has been slain by Dan Envy; Dan Hatred has expelled Dan Unity. Dan Patience has lost his temper; Dan Obedience has departed; it is Dan Pride, Dan Murmur, and Dan Backbiter who reign nowadays; and, what is worse Dan Unchaste and Dan Incontinent.[12] Thence, turning to the Canons Regular and the Friars, he is equally plain-spoken and uncomplimentary. And, though here in the *Mirour* he says nothing either way about the Nuns, in the parallel passage of *Vox Clamantis* he gives them no better character than the Monks.[13]

Let us next take Langland's evidence. Here, politically, we have a radical, in contrast to the conservative Gower; and, in religion, a stirring broad-Churchman in contrast to something of a conventionalist. Moreover, Langland's main interest is in the moral betterment of the whole world, and he refers to the clergy, as a rule, only in incidental connection with that betterment. Yet his testimony, on the whole, supports Gower's. We have first Sloth, the careless parson, who can scarcely read his own Mass-book, and cares only for his tithes and his hunting. Then the negligent bishops, who ordain men unable to read the Mass or the Psalms, and proportionally neglectful of their other duties, with the result that few clergy will come to heaven in comparison with simple layfolk. The root of all this evil is at the very foundation of the Church—in the Pope himself.

God amend the pope, that robbeth holy church
And claimeth before the king to be keeper over Christians,
And counteth not though Christians be killed and robbed
But hire folk to fight, and Christian blood to spill.

Next to the Pope, the greatest power in the Church is wielded by the friars; and these are as bad or worse than he; for it is well known that, when a man cannot get absolved by his parish priest from his sins, he can bribe a friar to whitewash him.[14]

In Chaucer we have a very different poet from either of these. In his wit there is always the flavour of reticence; and our clearest clue to his attitude is the fact that, of all the clergy who went with him to Canterbury, there are only two for whom we can feel respect. The Poor Parson is admirable: but, as we have seen, the very praise of this particular man is a criticism of his class in general: *he* did *not* do (Chaucer tells us) what was commonly done around him. The Prioress, again, is a dignified figure; and the respect which she commanded from the whole company is obvious. Yet, in Chaucer's detailed description of her dress and her manners, satire lurks under his very praise. Apart from that French of Stratford-atte-Bowe, her seemly-pinched wimple, her conspicuous forehead, her pet dogs, and her brooch with *amor vincit omnia* were all things which a strict bishop, at his visitation, would have been bound to disapprove. Thus Chaucer himself, like our ecclesiastical satirists of the twelfth and thirteenth centuries, and the Oxford Chancellor Gascoigne in the fifteenth, is no exception to what has been confessed by a most orthodox French historian: that, "whether rightly or wrongly, medieval literature does censure monastic morals in crude terms and without distinction".[15]

"Whether rightly or wrongly"; there, of course, is the real question. It is certainly dangerous to rely too much upon literary sources, and historians have often fallen into that trap in the past: for it is the line of least resistance. Yet it is still easier and more dangerous to dismiss such sources with a shrug of the shoulders, and a facile "nous avons changé tout cela". The literary evidence must be tested by side-lights from cold-blooded documents: we may then have to make very heavy discount, or even sometimes to reject our author's conclusions altogether. But when we find, wherever we can test him, that the cross-lights show his substantial veracity, then we may place upon him the same reasonable reliance as we do, in practical affairs, upon our banker or our lawyer or our doctor. At this stage, then, we may now pass on to weigh and test from official sources, point by point, that picture of the clergy which Gower and Langland and Chaucer have given us.

13. CHURCH STATISTICS

This chapter deals with a number of subjects important for the comprehension of English social life. Amid this multiplicity, logical sequence seems preferable to chronological. Sufficient dates are given to guide the reader, who can thus judge roughly for himself how far conditions improved or deteriorated during our period. He will probably conclude that time wrought here its usual effects. Men were struggling onwards to something better, but fitfully and sometimes blindly, as in other ages before or since. Wherever the betterment was only piecemeal or superficial, the old abuses went on wearing deeper and deeper ruts; so that Hildebrand's reforming efforts cannot be fully understood without reference to the state of things in More's age; nor is More's age fully comprehensible except in the light of Hildebrand's struggles.

We have seen how often the better livings either went to influential young men or were absorbed by monasteries and cathedrals who put in vicars, generally at starveling wages. But an even greater abuse was that of pluralism, with its natural consequence of non-residence. It was not only that the fattest benefices were often distributed for unspiritual reasons; this has been the case to some extent in all ages, although the last two or three generations of our own time have made an enormous difference, and the Anglican Church has at last the theory, and to some real extent the practice, that a curate, by efficient work and steady merit, shall within a reasonable time find his way into a benefice. That was not so in Trollope's time, nor was it so in medieval England: and, far worse, the less spiritual candidate might hold not only one rectory as rich as four or five vicarages put together, but a multiplicity of such benefices: it might almost be said, an infinity. Alexander III, one of the strongest of medieval Popes, rebuked the Archbishop of Genoa for introducing into his diocese this custom of pluralism, which (he writes) is a vice of the French Church, "contrary to Canon Law, and disapproved by Us, although the multitude of offenders renders it impossible to amend it". Some clerics, he says, are reported to have six benefices or even more.[1] In his great Lateran Council of 1179 he legislated expressly against it, as "involving the certain peril of souls". At the next Ecumenical Council (1215) Innocent III repeated this with greater emphasis and the addition of fresh sanctions. Yet twenty-two years later, when the papal legate Otho held a reforming council at St Paul's, London, he needed a strong armed guard of nobles and soldiers to protect him against the vengeance of the pluralist clergy to whom he proposed to apply these sanctions.[2] The later years of that century saw the worst abuses of English pluralism. Bishop Cantelupe of Worcester, uncle to St Thomas Cantelupe of Hereford, protested quite frankly: "Many like ourselves, of noble blood, hold a plurality of benefices: if we are to be deprived of one, we will resign them all in a body." John Mansel, a royal minister, is said (though doubtless in unfriendly exaggeration) to have held 300 benefices. His younger contemporary, Bogo de Clare, who had not even Mansel's excuse of great learning and ability, but was simply a younger son of an Earl of Gloucester, can be traced step by step in Professor A. Hamilton Thompson's *Pluralism in the Medieval Church* (*Ass. Archit. Soc. Reports,* vol. XXXIII). Professor Thompson writes: "This [man's] astonishing list [of pluralities] includes two canonries and prebends, which were sinecures, three dignities in cathedral and collegiate churches, and twenty-four parish churches or portions of such churches with cure of souls. London, Bath and Wells, Carlisle and Worcester were the only four English dioceses which did not reckon Bogo among their clergy. That he personally served any of his churches is most unlikely: it is to be hoped, at any rate, that he paid chaplains to officiate in them in his absence." It is certain that he was not yet a priest in 1283, when he had amassed the twentieth of these endowments: probably he never was. He died in 1294. Walter Langton, who was a contemporary of Bogo, though not quite his equal, is fit to be mentioned by his side. Perhaps there has never been any prohibitionist law which has lent itself to such open and systematic bootlegging as this of ecclesiastical pluralities. The more illegal endowments a man succeeded in amassing, the more dispensations he could buy from Rome. One of Bogo's dispensations gave him leave to hold pluralities not exceeding 400 marks (about £10,000 modern); he took advantage of this inch to take an ell. Here is a fairly ordinary specimen from papal letters to the Archbishop of York in 1289. "Transumpt of a dispensation from Pope Nicholas IV under the seal of the Bishop of Exeter, to Boniface, a clerk, son of Thomas, Marquess of Saluzzo, in the diocese of Turin, to hold [in England] two benefices with cure of souls, without being obliged to be ordained or to reside, notwithstanding any defects in orders or age."[3] A large proportion of the richest English endowments went to such papal protégés who never set foot in this country. The significance of this clause "without being obliged to reside" will be obvious. Our universities were staffed mainly by absentee rectors; that was a natural and comparatively pardonable form of endowment for research; we have seen how Wyclif profited by a system which, however indefensible in strict theory, had been a matter of course for more than a century before his day. But elsewhere the wholesale growth of pluralism spelt equally wholesale absenteeism. The episcopal visitation of the county of Oxford in 1520, covering 193 parishes, reports 58 absentees, i.e. 30 per cent.

Nor, as we have already seen, was that common-sense papal and conciliar decree strictly kept, that the rector of a parish should be in priest's orders, and therefore competent to celebrate Mass and perform the other necessary parochial duties. In 1282, eight years after this decree, even a strong prelate like Giffard of Worcester, backed up by the Archbishop of Canterbury, had great difficulty in applying the specified sanctions, and depriving a noble presentee who held the valuable living of Chipping Campden, yet refused to take priest's orders. The already quoted statistics from the registers show how, before the Black Death, this decree had become almost a dead letter; and, even in the improvement which followed upon that plague, there was still a proportion of non-priestly incumbents which could not be remotely paralleled in any civilized country of to-day. In the later generations of the Middle Ages, there grew up in England a class of brokers called "chop-churches", who dealt in benefices and arranged exchanges. In about 1470, for instance, there came before the Chancery Court the case of Sir John Thomas, parson of Flamstead, against William Lincoln, parson of Great Hallingbury and William Wever, "chopchyrch", of Markyate, "for false representation of the value of Great Hallingbury Church, on a proposed exchange". Later on, the records give us "John Polyng, clerk, alias Chopchirch, of Exeter".[4]

The ordinary priest was not what would be called, in any country of to-day, an educated man. Even in the exceptional case of his having completed his course of study at a university, he would have found there no faculty of classics or mathematics or history or science. The *Gesta Romanorum*, stories from Roman and other history compiled for the use of preachers, was a classic in its way; yet it informs us at the outset that "Pompey was a great and noble *king*", and goes on to confuse Marcus Aurelius with the legendary Mettus Curtius who closed an earthquake-gulf in the Forum by leaping, horsed and armed, into the chasm! Even of Latin, the priest needed to know scarcely more than what would enable him to read aloud correctly, without construing, the services of the Church. Yet, incredible as it might seem, we have definite evidence that a small minority could not even go so far as this. At the great Lateran Council of 1215, Innocent III had made a determined effort to raise the level of clerical education. In 1222, the Council of Oxford stigmatized some of the clergy as "dumb dogs", and doubted whether they could read even the Canon of the Mass; that is, the essential portion of the Eucharist, not so bulky as a page of this present book. Archbishop Pecham, in 1287, issued a statute in council which begins: "The ignorance of priests casteth the people into the ditch of error; and the folly or unlearning of the clergy, who are bidden to instruct the faithful in the Catholic Faith, doth sometimes tend rather to error than to sound doctrine." Similar complains meet us again and again in the records of later Synods; and, as late as 1518, Wolsey found himself compelled solemnly to reissue Pecham's statute, *Ignorantia Sacerdotum,* in the very same words.[5]

Let us try to fathom this ignorance, bearing in mind that the whole services of the Church, from beginning to end, were in Latin; that the only Bible authorized by Rome was in Latin; so also was every accessible commentary, and, until the last few generations of our period, nearly every religious book. The Venerable Bede [730] speaks of "clerics or monks who are ignorant of the Latin tongue . . . on which account I myself have often given to many unlearned priests these two things, the Apostles' Creed and the Lord's Prayer, translated into English".[6] This may be compared with that which Tyndale asserted and St Thomas More, I believe, never denied: "I dare say that there be twenty thousand priests, curates, this day in England, and not so few, that cannot give you the right English unto this text in the Paternoster, *Fiat voluntas tua, sicut in coelo et in terra,* and answer thereto." Bishop Hooper's visitation of 1552 shows that there were scores of clergy who could not tell who was the author of the Lord's Prayer, or where it was to be found.[7]

But to return to our earlier times. St Boniface [750] referred to Pope Zacharias the question whether a child had been effectually baptized by "a priest who was utterly ignorant of the Latin tongue, and who, in his baptism, not knowing the Latin speech, broke that language and said 'Baptizo te in nomine Patria et Filia et Spiritu sancta'" [for *Patris et Filii et Spiritus Sancti*]. The Pope replied that, since the priest had introduced no theological error or heresy, but "had simply broken the language in his ignorance of Roman Speech", therefore the sacrament was valid. King Alfred, in his complaints of English ignorance, includes the priests. Giraldus Cambrensis [1200] quote startling concrete instances: two may here suffice.[8] One priest, reading in his Breviary *In die* (and then, on a fresh line) *bus illis* (Luke ii. 1) thought this must mean "in Busillis's day", and asked who Busillis was.

Another explained to the congregation that the *piscis assus* (broiled fish) of Luke xxiv. 42 was an "ass fish", according to the medieval notion that the ocean-world is in every way a counterpart of our own. Yet all this pales before the cold-blooded documentary record of that priest who, examined by the Bishop of Sarum's commissaries in 1222, could not construe the first sentence of the first prayer in the Canon of the Mass, or reach even lower-form standard in parsing. The words run: *Te igitur, clementissime Pater . . . rogamus,* "we beseech thee therefore, most merciful Father. . . ." Let us hear the examiners' exact report. Simon, curate of Sonning-on-Thames, asserted that he had been ordained subdeacon "at Oxford, by a certain Irish bishop named Albin, then suffragan to the Bishop of Lincoln. *Item*, from him he received the Order of deacon. *Item,* the Order of priest from Hugh [of Wells], now Bishop of Lincoln, four years ago." In all this he may possibly have lied; but the certainty is that "he was tried in the Canon of the Mass, *Te igitur, clementissime Pater*, etc. He knew not what case *Te* was, nor by what it was governed: and when he was told to look more diligently and see what part could most properly govern *Te*, he said *Pater*, for He governeth all things. Asked what *clementissime* was, or what case, or how it was declined, he knew not. Asked what *clemens* meant, he knew not. . . . Moreover, he said that it seemed indecent to him that he should be tried before the dean, seeing that he had already been ordained. Examined as to where he had been when he received the Order of priesthood, he said that he did not remember. He is sufficiently illiterate"—*sufficienter illiteratus est.* In the seventeen parishes visited on that occasion, all of which were in the gift of the dean and chapter of Salisbury, four others beside Simon were found unable to construe that familiar and crucial Latin sentence. "After [the second of those priests who had been found utterly wanting] had left the church after the examination and had come to the others, all with one accord agreed that they would not answer; yet some separately answered afterwards under great urgency on the dean's part."[9] A generation later, the Archbishop of Rouen notes several similar examinations in his register; these tell much the same tale; yet Normandy was one of the most civilized corners of Europe in that day.

Instances of this kind were ubiquitous and notorious. "There are", wrote St Bonaventura [1260], "so many inexperienced clerics that, even if they be well taught in grammar and other knowledge, yet where 100 or more rectors and vicars are gathered together, there are scarce any who have in fact enough knowledge of the Scriptures to manage either the souls committed to their care, or other things necessary for salvation." He speaks here specially of Italy, and says that things were better in France and England. But St Thomas Aquinas, writing at Paris, complains of "the inexperience of many priests, who in some parts are found to be so ignorant that they cannot even speak Latin, and among whom very few are found who have learnt Holy Scripture". Roger Bacon, writing about the same time in England, and wishing to give an instance of mere parrot-learning, says "just as boys gabble through the Psalter which they have learnt, and as clerks and country priests recite the Church services, of which they know little or nothing, like brute beasts". Gerson, at the beginning of the fifteenth century, speaks equally strongly and far more frequently on this subject. He contrasts what he calls the restless and ill-digested Scripture studies of the heretics with the supineness of even "great prelates", who neglect "the wine of sacred wisdom", and cry, "What is this ye say to us of faith? It is enough that we are Christians, in good simplicity: that is enough; for he who pries into majesty shall be oppressed by its glory; and there is no need to seek things so lofty for us." Again he asks: "Are all ecclesiastics bound to study God's Law? It would seem so . . . yet on the other side it may be argued that to assert this is to place by far the greater part of ecclesiastics outside the way of salvation, and to assert that they are doomed to damnation." He speaks of the lamentable lack of religious books of any kind among the parish clergy, and complains that there is no organized attempt to multiply good writings against the rising tide of infidelity: to this supineness, and to the ignorance of the beneficed clergy, he attributes a great deal of what he calls the notorious decay of the Catholic Church. To omit much intermediate evidence, we have evidence of the same kind from the verge of the Reformation. When Dean Colet, in 1509, complained that all applicants were admitted indiscriminately to Holy Orders, so that the Church swarmed with " a multitude of unlearned and evil priests ", he was only repeating, almost in so many words, what the Bishop of Mende had said to the Pope at the Council of Vienne in 1311. Moreover, both Colet and the bishop lay stress on the fact that laws had been frequently enacted against these abuses, and that the Church needed no new legislation, but simply sufficient courage to enforce those time-honoured and repeatedly enacted laws. More, even in the heat of his controversy against Tyndale, quoted the case of " him that, because he read in his Mass-book *Te igitur clementissime Pater,* preached unto the parish that Te Igitur was St Clement's father ".[10]

I have heard a distinguished Roman Catholic layman maintain that his Church does not want a learned clergy: that the Faith is enough. He, like William Morris, was fascinated by Gothic art, and the picturesque side of medieval life. There is much in this plea; for the claims of the medieval Church were strong in imponderables, though far weaker on those sides which she tried to buttress with considerations vulnerable to scrutiny and to reason. The man who daily " made God's Body " found in that a claim far above all others. Just about the time of the Norman Conquest the righteous and courageous Gregory VII submitted the clergy, practically, to the moral judgment of their congregations, by forbidding the laity to attend the Masses of concubinary priests. But it soon became evident that this would eliminate from the Church not so much the offenders as their congregations. Therefore this Pope, who dared to bring the Emperor to public penance, shrank from pushing these sanctions to their full limit; and, in later generations, it became a definite note of heresy to maintain that a priest's morals affected the efficacy of his Mass. Here, therefore, in the superhuman character of the Mass, was a superiority unassailable because it was so intangible; and

Quivil, Bishop of Exeter in 1287, used no more than the ordinary clerical language of his time when he issued a decree complaining against those layfolk who, *modernis temporibus,* are mad enough to outrage clerical immunities. "Alas! unhappy wretches, walking in darkness! Is not God our Father who created us? and is not the Church our Mother in whom we were born again by baptism? and is it not written in Canon Law: 'He that stealeth anything from his father or his mother and saith: This is no sin, is the partner of a murderer'? Is it not evident and marvellous madness that the son should attempt to lord it over his father, the disciple over his master? and that a man should strive to subject by unjust obligations those whom he believes to have the power of binding and loosing him not only on earth but in heaven also?"

For the Mass, according to Church teaching in our period, was an *opus operatum*; a ceremony which affected the congregation quite apart from their attention to the service or their state of mind. In Myrc's *Instructions*, the parish priest is bidden to explain to his people the virtue of attendance at the making of the Consecrated Host:[11]

For glad may that man be
That once in the day may Him see;
For so mickle good doth that sight,
(As Saint Austin teacheth aright,)
That day that thou seest God's Body,
These benefices shalt thou have securely;
Meat and drink at thy need,
None shall thee that day begrede; [*reproach, accuse*
Idle oaths and words also
God forgiveth thee both;
Sudden death that ilk day,
Thee dare not dread, without nay;
Also that day, I thee plight,
Thou shalt not lose thyn eyë-sight.

It need hardly be said that St Augustine had never taught anything of this kind. But the superstition was ineradicable as many others which falsely claimed that great doctor's name; and, in the next century, we find Gerson, the great Chancellor of Paris, writing bitterly of the priests who still taught it. Here (he said) is a falsehood which, often enough, men find plainly contradicted by experience, and which can only help to weaken their faith. Yet the great scholar's protests had little effect; the priest could always promise such miracles that he was thereby raised to an untouchable height.

Yet medieval society oscillated between this childish credulity and childish indifference or petulance. Our earliest records show the priest, despite his lofty spiritual claims, greatly depressed on the material side. For Merovingian and Carolingian France, Imbart de la Tour emphasizes the menial or even servile relation of the village priest to the lord who " owned " the church.[12] Charles the Great had to legislate against the tendency towards drawing clerical recruits mainly from the servile class. For Norway, L. M. Larson quotes from the eleventh-century civil code: " As often as the priests give us wrong directions, or disobey the orders which the bishop puts forth . . . they shall atone to the bishop with a money fine; *for we have abolished the custom of punishing them with blows*, since we have entered into marriage relations with them and allow them to give our sons instruction."[13] William of Malmesbury describes their menial position in the houses of the Saxon nobles; and St Thomas More, on the verge of the Reformation, deplored the number of grovelling chaplains and hedge-priests in his own day.

The question of the priest's fees and dues is very important; the power of the purse was almost as weighty a factor in the Reformation as in the Rebellion of 1642. The " great tithes " (on crops and cattle) formed the greater part of the priest's income; and, except in cases where custom softened the strictness of the law, it imposed upon every parishioner an income-tax of 10 per cent. on his *gross* revenue, making no allowance for working expenses. It is sometimes asserted that this was cheerfully paid;[14] but this is contradicted by multiple and notorious documentary evidence. It is irreconcilable with the fact that one of the priest's most definite duties—far older and more insistent than that of preaching at Mass—was that of excommunicating periodically and publicly all who had defrauded the Church of this tax. It was one of Chaucer's Good Parson's conspicuous virtues that he was "full loth to cursen for his tithes"; yet curse he must, and in the grisliest earnest. Chaucer's contemporary, the Canon Myrc, gives the text in his *Instructions for Parish Priests.* It runs, "we curse them by the authority of the Court of Rome, within and without, sleeping or walking, going and sitting, standing and riding, lying above earth and under earth, speaking and crying and drinking; in wood, in water, in field, in town. Curse them Father and Son and Holy Ghost! curse them angels and archangels and all the nine orders of heaven! curse them patriarchs, prophets and apostles and all God's disciples and all holy Innocents, martyrs, confessors and virgins, monks, canons, hermits, priests and clerks, that they have no part of Mass nor Matins nor of none other good prayers that be done in Holy Church nor in none other places; but that the pains of hell be their meed with Judas that betrayed our Lord Jesu Christ, and the life of them be put out of the Book of Life till they come to amendment and satisfaction made. *Fiat, fiat! Amen.*"[15]

The "lesser tithes" were on everything except crops and beasts; here is a fair specimen. The monks of Sawley granted to the vicar of Tadcaster, in 1290, that he should have, as part of his stipend, "the tithes of wool, flax, pot-herbs, leeks, apples, cheese, butter, milk, eggs, calves, chickens, geese, hens, sucking-pigs, bees and honey, together with the tithes of servants in Lent, to wit, of hirelings, hawkers, bakers, carpenters, quarrymen, masons, *caprarum* [coopers?] and limeburners, while for a time such exist in the parish; *Item*, of carters and brewsters . . ." together with half a dozen other small dues from his parishioners.[16] This, though characteristic enough of England, would in one sense have been exceptional elsewhere; for Continental customs seldom recognized these "personal" tithes imposed on men's wages, even on those of all menial servants except the poorest. This formed the subject of serious complaints early in the sixteenth century, when the lay spirit was beginning to assert itself. The discontent was so serious that, in 1518, Wolsey decreed for his province of York that a labourer receiving no more than *6s. 8d.* a year (he would also have board and lodging, let us say 1*s.* a week) must not be compelled to pay personal tithes.

To put this in modern terms, a labourer at £2. 10*s.* a week would be excused; but one whose wages were £2. 11*s.* would have to pay a yearly tithe of more than a week's wages to his rector. That this was felt as a real burden by the poor can be proved from one of the fragmentary Yorkshire visitations published by Canon Raine. The parishioners of Masham are found enquiring of the visitors in 1510: "Also we desire to know what a servant should pay to tithe for his hire, for as much as draws ten shillings, for poor servants that hath but a small wage to find them, it is sore for them to take so mickle." The neighbouring parish of Kirby Malsherd put a similar question in a briefer and more grammatical form: "We desire to know what a servant should pay to tithe for ten shillings wage."[17] But, for many centuries before this, the tithe system had been a fertile source of quarrels and bad blood; it was responsible for more litigation, we may safely assert, than any other subject. There is a decree from Bishop Quivil of Exeter (1287) which, though specially piquant, tells us nothing more than we could prove in the main from other sources. "Seeing that certain persons for their tithe which hath hitherto been given in cheese (according to the custom hitherto approved in our diocese), maliciously bring the milk itself to Church and—what is more wicked still—finding there no man to receive it, pour it out before the altar in contumely to God and his Church." The bishop continues with a long list of similar frauds and subterfuges on the part of tithe-payers.[18] In 1419, Convocation dealt solemnly and very heatedly with the Franciscan Russell, who, with certain fellow-friars, had so heretically championed the people's cause as to teach the non-payment of tithes. Moreover, the whole system of "mortuary", or "corpse-present", which had become strictly compulsory long before the end of our period, reposed upon the assumption—one may say, the almost certainty—that the dead man must at some time have withheld some of his tithes, so that the mortuary, by redeeming this fault, would save him from hell or shorten his purgatory.

There were many other dues which became either strictly or practically compulsory upon all but paupers, even when the priest did not break Church law by exacting money for the Sacraments, an offence which disciplinarians stigmatized as only too frequent. And, finally, the priest had a strong hold upon the man's death-bed. He who had not made a written will (and only an infinitesimal fraction could do this) was expected to make one by word of mouth to the priest or to two unexceptionable witnesses. It was the Church, again, which had exclusive jurisdiction over the probate of wills. Thus "There arose a feeling that intestacy, except in the case of sudden death, was disgraceful. We have seen that there were traces of this feeling as early as the reign of Cnut. It was intensified after the Conquest."[19] Let us put ourselves for a moment in the dying man's place. Whatever else the poor wretch may believe or disbelieve, of hell and purgatory he has never been allowed to doubt. Whenever he entered his parish church, there stood the great ghastly picture of the Last Judgment staring down on him from the walls—blood and fire and devils in such pitiless realism that, when they come to light nowadays, even sympathetic restorers are often fain to cover them again under decent whitewash. A picture of that kind, seen once or twice a week for fifty years, is indelibly branded into the soul of the dying man; and, however little he may have allowed these things to influence the conduct of his life, however deliberately he may have overreached and cheated and robbed in his generation to scrape this little hoard together, here on his deathbed he has at least the faith of a devil—he believes and trembles. He knows that gifts to the Church are universally held to be one of the surest preservatives against the pains of purgatory; he has perhaps even seen men burned at the stake for denying a truth so essential to the Roman creed. What wonder, then, that deathbed legacies to the clergy and to the churches became so customary that the absence of such pious gifts was sometimes taken for proof presumptive of heresy, and that the intestate was in consequence buried in unconsecrated ground.

The priests' incomes varied even more than now. In parishes

where much land had been gradually reclaimed—moorland, as in Blackburn, or fenland, as in Doddington, the tithes sometimes ran into four figures in modern values. William Hudson worked out the average value of an incumbency in Norwich diocese (more wealthy than most) at nearly £11 towards the end of the thirteenth century. We may compare this with those of a knight and a peasant farmer. In 1353, all holders of land to the value of £15 and over were decreed worthy of knighthood, and were fined if, in order to avoid the duties and burdens of that order, they neglected to seek that honour. On the other hand, Thorold Rogers calculates that a peasant farming 20 acres of ploughland would spend about £3 a year upon himself, wife, and children.[20] The incumbent, if rector (and sometimes even as vicar), had the upkeep of chancel and service books to face, with traditions of almsgiving and hospitality: we shall see later what this meant. On the other hand, he had not, or ought not to have, a wife and family. The vicarages were, of course, definitely poorer than the rectories: orthodox writers constantly complained that the appropriation system was starving the parish clergy. The bishops, therefore, often stepped in to do what they could against this sweating system. The earliest statistics we have for such "ordinations" of vicarages are for Lincoln diocese in 1209 and following years. Out of the 134 thus "ordained", 113 amounted to less than £4; that is, scarcely more than the peasant farmer's income. The amounts required for a "title" help us also here. In Durham diocese, 1334-44, 96 per cent. of the ordinands assessed their title at 5 marks (£3 6*s.* 8*d.*), which was evidently the regular requirement. In Carlise diocese, 1292-1324, 75 per cent. claimed 5 marks, but 25 per cent. only 3. In Worcester, 1302-13, only 3 marks were required: one candidate alone was able to boast 5. Vicars' wages rose slowly even to the end of our period, but not more than the cost of living. Mr H. G. Richardson sums up judicially: "If we suppose the average [stipendiary] Chaplain to have had from all sources before the Black Death an income of from six to seven marks, and accept forty-eight shillings as a moderate estimate of the income of a first-class agricultural labourer, such as a ploughman or carter of the same period, we have some indication of whereabouts in the social scale to place the great mass of poorly-paid parish clergy."[21]

The facility with which the clergy accepted first Henry VIII's revolutionary measures and then the final change of faith under Elizabeth cannot be wholly dissociated from the natural discontent of a numerous and underpaid class. Professor E. F. Jacob has noted the contrast between the attitude of Convocation towards taxation in the thirteenth and the fifteenth century. When the legate Otho demanded heavy contributions (1237), there was apparently no discussion; the levy was forced upon the clergy without delay. In 1424/5, however, the proctors of the lower clergy pleaded that their constituents would not permit such a levy; they complained that fraudulent pardon-mongers were unusually active—*plus solito*—and demanded closer restrictions. The discussions lasted from October 18th to November 20th, when Convocation adjourned till after Christmas. Thence they sat till February 8th, when the lower clergy still refused assent, and Convocation was dissolved. Earlier, in 1401, special exemption had been made for "scanty" livings: the limit was set at 8 marks.

In these circumstances, the time-honoured theory of clerical almsgiving could not be strictly practised by any vicar; and, even if there were a few rectors who attempted it, as St Gilbert of Sempringham seems to have done, these are cited as marvels. The theory, in the earliest times, had demanded a fourfold division of the parish revenues, between the bishop, the poor, the upkeep of church and services, and the serving priest. The bishop dropped out at an early date; later canonists speak only of the other three. But a vicar who, by the settled custom of the time, scarcely ever got more than a bare third of the revenues, and more often got less, was obviously incapable of giving that third to the poor. Nor did the appropriating monastery fill up this gulf. After all the emphasis with which Archbishop Stephen Langton had decreed in 1222, and Archbishop Pecham in 1279, that the poor parishioners should not be defrauded of their share of the tithes, it was still necessary for Archbishop Stratford to repeat their decrees even more emphatically in 1342. In spite (he complains) of theories to the contrary, "yet monks and nuns of our province, procuring appropriations of churches, strive so greedily to apply to their own uses the fruits, revenues, and profits of the same, that . . . they neglect to exercise any works of charity whatsoever among the parishioners. Wherefore, by this their exceeding avarice, they not only provoke to indevotion those who owe them tithes and ecclesiastical dues, but also teach them sometimes to become perverse trespassers on, and consumers of, the said tithes, and abominable disturbers of the peace, to the grievous peril of both monks' and parishioners' souls, and to the scandal of very many."[22] The system, it is true, was not quite so bad as some of the malpractices which had preceded it. When the tithes were thus appropriated to a monastery, the church and the priest and the poor might get a little more than in those cases where, by a frequent abuse, the lay patron of the benefice had robbed the church which it was his duty to protect. But in England these lay robberies had been far less frequent than on the Continent; nor, again, did the lay abuse of paying royal ministers with Church livings affect one-tenth as many as were absorbed by the monastic appropriation system. The undeniable result of this was to render the poor man's portion ludicrously small in comparison with the time-honoured theory. The English parliament, a little before and after 1400, dealt over and over again with this scandal; but to no effect, since Popes and bishops had a pecuniary interest in it. At last parliament, losing patience, prescribed that the bishops should definitely earmark a reasonable proportion for the poor. But this prescription, again, was constantly neglected; and, in the few cases where the documents permit us to trace the actual sums, these come on an average not to the statutory one-third of the parochial income, but to about one-sixteenth at most.[23] The monasteries which thus drew two-thirds of the income from nearly one-third of the English parishes were, it is true, the main distributors of such charities as could be counted upon by the medieval poor: but we have irrefragable evidence that they thus gave back far less than they took. The monks' own account-rolls, where they survive, have never yet been found to record charities even to the extent of one-tenth of the abbey's gross income. Moreover, the documents show the monks sometimes even embezzling moneys which had never been their own, but had simply been left to them as charity trustees. At Finchale, a cell to Durham, they were able to claim income-tax reduction on 26*s*. 8*d*. which they held in trust for distribution to the poor every Maundy Thursday: yet their private accounts show them distributing only 10*s*. of this sum. At Dover Priory, they had endowments in trust for the poor to a total amount of £13. 19*s*. 2*d*.; their account-roll for the year 1530 still exists, and shows that they distributed only 8*s*., that is, one-fortieth.[24] Peter of Blois, at the end of the twelfth century, drew a harrowing picture of monastic luxury and neglect of the poor. This description was felt to be so true that the Franciscan Gilbert of Tournai, when the Pope consulted him for the General Council of Lyons (1274) repeated the same accusations, often in Peter's own words; and again, about 1450, Dionysius the Carthusian utilized the passage in his description of the monasticism of his own day. Christ crucified (these three writers said) lies at the gate, in the shape of His poor; and the dogs do not lick his sores but bite him; meanwhile the abbot, like Dives, is feasting within. At that same time the great Oxford Chancellor Gascoigne described the Seven Rivers of Babylon, the seven floods of iniquity; one of these was this absorption of parochial funds by the monasteries. In the north of England, where parishes were fewer, the loss of monastic doles at the Dissolution was more severely felt than elsewhere; but, during the centuries succeeding that event, the English poor have suffered less, on the whole, than those of France and Austria and Italy and Spain. The ecclesiastical visitation of Oxfordshire in 1520 deals with 193 parishes; in 35 it is complained that alms-giving is neglected.[25] Ten of these are monastic vicarages. The rich Abbey of Oseney had appropriated six Oxfordshire churches; five of the vicars do not give alms, and one of them has even embezzled from moneys that he had in trust for the poor: so, again, did one vicar under the rich Abbey of Eynsham. That friar, contemporary with Chaucer, who wrote the moral dialogue called *Dives and Pauper*, says no more than others said who were equally orthodox. He writes:[26] "Thys poynte of manslaughter toucheth moche men of holy churche; for, as the lawe saythe, The tythes of holy churche be tributes of them that be in nede, to releve theim in ther nede; and alle that men of holy churche have, it is the pore mennys goodys, and ther housys shulde be comon to alle men at nede. . . . But they be not bounde to fede the rych folke, but goostly, and them that have noo nede wythe holy churchys goodys. And of the pore folke yeve they no tale, but to pylle [pillage] them and have of them and get of them what they may by hypocrisy, by fraud, by dread and violence; and therefore God undermynethe [warneth] them by the prophet Ezechiel and saith thus to them: 'woo be to the shipherdis of israel, that is to saye to the prelatys and curatis of holi churche, which shuld be shepherdys of goddys shepe, and of the soulis that criste bought so dere, woo be to the shepeherdys, for they fede theimsylfe and of the pore people yeve they no tale.' And therefore God acceptethe not the praier of such men of holy churche, for they be wythoute charite and ful of crueltye in pyllinge of the pore people."

An excellent conspectus of medieval poor relief may be found in Sir W. Ashley's *Economic History* (vol. I, pt. ii, p. 338). He writes: "No attempt was made by the State as a whole, or by any secular public authority to relieve distress. The work was left entirely to the Church, and to the action of religious motives upon the minds of individuals. If it had ever been attempted to organize charity in a systematic way, making the parish priest the 'relieving-officer' for his parish, and the tithes the fund whence aid was to be furnished, that attempt had altogether broken down. Well-nigh all the assistance that was given to the poor was in the form of almsgiving; almsgiving by magnates, ecclesiastical and lay, by monasteries, by hospitals, by gilds, by private persons; and almsgiving that was in the vast majority of cases practically indiscriminate, whatever it may have been in theory. No attempt was made by any public authority, secular or ecclesiastical, to take a comprehensive view of the situation, and to co-ordinate the various agencies. The reckless distribution of doles cannot have failed to exercise a pauperizing influence in many localities, by rendering it easy for those who did not care to work to live without. But it has been well observed that if the poor relief of the Middle Ages in some directions did too much, in others it did too little. Voluntary charity always has the defect of being more abundant in districts which need it least, and least abundant where there is most want. The towns get more than their share; the fertile and prosperous districts have their richly endowed foundations; while the unhealthy or barren regions are left unprovided for. Thus, in Italy, where medieval conditions have been retained more completely than in any other country, owing to the power of the Church, districts containing scarcely a fourth of the population received until lately three-fourths of the revenue of charitable endowments; while, to give a further illustration, the healthier districts have most of the hospitals (in the modern sense of the term), and those constantly troubled by malaria and pellagra scarcely any. No doubt the same condition of things existed in England. Shameless beggars who were ready to wander from place to place in search of alms had an easy life: the honest hard-working poor, who were visited by misfortune and unable or afraid to leave their homes, would often find no relief at hand."

14. THE SHEPHERD

At this point, we may try to picture the priest in his parish as revealed by surviving official visitation records. Such records must, of course, be discounted by the consideration that the visitor's direct duty was that of noting faults for future amendment. Yet, with this discount constantly in mind, we shall be able to observe the extent to which our literary testimonies are borne out by the cold-blooded evidence of commissaries and clerks who were thinking of nothing less than of possible readers four or five centuries after their death.

The routine was always pretty much the same. The bishop's commissary, or the archdeacon, went round the district, and heard evidence either in each village or, more often, at certain accessible points. The clergy were supposed to attend in person; and from each parish came four "synodsmen" (*sidesmen*, by modern corruption) to answer a regular questionnaire, the points of which were nearly the same in every case.

One of the first and most important questions touched the cleric's morals; and on that point we must begin with a brief explanation. Though priestly celibacy had been decreed from very early times in the Roman Church, the law was very generally neglected both in Saxon England and in Normandy. The story was told fully and accurately by the late Dr H. C. Lea of Philadelphia, whose essential fairness and whose laborious scholarship, in spite of occasional lapses, have on the whole survived even the most hostile criticism from those who are interested to contest his conclusions.[1]

Lea begins by tracing the vain attempts to enforce the celibacy rule from 1049 to 1063. In 1074, the great and resolute Hildebrand (Gregory VII) took the extreme step of forbidding attendance at the Masses of concubinary priests, thus making the laity judges of their pastor to an extent which even he dared not push to its conclusion, and which gave excuse for later heresies. In 1076 the Council of Winchester set itself to enforce celibacy: yet William gave no help here, although in Normandy he had sided with the prohibitionists. In 1102 St Anselm faced the problem with his usual straightforward determination. The decrees of his council contained no sanctions; but Anselm for his own part threatened the offenders with deprivation of their benefices. Yet the Pope himself, Paschal II, though a strong man, definitely gave way here, and frankly abandoned the Hildebrandine attitude; it was better, he said, to suffer an unchaste priest than to die without the rites of the Church. And, though Henry I approved Anselm's policy, yet Eadmer, the saint's biographer, confesses its failure. Many priests went on strike, and locked up their churches. Even in Anselm's own diocese of Canterbury, many more flatly defied his excommunication and went on in their usual way. In 1107, Paschal II again yielded, and gave dispensations to priests' sons: "in England, the larger and better portion of the clergy fall within the scope of the prohibition" of marriage. It is significant that, by this time, the mere unchastity of a priest was far less offensive to the authorities than his formal marriage. In 1108, Henry I held a council which supported Anselm's contentions; but next year the saint died, and Eadmer admits the increase of secret and scandalous unchastity: "There were few indeed who continued to preserve the purity with which Anselm had laboured so strenuously to adorn his clergy". The papal legate himself, sent in 1126 to lead the orthodox campaign, was caught by night with a harlot after celebrating Mass that day; and, though Henry I professed to enforce the law, Matthew Paris suggests with much probability that he used prohibition as a lever for blackmail. In Wales and Ireland, clerical concubinage was even more widespread. This story of councils repeating prohibition, and by that very repetition tacitly confessing the past failures, need be continued no farther here. It must be added, however, that the Papal Court was notoriously the most immoral in Europe relatively, and perhaps even absolutely. When Durand, Bishop of Mende, was asked what reforms were most needed to be carried out by the Ecumenical Council of Vienne (1311), he began by insisting that all amendment must begin at the fountain-head, and specified, among other things, that brothels were kept at the doors of the Pope's palace, and that his marshals made an income by their upkeep. Thus, in process of time the great cities of Europe, London included, learned to defy those papal laws which protected clerical sinners from condign punishment. Priests caught in open unchastity were dealt with like other folk, and the Londoners kept a separate prison for them.

Without this preamble, it would not have been possible to realize the exact significance of these episcopal visitations: for clerical marriage was a primary question, not only moral but economic. Peccant priests had not only a partner and children to support, but might also be paying blackmail to the archdeacon, though this was not quite so general a practice in England as in Wales and Ireland. Even though there were no such secret bootlegging, there was the specified legal fine, the significance of which was brought out by the late Master of Balliol in his Ford Lectures. He wrote: "There is in existence a set of canons for Coventry diocese; they are dated 1237, but are evidently prior to those of Otto, and curiously timid in their attitude to clerical sinners. For incontinency a priest on the first two convictions is to be fined only. 'We fine in money because men fear money penalties most, and because it is wealth that is the cause of wantonness. . . . But for all our threats of excommunication we fear they will not return to the Lord, for the spirit of uncleanness is among them.'"[2] This, with masses of corroborative evidence which might be quoted, is even more significant than the bare statistics which are gleaned from the reports. Such cases as are reported on those visitations might easily be abused by an historian, consciously or unconsciously, to give an exaggerated picture, yet there is one point which tells its own incontrovertible tale. Whenever, beside the actual fact of the transgression, we note its comparative tolerance by the community and even by the authorities, there we are on safe ground. A law broken not only frequently but with comparative impunity, is scarcely a law at all. Although systematic breach of chastity was legally punishable by deprivation, yet it is extremely rare to find the very strongest bishops, even once in a way, applying that final sanction among the multitude of lawbreakers. Wherever the official records give us a glimpse behind the scenes, there we find the same story. The Chapter Acts of Ripon and Southwell, for instance, record many cases which, by law, should have resulted in deprivation, but in which a money fine sheltered the sinner even from public penance. "At Ripon, for instance, the full sentence on erring priests is recorded in 5 cases; in only one was it actually performed. In one case the culprit redeemed it for a private penance and a fine of 3*s.*; in the other three, it was redeemed for similar fines without even the private penance."[3]

In the 281 parishes of the Hereford visitation (A.D. 1397) 72 clerics, nearly all priests, were presented by the parishioners for incontinence: this gives more than 25 per cent. Even if we omit the 9 cases where the accused "purged himself", by a process of ecclesiastical swearing which the Oxford Chancellor Gascoigne branded as "an occasion of intolerable iniquity", the fraction is still more than 22 per cent. Moreover, in these same records we find the usual sidelights upon the actual working of this "compurgation" system, by which a man was acquitted if he would swear innocence, and procure a specified number of "compurgators" to swear that they believed him. At Dodynzob [*sic*] the report runs: "Sir William Westhope is incontinent with one Jane Stale, whom he keepeth always in his house." A later hand adds: "The man appeared, denied and is given a day to purge himself with five compurgators: he was also admonished to remove her from cohabitation within six days." Here we have practically the verdict of "Not guilty: but you must not do it again!" Next, at Colwall, the probable birthplace of William Langland: "Richard of Reye complained publicly in the presence of me, the Registrar, and of the parishioners, that Sir John Comyn, curate of Colwall, hath held his [Richard's] lawful wife Jane by night and day, against his will, wherefore he holdeth them grievously suspect of sin committed. Moreover, that the said Jane absenteth herself from the society and cohabitation of the said complainant her husband, and hath absented herself these six years past, because the said Sir John enticeth her to absent herself." [Added in another hand: "the man purged himself."]

The priest's position being such as it was, his social and moral relations with his parishioners form one of the most important chapters in the history of medieval civilization. It would overburden this volume to give any reports in full beyond that which I have relegated to my notes; readers who wish to pursue the matter into all its details may find the whole original documents in *The English Historical Review* for 1929 (p. 279) to 1930 (p. 444),[4] and Canon Bannister's article upon them in *The Nineteenth Century* for 1927 (vol. CII, p. 399). There are ten parishes among which it is difficult to assign the palm of bad pre-eminence; Goodrich, Westbury, Monmouth, Kempley, Coddington, Taddington, New Radnor, Ullingwick, Wentnor and Clunbury. The last will be found fully translated in my Appendix[5]; it will remind some readers of the rhyme quoted in *A Shropshire Lad*:

Clunton and Clunbury,
Clungunford and Clun
Are the quietest places
Under the sun.

Goodrich and Westbury show how prejudicial an ill-governed monastery might be to village morality. Three parish priests were presented for incontinence by the sidesmen at these two places, and thirteen laymen, one of whom was an abbey servant. The incontinent monks were nine, including the Prior of Flanford and the Abbot of Flaxley. The latter was "defamatus" with three separate women; so was another of his monks, and another with two. These are by far the two worst parishes in this particular respect; yet others show even more neglect and indiscipline under other heads, and few parishes show anything like a clean bill. In 45 cases the church fabric is presented as more or less ruinous; frequently, the roof is not watertight; as the Herefordshire author of *Piers Plowman* puts it, the clergy "care not, though the rain fall upon their altar". In 22 cases Mass is neglected. In 13 the priest, for the sake of extra fees, sings two Masses daily for different places, in flat defiance of Church law. In 14 churches there is not even a

Breviary, the book indispensable for Matins and Vespers; in 7 other cases service books are missing, and in 2 others "insufficient". In 21 parishes the churchyard was not properly enclosed and protected from beasts. Nine of the priests were presented for usury, 2 for forgery of wills, and 1 for sorcery. In 3 cases even the statutory alms were not given, and in 9 cases the font was not locked, though this was a statutory precaution lest folk should practise witchcraft with that "sanctified" water. This point, upon which medieval visitors always laid great stress, can be verified by any tourist in any church: it is an infallible test of a medieval font. Unless the remains of iron hinge and hasp be found opposite each other on the rim of the font, or at least the scars which betray their removal, then the font is certainly post-Reformation.

But to return to personal reports of these Herefordshire parishioners upon their clergy. We find priests tavern-haunting "and chattering indecently there", celebrating clandestine marriages for small bribes, trading, embezzling, neglecting Mass and other church ceremonies, selling the Sacraments, and in one case even revealing confessions made under the Sacrament of Penance. At Curshope (p. 448) half a dozen lines reveal the state of the parish: "The chancel is defective in roof, walls and windows, by default of the rector. *Item*, they have no Masses or other divine services except only Mass on Sundays, and that at their own expense [by hiring a priest], by default of the rector. *Item,* children are not baptized there, by default of the rector. . . . *Item,* Sir Owen, curate, is incontinent with a certain Gladys, Jokkyn's daughter."

Hereford diocese was, of course, considerably influenced by "wild Wales"; and this report is the worst I know except the almost contemporary visitation of the diocese of Lausanne (i.e. the most civilized part of those districts which are now called Switzerland) which I have analysed in my *Medieval Village*. But we have other evidence as to the extent to which Hereford may be taken as typical. The Oxford Archaeological Society's *Report* of 1925 reproduces in full an episcopal visitation of Oxfordshire in 1520, dealing with 193 parishes. Of these, 37 have a clean bill (19 per cent.). In 58 cases (30 per cent.)

the parson was an absentee: in 15 more the services were defective. In 109 cases (62 per cent.) there was serious disrepair. In 47 waste or embezzlement was reported, and in 35 (10 of which were monastic vicarages) almsgiving was defective.

Nor can we here bring in the Black Dean. Our records for the pre-plague period, though much scantier, tell essentially the same tale. A visitation of Norwich city in 1333 is preserved in the Bodleian Library (Norfolk Rolls, No. 18). It shows 10 parish clergy accused of incontinence. Three of these "purged" themselves, for what that record may be worth; the remaining 7, even when they "purged" themselves of the crime in the present tense, admitted it in the past. The last few paragraphs may be given here. "Robert, nephew to the vicar of Costessey [and apparently himself chaplain or incumbent of St George at the Gates] keeps incontinently, and has kept for 3 years, Beatrice of Brok. He denies this from all time; let him be admitted to purge himself with 4 compurgators. Roger, rector of Drayton, is ill-famed [*notatur*] with the same woman; he confesses the sin and abjured it (Jan. 31st) under penalty of 5*s*. Master Robert of Knapton, chaplain of St Magdalen, is ill-famed with the same woman, and with Margaret of Hampton; this he denies from all time; to purge with 6 compurgators; also with Jane of Whitlingham, this he denies since he was corrected [*word illegible*]; to purge himself with four; purged himself on Jan. 31st. Ralph Pecke, vice-dean of Rockland, is ill-famed with the same Beatrice and with Juliana Methelound of Shropham; he confesses the sin and abjures it Jan. 31st under penalty of 5*s*." These are the worst cases, on the whole; but the cumulative effect of such details can be imagined. In this same visitation, the parishioners present only 19 layfolk for incontinence, as against these 10 clerics; yet Norwich, even with her many churches, cannot possibly have had more than one cleric to every 50 adult layfolk: more probably one to 100. Therefore, though it is likely that many lay sinners escaped presentment through their comparative obscurity, yet the fact that the defamed clerics should have been so incomparably more numerous, in proportion, cannot fail to have produced its effect. The Bodleian Library possesses also a visitation of a Norfolk archdeaconry in 1499 (M.S. Tanner, 100, fol. 56ff.). There, among the 73 accusations of incontinence, 15 were against the clergy. In the Ripon Chapter Acts, to take the most favourable estimate, the numbers run 126-24. A visitation of 1498 (Lambeth, *Reg. Morton*, fol. 75ff.) gives 48-9. On the aggregate of these four records, therefore, we have 58 clergy to 251 laity, or 23.5 per cent. Yet the clergy cannot have formed more than 2 per cent. of the total population of these districts: probably a good deal less.

Here, again, are one or two Devonshire cases. At Clyst Honiton, in 1301, the parishioners reported their "capellanus" as honest and pious; but he is now past work. "The chancel is so ruinous that Mass cannot be said at the high altar; the service books are imperfect; there is no chalice, and all other appurtenances of the church may be said to be insufficient." In 1330, King Log has been replaced at Clyst Honiton by King Stork. The present chaplain is defamed with three different women, one of whom "he keepeth and hath long kept, as it is said", while another is the wife of one of the sidesmen. A long list of church appurtenances, including the Missal, are reported as "insufficient". At Dawlish (1301) one of the two chaplains "hath kept his concubine for ten years and more, or longer still; and, though often corrected on that account, he incorrigibly persists". At St Marychurch (1301) there is no pyx for the Eucharist, and no chalice for bearing it to the sick. The vicar is suspected of embezzling part of a legacy for the building-fund. "The sidesmen say that the said vicar puts all sorts of beasts into the churchyard, whereby it is evilly trodden down and foully defiled. Item, he appropriates the trees in the churchyard that are blown down, and uses them for his own buildings. *Item*, he causes his malt [*or*, his brewing] to be prepared in the church, and stores his corn and other things therein; whereby his servants, in their exits and their entrances, open the door, and at time of tempest the wind comes in and is wont to uncover the church [*discooperire*—loosen the tiles or shingles?]. He preacheth well and exercises his office laudably in all things when he is present; but he often absents himself and stays at Moreton-Hampstead, sometimes for 15 days, sometimes for 8, so that they have no chaplain, except when Sir Walter the archdeacon's chaplain is present, or when they beseech another to come from elsewhere." Though these full reports deal only with comparatively few Devonshire churches (those appropriated to the dean and chapter), yet they are eloquent of neglect and disrepair. Of the service books, 29 volumes are condemned as indifferent, 54 more as positively bad, and 19 as missing. The pyx itself, in 13 cases, had no lock; in two others it was otherwise deficient, and in 3 cases it was altogether missing (in one of these, stolen). Roofs out of repair were 13, often very badly: 12 chancels were condemned for the same reason, and in 4 cases the whole church. The statutory image or reredos over the high altar was bad in 5 cases, and altogether wanting in 12. The reports on vestments and other church furniture were in proportion.[6] The same tale is told in a visitation of Totnes archdeaconry (1346) which I edited textually in vol. XXVI (1911) of *The English Historical Review*.

In face of these records, who can reject Langland's picture of the clergy as mere slander, or see nothing but sectarian malice when Wyclif writes indignantly: "[The clergy] haunten tauernes out of all mesure and stiren lewid men to dronkenesse, ydelnesse and cursed swerynge and chydynge and fighttynge. . . . Thei fallen to nyse pleies [foolish games], at tables, chess and hasard, and beten the stretis, and sitten at the tauerne til thei han lost here witt, and than chiden and stryuen and fighten sumtyme, and sumtyme neither have eighe ne tonge ne hond ne foot to helpe hem self for dronkenesse."

15. THE FLOCK (1)

Sicut populus, sic sacerdos—" As the priest is, so are the people ". Those words of Isaiah were echoed from mouth to mouth, throughout our period, by men who were seriously concerned for the religion and morals of their own day, and who often saw no hope but in the Second Coming of Christ. Certainly we must not lend ourselves to the injustice of blaming our forefathers wherever they aimed high, and attempted to take the Kingdom of God with violence. But we should have had all the best of those men upon one side in the effort to see the past exactly as it was, and thus to estimate its true relations to the present.

St Thomas More, in reply to the outspoken criticisms of the lawyer St Germain, pointed out with some real truth that these, by implication, struck at the laity also, since it is from the laity that clerics are recruited, and a stream cannot rise above its source. If medieval society had been more advanced in civilization, it would have demanded, and would have got, a better clergy. It is good for us to-day to remember this, and not to ignore the fact that our criticism of Christianity and its professional exponents is necessarily to some extent a criticism of our own time and our own selves. Let us bear this in mind with regard to the village parson, present and past in all ages. Until those who reject his creed as no longer credible, and who take no stock of his advice on morals or politics, can find similar points of crystallization in town and country, around which beneficent impulses and societies will naturally group themselves, and in communion with which, at frequent meetings, all classes can assemble naturally and habitually to confess their brotherhood and to mingle their ideal aspirations—until Secularism can construct something of this kind, the Church will remain, what with all its shortcomings it always has been, the chief school of moral co-operation. We may emphasize this consideration the more unhesitatingly, because it raises us from mere negative criticism to positive effort, from destructive rivalry to St Paul's "covet ye the best gifts". The faith of the Christian, and the Agnostic's resolve to follow Truth alone, so far as he can apprehend it, are alike satisfied in the mutual promise: "Show me something better, and I will embrace that."

In that spirit, then, let us pass on from the priests to the people. Here, again, we may take those parochial visitations for our main text, and illustrate them by parallel evidence.

The priest, with the hierarchy at his back, was in theory almost everything to his people. It is still imperfectly realized that the extreme domination over men's morals, and sometimes over their smallest actions, which we think of as the main characteristic of Puritanism in the sixteenth and seventeenth centuries, was a direct inheritance from the Middle Ages. The medieval theory of usury may be taken as an instance. This (as apart from men's practice) was so impossibly strict, even when modified by the later schoolmen, that the Papacy of the nineteenth century finally forbade confessors to trouble their penitents with questions about so difficult a matter. The greatest saints often proclaimed an indifference to painting and sculpture and music, or even a dislike and suspicion, from which many of the later "Puritans" were quite free. As we shall see presently, that which is popularly called "Calvinism" has its roots in the medieval Scholastics. Again, it was practically taken for granted that the majority of mankind would go to hell; upon that point there was greater unanimity among orthodox theologians than on any of those which divide the Roman Church of to-day from other Christian bodies.*

* One of the heretical propositions for which Raymund Lull was condemned in the fourteenth century runs thus: "God hath such love for His people that almost all folk in the world shall be saved; for, if more were damned than saved, Christ's mercy would be without great charity" (Eymericus, *Directorium Inquisitorum*, pars II, quaest. ix). Long after the Reformation, Malebranche takes it as an admitted fact. One of his characters argues: "But if you are so charmed with the idea that God acts solely in pure kindness to men, how comes it that

Laughter and dancing and play, as we have already seen, were often reprobated : against dancing, the orthodox were almost as unanimous as they were in favour of hell-chances. The best minds often discouraged elaborate Church ritual : St Francis's biographer tells how an otherwise excellent friar was damned everlastingly for his share in the construction of that splendid basilica which still stands in honour of the saint's bones at Assisi.[1] The constant medieval wars resulted in frequent destruction or mutilation of sacred buildings : and even deliberate vandalism was not unknown. The Puritans of our English Reformation owe their unsavoury reputation less to their actual tenets than to their honest, but mistaken and blundering, attempt to enforce those ideals. The Covenant for which they fought was essentially the Covenant drawn up by medieval orthodoxy; but they blundered over the Sanctions. All this I have argued at such length in my *Ten Medieval Studies* and the first volume of *Five Centuries of Religion* (Appendix 23) that I may be excused from repeating it here. That journalistic parrot-cry of our own day, " Merrie England " is (it must be repeated here) a phrase almost unknown to the Middle Ages. As misused at present, it belongs to the mentality which mocks our countryside with *Ye Olde Inne* and *Ye Olde Shoppe.*

The Goodrich, Westbury, Clunbury cases have shown us how the bishop or archdeacon reckoned with the flock—and, directly or by implication, with their pastor—in matters of parish finance. In these 281 parishes, no less than 109 cases of misapplication or embezzlement of funds were reported. The other main subjects of inquisition were unchastity, usury, witchcraft, quarrelsomeness, churchgoing and Sabbatarianism. *Non venit ad ecclesiam*—he cometh not to church— is reported in 46 cases. In 31 more, a parishioner is denounced for Sabbath-breaking : he is *communis operator* on Sundays or

---

there will be twenty times, or a hundred times more damned than saved?" (*Entretiens sur la métaphysique*, 1688, ent. 9, q. iii; *Œuvres*, ed. Simon, 1846, vol. 1, p. 194.)

Holy-Days, and must therefore be punished unless he redeems himself by repentance and promise of amendment.

Here is an important subject ordinarily ignored or distorted by social historians. So far is Sabbatarianism from being a later English and Puritan invention, that it is part of a very early and widespread Christian tradition, Catholic in a far truer sense than many other observances which claim that title.[2] Tertullian [220] alludes to a Sunday rest; and Constantine I decreed it for all his subjects. Two councils, at least, prescribed that the faithful should spend all day in prayer, except, of course, for meals. In about A.D. 590, a sabbatarian letter appears, claiming to have been written by Christ and to have fallen from heaven: this reappears at intervals; at Cologne, it was reprinted even as late as 1648. Theodore of Tarsus, who became Archbishop of Canterbury in 669, "assures us that his fellow-Greeks would neither sail nor ride (except to church) or bake or bathe or write any unnecessary letters on Sunday". A Spanish council, in 1050, forbade all travelling except in cases of necessity: so did a version of the Christ-Letter written in Germany about the same time. And, though England was the scene of a great sabbatarian revival about the year 1200, the impetus for this came from Rome.[3] Roger of Hoveden, followed by Matthew Paris and Walter of Coventry, tells the old story of this miraculous letter; how it fell from heaven upon the altar at Jerusalem, straight from Christ Himself, with terrible threats against Sabbath-breakers.* A brief excerpt from its commands and its causes may suffice. "It is My will that, from noon [or, perhaps, 3 p.m.] on Saturday to sunrise on Monday no man do any work, unless it be good, and that whosoever doeth work shall make amends by penance." In case of continued disobedience: "I will send upon you beasts with heads like lions and hair like women and tails like camels; beasts so hungry that they shall devour your flesh and ye shall desire to flee to the

* We may use this word *Sabbath* safely; for the later Middle Ages habitually summarized the 4th Commandment in two words *Sabbata sanctifices.* Abailard, in his famous hymn, speaks of the blessed in heaven as "sabbatizing" to eternity: *perpes laetitia sabbatizantium.*

tombs of the dead and hide yourselves there for fear of them. . . . Ye shall perish like Sodom and Gomorrah. . . . I will send upon you worse beasts, which shall devour the breasts of your women." This letter, say the chroniclers, so impressed Innocent III that "he forthwith ordained preachers who went to divers parts of the world and preached everywhere according to the tenour of this letter, the Lord working with them and confirming the word with signs following". The missionary to England was Eustache, Abbot of St-Germer-de-Fly or Flai, among whose many miracles was one in exact accordance with the Heavenly Letter. A Norfolk woman, despising the warnings of the man of God, set out to wash linen one Saturday afternoon. A man of imposing figure warned her: but she persisted, "pleading her poverty, saying that she had hitherto earned a miserable livelihood by this kind of work and that, if she ceased from her accustomed labour, she would be in peril of starvation". The heavenly monitor disappeared; but the perverse female "hastened more busily than before to wash her linen and hang it to dry in the sun. But God's vengeance was not withheld; for straightway a beast like a sucking-pig, of coal-black hue, fixed upon the woman's left breast and could not be torn away; nay, sucking assiduously and drawing her blood, it had soon consumed almost her whole body." With the aid of such miracles, Eustache reaped a rich harvest of conversions. "He so strictly forbade Sunday fairs and markets that nearly all those which had customarily been held on Sundays throughout England were now fixed for some week-day; and thus the people spent their Sundays on divine service alone, and altogether abdicated all servile labour. Yet, in process of time, many returned like dogs to their vomit."* True, Church Councils went on to forbid Sunday markets: but it is characteristic of the medieval gulf between law and practice that the Prior of Walsingham habitually held market on Saturday and Sunday, finding this a very lucrative arrangement.[4]

* Another of his missionary themes was to "admonish rectors and priests, with their parishioners, to keep a light always burning before the Eucharist"; a custom which was not made general in Switzerland until two centuries later.

The fifteenth-century canonist Lyndwood writes: "Canon Law tells us that we must do nothing on the Lord's Day except to spend our time on God. No work is done on that holy day, but it is spent exclusively in hymns and psalms and spiritual songs." We must abstain from all *opera servilia;* i.e. works which primarily benefit the body, as distinguished from *opera liberalia,* pious and intellectual work. Thus field-work is explicitly forbidden, and markets, and pleas in court, except in cases of necessity. In Lyndwood's judgment: "The man who doth such work sinneth mortally, if by reason of such work he knowingly omits that which pertaineth to God's worship, and whereunto he is bound."[5] Charitable works, on the other hand, though wrought with our hands, are lawful, as when Christ permitted men to carry the sick man on his couch for healing.

Naturally, therefore, in the Durham records, we find a series of sabbatarian punishments.[6] In 1435, seven men and one woman of Hesilden are presented for "working on Sundays and holy-days". In 1441, "John Huchonson of South Shirburn worked with three carts on the day of the Decollation of St John Baptist. [The judgment is] suspen[ded]." In 1443 two women "are accused of having mown on the feast of dedication of St Oswald's Church; and they have to purge themselves with the 6th hand of honourable women, their neighbours".† In 1448 John Robinson, "walker" (i.e. fuller) is accused that he violated the Sabbath [*diem Sabbati*] in that he laboured at the fuller's art on the day of the Lord's Epiphany. He confesseth, and hath submitted himself to correction; and it is enjoined upon him that he do not so in future under pain of *6s. 8d.*" In 1450 it is alleged against James Dennant "that he was at the mill, with his cloths to be fulled, on the day of the Lord's Ascension. He confesseth, and for this he hath to go before the procession on three Sundays in his shirt and drawers, after the fashion of a penitent, and that he abstain henceforth under pain of 10*s.*, to be applied to the Lord Prior's almoner." In 1450, a woman is condemned

† That is, they must each find five women to swear belief in her innocence. Her own hand made the sixth.

for a similar offence "to go before the procession for two Sundays after the fashion of a penitent". Next year, two women confessed to washing linen on St Mary Magdalene's day: "they are to have two fustigations with a hank of linen yarn." In that same year, at Billigham: "William Dalby practiseth servile work almost habitually, and keepeth shop outside the churchyard on holy-days and on Holy Cross Day. He had two women winnowing corn at the time of Matins." Four others commonly fish for salmon on Sundays and holy-days. Two tailors and a mower are presented, and five in an adjacent hamlet "leave their parish church to frequent markets on Sundays in Lent". The sentences on that batch are not recorded; but two others, who confessed to mowing a meadow on St Oswald's Day, "have to go before the procession, with four fustigations around, and each having in his hands a bundle of hay [*botell feni*], and that they do no such work henceforth under pain of 10*s*." A woman "violated St Mark's day by washing her garments. She confesseth, and hath for her sin two days before the procession, bearing her shift in her hand, under pain of 6*s*. 8*d*. [for repetition of the offence]." In 1455, a man is accused of absence from church on Sundays and holy-days: another, for not having received Holy Communion since he has been in the parish. In 1436 Adam Gray of Acle "cometh not to his parish church on holy-days, as was enjoined upon him at the last visitation under pain of 4*d*. for every time, in default of impediment or lawful excuse. He confesseth; therefore he is at the judge's mercy; and again he was warned to come to church on Sundays under the same penalty, to wit, 4*d*., and on other holy-days on pain of 2*d*. every time, to be applied to the fabric fund of Durham Cathedral." So, again, a great Archbishop of Rouen twice records in his diary [1250] how, finding peasants working on Sunday, he punished them. Erasmus (as we shall see in Chapter LI) exposed the folly of ecclesiastics who made it a crime for a cobbler to do a little work on the holy-days, yet who shut their eyes to far more serious infractions of divine and moral law. In his *Praise of Folly* he pillories those who dispute "whether it is a smaller crime to kill a thousand men than to mend a beggar's shoe on Sunday".

Though sensible priests made sensible allowance (this is well brought out by Fr Thurston, with a little natural exaggeration), and though the multitude very commonly went their own way without too strict attention to the priests, it was always possible to suffer in the Middle Ages from rigid Sabbatarians.

Let us now pass on to the question of medieval religious education.

Of the Bible, the ordinary man knew only a few stories like that of Adam and Eve, and a little of the Gospels. It has been claimed that the church walls were his Bible; but wall-paintings, statues, and stained glass told far more of the saints' legends than of Bible history. I have dealt fully with this subject in *Art and the Reformation.* The Knight of La Tour-Landry's book, written for the education of his daughters, became a classic: there are two medieval translations of it into English. He tells us that he composed it with the help of two priests, and two clerks of his household. For the girls' edification, he tells the story of Ruth at length: it is a pretty story, but has no contact whatever with the actual Bible narrative except in the heroine's name and the fact that she was a widow. Many such instances might be quoted. Chaucer's Clerk Nicolas knows that the Carpenter will recognize the most un-Biblical of all the stories that had gathered around Noah. *Gesta Romanorum* was one of the most approved among the many manuals for preachers. Its fifteenth-century English translator quotes, as from the Gospels, texts from Revelation, Ezekiel, and Canticles. He attributes to St Paul a text from Job. Genesis is confused with the Psalms, Isaiah with St James, and scraps of the Fathers are palmed off as Bible texts. St Thomas More tells how a lady of his time was shocked to discover that Mary was a Jewess: she confessed that, thenceforward, she would love her the less all her life long. The Dominican Étienne de Bourbon, one of the most prominent of thirteenth-century heresy hunters, confesses frankly that one of the main characteristics of these men was their Bible knowledge, even among their poor, in contrast (he says) to the shameful ignorance of the orthodox. The result was that, gradually, Bible knowledge on the part of any but a cleric or a great person aroused almost as definite suspicions of heresy as were aroused by the objection to profane oaths: Chaucer's Shipman is one of our many witnesses on that point. If any complete translation of the Bible into English was ever made before Chaucer's day (which is more than doubtful) it never became public in any real sense: the task was left to Wyclif or his followers. A few earnest clerics, like the author of *Dives and Pauper,* were shocked at this policy. The author, complaining that "now men say that there should no lewd folk entermit them of God's law nor of the gospel nor of holy writ, neither to conne it nor to teach it", continues: "This is a foul error and full perilous to man's soul."[7] Archbishop Arundel's notorious decree of 1407, by which the making or the use of translations unlicensed by the hierarchy was forbidden under the ultimate penalty of burning alive, amounted practically to a heretication of Bible knowledge. For, as St Thomas More confessed even in his defence of the Church, it was most regrettable that, while unlicensed translations were thus forbidden, no licensed versions were made. No Roman Catholic version of the New Testament in English was printed until 1562; and 27 years elapsed before this was followed by the Old Testament. In 1870, Lord Acton wrote from Rome: "Here you may find a lottery-book in almost every house, but never a New Testament, and extremely seldom any religious book at all."[8] Facts of this kind must necessarily be emphasized in the face of persistent modern falsifications which have no excuse but the slender plea of ignorance. Cardinal Gasquet is still quoted as an authority for the admirable religious education of the past; and *The Catholic Times* refers his readers to this "age when there would have been no difficulties over an Education Bill; a time when the Church had it all its own way, and yet the Bible was taught . . . when such immense portions of Scripture were committed to memory, and that by Catholics".

We find no trace in the Middle Ages of anything resembling the modern Sunday-school system. No doubt individual priests sometimes taught individual children, and one in a thousand like St Gilbert of Sempringham, might be a most zealous missionary in his own village. But many indications go to support Étienne de Bourbon's complaint that the average orthodox parent did not even teach the Lord's Prayer to his family or servants. Haymo of Hythe, Bishop of Rochester in the fourteenth century, founded an almshouse not for the very poor, but expressly for middle-class folk of decayed fortunes. He made it a primary condition that the candidate should know the Lord's Prayer, the Ave, and the Apostles' Creed. We have seen how, at the Reformation, some priests were found who could not repeat the Lord's Prayer, nor name its author.

16. THE FLOCK (2)

Church behaviour was childlike in both directions: it had the child's happy familiarity and, sometimes, the child's embarrassing lack of restraint. Even unwilling Protestants have often admired, in Continental churches, not only the figures constantly flitting to and fro for private prayer, but the engaging bonhomie with which the women, in especial, make themselves at home in the Father's House; one sitting at the sermon with her basket full of cabbages from the market on the floor at her feet: another with the company of her pet dog. The earliest mention of a private pew is Italian, of about 1200. In England, not later than 1320, the Lady de Dalton had her private pew, and "of her humility" did not allow her servants to eject the stranger who was found kneeling in prayer there. In some of our thirteenth-century churches a stone bench runs all round the walls; but the Friar Salimbene, in 1248, found Louis IX of France, with his retinue, sitting on the ground in a wayside village church to which they had repaired for prayer. Hence the nave lent itself to that abusive use which we have seen at St Marychurch in Devon, and which meets us in many other records; the storing of corn, barrels, and similar unecclesiastical furniture. Many indications show that talk at divine service was rather normal than exceptional. The sermons of Berthold v. Regensburg and St Bernardino of Siena testify to this; cathedral canons, as we have seen, had statutory permission to converse during service, as far as to the third or fourth stall away. Chaucer's Host describes his wife's fury if any rival lady competed with her in priority for the Kiss of Peace at Mass: hence arose vendettas which, he intimates, might even end some day in bloodshed. Such bloodshed, official documents assure us, did not infrequently result from quarrels between parishes in the solemn cathedral processions, the struggle for precedence ending in a fight with banner-poles. Bishop Quivil of Exeter solemnly warned his diocese against the "grave scandal in the churches, and frequent hindrances to divine service" generated by the scrambling of parishioners for seats at Mass. The Knight of La Tour-Landry warns his daughters: "Some clerks maintain that none should speak no manner thing whiles they be at Mass, and in especial [while the priest readeth] the Gospel." He tells us of a case when there was such "chattering, laughing, jangling and jesting aloud", that the priest "smote his hand on the book to make them hold their peace; but there were some that did not".[1] At King's College, Cambridge, a special home of orthodoxy in the fifteenth century, the royal founder prescribed by statute that, in chapel, the students should not "in any wise make murmurs, babblings, scoffing, laughter, confabulations or indiscreet noises, lest, through their inordinate tumult and the various sounds of voices and other talk among themselves, the devotion and exercise of those singing psalms in the choir be in any wise impeded". The writer of *Dives and Pauper*, in Chaucer's day, thinks that the glories of architecture and church furniture are signs less of devotion than of "pomp and pride of this world, to have a name and worship thereby in the country . . . or else by sly covetise of men of Holy Church". "For" (he argues) "the people nowadays is full undevout to God and to Holy Church, and they love but little men of Holy Church, and they ben loth to come in Holy Church when they be bound to come thither, and full loth to hear God's service. Late they come and soon they go away. If they be there a little while, them thinketh full long. They have liever go to the tavern than to Holy Church. Liever to hear a song of Robin Hood or of some ribaldry, than for to hear Mass or Matins or any other of God's service or any word of God. And since the people hath so little devotion to God and to Holy Church, I cannot see that they do such cost in Holy Church for devotion nor for the love of God. For they despise God day and night with their evil and wicked living and their wicked thewys [manners]."[2] St Bernardino of Siena [1440] puts it more pithily still: folk come in late to Mass, and hasten out the moment after the Elevation of the Host, "as though they had seen not Christ, but the Devil".

Kings and magistrates, as we shall see, might turn the hour and place of Mass into a regular business office; and even exceptionally pious bishops might do this on occasion. Ordinary folk had only a vague inkling of the service itself, for the Mass was an *opus operatum*, independently of the hearer. Berthold of Regensburg, that Franciscan whom Roger Bacon extols as the greatest mission preacher of his time, says in one of his sermons: "It irks some to stand decently for a short hour in church, while God is being served with singing or reading; they laugh and chatter as if they were at a fair. . . . And ye women, ye never give your tongues rest from useless talk! One tells the other how glad the maidservant is to sleep, and how loth to work; another tells of her husband; a third complains that her children are troublesome and sickly!" At this a cry of expostulation rises from the audience: "Yea, Brother Berthold, but we understand not the Mass, and therefore can we not pray as we had need, nor may we feel such devotion as if we understood the Mass. The sermon indeed we can follow word by word, but not the Mass; we know not what is being sung or read, we cannot comprehend it." St Thomas More also tells us how little the congregation understood the Mass. The *Lay Folk's Mass-book* was composed by Dan Jeremy, a cleric, Norman or English, who wrote in French about 1150, for readers of the upper class. It was translated into English about 1300, and repeated in other versions down to the fifteenth century. In this book, as in those commonly used at Mass on the Continent nowadays, "the devotions are not a translation from the Missal", except in four places. "There is a version of the Apostles' Creed instead of the Nicene Creed." Moreover, that version itself is falsified at one point in favour of the doctrine of Transubstantiation. The last section begins:

> *Well I trow in the Holigoste*
> *And Holi Kirk that is so good;*
> *And so I trow that Housel is* [*the consecrated Host*
> *Both flesh and blood.*[3]

Again, bishops and disciplinarians struggled, with indifferent success, to put down the irreverences of dancing, theatrical performances, and markets (with their attendant quarrels and occasional bloodshed) in churches and churchyards. The late Cardinal Gasquet, in his attempt to minimize the treatment of churchyards, speaks of these customs as only "growing" in the latter part of the fourteenth century, and as first mentioned in a constitution of 1367. This statement is made in favour of his theory that the later medieval Church was an innocent victim of the Black Death. But, in fact, that constitution of 1367, in which Archbishop Thoresby fulminates against holding markets on Sundays in churchyards *or in churches* (these italics mark another of the Cardinal's suppressions), is not the first but nearly the last of its kind. Between 1229 and 1367 there are eleven such episcopal injunctions recorded; while from that date to the Reformation there seems to be only one. Bishop after bishop had thundered in vain, long before the Black Death, against those who "turned the house of prayer into a den of thieves"; and, if such anathemas grow rarer in the century before the Reformation, it is probably only because a large number of prelates were then non-resident, and the bonds of discipline were notoriously relaxed. Gasquet's picture is further falsified by the omission from his quotation, without the least warning, of Quivil's complaints of the scandal caused by Mass-scrambling. Moreover, he silently ignores 16 other clauses of that bishop's decrees which reveal parochial scandals scarcely less grave: for instance, the gross superstitions which in Exeter diocese, as in some others, led ignorant folk to "abhor" one of the pillars of medieval theology, the Sacrament of Extreme Unction. Again, the rite of Confirmation was disgracefully neglected by the bishops: it was performed only sporadically as they journeyed (when indeed they did so) through their dioceses. Archbishop Pecham [1280] complains of the "numberless people, grown old in evil days, who had not yet received the grace of Confirmation"; and we have similar evidence for Continental countries. Sacchetti, whom Chaucer might have met in Italy, speaks of "a good many" who did not even feel certain that they had been baptized, and consoles them with the assurance that God would take their faith as equivalent to the deed. Gascoigne says that many children died unbaptized through the fault of the monastic clergy.

Preaching was another weak point of the medieval Church. Such preaching as was done in all these thousands of English parishes, after the middle of the thirteenth century, was mainly performed by a few scores of itinerant friars.[4] Originally, it was only bishops who normally preached; others did so, very occasionally: sometimes never. Confessions, again, could not be effectually heard and dealt with but by some physician of souls far better technically instructed than the ordinary parochial clergy, as described by their orthodox contemporaries. It is almost common form for disciplinarians to complain that the average rector or vicar was quite unable (in Biblical language) "to discern leprosy from leprosy": i.e. to deal with really difficult cases. This defect, with that of preaching, was to some extent remedied by the friars in the thirteenth century: but, when these in their turn lost their savour, England possessed two sets of soul-physicians lending themselves almost equally to criticism. Chaucer's infallible eye caught both sides of this truth. His friar boasts his own preaching against that of the parish priest, and claims quite truly to have received from the Papacy powers of confession and absolution far beyond those of his rival. On the other hand, we all know how far Chaucer felt that this particular man of God had the true God behind him.

What Chaucer felt was echoed more plainly and fully in *Piers Plowman,* and was expressed to some extent even by a broad-minded friar of that age, the author of *Dives and Pauper*. For the friar of this day was already turned to conservatism; he was even readier than his older rivals to persecute all innovators.[5] The author writes: "Also men of Holy Church slay men and women ghostly of God's word and of good teaching. . . . Since that God's word is life and salvation of man's soul, all those that let God's word, and let them that have authority of God and by order take to preach and teach, that they may not preach and teach God's word and God's law, they be manslayers ghostly, and guilty of as many souls as perish and die ghostly by such lettyng of God's word; and namely these proud covetous prelates and curates that neither can teach nor will teach, nor suffer others that can and will. . . . As Saint Austen saith, God's word ought to be worshipped as much as Christ's Body. . . . There the Gloss sheweth, that it is more profitable to hear God's word in preaching, than to hear any Mass; and rather a man should forbear his Mass than his sermon. For by preaching folk be stirred to contrition and to forsake sin and the fiend, and to love God and goodness and be illumined to know their God and virtues from vices, truth from falsehood, and to forsake errors and heresies. By the Mass be they not so; but if they come to Mass in sin, they go away in sin; and shrews they come, and shrews they wend." It will be noted how boldly this thinker rejects the cruder forms of the *opus operatum* doctrine, and how he appeals to the [pseudo]-Augustinian text, enshrined in Canon Law, against the excessive importance attached to mere attendance at Mass. A far greater friar, St Bernardino of Siena himself, is even more emphatic in the same sense.[6]

So, again, we learn from the Dominican Minister-General, Humbert de Romans. In his *Book on the Preparation of Sermons* he reminds the young preacher "that men of exalted position are rarely wont to hear sermons. . . . Note also that poor folk come seldom to church, seldom to sermons."[7] Important as this subject is, it need not be laboured further in face of the evidence now accessible in Dr Owst's two learned and attractive volumes. It will suffice here to give two characteristic extracts from these.[8] Dr Owst is describing the sermon: "How, then, will our audience behave? Whether within the sacred precincts or upon the public square, in its motley character, it will probably reflect most of the great feudal class distinctions and class prejudices which seem to run deeper in medieval flesh and blood than even differences of nationality. Some of the portraits sketched in our manuscripts are wonderfully realistic and amusing. The lord and lady of the manor with their circle will probably be present. They have a bad habit of sleeping late in those too cosy new-fangled bedrooms of theirs. By the time my lady has completed her extravagant toilet, and sets out churchwards with her spouse, the parson and all the people of the parish are weary and exasperated with waiting for them."* Again: "Bishop Brunton makes it clear that then, even as now, men were in a minority, and the churches were attended mainly by the womenfolk. The sexes are probably separated,† the latter 'sitten all a rewe', as we have seen, and with good reason. For strange things are done in churches and strange folk go there. Gower's lover, like Dante, is amongst those 'in chirches and in minstres eke, That gon the women for to seke'; harmless enough, in his case, it is true. But the 'lechour' may go, too, as the preacher describes."‡

One word must be added concerning the Sacrament of Penance. The evidence is not in favour of its beneficent effect, on the whole. Dr H. C. Lea's exhaustive study in his *History of Confession and Indulgences* is almost as conclusive as his other volumes. The testimony of the Hereford visitation, and others of the kind, is definitely unfavourable to the laity. But we must bear in mind that the medieval parishioner usually confessed only once a year, before his or her Easter Communion. And the complaints of the clergy themselves, supported by the testimony of neighbours at the parochial visitations, and even to some extent by medical evidence, give us no reason to suppose that the pre-Reformation village or town was more moral than that of to-day. St Antonino, Archbishop of Florence, was reputed to have heard more confessions than any other of his day, a generation after Chaucer. His was perhaps the most civilized corner of Europe, almost under the shadow of the Seat of the Apostles. In reading him, we have only to discount the bitterness of a disciplinarian and mission preacher who saw disappointingly little fruit from his labours, and who, like all missioners from Elijah and John Baptist to Wesley, found

* The Knight of La Tour-Landry also shows how the common folk were sometimes kept waiting at Mass for the squirearchy. It was the great folk alone, also, who might sit with the clergy in the chancel. (G.G.C.)

† The Hereford visitations show this plainly in one church. (G.G.C.)

‡ Italian tales, especially, show us amorous young men frequenting church in order to ogle the ladies, as in the Introduction to the *Decameron*. (G.G.C.)

average humanity no very malleable stuff. He writes concerning the Tuscan peasants of the fifteenth century: "In the churches themselves they sometimes dance and leap and sing with women. On holy-days they spend little time on divine service or hearing of the whole Mass, but in games, or in taverns and in contentions at the church doors. They blaspheme God and His saints on slender provocation. They are filled with lies and perjuries: of fornication, and of worse sins still, they make no conscience. Very many of them do not confess once a year, and far fewer are those who take the Communion, under the false belief that they need not communicate except when they grow old or are sick unto death. They do little to instruct their families in the manner of faithful folk. They use enchantments for themselves and for their beasts. Of God, or their own soul's health, they think not at all. And, being commonly ignorant, and caring little for their own souls or for keeping God's commandments, which they know not, this it is which helps to bring them along the broad way leading to destruction, to wit, their ignorance of their own vices and the carelessness and evil conscience of their parish-priests, who, caring not for the flock committed unto them, but only for their wool and their milk, do not instruct them through preaching and the confessional, or by private admonitions, but walk in the same errors as their flocks, following their corrupt ways and not correcting them for their faults; whereby it cometh to pass that, living like beasts, they sometimes die the death of a beast."[9] His contemporary, St Bernardino of Siena, writes in equal fire of indignation: men often "believe in nothing higher than the roof of their own house"; and this is directly traceable to "the evil lives of the Religious [i.e. monks, friars, and nuns] and of the priests".[10]

We shall see later how, under Henry VIII, the Spanish envoy could report from London to his master: "Nearly all the people here hate the priests." For nearly a thousand years before this, the maxim had been current in Church Law that "the laity are thoroughly inimical to the clergy"; Boniface VIII took that sentence as the text for his famous bull *Clericis Laicos*. The priest was too often then such as Lina Duff-

Gordon describes in her *Home Life in Italy*; the man in black who takes toll of the parish and who is seldom seen in the house until he brings with him the Last Unction, and the shadow of death. *Dives and Pauper* alludes to the medieval superstition that it was ill-omened to meet a priest by the way. "Some man hadde levyr to mete with a [toad] or a frogge in the way than with a knight or a squier or with any man of Religion or of Holy Church; for than they say and believe that they shal have gold." Again, it is unlucky to hunt with a priest; or, again, if men meet "a man of Holy Churche or of Religion, and namely with a frere" in the road, "they will leave him on their left hand".[11] Two centuries earlier, Cardinal Jacques de Vitry had testified to a similar superstition. "I have seen how, in certain parts, when men met a priest, they crossed themselves at once, saying that it is an evil omen to meet with a priest. Nay, I have learned for certain that in a French village, seeing that many died on all hands, they said one to another 'This plague and mortality can never cease unless, before burying any corpse, we cast our priest into the same grave.' So it came to pass that, when the priest came to the grave to bury a dead parishioner, then the peasants and women, with one accord, seized upon him in his holy vestments and cast him into the pit. These are devilish inventions and illusions of demons."[12]

It must be added that Church life was still more irregular in Wales, Scotland, and Ireland than in England. I have given some detailed evidence for this in my *Scottish Abbeys*; but readers may easily verify it for themselves by taking, at random, any volume of the Calendar of Papal Letters.

There was a dualism in our ancestors' ordinary religion which comes out well in Froissart, a witness almost as valuable for England as for France, and all the more trustworthy when his evidence is merely incidental; merely an "aside" from a speaker mainly intent upon something else. He shows us a curious mixture of reverence and disrespect. "In our faith", he writes, "there ought to be no variation; for, as there is one God in heaven, so also there ought to be but one God on earth." Again, he disapproved the anticlerical policy of Gian

Galeazzo Visconti: "He held the error and opinion of his father that was, how one should neither honour nor worship God. He took from abbeys and priories much of their revenues and took them to himself. . . . These lords in their days lived like popes: they did great despites in their time to men of Holy Church: they set nothing by the pope's curse, and specially after the Schism began and that there was two popes; that the one cursed, the other assoiled." Yet when we look carefully into some of Froissart's other pages, we may find certain significant tales and side-remarks for which he evidently counted on sympathy from his aristocratic audience. The tragedy of the unpopular minister Bétisac shows how easily the Inquisition could be used by a political party in a purely political quarrel; it throws much light on the story of Joan of Arc. Again, Froissart is perfectly aware that, though much could be pleaded in his day, as in our own time, in favour of an established and endowed Church, yet establishment and endowment can never be quite compatible with religious freedom in the strictest sense. In 1399, the most Christian King of Aragon "saw well the Pope's letters, but he made no force of them, and said to his council that were about him . . . 'Let the clergy alone; for, if they purpose to live, the prelates must obey the great lords under whom their rents and revenues are.'" Again, he shows us how little the King of England cared for the excommunication even of an undoubted Pope. The Great Schism he traces to the personal fears of the cardinals, intimidated by the Roman populace, "for they had rather 'a died confessors than martyrs". He sees clearly enough the seamy side of the Indulgence system. When the disbanded soldiers, the "Companies", were wasting France, "even as the Vandals had done in times of old", then Innocent VI offered the Plenary Indulgence of a crusader—complete "pardon from penalty and guilt" up to date—to "all those that would take on them his croisey, and that would abandon their bodies willingly to destroy these evil people and their companions". The Cardinal Bishop of Ostia "retained all manner of soldiers, such as would save their souls in attaining to these said pardons, but they should have none other wages; wherefore that journey [expedition] brake, for every man departed, some into Lombardy, some to their own countries, and some went to the said evil Company, so that daily they increased ". One day he found himself talking with " a squire of England, called Henry Christead, an honest man and wise ", who had been much in Ireland and who explained that Richard II had now subdued that country " by treaty and by the grace of God ". To which our good Canon Froissart replied : " Indeed the grace of God is good; who-so can have it, it is much worth; but it is seen nowadays that earthly princes getteth little without it be by puissance."[13]

17. THE SILVER LINING

Let us turn now to the other side of the ledger. With all these undeniable failings, I cannot doubt that the Church was, on the whole, a power working for good, and that she would have been far the greatest of then existent powers for good, if only she had been able to work in harmony with other religious, moral, and intellectual movements, instead of threatening and even employing fire and sword against them.

Even the priest's unpopularity had its other side, illogical perhaps but most natural psychologically. The man who hated his parson most might well be he who most deeply felt, and shrank from, his supernatural powers. A modern French-Canadian, in a penetrating study of the Church there, quotes the words of a peasant farmer from whom the priest had turned haughtily away in the course of a heated dispute about tithes. "I longed to plant him a hearty kick on the part which he exposed to me; but then I thought my leg might shrivel up!" For many centuries the feudal lord had been tolerated, and even in a sense welcomed, as a protection against worse evils; and the priest, even at his worst, wielded the most effectual weapons against the Devil. He might damn his own soul every day that he touched the Lord's Body with sinful hands; but his Mass was none the less an *opus operatum*. One of the *Gesta Romanorum* tales was composed expressly to illustrate this doctrine. It tells how men drank from a stream of perfect clearness and purity; yet, traced to its well-spring it was found to gush forth from the very jaws of a dead dog! The scientific practical possibility of this was no more doubted by the faithful man than its theological and allegorical truth.

But we may truly go a great deal farther than this. Though the brighter touches are not always so explicit and emphatic as the darker, yet, amid that multitude of clergy, there were doubtless many in every time and country who were the salt of the earth. We must think here not only of the saints whom Rome has canonized; though but a small proportion of those were indeed parish priests, as a still smaller proportion were peasants or artisans. Behind those striking, and often theatrical, figures, we must think also of the hundred and forty-four thousand who, if all could be seen, would be worthy of the same crown and palm. Chaucer's Poor Parson was the forerunner of men who have lived serener lives in less troubled times, such as George Herbert's Country Parson, or convinced and unquestioning clerics of the Clapham School and of the Oxford Movement. Side by side with those others whom our documents brand as a dishonour to their profession, we must not forget those who lived and laboured unknown, though they daily faced their duty in the spirit which Keble holds out as a modern model:

Think not of rest: though dreams be sweet,
Start up, and ply your heavenward feet.
Is not God's oath upon your head,
Ne'er to sink back on slothful bed,
Never again your loins untie,
Nor let your torches waste and die,
Till, when the shadows thickest fall,
Ye hear your Master's midnight call?

The life as parish priest of St Gilbert of Sempringham (d. 1189) is told us in detail 300 years later by Capgrave, the Austin Friar of Lynn. He was of noble birth; his mother was English, his father a Norman knight who had come over with William the Conqueror. When he was promoted to the order of priesthood he was a model to his parish. He taught wisely in his preaching and his good example. In his parish there were no insolent drinkings, no wrestlings, bear-baitings or other unthrifty occupations to interfere with divine service. His parishioners prayed devoutly in the church, paid truly their tithes, visited the poor and spent their wealth in ways pleasing to God; in church they might be distinguished from others, since he had taught them to bow their knees to God and so devoutly to "bid their beads". In process of time, he founded the only purely English monastic order, for monks and for nuns. Even this man, with his social advantages, seems to have begun as a parish clerk; he certainly acted also as parish schoolmaster. Again, in those earlier generations when, apparently, a larger proportion of priests were ordained on their own title, and certainly there was less appropriation of the wealthier livings by monastic and other bodies comparatively disinterested in the parish, then we not infrequently find a handsome chancel, or a whole church, built by the rector himself. At Great Shelford, near Cambridge, the monumental brass of such a priest still exists, within the altar rails. Gascoigne, again, tells us: "I knew a Rector who had but one living, yet from the profits of that single church he sent twenty youths, [one after the other], to school and to the University and made priests of them."

Again, Professor Chambers has taught us to see the great literary and cultural value of those English religious pieces, in prose and in verse, which run on from Anglo-Saxon times in a stream never quite dried up, growing fast in the fourteenth century, and flowing most abundantly in the fifteenth. From that source, with the rich tributary stream of studied talk in court and council, flowed quite naturally the prose of Malory, of More, and (when Renaissance and Reformation had enriched it) of Bacon and Hooker and the Authorized Version. It is true that even the most orthodox of these religious pieces are sometimes directly traceable rather to the village prophet than to the village priest, or to one who combined both capacities; and certainly neither the literary nor the theological student can ignore the parallel influence of semi-orthodox and frankly Lollard writers. Yet, from one source or another, all this mass of writings must be taken fully into account in any survey of parish life. It is to the later Middle Ages that we owe the charming prayer which, to-day, is so often sung as a finale in Anglican services:

God be in my head,
And in my understanding;
God be in mine eyes,
And in my looking;

God be in my mouth,
And in my speaking;
God be in my heart,
And in my thinking;
God be at my end,
And at my departing.

Here, again, is the metrical prayer which Myrc [1400] gives for the parish priest to teach his people, that they may say it to themselves while he goes on with his Latin after the Elevation of the Host:

Jesu, lord, welcome Thou be,
In form of bread as I Thee see!
Jesu! for Thy holy name
Shield me to-day from sin and shame;
Shrift and housel, Lord, Thou grant me bo[th]
Ere that I shalle hencë go,
And very contrition of my sin,
That I, Lord, never die therein;
And as Thou wert of a maid y-bore
Suffer me never to be for-lore,
But when that I shall hencë wend
Grant me Thy bliss withouten end.

Most frequent of all, perhaps, are the rhymes that remind worshippers of the bleeding Crucifix and of their own latter end. In several cases, the poet gives a traditional computation of the actual wounds: these differ in different versions, but one may be taken as typical:

Five hundred wounds and five thousand,
And thereto sixty
And fifteen
Was told and seen
On My body.[1]

Sometimes, but far less frequently, these treatises contain episodes taken directly from Christ's parables, and treated with charming freshness and spontaneity. Perhaps the best of these is the parable of Matthew xx, as told in the poem of *Pearl,* where however the difficult English demands some modernization for unspecialized modern readers.[2] The poet sees the soul of his infant daughter in heaven, clad in the white robes of the Apocalypse, and jewelled with transcendent pearls. She bids him cease to mourn for one who is now, by God's courtesy, a queen in heaven. At this, he expostulates:

That courtesy is too free in deed,
If it be sooth that thou dost say;
Not two brief years with us didst lead,
Too young to please thy God or pray,
Nor never knew'st thou Pater or Creed
And yet made queen on thy first day!
I may not trow it, so God me speed,
That He would deal so wrong a way.
Of countess, damozel, par ma fay,
'Twere fair in heaven to hold the state;
Or e'en to be lady of less array;
*But a queen! That is too dear a date.**

She answers him with the Gospel parable, concluding with the dialogue between the lord and his labourers.

At the date of day, at evensong,
One hour before the sun went down,
He saw there idle men full strong
And said to them with sober sound:
"Why stand ye so idle this whole day long?"
"Our hire", said they, "is nowhere bound."
"Go into my vine, ye yeomen young,
And work as ye may ere the sun go down."
Soon the world became right brown,
The great sun sank and the hour waxed late;
To take their hire he made summoun;
The weary day was past its date.

The date of day the Lord did know
And called to the Reeve: "Let pay my meinie:

* End, goal, aim.

Give them the hire that I them owe;
And further, that none may me repreny,
Set them all upon a row
And give to each alike one penny.
Begin at the last that standeth low
Till the foremost thou atteny."
And then the first began to pleyny,
And said that they had travailed sore;
"These but one hour did strive and streyny;
Us think us ought to take ful more.

More have we served, us thinketh so,
That suffered all the long day's heat,
Than these that wrought not hourës two;
Yet to us thou dost them counterfeit!"
Said the lord to one that answered so:
"Friend, no wrong dost thou here get,
Take that is thine own and go:
Our bargain was at a penny set.
Why beginnest thou now to fret?
Was not a penny thy hire of yore?
No man may claim beyond his debt,
Why then shoulds't thou thus ask for more?"

Thus it is (says the daughter) with your own child:

More have I of joy and bliss herein,
Of ladyship great and life's full bloom,
Than all the wives in the world might win,
Seeking their own by righteous doom.
Though night was nigh ere I could begin,
(So late was I to the vineyard come,)
First of them all my hire did I win,
And was paid outright the whole full sum.
Yet others had labour more burdensome,
Toiling and sweating from hour to hour,
Whose time of reward is not yet come—
Nor shall be, perchance, for a whole year more.

How the poet's theology diverges here from Dante's, we shall see in the next chapter.

There are certain imponderables which no true historian can afford to neglect; least of all, those who deal in any way with the Middle Ages. The intuition of survival after death, apparently absent from some minds, faint in others, overmastering with a few, cannot be destroyed by any formal logic. Those who feel it have the same right to that conviction as to other ultimates: a right as legitimate as any doubter or contradictor can have. This belief, reasonably regulated like other beliefs, does unquestionably give greater significance to life. A Persian envoy in England, some eighty years ago, wrote home to a friend that there were people here who worried themselves with the fear lest, fifty years hence, the coal-mines should be exhausted: "Who is there, in Persia, that would care twopence for what happens fifty years after them?" Anything must be a gain which suggests to the multitude, even fitfully, that our present actions may be of abiding significance for good or for evil; and the world will not gain much by swinging back from medieval eschatology to a scramble for mere momentary advantages. Those who feel most deeply the liberation from a tyrant-god of past imagination—"our soul is escaped even as a bird out of the snare of the fowler"—are most strictly bound to face whatever flaws may exist in these modern ideals which take his place. No doubt it is a gross anachronism to take for granted that this or that pious man of the past, if confronted with all the alternatives which face the modern world, would have thought and written and acted as he did then. But, on the other hand, we must not exaggerate in the contrary direction. A modern Aquinas, familiar with Einstein and wielding the motor car with consummate skill, might still conceivably think essentially as the old Aquinas did. Renan, in his *Souvenirs d'Enfance et de Jeunesse* (p. 258), points out how a modern philosopher may still adapt himself to those words of Antonius in the fourth century:

Discussi fateor sectas attentius omnes,
Plurima quaesivi, per singula quaeque cucurri,
Nec quidquam inveni melius quam credere Christo.

We cannot fairly expect from the Church more than there is in human nature. Both the strength and the weakness of medieval Latin Christianity lay in this, that there were normally no parties, but one single State to which every man must conform, on peril of his life. The liberal Bishop Thirlwall, when first the question of relaxing statutory attendance at college chapels was seriously discussed, found himself confronted with an opponent who argued: "It comes to this plain question: Are we to have compulsory religion, or none at all?" The bishop replied: "My powers of logical analysis do not enable me to grasp that subtle distinction." Yet, to the enormous majority of English folk in our period, the question never presented itself at all: like the majority of all times, they did not think deeply enough. The parishioner's attitude, in most cases, was at worst that of Tennyson's *Northern Farmer*. He heard the parson dutifully every Sunday:

An' I niver know'd whot a meän'd, but I thowt a'ad summut to saäy,
An' I thowt a said whot a owt to a said an' I coom'd awaäy.

There was much of the herd-instinct in all that; but the exaggerated modern scorn of this herd-instinct is warranted neither by history nor by common everyday experience. Humanity is not predominantly evil; and men are the better for acting and thinking normally in masses; thus they keep their ideals warm; and there is, on the whole, more good than evil in every ideal which appeals to the multitudes, be the Intelligentsia never so impatient. "The inner life of Christianity, its very essence, resides in the social character of religion itself, what it has of most spiritual."[3] The words "Our Father", and the insistence on the brotherhood of man, represent ideas which humanity will never let go, whatever may be the language in which men will clothe them. And there is nothing in our medieval documents to weaken the probability that, to very many, the Lord's Prayer was a religious reality, whether taught by the parents or by the priest. "Thy kingdom come" is a call to effort, and "Thy will be done" is a call to brave endurance, in every mind that realizes prayer not only as an asking for favours, but also as a loyal surrender to demands for action and patience.

A modern French scientist, not without malice, analysed the liquid in the holy-water stoup that happened to be nearest to his laboratory, and found in it a great diversity of bacilli. If he could have analysed with equal patience and accuracy the feelings of the multitudinous worshippers, then also he might have been surprised by the variety of spiritual bacilli that hang about a parish church. The best religion any man learns, with ordinary good fortune, is at his mother's knee. One of the most moving passages in St Joan's answers to her inquisitors runs: "I learned my Pater and Ave and Creed from my mother; nor did I learn any belief from any other than from my mother."[4] But behind that mother was the Village Church.

Moreover, the existence of the one great Church, with its stable traditional framework, had considerable influence upon that agricultural life which, after all, formed some 90 per cent. of the whole national life. Its ritual, of which it had inherited part from Roman or Germanic paganism, and created still more for itself, gave consistency to village routine even in some of its most important factors: this is well brought out in a recent essay by Mr G. C. Homans.[5] The farmer's calendar was pinned to the Church calendar: there were "a set of acts, to be carried out in a particular way, on particular occasions. . . . One of the functions of a religious calendar is to help people get things done at the proper times. . . . Arrangements like this accomplish two things. They make it perfectly plain to a man and to his neighbors when he is late with his work, and give the neighbors an excuse for laughing at him for it. They also allow a man to get through the routines of the year to some extent without taking thought, simply by doing the customary things at the customary times. . . . A religion of ritual, then, like that of the Catholic Church, gives rise to well-regulated conduct in at least two ways. It helps insure that the routines of life are carried on in the usual manner, since these routines are tied to the religious calendar. And it gives men's feelings of helplessness and those linked with the changing seasons adequate and orderly social expression." And Mr Homans clinches this by a quotation from a study of the modern Polish peasant: "The fact is that when the peasant has been working steadily, and has fulfilled the religious and magical ceremonies which tradition requires, he 'leaves the rest to God', and waits for the ultimate results to come; the question of more or less skill and efficiency of work has very little importance."

Thus, in the Middle Ages as in our own day, the parson and his church afforded a natural centre of good thought and good works; a point of brotherly crystallization. The hope of heaven may not be the highest of human motives; but, just as Dr Johnson's robust common sense drove him to point out that a man is, in point of fact, seldom more innocently employed than in making money, so he would have suggested that few people live in a mood so lofty that they can justly look down upon the Christian in his hope of heaven. Even when we have reduced all religions to the category of Enlightened Selfishness, and assigned a slightly higher pigeon-hole in that same cupboard to all other forms of humanitarianism and altruism, such ideals will still remain superior, if only by a few degrees, to Selfishness Unenlightened; and human society, up to the present, has been painfully unsuccessful in working out any third alternative. A prominent and deservedly beloved Agnostic of our own day has been heard to confess sadly that the religious folk seem, hitherto, to excel in getting things done. Nor, again, need the religious man share that fear of finding himself duped at the last, which seems sometimes so strongly to sway his opponents. Lord Acton quoted once from Fénelon that the most habitually incredulous persons are sometimes the most grossly duped. But let us face the idea just as crudely as it is suggested. If any soul, at the Last Day, having believed on the strength of no base or merely careless impulse, found itself face to face with some grinning, all-powerful deceiver, then, by any civilized ethical standard, that trusting soul represents something divine in contrast with diabolism. The mere belief of humanity in a law of order, and that instinct of order which, traceable even in the lowest man, rises in the chosen few to an overmastering passion, would seem in themselves a cogent argument for a fundamentally Orderly Universe, if not in being, at least in becoming. To that belief in Order, everything bore witness in the theory of the medieval Church: and, even in its practice, there was more order than in the rest of society; sometimes incomparably more. Her very disorders were those of the rudimentary civilization around her, magnified sometimes by the greatness of the stage on which they were played. Her insistence upon a higher and rational ordinance throughout the world ought, as Professor Whitehead has pointed out, to enlist the sympathy of all truly scientific enquirers of to-day. Whatever the science of the future may be able to bring us in the way of coherent explanation, this will be in a true sense continued not only from the Greek philosophers, but also from Judaism with its insistence on the Divine Ruler, and on Christianity its successor.

The Order of the Universe finds its highest expression in Dante; and, though there is so little direct connection between him and any medieval Englishman except Chaucer, yet the whole scheme of his *Commedia* is so exact an epitome of religious-philosophic thought at the crown of the Middle Ages, that he may well be used here in illustration of that thought, rather than any of the distinguished English Schoolmen. For in fact there was no very distinctively English Scholasticism. The use of one common Latin language, together with the constant drift of scholars from one university to another, and, especially, the unquestioned supremacy of Paris as a focus of theological thought, forbade the formation of definite national schools in our period.

18. DANTE'S *COMMEDIA*[1]

We come here to the first really learned layman of the Middle Ages in Western Europe, and the first great vernacular poet of the later medieval centuries. The Troubadours, the Trouvères and the Minnesänger were now definitely on the downward slope. Moreover, Dante is the greatest poet of the whole Middle Ages, more unrivalled there in his superiority than Homer in antiquity, or Shakespeare in modern times. And finally, even though he had written nothing, his life itself is full of dramatic interest.

He was born in 1265, the year of the battle of Evesham, epoch-making for England. Then, in 1266, came the battle of Benevento, equally fateful for Italy. The mid-point of his life, reckoning by the Psalmist's computation of three score and ten years, was the equally epoch-making Jubilee year 1300. His home was in Florence, the most civilized town in the Western World, at a moment when Italian city life was perhaps at its highest ferment. Individual effort was still strong, and Florence was one of the city republics still unsubdued by the rising tide of despotism.

This later thirteenth century was the climax of several movements, especially in Italy. In religion, Europe had seen the fermentation of the year 1000. A century and a half later came St Bernard; and, a century and a half further on, in 1300, the Franciscans and Dominicans had come and had already passed their meridian. On the other hand, there was great activity of heresies and freethought. Gerardo Segharelli, one of the most remarkable of these heretics, was burned in 1300; and then, in 1307, Fra Dolcino, whose heresy was of extreme political, as well as religious, significance. In learning and philosophy, again, we trace the revival from about the year 1000. Europe saw teachers like Lanfranc and Anselm and Abailard, and the classical school of Chartres; and by 1200 universities existed already at Paris and Bologna. When Dante was born, Oxford and Cambridge were already formed, and many more. Aquinas was already writing his great *Summa,* and Roger Bacon was thinking out more modern philosophy. Dante must have known the *Summa* well, and had studied also Aquinas's brother-saint and philosopher, Bonaventura. In politics, Italy had seen the growth of civic liberties, the Lombard League with its victory over the Empire at Legnano (1176), and its position secured by the Peace of Constance in 1183. From that time forward the civic autonomy of Italy was practically safe from serious imperial encroachments; and the cities were left each to work out its own salvation, except so far as each relied upon alliances with others, after the fashion of the modern nationalistic balance of power. Thence came intense political life, with kaleidoscopic changes and incessant war; as Dante himself confessed in later years, Italy was "a hostelry of pain". In art the French had been far ahead at the beginning of the century; and in 1265 they were still ahead in sculpture, despite the work of Niccolo Pisano. The French might then have been called the equals of Cimabue and his contemporaries in painting; but, by 1300, Giotto was in full work. Italy thenceforward led the Western World in painting, and was soon to be foremost in sculpture also. In poetry France, again, had held the first lead; then the Sicilians and Germans imitated the Troubadours, and Dante himself praises the poetry of Frederick II and his son Manfred. The great German lyric poet, Walther von der Vogelweide, had died shortly before Dante's birth. Then, in the second half of the century, the poetic laurels passed to the communes of Lombardy and Tuscany. If Dante had been born a century earlier, there would scarcely have been a language for him to write in. But now, in his youth, he found himself in a society where the interchange of sonnets and *canzoni* was a fashionable recreation. To this early education and healthy competition he added himself the *bel stilo* of Virgil, to whose mastership over him he bore such emphatic tribute. Most of all, however, he owed to his varied personal experiences. Sacchetti, Chaucer's contemporary, recording an anecdote of Dante's life, speaks of his eyes which nothing escaped:

"Dante, che tutto vedea." Dante, that is, who had been everything—lover, painter, scholar, ambassador, councillor of the Republic, and finally exile. That last was the hardest school of all; one which gave force to all the rest. He tells us of that stern discipline. He had learned (he says) "how bitter is the taste of another man's bread, and how weary a path it is to climb and descend another man's stairs"; and again he describes the *Commedia* as "this book over which I have grown thin all these years". It may have been begun just before his exile, but it was emphatically the work of that period, from 1302-21.

His life should be read in his own poetic autobiography, the *Vita Nuova*, which is now so easily accessible in D. G. Rossetti's translation. He first saw Beatrice when each was nine years old, and, steeped as he was in medieval symbolism, this for him had the utmost significance. Three is the perfect number, the number of the Trinity. Nine is the square of three; three raised to a still higher power. It was natural, therefore, that Beatrice should have been what she was, a lady of superhuman perfection. He first heard her voice speaking to him nine years later at a feast. Yet we do not know for certain who she was, or even her name, or whether she died unmarried or had a husband and a large family. Of two things, however, there can be no legitimate doubt. First, that she was a real woman; attempts to prove her a purely ideal and imaginary figure, though supported by enthusiasts like D. G. Rossetti's father, may be relegated to the limbo of Baconian theories. On the other hand, there can be no doubt that she was intensely adored, sainted after death in his memory; and that, penetrated as he was with the study of Augustine and his *City of God*, in this woman who had so deeply influenced his life he grew to see a type of Holy Church herself. After her death he confesses to have fallen into an irregular life, from which he was partly saved by the study of philosophy. That, however, was in itself not enough, until religion came midway in his life, in that year 1300, as mystic in its world-significance as in its particular significance to him. He makes this the central point of his *Divina Commedia*. It was the year of the first Papal Jubilee that was ever held, and of the first bloodshed of Blacks and Whites among Guelfs in Florence; bloodshed which was fateful not only for Dante, but to a certain extent for all Europe. We in modern England can scarcely realize the significance of the fact that, since 1066, so little blood has been shed in our political quarrels. When, shortly after the Great War and during a great coal-strike, one of the Labour Leaders went so far as to predict that there would be "bloodshed" if the men did not get their way, that word betrayed his ignorance of Continental politics. Great Britain is the only great country of Europe in which there is no deep stain of blood on the hands of politicians; in which neither party can say to the other: "You are they who put our fathers up against the wall and shot them, when the political pendulum had swung in your favour." Therefore our less instructed politicians are tempted to take this for granted as a piece of good fortune, without realizing the significance of cause and effect; they are too narrow-minded to understand what a strict and solemn account will have to be paid by any party which first starts a reign of bloodshed within this island. In that fatal year 1300, Dante was one of the six elected priors. Next year the French prince, Charles de Valois, and the Pope intervened, nominally as mediators, but really as betrayers of the Whites. Dante himself was exiled; and when, in 1302, the sentence was confirmed, it was added that he should be burned alive if he were ever caught on his native territory.

Already before this, however, Dante had produced two of the most remarkable books of the Middle Ages. The *Vita Nuova* is "the most ideal book of love ever written", and certainly the most remarkable autobiography between St Augustine's *Confessions* and those of the Renaissance artist, Benvenuto Cellini. His *De Monarchia,* again, is "the most ideal of political works ever written", at any rate since the *De Civitate Dei.* When he crowned these with his *Divina Commedia,* he put himself side by side with Homer and Shakespeare; and, if we take the general verdict of cultured classes throughout the world, he stands perhaps not lowest of the three; certainly he is not least read of the three at the present moment. The poem was christened "Divina" in the seventeenth century; "Commedia" Dante himself calls it in his letter to his patron Can Grande, the Prince of Verona. A tragedy, he explains in that letter, is a poem that treats of the transition from bliss to evil: but this poem travels from evil to bliss, and therefore he calls it by the antithetical name of "Commedia".

He plunges straight into his subject from the very first, disregarding the tradition of cautious advance recommended by the genial Horace, as definitely as Daniel does in his story of Belshazzar's feast—

In the midway of this our mortal life
I found myself in a dark wood, astray—

So wild and desolate was this forest, that he felt it as the bitterness of death even to think himself back there. How had he found his way thither? He scarce knew: a sleepy dullness had benumbed his senses and he had strayed from the path. But, as he climbs, the trees begin to thin off at the top of the ravine, and he emerges on a mountain-side just touched by the first rays of dawn. Here is hope, and he breathes again, looking back upon the dark forest of his wanderings as a spent swimmer lying upon the shore pants and looks back upon the waves that had so nearly beaten the life out of him.

Already in these few lines we see Dante's main characteristics as a poet. In the first place his consummate art; the opening line arrests our attention, and each fresh verse beats the image in. We see this again in his selection of metre, the *terzina*; a metre regular enough, like Milton's blank verse, to carry him steadily to the end of a long epic, yet varied enough, with its constant change of rhyme, to escape monotony. Again, we see how firmly he takes his stand on the solid facts of this world. Even in his wildest flights, as Macaulay noted long ago, his imagination was always based on things seen, and especially on his own dear Italy; the mountains (not only Apennines, but even Alps), the blue Mediterranean, the farmers and herdsmen, down to their very gestures and every movement of the cattle and wild beasts and birds. Equally microscopically he shows us the outdoor and indoor life in the crowded streets of his native Florence; the butcher at his stall, the tailor on his bench. His poem is, on the one hand, such a repertory of daily life as we ourselves may enjoy by looking through the back pages of *Punch;* and, far beyond this, all those similes are heightened by his powerful use of metaphor. It has been suggested by a modern critic that his preference for simile over metaphor was a piece of instinctive art; that, since his whole poem might be considered as one vast metaphor, therefore he might spare the metaphor in detail. Yet in one of the very passages selected by the critic for this thesis we find, side by side with an obvious simile, a metaphor which he has failed to recognize. One of the shades, surprised to see in this fresh wanderer something so nearly resembling a man whom he had known in Florence, " sharpened his eyebrows at me " as a tailor eyes the needle which he tries to thread in scanty light. That metaphor of the sharpening of the eyebrows is characteristic of Dante's intense poetic force; and, with regard to the similes, if we take at random two or three pages of the *Commedia* and the *Aeneid,* we shall find in the latter an even greater preponderance. This use of similes, in fact, lay in the classical tradition in which Dante was steeped. All this art, however, is bent in Dante to serve the purposes of the mystic meaning. He is possessed with that conviction expressed in Goethe's *Faust,* that the visible things of earth are an adumbration of the invisible things of God: that Nature may say,

Here at the roaring loom of time I ply
And weave God's garment that you see Him by.

The poem, then, may very truly have been called a great allegory, centred round a day and a year of the deepest mystical significance. The story begins on Good Friday in this year of Jubilee, which was the thirty-fifth of the poet's own life. Dante himself may very likely have believed in the pseudo-historical excuse given for that great celebration. According to a story written by Cardinal Stefaneschi, an intimate friend of Boniface VIII, a man had come to that Pope saying that he was 107 years old and that his father, in childhood, had told him, " If you live a hundred years longer you will see the great Jubilee which marks the beginning of each fresh century in

Rome." All historical evidence is against the truth of this, and in fact the Jubilee of 1300, so far from being long foreseen, was so hastily announced, even in the fateful year itself, that it scarcely gave time for distant pilgrims to take advantage of it at all. Multitudes, however, did come. It is calculated that two hundred thousand pilgrims came to reverence especially the *Vernicle*, the napkin with which St Veronica had wiped our Lord's face, and which bore the lineaments of it thenceforth to all eternity. The crowds were so great that they motived, for the narrow bridges of Rome, what is perhaps the first Rule of the Road recorded in history; and the whole event stimulated Giovanni Villani, the Florentine citizen-historian, to write his great work; much as the Franciscan friars, chanting their vespers in the erstwhile Temple of Jupiter, suggested to Gibbon his story of the Decline and Fall of the Roman Empire.

To Dante this year brought new spiritual life. This was the moment of his issue from the gloomy wood. He had felt himself unworthy after Beatrice's death; how unworthy, we do not know. Philosophy had only partially cured him. He had woken up to find half his life already spent; but here at last was a dawn of promise. On the other hand, the World, the Flesh and the Devil still haunted him. He needed grace directly from God. This grace came to him through his purified human love, which undergoes a final apotheosis in his mind, and elevates Beatrice to a type of the Church. But all must be in order; artistic gradation is here the gradation of truth. First, in the *Inferno* he must look back upon sin and realize all its loathsomeness; then trace, step by step, the Purgation of Souls; and finally catch a vision of Eternal Bliss as an incentive to perseverance. No other poem ever undertook to give so complete a picture of life as this, and no other of equal length has been so carefully planned. It consists of a hundred cantos, in three groups of 33 each, with one introductory in the first group. Each of these cantos is so exactly balanced, that between the longest of all and the shortest there is only a margin of 38 lines. To keep up the sacred number of three, *Inferno, Purgatorio* and *Paradiso* are divided each into nine sections.

On the mountain slopes, then, at sunrise, Dante is confronted by three wild beasts, the panther, the lion, and the she-wolf: Uncleanness, Pride and Greed. A figure appears as his guide; this is Virgil, the godlike poet of his study, who will conduct him through Hell and Purgatory, but may not cross the threshold of Heaven; there he must be left behind, and thenceforward Beatrice alone can lead the poet. For the present, however, Virgil is all-powerful. He drives off the beasts; and the two wayfarers climb this mountain by an arduous and savage way which brings them by nightfall to the gates of Hell. Here they find that inscription which has since become a byword in literature:

Through me you pass into the city of Woe,
Through me you pass into eternal pain:
All hope abandon, ye who enter here.

They come first to an Ante-Hell, the place of the cowards and irresolute, peopled first by those angels who were neutral in the conflict between God and Satan, and whom therefore Heaven had spewed forth, while Hell itself disdained to receive them to its full hospitality. There it is that Dante finds the shade of "him who made the great refusal"—Pope Celestine V, sainted by the Church, but odious to many as having despaired of that worldly machine which it was his task to control as pope, and as having, by his resignation of that divine office, made way for Boniface VIII, the despot who had wronged not only Dante and his Florence, but, in Dante's opinion, the whole Christian world. Hence the poet and his guide pass the river Acheron in Charon's boat (for he owes much to Virgil's story of Aeneas' descent to Hades), and they enter the first circle of Hell proper.

Here is the Limbo of the Unbaptized. The air is thick with the sighs of these souls, though they suffer no physical pain. The multitude consists first of heathens, concerning whom Virgil explains: "for defect [of baptism] and no other fault, are we lost; and only in so far afflicted, that without hope we live in desire." Here (he says) am I myself with Homer and Horace and Lucan and Ovid, Hector and Aeneas and Caesar; nay, even the semi-divine Aristotle, the Master of all Science, with his fellow-philosophers of Greece and Rome. With these heathens are the unbaptized children of Christian parents: for no orthodox Latin theologian of that day admitted the salvation of the unbaptized since Christ's coming, apart from a few miraculous or semi-miraculous instances, some of which legend might have consecrated. St Augustine even laid such weight upon the doctrine of original sin that he assigned eternal physical torture to the unbaptized children of Christian parents; and medieval writers speak with horror of those priests or midwives who, in their negligence or ignorance, failed to baptize truly and effectually. St Thomas, it is true, assigns to them no punishment but the deprival of the Beatific Vision; but, seeing that this deprival was also reckoned by philosophers as the bitterest of all the woes suffered by the damned, the subtle logic by which he convinces himself that this Limbo of the Unbaptized is compatible with a certain degree of natural happiness can scarcely have comforted any but a small minority of bereaved mothers. Dante, as we have seen, does not follow his master quite so far; and Boccaccio, in his Commentary, speaks plainly of physical pain.

We have here the keynote of the *Inferno*, and the rest may be told more briefly. If Original Sin, the taint we all inherit from Adam and Eve, must be paid so dearly, how much heavier is the debt of wilful transgression! The travellers climb down from circle to circle, which are like mountain precipices. The second is peopled with those who suffer for crimes of passion overbalancing reason; and here comes the famous episode of Paolo and Francesca. He finds in this circle a hurricane whirling the souls for ever through the air. They are driven round like flocks of starlings in the winter blast, without hope either of rest or of lesser pain for all eternity. Here are Cleopatra, Helen, Dido, Tristram—heroes and heroines of the greatest romance—and here is a couple who move Dante immediately to cry: "Poet, I would willingly speak with those two that go together and seem so light upon the wind." Virgil here gives Dante an unfailing spell; and Dante, obedient to his teaching, cries: "In the name of that love that leads you, come and speak!" At those compelling words the two left the flying multitude, "gliding as swiftly as a dove glides on steady pinions to her nest", and Dante recognizes clearly now that he has spoken to Francesca, aunt to Guido da Polenta, who was his own great patron in his last refuge at Ravenna. She answers his challenge in those words of Boethius: "There is no greater pain than to remember one's happy days in times of misery." But his appeal was irresistible, and she must tell her story:

Amor, che al cor gentil ratto s' apprende,
Prese costui della bella persona
Che mi fu tolta, e il modo ancor m' offende.

Amor, che a nullo amato amar perdona,
Mi prese del costui piacer sì forte,
Che, come vedi, ancor non m' abbandona.

Amor condusse noi ad una morte;
Caina attende chi vita ci spense.

Love, that in gentle heart is quickly learnt,
Entangled him by that fair body, which I
Lost in such cruel sort, as grieves me still.
Love, that denial takes from none belov'd,
Caught me with pleasing him so passing well,
That, as thou seest, he yet deserts me not.
Love brought us to one death. Deep Hell awaits
The soul, who spilt our life.

The force of this triple repetition may be compared with one of the most wonderful passages in the Bible, where David receives the news of his rebel son's death: "And the king was much moved, and went up to the chamber over the gate, and wept; and as he went, thus he said, 'O my son Absalom, my son, my son Absalom! Would God I had died for thee, O Absalom my son, my son!'" In both cases we have primarily not art, but passion; the words that strike the hearer with this almost intolerable repetition of pathos are the very words that must burst from a heart that could bear no more. So it was with Dante; if the syllables come back again and again to the same point, it is because the heart beats again and again upon the same theme. The throb of the verse echoes the actual pulsation; here we have primarily the reality of passion; all that art had to do was to fix this in an abiding form. We are told of Michael Angelo that his chisel, even in old age, stripped and flaked the marble with such direct vigour that it seemed as though he were not hewing from an inert block, but removing foreign accretions from a pre-existent statue. So with Dante; we feel not so much that he is relating, nor that he is creating, as that he stands by, removes a veil, and shows us a truth pre-existent from all eternity and living to all eternity; a picture that impresses itself as irresistibly upon the mind as (to use his own simile) the seal impresses itself upon the wax.

The *Inferno* is the most scathing satire in all literature—devastating because it is so inevitable in its justice, which, after all, is the true touchstone even in satire. He finds the angry and sullen together in one circle; the first tearing each other through endless ages as they sought to tear each other in life, and the second sunk in a filthy marsh in which their very existence was seldom revealed except by the bubbles that rose to the surface from their sighs:

> *Fixed in the slime they said: " Sad once were we*
> *In God's sweet air made gladsome by the sun,*
> *Carrying a foul and lazy fume within us;*
> *Now in this dismal sediment are we sad."*

Here and everywhere, we have a punishment that fits the crime; and thus we pass on from circle to circle, as through terrace after terrace of a great Alp; not up into the clouds here, but down into the deepest pit. No earthly rank or profession saves them from Dante's judgment. Even with Popes and cardinals and proud prelates, we must say of the *Inferno,* as the Psalmist says of the proud sinners of his own world, " they lie in hell like sheep ". Here are five Popes and one Emperor; Anastasius among the heretics, side by side with the godless Emperor Frederick II; but Dante here was probably mistaken: he apparently confused Pope Anastasius with the Emperor of that name. In the circle of the fraudulent, again, Dante places three Popes of his own lifetime—plunged head foremost into circular cavities of white-hot rock, with tongues of flame flickering up from their protruding feet. It is one of these who utters that sentiment familiar to moralists of the Middle Ages:

> *Ah Constantine, to how great ill gave birth*
> *Not thy conversion, but that plenteous dower*
> *Which the first wealthy pope received of thee!*

In the lowest pit of all are the traitors; Brutus and Cassius, who, by murdering Caesar, betrayed the Empire; and Judas, who betrayed his Lord. Last of all comes Lucifer, cast down head-foremost from Heaven to mid-earth, a gigantic figure, past which they climb through the chasm made by his fall, and at last, emerging, find themselves beneath the stars of the Southern Hemisphere; for Dante knows of the Southern Cross.

Here, then, they find Purgatory; a mountain rising in terraces that correspond to the falling terraces of Hell. We have here that most natural idea of purgation by pain before the soul can be pure enough to endure the presence of God: a doctrine naturally evolved as a spiritual counterpart of the public and visible penances required by the early Church before the faithful would restore a sinner to communion with the rest. But between those days and Dante's it had gone through a treble current of debasement. First, spiritually, through even so great a Pope as Gregory I, who did much to systematize the idea, and may be said practically to have originated it as a dogma of the Church; and secondly, in practice, through the custom of commutation. Originally these public penances necessary for restoration to communion had sometimes been commuted, by an equitable compromise, for something equally difficult in itself, yet bearing less hardly on this particular case. Then, by a natural transition, the commutation was softened to something not equal, but easier. Augustine had shown this in the case of Victorinus, where it was suggested that, in deference to his specially dignified position in the intellectual and social and political world, he might be allowed to make his baptism and profession of faith in private. Then, thirdly, came the worst debasement of all, a money commutation. This led naturally, and it may be almost said inevitably, to such doings as Chaucer satirizes when he depicts the friar as pleading on behalf of those sinners who are too hard-hearted to weep or sorrow for their sins, and must therefore atone for them by giving money to the professional Religious, who will do the mourning for them. This, again, bred that whole system of Indulgences, in which remission of sins was almost invariably bound up with more or less of money payments. It is true that, in theory, the Indulgence was valid only in cases where the sinner was already repentant and confessed; but in fact the great Franciscan preacher Berthold of Ratisbon, contemporary with Dante's father, speaks of "penny-preachers" who promise so much Indulgence, as from the Pope himself, for a penny or a half-penny, that many thousand Christians imagine they have got rid of their sins for money, and go to hell. Two centuries later, on the verge of the Reformation, we shall find Gascoigne, the Chancellor of Oxford University, writing in even stronger terms. But of such abusive views there is no trace in Dante; and many feel the *Purgatorio* to be, on the whole, his greatest poetical achievement, though the general opinion will place the *Inferno* as the most powerful and the *Paradiso* as the most beautiful. He had entered Hell on Good Friday. He emerged at the foot of the mountain of Purgatory on Easter morning before daybreak. He and Virgil climbed thus, terrace after terrace, up this island mountain; for Dante, like the most enlightened geographers of his time, believed the Southern Hemisphere to be purely oceanic, apart from this rock on whose summit was the Paradise from which Adam and Eve had been expelled. The Pit of Hell, according to his cosmography, was exactly below Jerusalem, and the Earthly Paradise exactly opposite. The place of Adam's sin was thus, not only spiritually but geographically, the Antipodes to that of Christ's redemption. There is here an Ante-Purgatory, as there was an Ante-Hell. Then come seven terraces, one for the purgation of each of the Seven Deadly Sins; and these, together with the Ante-Purgatory and the Earthly Paradise, form nine divisions, as Hell was in nine circles. Here from terrace to terrace they climb, by stairs steep and narrow and rough, but easier in gradation as they ascend. At each stair stands an angel chanting one of the seven Beatitudes to comfort the toiler as he reaches the next.

Some of the punishments here are almost as painful as in the *Inferno*; but there is this essential difference, that here we have no abiding sense of pain; and not only is there this alleviation in time, but (and herein we feel Dante's greatness) the toiler's will is felt to be in unison with his fate. Even great theologians in the Middle Ages speak of haste through Purgatory as a mercy. It is the constant theme of preachers that money must be given for Masses and prayers which will shorten this passage; and even nowadays, in the wayside shrines of Italy and Roman Catholic Switzerland, we see souls writhing in the flames and the money-box by their side for charitable alleviation. In Dante, the spirit of these souls is "we would not abbreviate one moment of the process, any more than we would quarrel in any other way with our final good". Moreover, Dante exercises the same independence of judgment here as in his *Inferno*. The first soul he met in Hell was a Pope canonized by the Church; and the first with whom he spoke in Purgatory was that Manfred, arch-enemy of the Popes, who died excommunicate in battle against them. "Horrible were my sins", he confesses, "but God's mercy is even greater. True, I died with the full curse of the Church upon me, yet the trunk is not so blasted but that one green shoot can sprout and the whole tree be some day restored."

The most beautiful cantos, except the Earthly Paradise, are perhaps the 2nd [Casella] and the 7th with the 8th—the Valley of the Princes. Here, Dante found the most conspicuous figures of an age almost unrivalled in its wealth of such men—the Emperor Rudolf, Charles of Anjou, with his mortal enemy, Peter of Aragon, Henry III of England, and many more, resting at eventide in the Valley of Flowers: a flock of majestic souls nestling humbly under the guard of two angels assigned to watch over them through the night. Finally, at the top of the mountain, they come to the wall of fire that rings the Earthly Paradise; and here Dante's flesh shrinks naturally, while the disembodied Virgil and his fellow-poet Statius were at their ease.

I still, though conscience urg'd, no step advanced.
When still he saw me fix'd and obstinate,

Somewhat disturb'd he cried: " Mark now, my son,
From Beatrice thou art by this wall
Divided." As at Thisbe's name the eye
Of Pyramus was open'd (when life ebb'd
Fast from his veins), and took one parting glance,
While vermeil dyed the mulberry; thus I turn'd
To my sage guide, relenting, when I heard
The name, that springs for ever in my breast.

He shook his forehead; and, " How long ", he said,
" Linger we now?" then smil'd, as one would smile
Upon a child, that eyes the fruit and yields.
Into the fire before me then he walk'd;
And Statius, who erewhile no little space
Had parted us, he pray'd to come behind.

I would have cast me into molten glass
To cool me, when I enter'd, so intense
Rag'd the conflagrant mass. The sire belov'd,
To comfort me, as he proceeded, still
Of Beatrice talk'd. " Her eyes ", saith he,
" E'en now I seem to view." From th'other side
A voice, that sang, did guide us; and, the voice
Following, with heedful ear, we issued forth
There where the path led upward. " Come ", we heard,
" Come, blessed of my Father." Such the sounds,
That hail'd us from within a light, which shone
So radiant, I could not endure the view.

Then comes the culmination of all—the Earthly Paradise.

From this Earthly Paradise we pass now to that of the Heavens, with Beatrice as guide. To Dante, as to his contemporaries, the earth was the centre of the universe, surrounded by concentric hollow crystal spheres in each of which a planet was set like a gem in a ring. Each planet, as it circled farther from the earth, offered a higher stage of beatitude. Here again Dante follows the ordinary scholastic teaching of his time, that there shall be different degrees of perfection in the bliss of souls in Heaven. The only great philosopher, perhaps, who gave equality to all, was our English Archbishop Bradwardine; and, among remarkable poets, only the author of *Pearl*, who here follows literally Christ's teaching in his parable of the Vineyard and the Labourers. With Dante, as with Aquinas and Bonaventura, the difference of gradations is no obstacle whatever to the perfect and supreme content of each soul, which has no will outside the sovereign will of God: *E la sua voluntate è nostra pace.*

Those words are what our poet hears in the first and lowest Heaven—that of the moon, a planet which Dante conceives as one vast eternal pearl wherein move souls yet whiter than itself—just so much whiter, just so delicately visible, as a pearl itself is on the forehead of a beautiful girl. Thus they passed on from sphere to sphere, from Heaven to Heaven, speaking with saints that will always live in history—Bernard, Bonaventura, Aquinas, and with other folk of whom we should never have heard but for Dante—men and women that had lived with him, at the sight of whose faces and the sound of whose voices his pulse had beaten—souls to whom he wished immortality because he loved them in the flesh, and to whom his poem has given immortality. Such was Cunizza, the tender-hearted and high-born, multi-adulteress; so also had Dante done already in his Purgatory, immortalizing Pia, the obscure victim of a husband's murder in a desolate Italian "moated grange", and his friend Casella, the musician, whom he makes to sing, among those suffering souls, as he had sung on earth; a song, moreover, of Dante's own. At last they reach the Empyrean, that Heaven of Flame above all other Heavens, in which dwells the Godhead Itself. Here he sees the Mystic Rose, formed of the palpitating souls of all the saints. Here St Bernard intercedes for him to the Virgin Mary, and the Virgin grants him grace to see for one brief division of a moment that Beatific Vision of the Divine Essence to which it is the whole aim of his life to attain one day for all eternity. And here we must remember what the man was—how rich were the faculties and the experience which in this moment were to receive their intensest possible satisfaction. Let us remember

Dante's love of visible things— *Dante, che tutto vedea*— and the ignominious Hell he created for those who were sad even while they trod God's good brown earth, and were bathed in His genial sunshine. Let us remember his love of abstract thought and dialectics; the extreme—the pedantic—minuteness with which he comments on his own poems in his *Vita Nuova.* And then, reading the last few lines of the *Paradiso*, we see how these and all his other faculties were for once swallowed up in one supreme moment of direct intuition. All visible things, all thinkable things, were seen suddenly as existing only in God, narrowed down, at that indivisible point of space and time, to a single ray of light, into which the rapt soul plunged its gaze—plunged dizzily on ("I had been lost, had mine eyes turned away from it")—plunged on and on, and saw "ingathered within its depths, bound by [Almighty] love into one volume, all that which is scattered in single [Sibylline] leaves throughout the whole universe". Dante, thus seeing, felt himself for the moment in fact, and to some extent for ever afterwards in recollection of that fact, in absolute harmony, through every fibre of his being, with the infinite invisible forces of this vast universe: "My will and desire were rolled, with the even motion of a wheel, by that Love which moveth the sun and the infinitude of the stars." Here, again, the feeling is no less truly Dante's own, although the words are an echo from Boethius.

St Augustine had given, as his briefest and best definition of Virtue: "it is the setting-in-order of Love"—*Ordo est Amoris.* The Franciscan poet-mystic Jacopone had cried: "Set this love of mine in order, O Thou who lovest me"—*Ordina quest' amore, o Tu che m' ami!* Dante sums up all this, in a poem not only inspired by the characteristic medieval passion for order, but displaying its completest artistic exemplification. No other epic can rival this steady and effortless passage from the tumult of Hell, through the gradual pacification of Purgatory, to the perfect peace of Paradise.

19. THE ROYAL COURT

With Dante, we are on the Mount of Transfiguration. It is good for us to be here; it is good to repair hither again and again; but at the foot of this mountain the world is going very much its own way: that motley world, that Vanity Fair, from out of which so many struggling souls cry: "Lord, I believe, help Thou mine unbelief!" We have taken stock of the true foundation of lay society, the Village; let us look now at its apex, the Court.

The Conquest made England the home of a more powerful monarchy than any other state of equal size. Not that the general population was worse off; quite the contrary; but the barons were more restricted. From William the Conqueror to Henry II, the power of the English king was far greater than that of his contemporary in France—let alone Germany. King and barons alike were foreigners, and were compelled to hold together in face of a hostile population. Again, the king had made himself, and had made the barons. The Duke of Normandy had become King of England; and the adventurers, distinguished or undistinguished, who shared his fortunes, thus became great nobles. Hence, William being a character strong enough to take advantage of this position, the feudal nobility was curbed here as nowhere else on the Continent. Michelet says truly: "The Anglo-Norman State and Church were organized with a firmness which was a model to the rest of the world. Continental kings envied the omnipotence of their English brethren; continental peoples envied the despotic but orderly discipline which reigned in Great Britain." Much importance must be given to the predominantly northern character of our constitutional development. Upon Anglo-Saxon civilization was grafted that of these Norman customs. On both sides, we find little or no trace of direct Roman influences, in spite of modern attempts to extol these as a primary factor. Thus this baronage, disciplined at first to stand by the king, became gradually a class disciplined to resist him in turn. For the Norman kings, by restricting the powers of the barons, made them gradually drift into alliance with the people. In France some barons became, while others might hope to become, petty sovereigns, almost absolute on their own lands; these were able to defy the king, sometimes even singly, and at any rate by twos and threes. In England there was no such possibility: barons could not thus assert themselves except in large numbers; and, since a strong minority would always stand by the king, they could not even do that without the help of towns and the lower gentry.

Again, our French possessions were disadvantageous to royalty, and advantageous to the opposition. Kings were constantly involved in Continental affairs to which they attached equal or greater importance than to home affairs. Therefore this created a baronial-popular opposition such as we find in the famous case of Edward I in 1297, when Roger Bigod refused to go on one of Edward's oversea expeditions, and the king insisted: "By God, you shall either go or hang!" only to provoke the retort: "By God, my Lord King, I will neither go nor hang!" It took long, however, to produce the beginnings of such reasoned resistance. Constitutional monarchy began under John. It is true that Magna Carta was at bottom an opportunist document, voicing mainly the class grievances of the baronage, with which popular grievances were bound up in virtue of the popular-baronial alliance; yet it gained in fact far wider significance, at least in the form in which it was later republished and repeated from reign to reign. Although its provisions about taxation were in themselves temporary, they formed the basis of that pressure on the king through the power of the purse, which has been so remarkable a factor in the English struggle for liberty. So again with other clauses; practical and opportunist in themselves, they "gave a solemn sanction and a definite statement, to which appeal could ever after be made, to certain fundamental principles of liberty, much wider in their application than their framers knew"; so that nearly every insurrection against absolutism in England has been able to appeal to Magna Carta. Its value is best expressed by Maitland in Traill's *Social England* (ch. IV, § 4, p. 409); and, as Maitland insists, its main significance lies in the fact that it is "a grand compromise, and a fit prologue for all those thousands of compromises in which the practical wisdom of the English will always be expressing itself. . . . And then in its detailed clauses it must do something for all those sorts and conditions of men who have united to resist John's tyranny—for the bishop, the clerk, the baron, the knight, the burgess, the merchant—and there must be some give and take between these classes, for not all their interests are harmonious."[1]

The next great step came under Henry III, with government by a committee of barons. This broke down; fortunately, for it would have meant an oligarchy. Then, with Edward I, we get what may be called a parliament; and, within a generation of this, England is politically in the forefront of Europe and destined to outpace the rest more and more. This, again, had a definite effect upon our literature. Mr V. H. Galbraith, in his valuable paper on *The Literacy of the medieval English Kings*, read before the British Academy in 1935, has shown how early-ripe our vernacular prose was before the Conquest. Alfred had consciously stimulated what had already begun through natural causes, "the precocious development of English as an educational, even literary language and as the language of government. . . . In so far as [this] affected law, government and business, lay society must have been more developed in England than abroad, where the force of tradition and a higher standard of clerical Latin retarded the development of the vernaculars, and thus kept the layman a stranger to the written word." The immediate effect of the Conquest was to strangle this vernacular prose through the importation of Continental clerics, well versed in Latin, by whose help our kings did their business; our Anglo-Saxon Chronicle flickered out in the next generation but one. But the literary student cannot ignore the fact that our later writers grew up among a people rapidly outdistancing other European peoples (except in corners: e.g. Aragon, and Sicily during certain periods) in the assertion of liberty and the practice of liberty. This gave us very early a spirit of independence even in literature; not in the narrow sense of that word, for we borrowed enormously from other nations, more perhaps than any other people; but true independence in our use of this material. Chaucer's works and *Piers Plowman*, with the Pearl-cycle, are more truly national, more original in the modern sense, than anything in French literature of the time.

Yet, for some time, the only post-Conquest vernacular encouraged by our kings was the French. Mr Galbraith points out very truly that the Middle Ages divided society into three classes, "those who fought, those who worked, and those who prayed", and that "the social prejudices of the military class discouraged learned tastes in its members; and the occasional exception, as we learn from Ordericus Vitalis, was nicknamed 'the Clerk'", i.e. Henry I. Mr Galbraith dismisses as "pure journalism" the story that Henry I as a youth was given to quoting, even in his father's hearing, the proverb "Rex illiteratus, asinus coronatus". But he points out that this *cliché* must yet be taken into account, and that the ordinary opinion of the later twelfth century was "that kings needed to be 'educated'": i.e. that, if they could not themselves read Latin, at least they should take real interest in what might be heard from men who could. He sums up briefly: "From 597 to 1100 it is exceptional for a king to be able to write at all, or to read Latin; in the twelfth and thirteenth centuries kings learn to read Latin but do not (even if they can) write it; in the fourteenth and fifteenth centuries they are taught in youth both to read and write Latin, but in fact are far more occupied with French and English."

But "literacy" in the ordinary medieval sense, i.e. the knowledge of Latin, was not necessarily "education" as understood nowadays; and Mr Galbraith argues very truly "that the medieval potentate did not read and write (if indeed he could not) because he had neither the need nor the wish, having others [i.e. the clergy] to do these things for him; that social prejudice rendered reading and writing *infra dig*. for the noble class; and that in any case they are no necessary index to the level of education". In those days men were wont to read aloud even when they read only for their own enjoyment; therefore it would be natural to find, quite apart from the class of professional reciters, an amateur here and there who advanced as far in knowledge of the available literature of his day as the non-performing musical amateur does in modern music. We see this in Froissart's noble patron, Gaston de Foix, for whose entertainment our chronicler read during so many weary midnight hours. Thus, throughout the pre-Chaucerian period and for a good while later, royal and baronial life exercised a very direct influence on literature. Except for religious writings, the author's best hope of patronage was either in a royal or noble household; or at least by attracting royal or noble attention; Chaucer and Froissart are stock examples here. It was in such courts that the English language was formed as a literary tongue, quite apart from written literary work. Courts and castles were regular schools of manners; and we must here include the households of the spiritual barons also—bishops and abbots. The influence of Theobald of Canterbury in this way, and of his successor Becket, are well brought out by Miss Norgate. All our kings, down to Henry IV, spoke French; even of Edward I we only know that he was master of just enough English to make that simple and irreverent pun upon *Bigod*. His grandson, Edward III, is sometimes credited with something more by modern writers; but there is no clear evidence that he could talk English with any fluency. Yet the barons and prelates were becoming more and more English; and it seems probable (though I know no explicit text) that a good deal of English was spoken at their courts even during the first half of our period. The result was a gradual formation, on the tongues of able and cultured men, of a real literary taste. Choice and elaborate speech, as we shall see, was counted as an accomplishment of the perfect knight.

Let us come, therefore, to a more detailed and intimate glance at a royal court, contenting ourselves with a single specimen. Let us take as typical that of Henry II. In the first place we have here many first-rate literary witnesses; again, this was specially a resort of literary men; and, thirdly, it stands roughly midway in our period, both in time and in evolution.

Henry II's court was far more civilized and national than William's, less civilized and national than that of Henry VIII. This king's crowning marked, "scarcely less than that of William the Conqueror, the beginning of a new era . . . and it was distinctly recognized as such by the men of the period". We have his portrait from different contemporaries. We cannot trust that which is on his sculptured monument at Fontevraud; not only because this was made whole generations after his death, but also because monumental sculpture did not aim at exact portraits till a much later date. The earliest, probably, is that of Philippe-le-Hardi of France [1298], whose mouth is slightly distorted at one corner, evidently in reproduction of what the sculptor found on the death-mask. Henry II was of middle stature, thick-set, with broad shoulders and brawny arms; his hands were coarse and neglected, and his legs of iron. He was naturally given to corpulence, but he kept it down by temperance at the table and hard work. He had a large round head, short neck, reddish hair, and freckled skin. He was great in war and in the council chamber; always ready with his facts and with his words; a ruler who never forgot a face he had once seen, or a fact that had once interested him. Above all, his contemporaries describe his energy; when not at war, he was always hunting in his spare time; his legs and feet were chronically black and blue. If not on horseback, then he was on his feet; scarcely ever sitting. Thus he tired out his whole court: "Whensoever he can breathe freely from cares and anxieties, he busies himself with private reading, or labours to unravel some knotty question amid a throng of clerks." His sons all took after him, if only at a distance; all had more than average intellectual vigour and interests.

Here, then, will be a picturesque court; let us look at it mainly, though not exclusively, from the point of view of literary students. What were the court manners of that time? We may understand them best from a few concrete examples. We shall here again be reminded that there was far more room for impulse then than in our own drab age; in that respect our ancestors of 800 years ago were children in comparison with modern times. On the one hand was royal dignity, on the other, liberties all the greater because there was so little fear lest familiarity should breed contempt. Mr Galbraith here quotes very appositely from that half-unwilling tribute to William I in the Anglo-Saxon Chronicle: "He was very dignified: thrice every year he bare his crown, as often as he was in England. At Easter he bare it in Winchester; at Pentecost in Westminster; at Mid-winter in Gloucester. And there were with him all the great men over all England, archbishops and suffragan bishops, abbots and earls, thanes and knights." Solemn scenes of that kind impressed a very living conception of sovereignty not only upon beholders but upon thousands who would only hear the story told, with bated breath, at second or third or fiftieth hand. At other times, in contrast to this, the king might be a mere grown-up schoolboy in his passions or in his play. Many instances of this are well enough known; John, for example, after his disaster at Runnymede, rolling on the floor and gnawing the straws and rushes that littered it; or, again, Henry II pulling off Becket's costly cloak to give to the beggar: the whole street crowding round to see what the king and chancellor were fighting about. But far less known is that which Fitzstephen tells us in the same place—how the king would ride on horseback into the chancellor's hall, bow in hand, on the way to or from hunting; how he would dismount and leap over the table and sit by Becket's side and drink with him: "They played together like two boys of the same age." Less known, again, is what several chroniclers tell of Henry II's last year of life, when he burst out in fury against God, as he rode away for the last time from Le Mans and saw the town burst into flames: "For that Thou, O God, hast taken from me this day the city that I most loved in this world, [wherein I was born and bred and my father lieth buried, therefore] I shall requite Thee. For, from this time forward, I shall take from Thee the thing that should please Thee most in me, and that is mine heart." Salimbene, again, gives us a characteristic instance from the court of Henry III. A jester cried aloud in his presence: "Hear ye, hear ye, my masters! Our king is like unto the Lord Jesus Christ." "How so?" asked the king, hugely flattered. "Because our Lord was as wise at the moment of His conception as when He was 30 years old: so likewise our King is as wise now as when he was a little child." This Henry, like other weak men, had his fits of sudden fury; he ordered the untimely jester to be strung up out of hand. His servants, however, only went through an empty form of execution, and bade the unlucky fool keep carefully out of the way until royalty should have forgotten or forgiven.

As for Henry II, we may learn much from what is in every way an admirable book, the *Magna Vita S. Hugonis*, an intimate biography of St Hugh of Lincoln by his chaplain, which may be found excellently summarized in C. Marson's *Life* of St Hugh. This pious and bold Bishop of Lincoln had excommunicated the king's chief forester for infringing the liberties of the Church; again, he had refused the king's request for a Lincoln canonry in favour of one of his courtiers who was not ecclesiastically suitable. The king summoned him to Woodstock. Hugh found Henry sitting on the turf in his park, his courtiers in a ring round him. Not a soul rose to greet the bishop, and he realized that this was at the king's bidding. Therefore he "quietly laid his hands on the shoulders of a great councillor who sat next the King, and made a place for himself at the royal side". Still there was dead silence. Henry, to show his unconcern, told a courtier to give him a needle and thread, and began to stitch at a bandage on his wounded left finger. At this the bishop remarked: "How like you are now to your ancestors of Falaise!" an allusion to the fact that William the Conqueror's mother was daughter to a tanner of Falaise, and in those days leather-dressers were commonly leather-sellers and leather-workers, so that "the cobbler" may well have become a proverbial nickname. The king, "struck to the heart by this smooth yet razor-like stroke, clenched his fingers and burst into uncontrollable laughter, rolling over on the ground with his head in the grass and his face in the air; in which posture he long gave way to his laughter without control". The courtiers, even the most shocked, could not repress a smile. Henry explained the jest: then he turned to Hugh and argued both cases reasonably with him. He found himself wrong on both points, and was frankly reconciled. The chief forester and his accomplices were first publicly flogged and then ecclesiastically absolved; afterwards they became Hugh's firm friends. We must remember that Hugh the man is exceptional here; there is abundant evidence that his character gave him immense power not only over men, but over animals; yet his and Henry's manners are typical of the time, except possibly for the comparative politeness of Hugh's retort, the stroke "so keen yet so polished".

We may now pass on to see the same saint in contact with Richard I. Hugh had refused to render Richard military aid *outside* the kingdom; therefore Richard had ordered the confiscation of the Lincoln episcopal possessions [1198]. "St Hugh crossed the Channel", writes his biographer, "and went confidently to seek Richard. He found him in the chapel of his new castle of Château-Gaillard, hearing Mass on St Augustine's day; St Hugh immediately approached and saluted him. Now the King was hard by the chapel door, on his royal throne, and at his feet were the Bishops of Durham and Ely. To Hugh's greeting Richard answered no word; but, scanning him awhile with a frown, he turned his face away. Then Hugh unmoved by his wrath, said: 'Kiss me, my lord King': whereat the King averted his face all the more, turning his whole head away. Then the saintly bishop, grasping the two lappets of the King's mantle firmly at the breast, shook it with some force, saying again, 'Thou owest me a kiss, for I am come from afar to see thee.' 'Not so', replied the King; 'For thou hast merited no kiss from me.' Then the bishop shook him more strongly by the mantle, which he still held tight in his grasp, and made answer boldly, 'nay, but I *have* merited it; kiss me, I say!' Then the King, marvelling at his constancy, smiled faintly and kissed him. The two archbishops and five bishops [who sat betwixt the King and the altar, would then have made room for St Hugh]; but he went straight past them to the side of the altar, where he stood with his eyes resolutely fixed on the ground, attending now to naught else but the divine service."

If the saintliest of bishops conversed thus at Mass in certain circumstances, we may imagine how kings and nobles behaved habitually. This *Magna Vita* gives us a vivid picture of John at Lincoln minster, on Easter Day, 1213. The king was then humbled by adversity. A day or two before, when Hugh was preaching to him of the pains of hell, John had led him to the other wall of the minster (where the Blesssed were represented rising at the Last Day, with good kings resplendent in eternal crowns) and had said to Hugh: "Those are the men I aspire to imitate." Yet on Easter Day, approaching the altar to offer at Mass, he took the twelve gold pieces from his chamberlain and began tossing them about in play instead of offering them. The bishop asked him what he was doing. "I was thinking", he replied, "that, a few days ago, I would never have offered these; but take them now!" The bishop withdrew his arm on hearing this, and would neither touch the gold nor allow John to kiss his hand: "Cast them into the basin here", he said, "and depart." Then he addressed himself to his sermon, and dwelt long upon the punishment of evil princes, with the reward of the good. John, liking neither the theme nor the delay, sent thrice to the bishop to suggest that he might wind up, since the king was fasting and wanted his dinner. But the bishop continued preaching to the people, till all acclaimed him and some wept tears of devotion; then he summoned them to the altar for the Eucharist. John, "caring neither for the food of God's word nor for that of the Holy Sacrament, but hastening to saturate his flesh with the flesh of beasts, hurried from the Cathedral".

This was all very well in John, who would not communicate even on his Coronation Day, and was said never to have taken the Eucharist since he had come to years of discretion. But of Henry II, who was quite an average God-fearing man as medieval kings went, Giraldus tells us that, "either forgetting his own sacramental unction as King, or putting it out of his mind, he would scarce lend to God's worship the time of the Mass; and even during that time (perchance by reason of his royal cares and the heavy business of the State) he was more busy with his council and talk, than with devotion to the Sacrament". "When he went into his chapel", says another contemporary, "he would spend the time in whispering and scribbling pictures."[1] Numerous illustrations of these last words may still be seen in many of our English and Continental churches. Wherever the stone is soft, and not smothered in whitewash and paint, nor, again, too conscientiously scraped by the restorer, we may often find names and sketches and tags, moral, religious or satirical, scratched on the pillars and walls. At Sion in the Valais, on the pulpitum of the old cathedral church, there is an unusually rich collection of these graffiti, several of which represent just such knights and squires and castles and combats as Henry might have drawn. A still more significant story is told in the Chronicle of Battle Abbey. The Abbot of Westminster, a few days after Henry II's coronation, was so anxious to get confirmation of a charter of privileges for his abbey, that he came to the king during Mass and persuaded him to read and approve it; the king then sent for the chancellor and got it sealed: then, up came the Bishop of Chichester and protested against it; all this certainly went on during Mass, and apparently almost at the foot of the altar.

We have said that Henry II's was a specially literary court. He and his wife both patronized not only scholars, but poets. It was here that the troubadours of the south and the trouvères of the north met together; and literary historians date roughly from this marriage the beginning of written French vernacular poetry. Yet it was an unrestful court for the literary man, and we find those who frequented it complaining in terms which prove that the primitive conditions of twelfth-century life were sometimes very painful, not only to our own modern imagination, but also to the actual feelings of sensitive and cultured contemporaries. Giraldus Cambrensis, Walter Map and Peter of Blois, three of the greatest scholars then living in Europe, were all attached to Henry's court, and knew it only too well. Their verdict, from the point of view of comfort and personal respect, is unanimously unfavourable. Map institutes a formal comparison between the king's court and hell. "It is true", he points out, "that from the former we escape by death, though not from the latter. Otherwise" (he concludes) "there is about as much difference between the two as between a horse-shoe and a mare's shoe." The discomforts were doubtless aggravated by Henry II's physical strength and restless energy; but to a far greater extent they were inherent in the circumstances of the time. We have already seen how kings and nobles were obliged to flit from manor to manor to consume their supplies; and then to pass on elsewhere, where they could be fed. Thus that *Northumberland Household Book,* which tells us incidentally so much about upper-class manners at the end of the Middle Ages, shows us how the chaplains were treated in a great baronial household. The baronial order of removal, in that record, specifies minutely how many horses or vehicles there should be, and calculates " for six priests three beds, at two to a bed . . . and to have no more carriages [i.e. baggage] allowed them "; the narrowest possible allowance is made for these six men's luggage. Unquestionably, therefore, whether at court or at castle, the literary man must be prepared to rough it. It was the natural policy of the officials and upper servants to send the king out hunting all day, and meanwhile to work their own will at home. Our most eloquent witness here is Peter of Blois, one of those archdeacons whose weaknesses from the strictly religious and moral point of view are so plainly indicated by his contemporary John of Salisbury, Bishop of Chartres. Peter's whole letter is far too long for reproduction here; I have printed elsewhere all the relevant portions of it; but a few brief extracts may serve as samples of the whole.[2] The court's constant peregrinations (says Peter) condemn the scholar, with his love of sedentary life, to a continual purgatory. He finds himself served with the rough-and-ready meals of the traveller; " bread hastily made, without leaven, from the dregs of the ale-tub; leaden bread, bread of tares, bread unbaken. The wine is turned sour or mouldy; thick, greasy, stale, flat and smacking of pitch [from the cask]. I have sometimes seen even great lords served with wine so muddy that a man must needs close his eyes, and clench his teeth, wry-mouthed and shuddering, and filtering the stuff rather than drinking. The ale which men drink in that place is horrid to the taste and abominable to the sight. There, also, such is the concourse of people that sick and whole beasts are sold at random, with fishes even four days old; yet shall not all this corruption and stench abate one penny of the price; for the servants reck not whether an unhappy guest fall sick and die, so that their lords' tables be served with a multitude of dishes; thus we who sit at meat must needs fill our bellies with carrion, and become graves (as it were) for sundry corpses." Moreover, just when the unfortunate retinue hopes to dine or sleep, then the king suddenly takes it into his head to break up camp and start for a fresh stage. "Then may ye see men rush forth like madmen, sumpter-mules jostling sumpter-mules and chariots clashing against chariots in frantic confusion, a very Pandemonium made visible." "The abyss seems to have opened, and hell to vomit forth his legions." "We therefore, wandering for three or four miles through unknown forests, and oftentimes in the black darkness, esteemed ourselves fortunate if perchance we fell upon some vile and sordid hovel. Oftentimes the courtiers would fight bitterly and obstinately for mere huts, and contend with drawn sword for a lair which had been unworthy of contention among swine." When we read the further complaint that the chaplain or the man of letters must endure all this in company with the court jesters, sycophants, pampered menials who accept the proffered guerdon with scornful ingratitude, washer-women, and worse, we then realize that even the Maître de Philosophie felt himself less out of place in Monsieur Jourdain's household, than Peter and Map and Giraldus in that of Henry II.

20. CHIVALRY

Here we come to an institution more closely bound up with most men's ideas of the Middle Ages, perhaps, than any other. And, like most things distinctively medieval, here is one which has provoked the most opposite judgments. For Walter Scott, it came next in value to Christianity itself. To Arnold of Rugby it was the spirit of Antichrist; to J. R. Green "a picturesque mimicry of high sentiment"; and even the conservative Bishop Stubbs writes: "What is the meaning of Chivalry? Is it not the gloss put by fine manners on vice and selfishness and contempt for the rights of man?" All this, and much more, may be read in Professor F. J. C. Hearnshaw's essay on *Chivalry and its Place in History*, the thirty-three pages of which provide a useful collection of accurate facts, tempered with sympathetic and judicious reflections.[1] His last two pages are especially valuable; and few who have read the whole essay will dissent from its concluding reflection, that, taking it all in all, chivalry marked a distinct social advance. "Above all, it inculcated an ideal of social service; service without remuneration; service, however humble its nature, free from degradation or disparagement; service of the weak by the strong; service of the poor by the wealthy; service of the lowly by the high." Again, his earlier verdict deserves careful consideration: "In England, particularly, it set that tone which has been perpetuated in the great Public School tradition."

The fact is, that no other institution displays more clearly that contrast between theory and practice which was so characteristic of medieval society. The contrast is always with us, of course, but never so crudely as then. In the cathedral, the saint stood side by side with the demon or grinning buffoon; God's Body hung over the altar, but the king might be drawing and scribbling on the walls, or talking, or doing business; indeed, the Burgomaster of Strassburg's pew was one of his regular working offices at Mass time. In chivalry we have that same contrast of splendour and squalor; dresses of brocade and cloth of gold, of which the sleeves might dip into a sauce on the table, or the train drag in the filth of the streets or of the floor; and beneath the table dogs fighting for the bones and leaving whatever they had not consumed. Partly due to this, and partly a symptom of it, was the disproportionate stress (from the purely modern point of view) laid upon impulsive virtues, and the preference given to intuition over logic. In chivalry the stress lay always on the generosity of the moment rather than on plodding business-like justice; and, if the world in general gave special admiration to the impulsive virtues, still more did the minstrel. It was his life's business to give fame to the men who could give him gold. Henry II's eldest son—Henry III as he was sometimes called, Il Re Giovane of Dante's great poem—was held up after his early death as a pattern to all chivalry. Giraldus Cambrensis emphasizes that in his book on the *Instruction of Princes*.[2] " He had made it a fixed rule of conduct that he would never deny to any man any gift worthy of him, thinking it unworthy of his dignity that any man should depart from him either sad or lacking his heart's desire. In short, he counted every day as wasted whereon he had not drawn many men to himself by his manifold largesses, buying both their hearts and their bodies by his profuse liberality. . . . [When, as a rebel against his father, he fell into misfortune] it seemed miraculous that almost all men clung to this man who had utterly lost his lands and his treasure." Richard, again, with his energy and fiery spirit and unbounded generosity in largesse, " was second to his eldest brother only in age, not in virtue ". Salimbene tells us how on one occasion, when all were resting by the side of a spring after a hard hunt, and it turned out that the servants had brought only one flask of wine for the whole party, the Young King refused to take it for himself, and poured all into the spring that it might be shared by all. The *Novellino,* which may still be bought for a few pence in Italy, and which gives such a vivid picture of court life under Frederick II, has also much to say in honour of this Henry's impulsive generosity. Take, again, the romance of *Fulk Fitz-*

warine. Here we have a man who, after a long and adventurous life, had many sins to repent of; but he balanced his account by founding a great abbey; and "he was very hospitable and liberal, and he caused the highway to be turned [aside so that it ran] through the hall of his manor of Alleston, to the intent that no stranger might pass that way without meat or lodging or other reward or goods from him". The prisoner-king of Edward III, Jean le Bon, earned that complimentary title not from any wisdom as a ruler, for there he was sadly to seek, but from those chivalrous qualities which, blundering him into defeat as general at Poitiers, still sustained him in his hand-to-hand fight to the end; and which, when he was a prisoner in London, made him pay generously to the poor milkmaid whose pails the king's riotous greyhounds had spilled. John of Gaunt was typical of the great nobles here: "his almoner distributed twelve pence daily; John of Gaunt was accustomed to distribute twelve shillings and sixpence every Friday, and ten shillings every Saturday, amongst needy persons. He helped the poor also in other ways from time to time; in 1372, he sent the poor lazars of Leicester three cartloads of wood for fuel in winter, and the same year he gave the prisoners at Newgate a tun of Gascony wine."[3]

The same stress upon impulse is indicated by those unrestrained expressions of feeling which are even more significant, perhaps, than hastiness of action. The modern world may be excessive in its conventions for the repression of emotion; but to us the medieval man must seem to exceed in the other direction. Weeping and crying aloud were evidently rather encouraged. It is not only that we find this constantly in romance, as when Launcelot "wept as it were a child that had been beaten". It comes out frequently in the chronicles also. Joinville describes the tears and lamentations of fighting men confronted with what seems certain defeat and death; and again, when the barbers were called in to cut away those scorbutic growths from the soldiers' gums, he shows us the whole camp echoing as with the cries of women in travail. So again Froissart, when Sir John Chandos lay dying at the bridge of Lussac: "They wept piteously that were about him. . . . They wrung their hands and tore their hairs and made pitiful complaint, and specially such as were of his own house."[4]

As a rule, the young English noble had little literary training, or even none at all. Mr Galbraith appositely quotes Walter Map's words to Henry II's great justiciar, Ranulf Glanville: "The highborn of our country disdain letters, or delay to apply their children to them." They left that to the lower classes; to those whose ambitions might be served through book-learning. It was only in Italy, the least feudalized of all countries, that the nobles kept up some of the literate traditions of their Roman predecessors. On this side of the Alps "there was clearly no normal provision for the education of boys and girls of the noble class in the feudal age; and the 'palace schools' [of Charlemagne] are a myth". The young aspirant to knighthood, the squire, learnt his future job, like the apprentice to any other trade, mainly by rule of thumb. He is drawn by Chaucer not only in his personal attractions but in the helpfulness of his social service: "Curteis he was, lowely and servysable, And carf biforn his fader at the table." So also in the romance of *Blonde of Oxford*, where the hero, Jenan, is Blonde's special squire.[5] "He waited not on his lady alone, but up and down throughout the hall; knight and lady, squire and page, groom and messenger, all he served according to their desire, and thus from all he earned good will. He knew well to seize the moment for serving and honouring each guest; so that Blonde, the fair and shapely, found her needs none the worse supplied. After the dinner they washed their hands, and went to play, each as he would, up in the forest or down by the river or in some other sort of pastime. Jehan went with whom he would; and, on his return, oftentimes would he go to play in the countess's bower. . . . Well he knew all chamber-games—chess and tables and dice—wherewith he diverted the lady Blonde; often said he *check!* and *mate!* to her."

Knighthood itself we must trace briefly from its first origins. It was a prehistoric institution, much modified by the growth of medieval society, and especially by its connection with the Church, from which in its most flourishing times it derived a definite religious sanction. On the other hand, it was also influenced to a very real extent by the Muslim civilization of Spain. Tacitus shows the germ of it in his description of the Germans. "They transact no business, whether public or private, except in arms; but it is not their custom that any man should receive his arms [*arma sumere*] until the State has proved him and found him worthy. Then, in full council, the youth is equipped with shield and spear by one of their chiefs, or by his own father or kinsman. This is to them like our assumption of the *toga virilis*; this is the first honour of early manhood. Until now, the youth was part of his home; henceforward, he is part of the State." This national custom developed under growing civilization, and especially under the wing of the Church. As early as the ninth century we have scattered allusions to the formal arming of a young prince or noble. These multiplied as time went on. When we come to the twelfth century, we are at what many writers reckon to be the high-water mark of chivalry; this, however, is very likely an optical illusion, because it is certainly the time of the first great epics and romances. By this time we find knighthood established as a military gild; voluntary, but very much moulded by outward forces. It rested on the principle of co-optation; however nobly born a man might be (except, later, in the case of princes of blood) knighthood added something to his dignity. St Louis, again, steadily refused at the risk of his life, to bestow knighthood on the Muslim chiefs who had captured him. Being co-optative, therefore it was a free-masonry. All knights in theory were brothers everywhere. Froissart indeed complains that the Germans and Spaniards were often too rude to realize this; but it was clearly recognized between the English and French. The hundreds of French prisoners after Crécy and Poitiers were guests to the English nobles of Chaucer's day, sharing in their feasts and their sports: and the chronicler Walsingham gives us an admirable instance from the campaign of 1389, in which John of Gaunt and the King of Portugal fought the Spaniards and French. Famine and dysentery broke out in the Anglo-Portuguese camp, and the surviving English knights got a safe-conduct to go and convalesce among the French. The King of Portugal was scandalized: "They are deserting!" But John denied this; and in fact, after a brief period of convalescence, they came back to exchange blows with the French. "For", adds the chronicler, "both nations, French and English, though they be bitter foes in their own countries, yet abroad they often help each other like brethren, and keep inviolable faith one with the other." Thus chivalry was partly a check on feudalism, although it owed so much to that institution. In the first place, as we have seen, though the feudal fiefs soon became hereditary, knighthood was never hereditary except for blood-princes. Again, a fief was not necessary for knighthood. There were *knights bachelor*, who were not yet *bannerets,* but a sort of apprentice-knight. These, then, are sometimes treated in the romances as the stuff for the forlorn hope; if a deadly breach has to be stormed, then "The bachelors to the front!" Moreover, in its earlier stages even serfs were sometimes admitted; but this was forbidden by the later codes. Yet this freemasonry, like that of the gild, had its exclusive side. Froissart shows us plainly enough how, after the bloody capture of a town or castle, the gentles were spared, but the common soldiers were massacred without protest from their more exalted companions in arms. Sir E. K. Chambers pointed out in his paper on Malory how "in *Morte d'Arthur* itself, the distinction between noble and churl is fundamental. If there are sparks of nobility in a cowherd's son, like Tor, or a kitchen knave, like Gareth, you may be sure he will turn out to be a king's son in disguise."[6] And Miss A. Abram writes, from her studies in legal documents as well as in romance: "Class distinctions were far more real and important in the Middle Ages than they are to-day, and the distance between the upper and lower classes was much greater."[7] We may say, therefore, that chivalry was the blossom of a caste system, and that to some extent it rested, like the blossom of Periclean civilization, upon slave labour. Ruskin, with all his love for the Middle Ages, noted the weakness of chivalry in its contempt for the manual worker. He points out the gulf between *Aucassin and Nicolette,* with its Caliban-peasant, and that great literature of antiquity where noble and peasant were nearer to each other: Homer's Laertes working in his own vines with stout gloves to protect him from the thorns; or Virgil's pastoral heroes and his elegy for the dead ox. There was something of the parvenu, something of the Philistine, in the medieval descendants of these barbarian conquerors, except when religion brought them into the cloister at those times and places where the monk actually followed St Benedict's prescription of manual labour and study. Even their literary interests were small, apart from those who, like Lanfranc and Abailard and St Thomas Aquinas, gave up as boys the paternal inheritance and went out into the world as learners and teachers. It was only at the end of the twelfth century in France, and two centuries later in England, that great nobles like the Lord of Berkeley employed chaplains to translate for them from the Latin; and, even at the Renaissance, our authors found few patrons comparable to those of Italy or France.

In one respect, however, more important than is often recognized, chivalry did promote literature. Tacitus had noticed among the Germans that elaborate and effective speech was much esteemed by those fighting men, as it has been among the Arabs of the desert from time immemorial. It was the same in our own baronial courts. In *Sir Gawayne and the Green Knight*, when the hero came to the Enchanted Castle, and the lord, having first given him his fill of meat and drink, asked his name and discovered that the guest was of Arthur's Round Table, then:

Loud laughed he thereat,
And uch segge ful softly sayde to his fere, [*person, companion*
"Now schal we semlich se sleghtes of thewes [*curious arguments*
And the teccheles terms of talking noble!"[8] [*flawless*

In those days when literature was so preponderantly oral, much of it was fashioned at the tables of the great, as a sculptor fashions his work first in clay. It has been argued that, while Colonel Newcome is the natural ninteenth-century counterpart of Chaucer's knight, he is in one way markedly inferior:

"Colonel Newcome would have been ill at ease in the company of a housemaid." Such truth as there is in that contention tends, under analysis, in the direction indicated above. It is often the absence of essential and universally recognized differences which makes free social intercourse more difficult. King Edward VII was godfather to one of his gamekeeper's sons; both parties here knew that there was a gulf over which the gamekeeper had not the slightest temptation to trespass.

On its moral side, knighthood was based on two eternal principles. The first was that of *noblesse oblige*—privileges implying responsibilities—and the second, that indefinable something connoted by the word "gentleman" in its best sense; a person not only "gentle" as we say that a nurse is gentle with a patient, but also in the more literal sense of the word, a person of *gens*, of race; a pedigree-person, a thoroughbred, so long as his actions do justice to his breeding. The author of *Piers Plowman* speaks of the knight first on his political side:

Then came there a King, Knighthood him led;
Might of the Commons made him to reign.

Then, later on, when the knight promises to help this ploughman to set the world right:

By St Peter, quoth Piers, for thou profferest thee so low,
I shall swinken and sweaten, and sowen for us both
And eke labour for thy love all my lifetime,
In covenant that thou keep Holychurch and myself
From wastours and from wicked men that would us destroy.
And go thou hunt hardily to hares and to foxes
To boars and to roebucks that break men's hedges:
And fetch thee home falcons, the wildfowl to kill
For they comen into my croft and croppen my wheat.

Chaucer's definition is too well known to repeat. We need only note that his model knight was "worthy", that is dignified, as became an inheritor of a great name and wealth, who was conscious of the duty to use these profitably. On the other hand, he was meek and plainly dressed. Without forgetting his own rights, he had no wish to override those of others. We have here, therefore, a sort of social contract. The division of classes is frankly accepted—even a hereditary division of classes—but the higher class must live up to its higher fortunes. Knighthood is no mere soft option. So again it is in the philosopher John of Salisbury, from whom the words in *Piers Plowman* are very likely a dimly remembered echo. John writes; "What is the function of orderly knighthood? To protect the Church, to fight against treachery, to reverence the priesthood, to fend off injustice from the poor, to make peace in your own province, to shed your blood for your brethren, and, if needs must, to lay down your life." So again, does Malory define the ideal to which "were all the knights sworn of the Table Round, both old and young". They were solemnly bound "never to do outrageousity, nor murder, and always to flee treason. Also, by no mean to be cruel, but to give mercy unto him that asketh mercy . . .; and always to do ladies, damsels and gentlewomen succour upon pain of death. Also, that no man take no battles in a wrongful quarrel for no law, ne for no world's goods." Yet, as Sir E. K. Chambers points out, Malory was here contrasting the Arthurian theory with the too-frequent practice of his own day:[9] and similarly, from a distinguished contemporary of John of Salisbury, we have practice contrasted with that philosopher's ideal. We must discount the words as those of a rhetorician, but we cannot altogether ignore them. Peter of Blois, Archdeacon of Bath, writes to a friend: "I cannot bear the vaunting and vainglory of the knights your nephews. . . . The Order of Knighthood, in these days of ours, is mere disorder. For he whose mouth is defiled with the foulest words, whose oaths are most detestable, who least fears God, who vilifies God's ministers, who feareth not the Church—that man nowadays is reputed bravest and most renowned of the knightly band. . . . Even nowadays, aspirants receive their swords from the altar in order that they may profess themselves sons of the Church, acknowledging themselves to have received their weapons for the honour of the priesthood, the defence of the poor, the avenging of wrongs and the freedom of their country. Yet in practice they do the contrary. . . . If these knights of ours are sometimes constrained to take the field, then their sumpter-beasts are laden not with steel but with wine, not with spears but with cheeses, not with swords but with wine-skins, not with javelins but with spits. You would think they were on their way to feast, and not to fight."[10]

There was never any official written code of chivalry, but several unauthorized codes have come down to us. We must lay stress on the influence of the Church in moulding it; this may best be traced by showing the development of the ritual. There were three manners of conferring knighthood. In the first and commonest there was little or no religious ceremony, the king or great noble dubbing the worthy recipient on the field of battle or in his own hall. The knighting of an eldest son always entailed an expensive feast: this, therefore, was one of the occasions on which a king might tax his subjects. In the second method, although the consecrator was a layman and his language was the vernacular, yet there was a good deal of definitely religious ritual. The candidate kept vigil all through the preceding night in face of the altar on which his arms were laid. This, however, was not universal: there is no trace of it in Germany. Next morning he took formally a purifying bath; the Order of the Bath still bears testimony to this part of the ritual. Then he heard Mass, after which his spurs were put on; he was dubbed with the sword and exhorted in a formal sermon. A third and much rarer ceremony was purely clerical, performed by a bishop according to a service sometimes found in the liturgy, *Benedictio Novi Militis*.

So far the Church; but modern research seems to point more and more strongly towards emphasizing the influence of Mohammedan civilization, as imported from the south of Spain. We find Alvares of Cordova [950] complaining to his fellow-Christians that nowadays everything Mohammedan is fashionable among the upper classes. Again, Provençal poetry was confessedly influenced by the earlier romantic poetry of the Arabs. Chivalry, therefore (so runs the theory) spread first from Spain into Provence, and then northwards, eastwards and westwards through France. Certainly, there are considerable coincidences. This Arab civilization did place women on a high pedestal; that is, at least, the warrior's own woman. A great boot manufacturer once told me that when, in his early struggling days, he toured all Europe again and again to sell his own boots, the two districts where he could scarcely produce anything fine or expensive enough for men to buy for their women were Turkey and Asia Minor. Moreover, in Southern Spain military societies apparently crystallized into definitely religious form earlier than elsewhere; and, again, the Mohammedans unquestionably preceded the Christian countries of their day in refinement of social manners. The Arab chronicler Ousâma, in the twelfth century, expresses plainly his disgust at seeing the Christian knights amusing themselves by setting old women to run after a greased pig, and at other social manners which to him were equally barbarous.

Yet no doubt the code of chivalry did something in the long run to raise women's status. It brought greater politeness into a society in which, when a woman was left with a fief, she was naturally given to someone who could defend it and her. It was probably connected in some degree, both by action and by reaction, with that worship of the Virgin Mary which received such definite impetus from the Normans of the eleventh century. But the progress was slow; and, as we shall see in Chapter XLV, it did not prevent wife-beating. Even England, though it had no Salic law, could not quite do with Matilda as queen; and Fortescue in the fifteenth century rules out feminine sovereignty. It was not until Tudor times that this was possible; but unquestionably a good deal was done by the knight's theoretical duty to serve God and the ladies.

By Chaucer's time chivalry was in decay. Froissart, whose chronicles tell us perhaps more of its brilliance than any other source, cannot disguise its decadence from any searching eye. Yet we may here speak of decay not in the sense that Chaucer's knight and his fellows were in any way inferior to those of the twelfth century; that " golden age of knighthood " owes doubtless much to the effect of distance and mirage. Decay was only comparative, not positive; the real operating cause was the gradual rise and improvement of the middle and lower classes. The knight of Chaucer's day had as much courtesy and honour as in the days of Henry II and his son the Young King; perhaps even more. But at this later time he competed less advantageously with those outside his own class. Land cannot be multiplied: and nearly all the medieval clearing efforts or draining of swamps that was done with us had been completed before 1350. Therefore, since estates could not grow in size, and they were liable to constant subdivision for the sake of younger sons, the knight was at an increasing disadvantage as compared with the rapidly growing towns and the wealth of their merchants. This movement, inevitable in any case, was immensely hastened by the Crusades; nearly all monastic chartularies show us nobles selling their lands cheap to the monasteries in order to defray the expense of these expeditions. Thus they got into the hands of usurers, a trade by no means confined to the Jews but very commonly exercised, as we shall see later on, by merchants, and sometimes even by ecclesiastics. Therefore, not only was the knight obliged to be something of a trader, but the trader might become a knight, as for instance Walworth and others of Chaucer's friends. His contemporary, in *Piers Plowman*, puts this into one bitter epigrammatic line:

Soap-sellers and their sons for silver are made knights.

Doubtless the Black Death had some effect here, as it had upon all institutions. Chivalry was already losing something of its vitality, but by far the strongest operative cause was the Hundred Years' War, to which we shall come in Chapter XXXIX.

Without minimizing the beneficent working of the chivalric ideal, we must recognize that barons and knights were often, under the pressure of their circumstances, very hard business men. On every side, we may find scattered evidence for that state of things which is implicit in that manual for the great Percy castles and manors, *The Northumberland Household Book.* In England, especially, the increasing security of the kingdom tended to obliterate the distinction between the rich landowner and the rich trader. Castles, which in earlier times were shockingly uncomfortable, military considerations being paramount, were already far more habitable under Henry III;

it is remarkable how often that king granted licences to great men to "crenellate" their houses; in other words, to supply some great comfortable mansion with such moderate fortifications as would secure it under any other conditions than that of a formal siege by an army. Moreover, there was often the strictest business in their social relations. When a father died leaving children under age, these became wards of the overlord. Such tutelage was not, as nowadays, an honorary and burdensome duty, but a matter of considerable profit, since the guardian handled most of the endowment until the child's coming of age, and was able to dispose of him or her in marriage almost as he chose. Thus we find great nobles, lay or ecclesiastical, dealing in wardships as we deal nowadays in commercial investments. Again, when the eldest son married, he very commonly continued life with his wife in his father's castle. The heir of that Earl of Northumberland for whom the Household Book was compiled did in fact live many years in utter dependence, and on a miserable pittance, under his father. Marriage itself, again, was commonly a matter of business bargaining, as we see in the *Paston Letters*. Lastly, the laws for Distraint of Knighthood clearly emphasize the business side of that institution. The law of Edward I prevented rich men from shirking the duties attendant upon rank, by compelling everybody to be knighted who had a landed income of £20 a year or over: that is, no more than twice the income of an average incumbent of a parish in the diocese of Norwich. The account-rolls of the Lords of Berkeley, who were among the greatest of baronial families, show the lady superintending the dairy herself, and the lords selling the fruit from their orchards or the wine from their vineyards, just as nowadays we may approach a side-window at a count's palazzo in Florence and buy a bottle or two of the noble's own vintage. Miss Abram points out how in 1345 "the gardeners of the earls, barons, bishops and citizens of [London] . . . had been in the habit of standing at the side of the gate of St Paul's Churchyard to sell the garden produce of their master, 'pulse, cherries, vegetables and other wares to their trade pertaining', and they were allowed to continue the practice, but were ordered to stand in a different place."[11] In 1372, we find the Bishop of Ely selling vegetables from his garden in Holborn, where his beautiful palace-chapel still stands in Ely Place. And, as they followed mercantile methods, so also they often knew the merchant's burden of debt. The surviving fifteenth-century letters of the Plumptons, great landed gentry in Yorkshire, show them in perpetual difficulties. Mrs. Green, in her *Town Life in the fifteenth Century*, tells how "during an unwonted visit to Westminster in 1449, the poor Lady of Berkeley wrote anxiously to her husband, one of the greatest landowners in England, 'At the reverence of God, send me money or else I must lay my horse to pledge and come home on my feet'; and he raised £15 to meet her needs by pawning the Mass-book, chalices and chasubles of his chapel."[12] As the great men dealt in wardships and marriages, so also in prisoners' ransoms. Froissart is astoundingly cold-blooded on this subject: he estimates battles in terms of money with a frequency which must delight the Marxist historian.[13] At Aljubarrota, for instance, when a false alarm impelled the victorious English and Portuguese to kill their Franco-Spanish prisoners out of hand, he adds: "Lo, behold the great evil adventure that fell that Saturday! for they slew as many good prisoners as would well have been worth, one with another, four hundred thousand francs." There is no worse anachronism than to suppose that, because money in the Middle Ages was not plentiful enough to breed multi-millionaires, therefore the reign of the Almighty Dollar is a modern evil. In proportion to population, there are as many money-quarrels and money-murders among the thrifty French peasant-proprietors of to-day as in districts of Big Business.

21. CHAUCER AND MALORY

Let us take a final survey of chivalry as portrayed in two of the greatest achievements of English literature, Chaucer's *Troilus and Criseyde* and Malory's *Morte d'Arthur*. It need not embarrass us that the one is in great part translated from Boccaccio, and the other from "the French Book" which Malory had to his hand. For each has made the stuff his own not only by deliberate choice here and rejection there, but by additions and changes which, in Chaucer's case at least, have greater literary and human value than anything in the original.

If Chaucer's *Troilus*, which a good many readers have ranked even above the *Canterbury Tales,* is so little read in comparison, this is partly because it is so long. That is a very common defect in medieval literature, especially among the non-Latin nations: higher civilization means greater concentration. If every reader of *Troilus* would frankly mark off the parts that seem obviously redundant, these would probably amount to 1000 lines at least, and the different readers would be roughly agreed. And, on analysing these redundant passages, they would be found to fall under three heads, all of which are characteristic of Chaucer's time, and of the aristocratic society in which he moved as royal page and squire and member of parliament.

First, the speeches are often too long. As we have seen, speech was studied among great folk as a fine art: a knight of Arthur's Round Table might be counted upon to display "the flawless terms of talking noble", and it was for the new Round Table founded by Edward III that he had built the great Round Tower at Windsor. Here was a matter in which not brevity but verbosity was a note of highest culture; it survived long in England, and the Venetian Envoy of Henry VII's time was much struck by our elaborate ceremoniousness in this respect. The fact that Chaucer makes game of this in his Squire's Tale does not save him from falling into it at unguarded moments.

Secondly, we should eliminate most of the discussion on Freewill and Predestination. But, here again, this problem, especially in its crudest form of fatalism, was popular among the upper classes. Chroniclers tell us of it; Caesarius of Heisterbach cites a Markgraf who justified his moral lapses by pleading that, however he might behave, God knew already whether he would be damned or not. His physician, however, when urgently summoned in face of serious illness, cured him of this mental aberration by suggesting that, whatever he himself might prescribe or administer, God already knew the final result. In short, Predestination was still a comparatively new and living subject of discussion among the educated in Chaucer's day. We have abundant evidence that it was an exciting topic, not only among high-brows, but also in political and anti-clerical circles. It has lost its freshness now; but it was then quite as burning a question as the League of Nations. And, thirdly, Wertherism in love was a literary convention which had very real roots in the social conditions of that age. If we are to understand either Chaucer's society or Malory's, we must face what Sir E. K. Chambers calls " the queer spiritual tangle of the twelfth century *amour courtois* "; the spirit which inspired, or is said to have inspired, a solemn verdict of the Provençal Court of Love to the effect that real love is impossible between husband and wife. Professor Hearnshaw can write without injustice: " Marriage was, and always remained, to the troubadours, not the sacrament and consummation of love, but its most formidable obstacle and dangerous enemy. They deepened, indeed, the schism which feudalism had created between the two." Therefore we must compare and contrast medieval and modern love-making. Not, of course, that this contrast is absolute. Even sex-distinctions are not absolute; in a solemn public debate some years ago on the question of women's status in Cambridge, it was aptly pointed out that old women are not always of the female sex. We have plenty of medieval lovers among us to-day, and there were modern lovers long before Chaucer's birth; but, on the whole, there is a very real contrast in this matter between Chaucer's court environment and the ordinary modern public, even as it has been since the War. In Chaucer's society, woman-hunting was, it may be said, a normal sport. The Knight of La Tour-Landry speaks very emphatically here; St Bernardino of Siena more emphatically still. Chaucer himself, in his Doctor of Physic's Tale, lifts the veil for a moment; his contemporary, the Dominican Bromyard, tells enough to assure us that we are not misinterpreting Chaucer's hints. In such a society, where the men were commonly out for prey and all the women more or less on the defensive, and where the *mariage de convenance* was the rule, romantic love was nearly always illicit, difficult and dangerous. First, the woman's natural instinct of self-defence was here at its strongest. Next, the rival might very likely be murderous. Last, but not least, there was always a *tertium quid*, the "spier" of romance, or perhaps a multitude of "spiers", all agog with mean curiosity or jealousy or sheer love of mischief. The jealous husband, or the intrusive "spier", are almost as essential to the medieval love-drama as the hero and heroine themselves. It is difficult to exaggerate the want of privacy in the Middle Ages, or the influence of this overcrowding upon social intercourse, and therefore upon literature. Even in a great and roomy castle there was no more privacy than on a modern Atlantic liner; and, in those crag-castles that are so picturesque on French and German rivers, there can have been scarcely more solitude than on a tramp-steamer. Therefore it was almost a conventional necessity that the love-story of medieval romance should rest upon a basis of difficulty and pain, even where there was no nobler tragedy to account for this, as (for instance) in the story of Tristram. Chaucer begins the poem by announcing it as his own business to relate the "double pain" of Troilus. It was the first pain of Troilus to fall in love at all; Troilus's "Sorrows of Werther", which to us often seem tedious and artificial, were as much a court fashion as any cut of dress or hair was; so also was the secrecy of the lovers' final enjoyment. Chaucer took his society as he found it, spiced Boccaccio's story with a Pandarus who is practically a new creation in literature (though the poet probably took him to a great extent from life), and displayed in those first three books of the poem a psychology and a power of artistic development which have often been compared with Richardson's.

This brings us to a far more complicated question, and one which more deeply affects the question of Chaucer's art. It seems to me that Professor Jack is very right in indicating how Chaucer grows weary, whether consciously or unconsciously, of the more sordid elements in his story. He takes the plot as he finds it; he rules out mere common-sense solutions of the Antenor difficulty, but, it would seem, without genuine conviction. Again, the Diomede incident, which he might easily have treated in such prominent or cynical detail, and which his audience would probably have enjoyed in such detail, he dismisses with artistic brevity. And finally the epilogue, one of his greatest achievements in the matter of style, amounts almost to a retractation of all that he has taken such pains to narrate in the five preceding books: it is like his epilogue to the *Canterbury Tales*. Is it too fanciful to suggest that we have here something of an analogy to Thackeray's *Shabby-Genteel Story*? Chaucer had drunk deeply of Boccaccio; but he was not an "Italianate Englishman" in Ascham's sense. He remained, to the end of his life, too great a poet not to be something of a moralist; and he must have known more and more, as he worked through *Troilus*, that this subject was not compatible with the highest poetry of all. Here and there, indeed, Chaucer does not rise as high as his subject permits, for instance, in Troilus's waitings at the town gate, and in his faith that remains steadfast against all but the last ocular demonstration of Criseyde's fickleness, and in Criseyde's self-contempt at her own weakness. Moreover, in that epilogue, he turns upon himself and his public with no merely conventional criticism; he seriously asks himself and them: "Is this game worth a candle?" Surely the Chaucer of that moment meant this as sincerely as the Chaucer of other moments meant to ask that other very different question: What do we know, after all is said and done, about life beyond the grave?

If this, or anything like it, be the true interpretation, then we may read *Troilus* with even greater appreciation of its extraordinary beauty and interest. We may skip whole stanzas, and blocks of stanzas, as the mere conventional Wertherism of that day. We may skip a great deal more, as mere exercises in polite conversation; or, again, as attempts to talk the current philosophical talk of the day in language not too intellectual for the man in the street. We may skip here, in fact, just as all readers probably do skip when they read, for the second time at least, another love-story equally remarkable and still more popular, but which is debarred, like *Troilus*, by the nature of its plot from the very highest success of all; I mean *Manon Lescaut*. Both are very great books; both are growing rather than dwindling as time goes on; yet neither is in the very first rank of world-stories, and for much the same reasons. Both are either too immoral or not immoral enough. Their plot would give free scope to a frankly barbarian writer—free scope of a certain kind—but a man with some remnant of real decency left in him, like Chaucer or Abbé Prévost, was pulled up every now and then by breaking his shins over the stones of offence with which the whole ground is littered. Manon Lescaut knows her own weakness—knows and deplores it, as Criseyde knows hers—but she cannot mend it. She ruins a man's life; but the story forces us to ask ourselves what was the real worth of the life that she ruined. Both Manon and Criseyde fall very low; the Chevalier Desgrieux and Troilus are dragged down in the fall; but in neither case can we get the highest effects of tragedy, for in neither case was the fall from any such outstanding height; we cannot pity Troilus as we pity Hamlet, nor Criseyde as we pity Desdemona. The tragedy is that of Murger's stories in his *Vie de Bohême*—the tragedy that we sometimes think we demand so little from life—imagine that we ask no more than this, that love should endure—yet bitter experience disabuses us. But, on reflection, we must answer Chaucer and Prévost here as we answer Murger.

Few indeed are those who do truly ask so little as this from life. Not all men, far from it, even ask for this first of all, that love should endure; and are we sure that those few who do ask for love first, or who ask for love only, do not in fact get abiding love? The tragedy of bitter disappointment is very real; but must we not always ask ourselves, consciously or unconsciously: How far did the victims deserve success?

An able modern critic has argued that *Troilus* is difficult to understand because of the poet's religious attitude: " He was an English Catholic long before the Reformation—superficially more remote from us in religious sensibility than either Dante or Shakespeare. . . . Chaucer does not pass a moral judgment either upon Criseyde or upon Troilus or upon Pandarus; only a high and dispassionate view of the place of these persons in a fixed and firm moral order."[1] The whole article seems inspired by the belief, common enough, that it is not only very difficult for outsiders to grasp certain *nuances* of medieval Catholicism—a suggestion which is true of all dissenters from all *-isms*—but almost impossible to comprehend its *essence.* Yet, to begin with, we are faced with the fact that Chaucer does condemn, and that very plainly. For Troilus, from that " eighth sphere "

as he lookëd down,
He damned all our work that followeth so
The blindë lust, the which that may not last.

What is this but an explicit " moral judgment ", and one independent of sectarian difficulties among Christians? There was no orthodox writer of Chaucer's time who would not have condemned that " blindë lust ", which fills so much of the poem, as definitely as any modern Evangelical or Nonconformist does. Perhaps the greatest Churchman of the whole fifteenth century was Jean Gerson, Chancellor of Paris, who found it worth while to write a whole treatise in condemnation of the *Roman de la Rose.* If he had dealt in the same spirit with *Troilus,* might he not have condemned it as soundly as Roger Ascham condemned the *Morte d'Arthur*? This critic, if it be not rash to suggest this, has failed to realize how characteristic it was of medieval mentality to be, even more than the modern man, moral at one moment and immoral at another, without any great effort to paper over the cracks.

This is illustrated even more clearly by Malory, to whom we may now pass on. Here we have a book equally wonderful in its contrasts and in its harmony. It has all the violent antitheses which are so characteristic of medieval life, but, withal, the harmony of a single mind which has absorbed a mass of ancient legend and reproduced it not mechanically but organically, making it into flesh and blood of its own. Though medieval society was less simple than is often imagined, yet it was naturally far less complex than ours. The factors were simpler; men's fashions and manners were more elementary and more frankly displayed. We can even illustrate these factors, alike in their simplicity and in their contrasts, by putting the problem into the form of a colour-scheme, so long as we bear in mind that this is a mere illustration; no tangible argument, but only a parable. We may think then of that colour-scheme, dear to the medieval artist and especially to the simplest craftsmen, which illustrates two of the most striking lines in all medieval poetry. Walther von der Vogelweide writes:

die werlt ist ûzen schoene, wîz grüen unde rôt
und innân swarzer varwe, vinster sam der tôt.

The world is fair to look on, white and green and red,
But inly it is black of hue, and dismal as the dead.

We find the same picture again in Chaucer's Squire,

Embrouded was he, as it were a meede
Al ful of fresshë flourës whyte and reede;

a description which is equally to the point even though the actual cloak he describes may have been of any colour, powdered with those flowers; for that " mead " brings the green at once to our minds. The same, again, is implied no less distinctly, though not so briefly expressed, by Dante when he suddenly reveals to us the Earthly Paradise (*Purg.* XXIX). There he shows us the green boughs and the eternal verdure of the meadows, with flames of ruddy fire moving in the air and leaving rainbows behind them as they moved; and, finally, the whole place peopled with "a folk clad all in white, of a whiteness that was never seen among us". There, then, is the colour-scheme; green and red, the two most striking contrasts among strong colours that are common in ordinary nature, complemented by white, which stands out in equal contrast from both. We see it in young corn with poppies and marguerites and white campion, or in white houses and heavy trees massed against a crimson sunset. The other natural contrast, between orange and blue, is far less common in England; but we may see it, for instance, in the Black Forest wherever the foreground rises in ripe corn to the brow of the hill and then, without any softening middle-distance, we get the deep indigo of a pine-clad mountain twenty miles away. But to the ordinary country folk, under the blue sky, mother earth at her best and richest was clad in green and white and red. And that was the rustic painter's colour-scheme, still visible in much of its freshness on all the great Norfolk rood-screens such as Ranworth and Barton Turf. There then we have it on the art side; the simplest possible scheme of colour-contrast, getting its harmony not by the blending of the tints into one other, but by the balance and disposition of these three frankly contrasted factors. So also it was in medieval life. Men often held conflicting ideals; they did homage, as men must in every age, to things which in strict logic seem ultimately almost irreconcilable; but their conception of harmony between those opposites differed greatly from ours. We ourselves generally aim, as Aristotle taught, at the Golden Mean, striving by all sorts of concessions and compromises to temper one ideal with the other. They, on the other hand, strove far less to be all things at all times; to be, for instance, at every given moment just as warlike as we should be, and yet just as pacific and merciful as beseems a man dealing with his fellow-man. The medieval man aimed much less at this than at being frankly and unmixedly combative at one moment and counterbalancing this at a later moment with an equally unqualified generosity. We have seen how, when Geoffrey Malaterra described the Normans as "evenly balanced between greed and lavishness", he did not mean that they avoided both extremes, but that they oscillated with rough impartiality between one and the other. Medieval harmony, therefore, was reached not by the blending but by the balance of opposite factors. Here our own Black Prince is typical; at one moment he serves his captive enemy, the King of France, on bended knee; and then, another day, when he had recaptured the revolted city of Limoges, he was borne in his litter to watch an indiscriminate massacre that spared neither age nor sex. "There was not so hard a heart" (writes Froissart) "within the city of Limoges, an if he had any remembrance of God, but that wept piteously for the great mischief that they saw before their eyen; for more than three thousand men, women and children, were slain and beheaded that day. God have mercy on their souls, for I trow they were martyrs!"[2]

Thus, then, we may even venture to interpret this colour-scheme in terms of those elementary factors in human life which stand out most clearly in medieval society. Or, to put it more accurately, we can use this white-green-red picture as a sort of *memoria technica*, helping us to visualize the main elements of medieval romance. Blue we must not forget; blue the favourite colour of the missal-painter, blue of the all-pervading sky, just as the Church's teaching was almost universally accepted, in theory at least, and thus was taken in a measure for granted. But with that we are not here concerned; only with the colours of earth; green and white and red. Green, the colour of spring and summer; standing for the restfulness of earth, the fruitfulness of earth, the quiet content in earthly things. Red, the colour of passion and of conflict; red roses and red blood; the battles of this life, its victories and its defeats. White, in one sense the sum of all possible colours; so complete a blend of all that it has none of its own; the colourlessness of eternity, and of a peace beyond even the quiet green of the meadows, beyond even the blue of the Church and of all visible religion. As Shelley writes:

Life, like a dome of many-coloured glass,
Stains the white radiance of Eternity.

Or Henry Vaughan:

I saw eternity the other night,
Like a great ring of pure and endless light
All calm, as it was bright;
And round beneath it Time in hours, days, years
Driven by the spheres,
Like a vast shadow moved, in which the world
And all her train were hurled.

This imagery comes out even plainer in more definitely theological literature. Take that sermon of Newman's which fascinated Matthew Arnold. "After the fever of life; after wearinesses and sicknesses; fightings and despondings; languor and fretfulness; struggling and failing; struggling and succeeding; after all the changes and chances of this troubled unhealthy state, at length comes death, at length the white Throne of God, at length the Beatific Vision."[3] Or, to go back farther and higher, Isaiah i. 18: "Though your sins be as scarlet, they shall be as white as snow"; or Revelation vii. 9-14: "And lo! a great multitude which no man could number . . . clothed with white robes, and palms in their hands. . . . These are they which came out of great tribulation, and have washed their robes, and made them white in the blood of the Lamb." Those are the main notes of medieval life; the delights of the world and the battles of the world in brilliant contrast; and, apart from both, the pure white of unworldliness, the charm of deep and simple religion, not only of the official Church, but also that still more primeval religion; the unselfish love of friend for friend, of man for woman and of woman for man, with the conviction that this love is, in some most real sense, eternal. All these in startling contrast; yet always, in virtue of the purity and simplicity with which each colour is laid on, and of the just balance between contrast and contrast, the three colours grouped into one harmonious whole:

A meede—Al ful of fresshë flourës whyte and reede.

All these are admirably represented in Malory. Green, by the Queen's Maying, at the beginning of book 19: Red, by the fights on every page; White, by the Graal, from its very first pages, with Galahad nurtured in that Nunnery of Nuns, down to the very last, where the Sacred Quest is finally achieved. Nor is the sense of religion in that episode alone: it pervades the book, and comes out in the minutest touches. "Then heard they Mass and rode forth"; "There they came to a ruined chapel"; "Then to an hermitage", "Then to a great abbey of black [or white] monks", and so forth. Here is a whole paradise of romance; the idealized picture of an heroic past.

We must emphasize that last point; for days of knight-errantry, in so far as they ever existed, lay far behind when Malory wrote. Whether the late twelfth century was or was not the golden age of chivalry, certainly it was that of knightly romance. Not only had the Hundred Years' War come between, with its emphasis on the practical business side of warfare and its breach of many older class conventions, but the whole world had changed greatly between 1150 and 1450. A real knight-errant would have been as hard to find in that fifteenth-century society, and would have been quite as much out of place, as Charles Gordon and T. E. Lawrence were in ours. We cannot imagine the first John Paston in the rôle of knight-errant, nor either of the two Sir Johns, his sons! Yet all the mere body of chivalry was still there in Malory's time; heraldry, and feast in hall, and song and dance in bower, and the great abbey for hospitality, and the ruined chapel and the hermit. Men were familiar with these things as part of their daily life; these were the colours, so to speak, fresh to any painter's hand who wished to revive the ancient ideal before men's eyes. And, if that ideal was in one sense dead already, yet in another and deeper sense it has never died, from that day to this. André Maurois, in his *Silences du Colonel Bramble*, shows us something of this, inarticulate but none the less real.

But to Malory's contemporaries, it must be repeated, the Arthur story must already have had much of the same archaic charm which it has for us. Even where men could still see the outward things he described, the soul of those things needed imagination for its comprehension then as now. And the author's own life, as we now know, was very far from that of a hero of Arthurian legend.[4]

22. THE MONASTERY

All civilization proceeds by alternate emphasis on individualism and collectivism. In one age, men lay most stress on the unhampered development of the individual, in spite of the claims of his surroundings. In another, they most emphasize the fact that individuals must be disciplined to act in masses, or the world cannot advance. Man (they feel) shows his superiority to the brute in nothing more than in this power of forming groups, and then groups of groups, and still wider, still more complicated groups of groups of groups; so that, for such formations, self-control is even more necessary for the multitude than energy and self-assertion. It would be no gain to civilization that the exaggeration of "My country, right or wrong!" should give place to a counter-exaggeration: "My own personality, right or wrong!" Monasticism, Chivalry, and the Gild were perhaps the greatest collectivist movements of the Middle Ages. All of them are unduly depreciated by many people nowadays, while they are loaded with exaggerated praise by others; the difficulty is to reach a fair balance. We have to reconcile two widely different facts which seem equally indisputable in the light of historical documents. First, that monasticism grew up by what seemed an overmastering impulse, and became one of the chief social forces of the Middle Ages; at one time, even perhaps *the* chief. Secondly, that (apart from those boys who form the vast majority of converts under the Roman and the Greek Church) so few even of the chosen, even of the most religious men, adopt nowadays that life which, before the Reformation, was called *the* religious life *par excellence*. For it may safely be asserted that, at least from the twelfth century onwards, in nine cases out of ten, the word *Religion* is used by medieval writers in the technical sense of a monastic order, and the word *"conversion"* means entering

Religion, i.e. joining some monastic order. Those facts will perhaps be best explained and reconciled if we deal with the development of monasticism under three heads. First, the spontaneous and natural genesis of the ideal. Then, this ideal materialized in a formal and world-wide institution. Finally, the decay of that formal institution, and its loss of all special legal privileges; although, even nowadays, the fire of the ideal still glows to some extent amidst the embers.

Monasticism, then, represents a natural (perhaps even necessary) stage in the development of the Christian Church. In every generation a few earnest men have suddenly rediscovered for themselves, with overpowering force, that Christ may have meant literally what he said in those words "many are called and few are chosen". Such men realize with intense force that the majority of the baptized, in their own generation, are Christians scarcely more than skin-deep; that they cannot in the strictest sense be said to be Christians at heart; that we cannot strictly call our fatherland a Christian country; nay, more, that no steamship or airship can bear us away to any land which is thoroughly Christian. Therefore those individuals who in their own hearts say with St Paul "to me, to live is Christ and to die is gain" must almost of necessity be in some sense strangers to their own kith and kin. This has been true of every generation in every country, for the last 1900 years. Figgis, a true historian and devoted monk, emphasized this fact that, in the deepest sense, the Western World never has been Christian. However our further deductions may differ, the fact itself must be fully faced in its actual historical perspective. It is not that Christianity has been tried, and failed, but that it has never been strictly tried. St Augustine, in whose father's lifetime Christianity had won its world-wide political victory under Constantine, recognized as clearly as we can that many are called and few are chosen. Indeed, we can go back much farther than that; the conviction was already overmastering in many minds two hundred years before Augustine.[1] As early as about A.D. 170 arose the Montanists, Puritans for whom the official Church was already too worldly, and who were joined by the great Church writer Tertullian.

Indeed, the movement may be traced still farther back; and we find the germ of it even in the earliest days of Christianity, bringing with it a definite divergence of opinion as to how far the Christian should separate himself from the world. And, if the earnest Christian's attitude towards the world around him was not always quite simple, it grew more complicated in process of time, in proportion as the world changed, and, above all, as the Church herself changed. Men sometimes ask: "Was Christ a socialist?" At least He wished His more immediate disciples to be unencumbered with earthly possessions and family ties. Moreover, only thus could they have done their missionary work; and we must remember that they were in daily expectation of the second Advent. But, as years passed on, and generation succeeded generation, this exclusively missionary element naturally fell more and more into the background. Many men had their family, their business, their office; they were bound by ties of all sorts. Should they leave these, or could they not do better by using them for Christian purposes? Already in apostolic times, St Paul puts this problem in the form of marriage to an unbeliever: "For what knowest thou, O wife, whether thou shalt save thy husband, or how knowest thou, O man, whether thou shalt save thy wife?" Moreover, the problem naturally became more insistent as the end of the world seemed more and more remote. This, then was the individual's problem; and that of the Church, the Christian society, was similar. Should the Church (or, as we may say at first, the Churches) remain as obscure, as detached as possible, or should it enter into civic life, imperial life, form an *imperium in imperio,* and so pursue its missionary work by ordinary business methods? The Quakers of our own day faced with these alternatives, have definitely chosen the latter So, for the Church, it is difficult to find an answer different from that which history gives; and yet that meant relegating some very plain gospel precepts to the limbo of counsels of perfection. Property, family ties, office in the city or in the State, all meant either a silent abandonment of, or a difficult and perpetual struggle of adaptation to, certain distinctive Christian tenets of the first generation. Hence the growing worldliness of the Church was acutely felt for at least a century before Constantine made it a State Institution.

The history of Tertullian and the Montanists shows us two most important developments. First, in morals; the Church is losing her disciplinary hold over the congregations; she no longer exacts more than the minimum penance for sin as a condition of communion in the Christian rites; she is glad to retain all she can, and afraid of frightening any away. On the other hand, she is drawing tighter the reins of dogmatic discipline in proportion as she loosens the moral reins. These Montanists, for instance, in reward for their inconvenient zeal and their peculiar tenets, found themselves cast out from the pale of the orthodox Church. From that time forth, if not before, we may say that Christian society is no longer bound together mainly by the bonds of fraternal love, but by the framework of an official hierarchy. And the hierarchy, in order to keep its power over the mass of the baptized, has to make constant concessions to ordinary social customs; in other words, to the worldly spirit. When, therefore, a century after this Montanist expulsion (or secession, for, like Wesleyanism, it was half-and-half), Constantine made Christianity into a privileged Church, then the incompatibility of the two ideals became more evident. Some aimed at apostolic simplicity; others aimed at a great organization on the lines of the imperial bureaucracy; few indeed were able to reconcile both ideals. Therefore we find now an increasing stream of Christians going out to live the hermit life in the wilds of Egypt and Syria. "They fled from the world, and therefore from the Church which had admitted the world into her bosom." This separation was not in a controversial spirit, but in self-defence. The impulse came partly from Alexandria, which was then the centre of Christian thought; partly, again, it was in imitation of pagan ascetics who had long lived in the Egyptian desert. Concerning the earliest Christian hermits, Paul and Anthony, there is much uncertainty in detail: they lived about A.D. 250. But certainly, by about A.D. 350, Egypt contained thousands of such. And their manner of life was necessarily unsacerdotal, without being anti-sacerdotal: unsacramental, though not anti-sacramental; that was also a distinguishing mark of nearly all the monastic reforms of later ages. For the monk's ideal of the religious life, in the earliest times, differed widely from that of the official Church. To him, the essence of Christianity lay in asceticism. Personal self-denial and constant prayer were, in his mind, prior to Christian brotherhood, public worship with its common liturgy, and the bishop's teaching. It is difficult (as Monsignor Duchesne points out) to see how St Anthony ever received the Holy Communion during his twenty years of seclusion in the desert.[2] St Thomas More speaks of monasteries in the distant past which had only four priests to five hundred monks. Here he probably spoke without book; but the ancient *Historia Lausiaca*, a trustworthy source, shows only eight priests to the five thousand monks of the Nitrian desert; and one alone of these performed all the ordinary celebrations of the Holy Communion.[3] These recluses needed no more than Elijah did; the desert for quiet, the oasis for food, and the sustaining belief in God's final government. Yet there was as a rule no antagonism, or, at any rate, no conscious antagonism, to the secular Church, the World-Church. The difference was simply one of emphasis and division of labour. The monks, for their part, were devoted to prayer, contemplation, and mortification of the body; but the World-Church recognized all these things as very holy, and was very glad that others should do them. It said in effect to the monks: "Mortify yourselves, and pray for us." On the other hand, this World-Church had its imposing traditions, its organization, and its worship. But, here again, the hermits were glad that the hierarchy should impress and even control the laity. Thus each party comforted the other against heresy and paganism; and the divergence of ideal was settled in a sense acceptable to both. There need now be no general reform of the whole Church; each took one part, and each exaggerated it. The monastic ideal became more and more ascetic, while the World-Church became more and more worldly; so that, by A.D. 350, the contrast was enormous and there were thousands of such hermits. Then, gradually, these developed an organization of their own; and consequently, in process of time, the ritual and sacramental system of the Church became as necessary to the monk as to the rest: indeed, for the last five centuries of the Middle Ages, the abbey churches were in the front rank for size and splendour. The monks thus received an organization quite as rigid as that of the hierarchy; and their collective enthusiasm was often enlisted in Church politics. Hypatia [410] and, later, the Iconoclasts were routed by physical violence on the part of the monks; more than one Church council was overawed by their turbulent enthusiasm. The Emperor Theodosius, pious as he was, found it necessary to take measures against them; he wrote to St Ambrose: "The monks commit many crimes."[4] Their intrusion into secular life was constantly forbidden by State edicts: the cry of the public was: "Return to your own deserts!" Indeed, this it was which prompted the final recognition of the indelibility of monastic vows by Justinian in 532. For at first there were no vows at all; and, even after their introduction, for a long time they were merely conditional and revocable, if not from the strict ecclesiastical point of view, at least from that of the State. The modern indelibility of the vow has its origin far less in grounds of religion than of civic expediency.

We have thus reached the stage of organized monasticism; let us briefly trace its fortunes. In the Eastern Church, its main features have remained unchanged to the present day. The monk, withdrawing from the World, leaves the World-Church mainly to shift for itself. The monasteries are increasingly drawn upon to supply bishops; but the bishop is mainly a conservative and mechanical State officer; for such work, the best man is a monk trained under a conservative and mechanical system, which has stood almost unaltered for ages. Thus we get a curious contrast; the Eastern parish priests are regularly married, generally to daughters of priests, while the bishops are always celibate monks. We may contrast this with the West, where the Benedictines alone, beginning two centuries later, claimed to have produced, by the middle of the fourteenth-century, twenty-four Popes, two hundred cardinals, seven thousand archbishops and fifteen thousand bishops; the list was probably exaggerated, but nearer to the facts than large figures usually are in the Middle Ages.

This brings us to the central fact of Western monastic history. St Benedict's Rule, having been composed about A.D. 529, was thus contemporary with Justinian's work on Roman Law, and his closing of the Schools of Athens. There were already many monasteries in the West, and even monastic lawgivers. There existed a whole system of Celtic monasticism in early times, bound up with tribal organization. Again, Cassiodorus, Theodoric's great minister, and two other Western churchmen, Cassian and Caesarius of Arles, composed monastic rules after the types already classical in the East; Caesarius only a few years before St Benedict. But all these soon became obsolete, while St Benedict's survived. Partly, no doubt, because this came at a time of crying need for codification. For instance, the first chapter of the Rule complains bitterly of monks who were a law to themselves, sometimes mere pseudo-religious tramps. Again, it is significant that, in 532, Justinian began publishing that series of laws which made monastic vows irrevocable, and which allowed secular magistrates to clap apostate monks into prison. The circumstances, therefore, called for a legislator: but here also was the man, for Benedict was certainly a man of genius. His Rule shows a splendid combination of the ideal and the practical. It was possible for the great architect and medievalist Viollet-le-Duc to call it, without intolerable exaggeration, "the most important document of the Middle Ages". Reading it carefully, and interpreting it in the light of early practice, we find much in Benedict's own Rule different from the average medieval, let alone modern, monastic practice. In the first place there was still much of the *monos* principle. It insisted on strict claustration. Again, each house was an independent unit, except that the monks, originally, were under the authority of the diocesan bishop; their frequent later escape from this control was an abuse. Secondly, St Benedict insisted upon the necessity and moral value of manual labour; reading and writing were only by-occupations in his mind. Thirdly, there was still a good deal of unsacerdotalism long after St Benedict's death; we find monasteries which did not possess a single priest, and all early lists show us a decided majority of non-priests. It was only the Council of Vienne (1311) which at last compelled monks to proceed to priestly orders. "For the increase of divine worship", it directed every monk to take priest's orders if bidden by his abbot: the reason being that, by this time, the abbeys were saddled with multitudes of statutory Masses undertaken for the souls of past benefactors. From the first, therefore, there was in monasticism a strong temptation towards the "holy boorishness" which "profiteth itself alone"; *sancta rusticitas solum sibi prodest*, wrote St Jerome. But healthy monasticism was too strongly bent towards the real service of God to remain strictly obedient to that "boorish" side of the Rule. At first, Benedictinism seems to have been confined to the dozen houses founded by St Benedict himself. But the burning of its headquarters at Monte Cassino by the Lombards brought the monks to Rome, where Gregory I established them in his own palace, and probably became a monk himself [580]. Thence it was carried by St Augustine of Canterbury to England; thus Canterbury was probably the first Benedictine monastery founded outside Italy. The significance of these two facts is enormous: they strike the two keynotes of the world-history of Western monasticism. First, its close alliance with the Papacy and, secondly, the missionary spirit which inspired it wherever it was really fresh and living. It is no accident that Gregory the Great, who was in one sense the founder of the medieval Papacy, was the first monk (or, at least, monastically living person) to sit in the chair of St Peter. Nor, again, that Gregory's letters in answer to the difficulties propounded by his monastic missionaries constantly harp upon one theme: If you would win souls, you must conform yourself to others' points of view; be all things to all men, in so far as you can do so without sacrifice of principle.[1] In other words, to become a true missionary, the monk must break through many of the narrower prescriptions of his Rule. Here is the radical difference between Western and Eastern monasticism. If in the Western political world there was more disorder, at least there was more life, more abundant energy. And, again, this Northern climate is unfavourable to Fakirism : it " turns earth's smoothness rough, and bids nor stand nor sit, but go ". One cannot, even in Italy, exist as in the Egyptian deserts, lying in the sand and the sun, and eating a couple of dates a day. Therefore, in the West, the best monks were seldom able to school themselves into mere passive receptacles of the Holy Ghost. They were called to the world's work, and obeyed the call. Men like Anselm and Bernard were most unwilling to leave the quiet of their cloister; but, recognizing God's voice in the summons, they went out whensoever and whithersoever they were needed to do the world's work. Moreover, this spread of monasticism in the West coincided very closely with the decay of the Roman Empire. Thus, during the period when barbarian forces were everywhere working most busily for disruption, this institution was interpenetrating barbarism in the contrary direction, and making everywhere for consolidation. We cannot find a better example of this than the life and work of St Boniface the Englishman, with which I have dealt already.

The Western monks, then, at their best, became not only ecclesiastical statesmen, but often secular politicians also; historians, poets, even artists and schoolmasters, though far less than is generally supposed. But all these activities are in no wise contemplated in St Benedict's Rule; so that Benedictine disciplinarians frequently insisted that a monk can seldom mingle with the world, even in order to do good in the world, without contracting himself something of the worldly taint. The ideal monk should be, according to the twelfth-century *Speculum Monachorum*, " like Melchizedek, without father or mother or kinsfolk ". It is this conflict of ideals within monasticism which partly justifies Professor Grant's somewhat agnostic sentence: " The social influence of monasticism was very great, though it is difficult exactly to analyse it." Its social influence was indeed enormous, if only because the institution itself grew to such enormous proportions. Monks, friars, and nuns numbered about 8000 in Tudor England with its $4\frac{1}{2}$ millions; about 2 millions of these would be adult, and that proportion would make 80,000 Religious in modern Britain. Again, their income, though it can only be roughly guessed, was in all probability at least one-tenth of the whole national income, and very likely considerably more.[5] In 1200, both numbers and incomes were probably at least half as great again, in proportion to national population and income, as in 1500. Their numerical and territorial influence therefore, even apart from the influence of their ideal, was enormous.

And what, then, was the influence of their ideal? We may divide the monks roughly into three classes. First, those who kept strictly to the original principle of complete separation from their fellow-men. Of these the Carthusians are the type; always very few in numbers, scarcely more than one-hundredth of the general monastic population, but strictly secluded, and therefore able to boast with approximate truth: "We have never been reformed, because never deformed"—*nunquam reformati, quia nunquam deformati.* Secondly, there were those who relaxed this principle of retirement in favour of the stronger principle of charity, and made their monasteries centres of beneficent practical work, living a life not very ascetic, but as dignified and regular as in any other such institution known to history. Thirdly, those who relaxed the principle of claustration for their own comfort, and lived a worldly life under the religious habit. On the whole, the second and most beneficent type certainly preponderated during the best ages of monachism. An admirable example of this kind of average monastic life, or somewhat above the average, at Bury St Edmunds, may be read in Jocelin of Brakelond's Chronicle. Undoubtedly, again, there was no age at which the standard of cloistered practice was not on the whole higher than that of the average layman outside; and, in certain times and places, the monks were the very salt of the earth.

Their contributions to civilization (apart from their direct influence on Church life) may be briefly summed up as follows.

Their *charity*, though it is often much exaggerated by authors who quote exceptional instances as normal, was yet considerable. We have seen above that they took more out of the parishes than they gave back: but the alternative to the monk was often a layman who would have taken still more; and the monastic dole was certainly missed at the Dissolution, especially in the comparatively backward Northern counties of England. *Manual work* was an integral part of both Benedictine and Augustinian Rules, from which every monastic order of the later Middle Ages more or less directly derived except the Friars. But the actual amount of work done by monks is often ludicrously exaggerated. This Benedictine precept was soon neglected; and, often as monastic reformers recalled it, real manual work was short-lived in practically all those revivals. What the monks did for agriculture was far more as landlords than as labourers. Even such work as copying or binding books was scarcely ever practised by the majority in a monastery, and often for whole generations by nobody at all: this can be proved by their own records. Comparison of successive catalogues, even in flourishing monasteries, suggests that the actual rate of increase was no greater than would be accounted for by one monk out of every fifty spending all his spare time as a copyist. Moreover, in spite of frequent assertions to the contrary, the monks very seldom taught outside pupils; St Jerome's words, repeated by St Bernard, were often echoed afterwards: "The monk's businesss is not to teach but to mourn"—*monachus non docentis sed plangentis habet officium*. The nunnery schools, of which there were a few in the later Middle Ages, were generally of the most unpretentious description, and had grown up mainly from financial causes. For the nuns were often miserably poor; and, in spite of discouragement or even prohibitions from their ecclesiastical superiors, they received children to board or teach as one way of making both ends meet. But, although it was only in exceptional cases or times that the monks set a really brilliant example of labour, unquestionably the institution as a whole did a good deal to counteract that scorn of manual work which marked all the barbarian invaders. Monastic contributions to *Art, Literature* and *Science* will be considered under those heads in later chapters. Meanwhile, it must be noted that the monastery was to some extent an object-lesson in *democracy*. Here, again, however, we must beware of exaggeration. Much natural favour was shown to the rich and high-born; moreover, monks did not usually come from a stratum of society below the citizen class, and nuns were still less often of really humble extraction. Savine, using the word " democratic " in its strict modern sense, is right in saying that " the monasteries could not be democratic institutions : . . . the majority [of the monks] could not but sympathize with the upper and middle classes ".[6] But they were democratic in the sense in which the English parliament of the eighteenth century was democratic, oligarchical as it may seem to us in a more advanced age. Not only might the very poorest be admitted sometimes to a rich abbey, but he might be elected abbot, and, theoretically, have absolute sway. Popular election had been the strength of the early Church; bishops and priests were really elected by flocks at a time when municipal elections had become a farce in the Empire; and much of this system remained a reality down to the ninth century at least. Within the monasteries, in spite of illegal encroachments from popes, kings, and nobles, election remained the general rule in England down to the Reformation, thus keeping up some reminder of that republican maxim which Napoleon cherished: *la carrière ouverte aux talents*. On the Continent, election in the abbeys had given way almost everywhere to appointments by king or pope, or by both in collusion; scarcely one great house in France was free from what Montalembert called " this leprosy of monasticism "; that is, a " commendatory " abbot, who consumed nearly all the revenues, yet was commonly not a monk, and often not even a priest. From this plague England was saved by steady resistance from kings and layfolk against papal pressure; the " leprosy " was only beginning to take root with us when Henry VIII dissolved the monasteries. Thus, in their most living days, the monks had set an example of election and representative government to society around them; the elaborate representative systems of the Cluniacs and Cistercians, and the organization of Dominicans after them, could scarcely fail to exert some influence upon the parliamentary movements; especially in England, where monastic life was on the whole more regular than in any other great country.

23. CLOISTER LIFE

It remains to enquire rather more closely how the Rule worked out in practice. We must take the Benedictine, which was followed by far the most and the greatest houses, as type; the Augustinian, which comes next in importance, resembled it strongly, but was a little less strict.

Disciplinarians insisted that their Rule contained three essential principles—*tria substantialia*—viz. Obedience, Poverty, and Celibacy. From these not even the Pope could dispense the sworn Religious. He could, indeed, relieve him of the whole vow—could, as it were, annul his marriage to that ideal—but, short of this step, of which there are very few historical examples, those *substantialia* were as inviolable as matrimony itself. In reinforcement of them the authorities insisted on four main pillars of discipline laid down in the Rule: Propertylessness, Labour, Claustration, and Diet. But, even before the Black Death, those four pillars had been cut away in practice; the Canonist John of Ayton [1340] tells us this in so many words, and monastic records themselves bear him out. Between then and the Dissolution, they were not only neglected in practice but even whittled away in theory. The monk not only had pocket-money, from which he might amass a private hoard and lend it out at usury (we have definite evidence of this), but he would complain to the official visitor if that pocket-money were not regularly paid. Chapter 66 of the Rule prescribes, most emphatically, that he must not go outside the precincts, and early disciplinarians interpreted this in the strictest sense; yet in the fifteenth century such strict claustration was not the rule, but a rare exception. The English General Chapter of 1444 published a statute to the effect that a monk who called his brother "liar" should be restricted to the interior monastic buildings for three weeks; if he struck him with fist or knife, for a year. Diet, again, was by Rule quasi-vegetarian; butcher's meat was strictly forbidden except to the sick. Yet first the habit grew up of resorting to the infirmary in order to enjoy those forbidden flesh-pots; then, when this was prohibited by papal statute, of creating a sort of half-way chamber, in which meat was eaten without polluting (so the canonists argued) either refectory or infirmary. At Peterborough this was called "seyny house", at Durham, "loft" (it is now the Chapter Library); but its ordinary name was "misericorde"—the Chamber of Mercy. This, again, was definitely forbidden by papal statute (Gregory IX); but a century later (1339) Benedict XII recognized the concession as inevitable, and contented himself with permitting the misericorde to only half the congregation at a time; so that the alternate half would be maintaining their vegetarian rule in the refectory. Yet, only a few years later, the English Chapter General complained of that restriction as difficult to keep; and visitatorial injunctions bear this out. Finally, labour was abandoned earlier and more completely than the other three pillars. Field-work was first dropped, as superfluous for houses that were so richly endowed, and as scarcely compatible with monastic dignity: writers even pleaded here the example of St Maur, who had been St Benedict's own pupil. Then kitchen and house work went by the board; so that, during the last two or three monastic centuries in England, we find even shaving, gardening, washing, the mowing of the cloister-garth, done by paid servants, who, in the wealthier house, outnumbered the brethren, sometimes by 50 per cent. Moreover the monk's own special labour, that on which he fell back in excuse and by which he gained his endowments, was the *Opus Dei*, his psalmody and Masses. Yet, long before the Dissolution, even statutory Masses were being neglected in great numbers, to the defrauding of benefactors' souls. The other liturgical services, again, were so irregularly maintained even at such great and wealthy abbeys as Peterborough, Ramsey and Norwich Cathedral, that the visitors found less than half of the community in choir, and recorded the scandal which this caused among the laity. As to the rule of celibacy, though it is seldom that we find a house so ill-reported as we have seen of

Flaxley, yet the episcopal visitations leave no doubt that there were sufficient scandals to affect monastic reputation very seriously. Not only satirists, but the most unexceptionable witnesses, are practically unanimous upon this point. Most convincing of all is the comparative silence of anti-Lollard apologists. These men fill one folio page after another in defence of the monks on other points, yet they show striking diffidence and hesitations upon this, the most serious point of Lollard attack. St Thomas More, in his controversial discussions with the innovators, where he says the worst that could be said against them with any semblance of truth by an honest and indignant champion of orthodoxy, yet goes out of his way to relate three anti-monastic anecdotes which, from the pen of a modern Protestant, would be cried down as mere bigotry.

That, after all, is the most important question: What did the laity think of these Religious, for many generations before the Reformation? We have already glanced briefly at the evidence of Gower and *Piers Plowman*; let us here take Chaucer, the most Shakespearian among all medieval writers in his pictures and his estimates of all sorts of men. Let us consider, in the light of cold-blooded ecclesiastical documents, his Friar, his Monk, and his Nun.

With the Friar he had plainly least sympathy: the man is, as Professor Trevelyan pithily remarks, a medieval Stiggins. St Francis and St Dominic, almost at the same moment, had set themselves to inaugurate a new era in monasticism. The older orders had become rich: the monks' own friends were confessing that this child Wealth was destroying its parent Religion, and therefore the Friars adopted the principle of poverty, not only individual, but corporate also. The Friar must possess nothing, and his house must possess nothing: all life must be lived from hand to mouth. Moreover, the good monk's Rule had confined him for life within his own precincts; and the relaxed monk, when he broke that rule of claustration, had brought disorder rather than order into the society round him; for Chaucer's Shipman's Tale might be paralleled from visitatorial reports. The Friar, on the other hand, abandoned the whole principle of strict claustration; he used his monastery only as a base of operations: his main work was to be done outside, as evangelist and physician of souls. It was a golden ideal; but this gold had rapidly become encumbered with dross. Long before Chaucer's birth, those Friars who fought for their Rule in its primitive strictness had become a persecuted minority: in the lifetime of Chaucer's father (1318) four Franciscans at Marseilles had been burnt alive for disobedience when their General had commanded them to do things incompatible with St Francis's own Rule and Testament. Piers Plowman cites such "poor fools" as rare exceptions among the general Franciscan decay.[1] Therefore, much as the Franciscans and Dominicans, with their brother-orders of Carmelites and Austin Friars, had done at one time to rejuvenate Church life, yet Chaucer and his contemporaries already visualized them as men who professed to do the parish priest's work but were in fact his rivals, and too often mere stumbling-blocks in the way of true religion and morality. In so far as Chaucer is capable of flaming indignation, he spends that upon the Friar.

To the Monk his satire is far more genial; it is rather that of Thackeray, who has a good deal of good-humoured fellow-feeling with the human failings of the cleric, so that we cannot resist a sneaking sympathy with the Rev. Jedidiah Ramshorn, whom the Spirit has commissioned to go and convert the Pope of Rome; or, again, with that Bishop of Bullocksmithy of whom the club steward can quote, as a testimonial to the meat there served, that he has just eaten three chops from this same loin; or even with Charles Honeyman. Let us look at Chaucer's Monk, then, in this spirit and through the microscope of ecclesiastical records.

We see at first sight the humour of his hunting Monk; but what is that "text" at which he snapped his fingers, "that seith that hunters beth nat hooly men"? The Vulgate Bible, at the passage where our Authorized Version makes Nimrod "a mighty hunter *before* the Lord", has "*against* the Lord". He thus became a type of the godless despot, and finds his fitting place in Dante's *Inferno*. His case, equally naturally, was quoted in Gratian's *Decretum*, the first volume of Canon

Law, in support of the strict prohibition of hunting for all clergy, and, *à fortiori,* for the nominally cloistered clergy. There, Canon Law comes in again; one of its best known texts was that which smote monastic wanderers with the words of St Jerome: "A monk out of his cloister dies spiritually, like a fish out of water." Chaucer knew well, and most of his readers knew roughly, how many papal and conciliar injunctions might have been quoted against this hunter-monk, and how often he was the target for moral preachers who loved the habitation of God's house, and were not inclined to make their lives a portion for foxes. We hear his bridle jingle gaily in the whistling wind, as clear and loud as the bell of his own chapel: we see how his admirably supple boots are in exact character for this huntsman. Here are obvious unclerical touches; but few modern readers realize their full force. Few know how often and how earnestly such worldliness and expense had been forbidden to these men whose whole life was vowed to poverty; men who claimed to be *par excellence* "Christ's Poor"—*pauperes Christi*—and therefore to be even more worthy of alms than the non-Religious poor. Let us see how the contemporary *Dives and Pauper* treats this subject. "To them that have the benefices and the goods of Holy Church, it longeth principally to give almesse and to have cure of the poor people. . . . Therefore these men of Holy Church that boocle their shone with boocles of silver, and use great silver harneys in their girdles and knyves, and men of Religion, monks and chanones, and such other, that . . . ride on high horses with saddles harnessed with gold and silver more pompously than lords, be strong thieves and do great sacrilege, so spending the goods of Holy Church in vanity and pride [and] in lust of the flesh, by which goods the poor folk should live. A lady of a thousand mark by year can pin her hood against the wind with a small pin of laton [brass]; xii for a penny. But a monk that is bounden to poverty by his profession will have an ouche [locket] or a broche of gold and silver, in value of a noble or much more."[2] Here again Chaucer's Monk fits in most exactly:

For to festne his hood under his chyn
He hadde of gold y-wroght a ful curious pyn,
A love-knotte in the gretter end there was.

This Monk's scorn of study and manual work is in obvious keeping with his repudiation of his own Rule as "old and some-deal strait". St Augustine, it is true, laid even more emphasis than St Benedict upon manual labour; but "let Austin have his swink [work] to him reserved!" "Greyhoundes he hadde", while episcopal visitors were recording, over and over again, in words which this generation of ours can now at last read in print after centuries of historical neglect, that it was scandalous to nourish hunting dogs in monasteries, and to "give the children's bread unto dogs". Again:

I seigh his sleves y-purfiled at the hond
With grys, and that the fynest of a lond.

Gris was the fur of the grey squirrel, finest and most expensive of all except ermine and vair. It was expressly forbidden to monks, as also was *burnet* (fine black cloth of the quality we now call "broadcloth") as a luxury which belied their profession. Yet, in Chaucer's day, it was already common—the papal registers prove it—for individual cloisterers to buy from Rome private indulgences for this forbidden gris; bribing, as the boldest and most successful always do in every age and place, at the very fountainhead. Moreover, with regard to burnet, we find an Archbishop of Canterbury, Simon Langham, leaving by will to every monk of his great house a measure of this cloth for his frock or, if he preferred, its equivalent in the no less sinful money. Yet this man who thus drove his coach through two solemn monastic statutes, in order to earn the prayers of the brethren for his own soul, was himself monk and abbot, and had been Bishop of Ely before his translation to Canterbury.

Finally, our Hunting Monk has a good appetite, and is something of a *bon vivant*. On this point we need not rely upon Giraldus Cambrensis's account of the feasting that he found at Canterbury, for we possess the "consuetudinaries", the household-books, both of that cathedral priory and of its rival, the Abbey of Westminster. In these books and in many similar documents, we find the minutest and most stringent prescriptions as to the quantity and quality of meat and drink. Of bread and ale there are different qualities, and the brethren in each case are to have the finest. Here, as in all other cases where similar records have survived, the lowest allowance of ale is a gallon each *per diem.* At Westminster, the fish must be sought from the best in the market, and each monk's portion is six, whether of bream or mullet or "salted Cambridge eels" or flounders or herring.* Much of this may be accounted for by the superior wealth of Westminster, and its neighbourhood to the royal court. But at Spalding, a house definitely of the second or third rank, a contemporary abbot left money by will in order that, whereas in the past each monk had had four eggs or flounders or herrings, the future allowance should be six each. Not all of this, of course, was actually eaten; this may be proved, if in no other way, by the fact that, in all such specifications, the prior has always a double allowance. Nominally, all that was left was gathered up by the almoner and given to the poor. But in fact visitatorial injunctions very frequently turn upon the abuse of feeding the servants or dependents or friends with this food which the statutes had earmarked for charity; and the monk himself often employed his superfluity for hob-nobbing with his cronies in the town. There, again, Chaucer gives us an illustration of this custom in his Shipman's Tale with its monk of St-Denis. The Middle Ages, like ancient Greece, recognized the custom of reciprocal dinners or suppers, each guest bringing his own contribution to the common feast (ἔρανος). The Monk of Chaucer's tale, who could bring from a wealthy abbey his "jubbe of Malvoisie"—his great pitcher of rich wine—was a welcome guest in any company.

Let us turn now to the best known and most sympathetic of all Chaucer's Religious. There is perhaps no single phrase of his that is so often quoted as that *French of Stratford attë Bowe*; and his dear Prioress is perhaps the character whom we

* It is possible (though the context makes it improbable) that these specifications are not for each *separate* monk, but for each *pair,* eating from one dish. In that case, each monk would have only three fish for that course.

have most clearly visualized from the first, and with whom we have lived most familiarly ever since. From our schooldays onwards, if asked to name the most conspicuous instances of Chaucer's sly humour, we should probably have turned to her. Yet I will venture to say that some of his most delicate touches here, and not his least humorous, are missed by those who do not know something (if only indirectly and at second hand) concerning the most formal ecclesiastical records. Even her French of Stratford-attë-Bowe gains something from a glance at those visitatorial injunctions in Norman-French which bishops often addressed to the nuns, at a time when similar injunctions to monks were still drawn up in Latin. And even the Prioress's favourites and ours, those *smalë houndës*, gain something in effect for those readers who have realized how stubbornly the orthodox visitors tried to eliminate such pets from the convents, and with what small success. At Romsey, in 1387, the bishop found two nuns bringing into church birds, rabbits, and hounds; at Queen Matilda's *Abbaye aux Dames,* they brought their squirrels. Then our Prioress's dress: " full semëly hyr wympul y-pynched was ". What a charming picture of this demure lady in her cleanest of black and white, as dainty as the daintiest worldling, yet with all the added charm of pure religion! Chaucer meant all this, no doubt; nothing is more significant than Harry Bailey's natural and unfeigned respect for the Prioress. But (and here is the point) Chaucer meant something more, which contemporaries saw at a glance, but which we can only see when some historical Dryasdust serves us by focusing his microscope upon it. This seemly pinched wimple was, ecclesiastically, most unseemly; disciplinarians warred against such fashions even more persistently than against pets, and with more unquestionable support from the law, both in letter and in spirit. A wimple so pleated as to earn Chaucer's commendation was technically as irregular as a guardsman's moustache would be on the quarter-deck of a man-of-war. Those who miss this fact are almost as far from the full comprehension of this particular verse as the old lady who is said to have loved Gibbon's *Decline and Fall* for the inexhaustible mine of pious reflections which she always found in his footnotes. Let us read on for the next three lines. The Prioress's nose and eyes and lips are as attractive as those of our favourite partner at the dance. This she could not help, of course; God may have made her to dance, and the world may have made her into a prioress. The large majority of nuns were of the upper or upper middle class—younger daughters lacking the necessary dowry for marriage—and, in the cloister, promotion naturally went very often by good birth and good connections; it may well have been that Madam Eglantyne was of nobler lineage than the Knight himself. "But sikerly she hadde a fair forheed"; there comes the crowning glory of her features, and it lifts us to a higher plane; she has charmed us as a woman, and now she impresses us with her intellect. Here again we need not doubt Chaucer's good intentions; yet to his original hearers this very praise must have suggested something beyond his plain words, and something very different. The nun's wimple was officially supposed to be not only puritanically plain, but also of Mohammedan amplitude and efficiency; let it hide as much of the face as possible (so ran episcopal injunctions); let it come down to the very eyebrows. This was distressing; for the forehead was one of the great points of medieval comeliness, and those girls who had the misfortune to be formed by nature for the Rossetti type of beauty would painfully standardize themselves by plucking out the superfluous hairs. Those, however, were mere worldlings. In the world, if you had not a forehead, you might make yourself one; but this nun had no business to possess any forehead at all, so far as Chaucer was concerned. She had no more right to a forehead than the young lady in Richardson's novel had to possess ankles or toes.

Let me not be taken to suggest that either Chaucer or his hearers sympathized with all this official puritanism; I only mean that they cannot possibly have ignored it. Chaucer meant to show the Prioress as she really was; an individual portrait, yet true to type; a caged creature charming even to worldlings, and scarcely less dignified because hers was not merely the angelic and incorporeal dignity of Tennyson's nun, breathing out her soul in the winter moonlight. Chaucer knew the artistic value of contrasts as well as that of harmonies; especially of subtle contrasts; of those gleams of summer-lightning which quicken our general appreciation without disturbing it, making us laugh inwardly and read on with heightened expectation. And in this we are not disappointed, for now comes the climax in a touch of sly humour which must have set even Gibbon's old lady a-thinking. The Prioress wore "a brooch of gold ful sheenë, On which ther was first writ a crowned A, And after, *Amor vincit omnia*". Here Chaucer plainly wishes us to ponder over this equivoque. And later on, while the Miller and the Reeve tell their tales, he knows we cannot help glancing sideways at the Prioress and her two nuns, and wondering *que diable faisaient-elles dans cette galère?* For, at the very beginning of Chaucer's century, one of the boldest and most masterful Popes of the whole Middle Ages had undertaken to grapple with this perilous abuse (so the bull *Periculoso* phrases it) of the nun wandering outside her cloister. Strict claustration was commanded thenceforward by Boniface VIII for all, except at the rarest moments of extreme necessity; and disciplinarians were so far from admitting pilgrimages among the pious and justifiable exceptions here, that they thundered against this practice on the part of nuns with an emphasis which we can scarcely find outdone by the Lollards themselves.

Such, then, are the historical facts which supply a key to the poet's real meaning. This, the least tedious of our poets, is supported by the most tedious records of ecclesiastical legislation; records which have been among the most neglected down to our present day. Legislation may not be a poetical subject in itself; but in many different countries, and at many different times, poets have found their material either in legal humours or in legal tragedies. Thus, if we dream that we can ignore medieval law without missing something of the poet's mind, we deceive ourselves. We may, of course, understand a great deal of Chaucer at first sight; but we shall never comprehend the full Chaucer but by studying those minutiae which are matters of history to us, but which were present everyday commonplaces to the people for whom he wrote. Nobody who reads Professor Eileen Power's *Medieval English Nunneries* can fail to rise from that book with a deeper sense of the humour that lurks in those fifty lines of Chaucer.

Let us now leave our gentle satirist, and go backwards a century and a half to hear Hugh, that canon of the model Augustinian monastery of St Victor at Paris to whom Dante assigns a high place in heaven. Hugh, side by side with his mystical writings, composed a manual of behaviour for novices, which became classical not only in his own order but in others also. The evidence contained in this book is all the more important, because Hugh is writing for men drawn from one of the most cultured districts in Europe.[3] Naturally enough, he is much concerned with "deportment". "We should keep discretion of action in our limbs, so that each limb should do that for which it was made. Let not the hand speak nor the mouth listen, nor the eye usurp the office of the tongue. For there are some who cannot listen but with gaping mouth, and who open their palate to the speaker's words as though the sense thereof could trickle through the mouth into the heart. Others, worse still, when they act or listen, thrust forth their tongue like thirsty dogs. Others swim along with their arms, and, by a double monstrosity, at one and the same moment they walk with their feet on earth and fly with their arms in the air. . . . But, lest I should seem perchance to utter rather satire than teaching (though there are still many things which might be set forth) here also I must not forget moderation." Then he turns specifically to table-manners. "Taciturnity is necessary at our feasts [*epulas*] because the tongue, which at all times is prone to sin, is more perilously loosened to speech when it has been inflamed with liberal food and drink [*per crapulam*]; it was for that reason that the rich man who had given way to loquacity at his feasting, felt the more vehement fire in his tongue as he lay in hell. . . . Let nothing be done [at table] with tumult or noise. . . . Not as some do, who, when they sit down to eat, show their intemperance of mind in a certain restless agitation and confusion of their limbs. . . . They pant and groan in anguish, so that you might think they are seeking another wider orifice for their roaring maw, as though their narrow throat could not minister sufficient abundance to their hungry stomach. Though they sit in one place, their eyes and their hands roam around everywhere, far and near; at the same moment they crumble the bread, pour the wine into cups and goblets, draw the dishes round, and mount to the assault like kings against a beleaguered city, doubting at what point to attack first, since they hunger to take all at once by storm. It may be that we, writing thus, have too far forgotten our modesty; but sometimes impudence cannot be brought to blush unless it be plainly confounded." Thence Hugh goes on to speak not only of manners but of appetites. He depicts the cloisterer who finds that ordinary fare gives him indigestion or headache; and, again, the ascetic who tries to feed more plainly than his fellows. Some "seek after new and unwonted sorts of food, so that oftentimes, for the sake of one man's belly, a host of servants scour all the villages around, and, after all, can scarce quench the petulance of this single appetite either by tearing up roots from wild and distant mountains, or by profound investigation, dragging a few little fishes from the deepest whirlpools, or by collecting untimely berries from the withering bushes. . . . Others pay too fastidious attention to the preparation of food, excogitating infinite sorts of stewings and fryings and seasonings; now soft, now hard; now hot, now cold; now sodden, now roast; seasoned now with pepper, now with garlic, now with cummin, now with salt, after the fashion of women in their pregnancy." Above all, novices must shun one of the great temptations of the cloisterer, to whom, in his less inspired moments, dinner or supper are happy oases in a sea of monotony. "Some, at meals, in their anxiety to empty the dishes, wrap in their napkins, or cast upon them, the foursquare gobbets of the mess, dripping with the fat or the grease that has been poured upon them, until, having again scooped them out, they restore the remains to their former place. Others, while they drink, dip their fingers half-way down the cup. Others wipe their greasy hands upon their garments, and come back again to handle food. Others fish with bare fingers, instead of spoons, for their pot-herbs; so that they seem to seek, in that same bowl of soup, both the washing of hands and the refection of their belly. Others dip repeatedly into the dish their half-gnawed crusts and the sippets which they have bitten, and plunge the leavings of their own teeth, in the guise of sops, into the gobbets. These things, as I have said above, would have been shameful in those who relate them if they had not been presumptuously acted in deed; let that man now suffer discipline in hearing who would not keep discipline in his acts." Four generations later, the Franciscan David of Augsburg wrote more briefly, but in a similar vein: "Fall not upon thy meat with tooth and claw like a famished dog." Bernard of Besse, secretary to St Bonaventura, writes in greatest detail of all, quoting from Hugh but outdoing him in plainness of speech; I have translated his evidence in my *From St Francis to Dante* (2nd ed. p. 65). Humbert de Romans, the great contemporary Minister General of the Dominicans, makes similar complaints against his fellow-friars' table-manners.

With regard to behaviour in church, the Franciscan disciplinarians warn their novices against sleep, laughter, perambulation, late coming or premature departure, and talk during Mass: "for Canon Law forbiddeth this at such times even to the secular clergy". In brief, it is evident that the authorities were confronted at times with something of the same difficulties which beset Bishop Grandisson in his Cathedral of Exeter.

Yet this chapter must not end upon that note. Chaucer, like Thackeray, had at bottom a true reverence for religious goodness, and he would very likely have agreed less with the Lollards than with the apologists of his own day. The attitude of those apologists has been too little studied from this point of view, beginning with the Carmelite Netter of Walden and ending with the St Thomas More the Martyr. Each of these men, in his natural attempts to minimize, practically confesses a great deal of the accusation. Yet each pleads that we should not only look at the failings, but recognize also the better side; and, above all, that with one eye on the ideal we must keep the other on human nature; first of all, indeed, upon our own conscience. Netter, Pecock, More all ask in effect *Can you cast the first stone?* We have the League of Nations, at the present moment, as a parallel only too obvious and painful. An institution may aim at an ideal which all men confess to be lofty, and to which they will subscribe by the million; yet its history in practice may be one long record of disillusionment. There may be no alternative left but reform or extinction; and yet there will remain something of the generous impulses that prompted it and of the good work done by a devoted few: mankind will never be ashamed of it. These monastic ruins of ours, which attract more attention in these days of easy locomotion and cheap advertisement than in any other generation of the last four hundred years, were peopled by men and women who resembled mostly our ordinary selves, and who lived, if not strictly according to the Rule, at least with more regularity than the average of their fellow men and women outside. More can tell us Rabelaisian tales from the monasteries even while he is defending the institution as a whole; but there is real, though not conclusive, force in his reminder that, among all the loudest lay critics, there were not many who would face the ordinary requirements of monastic discipline.

24. THE TOWN

The modern distinction between municipal and village life had comparatively little force in the Middle Ages. The town was often scarcely more than an overgrown village, and indeed there were few whose population would raise them above village rank in Yorkshire or Lancashire of to-day. In this field, as in many others, many significant indications come from that record which Carlyle has made famous in his *Past and Present*—the chronicle of Jocelin of Brakelond. We see there how the townsfolk of Bury St Edmunds, at the end of the twelfth century, were still not only under village, but even to a great extent under servile, conditions. They paid yearly "reap-silver" as a commutation for the harvest work to which they had formerly been bound. They paid a "sor-penny" for free pasture. There were dunghills in the streets, as in any farm-yard. They had ploughing to do for the abbot, a remnant of their past condition as bondmen. Their sheep had to be folded in the abbot's field, in order that he might profit by the dung; and they were still subject to forced labour in the matter of fishing, or of carting eels. "The men of the town were wont, at the cellarer's bidding, to go to Lakenheath and bring a convoy of eels from Southery, and oftentimes to return empty and thus to be vexed without any gain to the cellarer; wherefore they agreed that, in future, each thirty acres should pay one penny yearly, and the men should stay at home. But, in these days of ours, those lands have been divided into so many parts that it is scarce known who owes that due; so that I have seen the cellarer one year take 27 pence, yet now he can scarce get 10½*d*."

Take again, the case of Leicester. There were, to begin with, the great fields in the suburbs in which the citizens pastured their cattle, and which by a fortunate concurrence of circumstances have become, since the nineteenth century, a series of public parks such as perhaps no other great town in England can boast. Then, about 1200, we find the citizens buying themselves free of the yearly payments which they owed to the earl in lieu of field service; and, thirdly, the borough financial year begins when the harvest was well gathered in, generally the first week in October. Again, we have definite traces of rural conditions in the presentment of a Leicester jury. The jurors say on their oath "that in the time of the same Earl Robert [d. 1118], the forest of Leicester was so great, thick and full, that it was scarcely possible to go by the paths of that forest, on account of the quantity of dead wood and of boughs blown down by the wind; and then, by the will and consent of the Lord Earl and of his Council, it was allowed to those who wished to look for dead wood, to have six cartloads for 1*d.* and a horse-load a week for ½*d.* and a man's load a week for ¼*d.*" Even in the case of London, Becket's biographer, Fitzstephen, says "the arable fields of the town of London are fertile"; not merely "fertile arable fields can be found in the neighbourhood of the town of London"; moreover, throughout the whole of the Middle Ages, the citizens enjoyed hunting rights throughout Epping Forest, and southwards "to the waters of Cray": i.e. far down into Kent. At Lynn, the small public park eastward from the town is still called "The Chase".[1]

How, then, did these agricultural communities become urban? How did the "township", in which land alone counted, become the modern "town", in which trade is the predominant factor? How did so many urban communities grow up and take place beside the comparatively rare survivals of Roman cities, so that Southampton rivalled Winchester, and Norwich probably displaced Caister altogether?

The process was perfectly natural, by a sequence which has created our political liberties. On the Continent, Professor Pirenne would find the normal origin of the municipality in the suburb of some city or fortress: in the outer enclosure (forisburgus=*faubourg*) of some *bourg*. Such settlements would be created by the great revival of commerce shortly before the year 1000. Enough men would specialize in trade to outgrow the mainly agricultural interests of the old community. Nestling at first under the protection of the city or fortress walls, they would soon become rich enough to entrench themselves in turn; and thus we get that very common Continental phenomenon of two or more fortified enclosures, one the nucleus of the rest. "There were no unfortified towns in the Middle Ages", writes Pirenne (p. 54).

This, however, will not do for England, as we shall see presently; for there are many English towns of note which never had even such rudimentary defences as the earthen bank which surrounded Wallingford. Cambridge would seem far more typical for England than the more artificially created cities from which Pirenne drew his evidence; and here we are on pretty firm ground, thanks to Miss H. M. Cam's excellent summary of all that previous historians and antiquaries have collected. At Cambridge both fortress and town sprang from the same cause—a bridge (or, earlier, a ford) where an important road crossed an otherwise impassable river. It was natural, again, that this same point of the river, should become less easily navigable; so that Cambridge was counted as a seaport even at the end of the thirteenth century. Thus, almost inevitably, traders gradually settled here; there is definite evidence of trade with foreign merchants as early as the tenth century, and presumptive evidence for a still earlier date. The Romans had already fortified the bridge-head; a Norman castle was built there afterwards; thus castle and town derived importance from each other. But there was no sudden and artificial creation, and no clear differentiation between merchant and agriculturalist, such as Pirenne has traced in so many Continental cities. Agricultural Cambridge became urban Cambridge by exactly the same slow and irresistible development which has gradually transformed England from a country of villages to a country of towns. Almost everywhere we can trace the same causes at work. The original village would find itself in a particularly fortunate position—a natural halting place on a great road hard by the bridge or the ford of a river, or a point commanding a pass through the forest or between the hills, or at the gate of a castle or monastery. This would cause a natural influx of inhabitants. They themselves would no less naturally evolve communal ambitions as they grew more numerous; and a wise lord would find it convenient not to discourage them too much. Otherwise he would always find himself with a miserable hamlet, instead of a multitude of subjects prosperous themselves and able to pay him heavy dues. Moreover, in many cases the lord granted these urban privileges mainly at other people's expense, in so far as he could do so without getting into trouble with the suffering parties. Here, for instance, is the first charter of the town of Cambridge, granted by Henry I about 1125: "Henry King of the English to Hervey Bishop of Ely and all his barons of Cambridgeshire greeting. I forbid that any boat shall ply at any hithe in Cambridgeshire, save at the hithe of my borough of Cambridge; nor shall barges be laden save in the borough of Cambridge; nor shall any take toll elsewhere, but only there." The natural result of that would be a large influx from the country around. Mr W. Hudson, whose studies on Martham we have already seen, has worked out similar results for the city of Norwich. He shows how, before the end of the thirteenth century, the city had attracted natives of at least 400 Norfolk and perhaps 60 Suffolk towns or villages or manors. Moreover, Henry I was doubtless heavily paid by the citizens in a lump sum for this monopoly. In the case of London we have an exact record; it paid King John £2000, at least equivalent to £80,000 in modern terms, for its charter. Therefore it is natural that we find the great grantors of charters in England to have been kings who were desperately in want of money, like John, or who had great and costly schemes. In any case, however, the charter was not only to some extent the result of past prosperity, but an earnest of prosperity to come. Cambridge, which had only about 325 habitable houses at Domesday, had 534 in 1279. At ordinary village rate of increase for the Middle Ages, there would have been only about 450 houses at that later date. We may get a rough estimate of the population in each case if we multiply the houses by five.

All this was done, then, on a definite money foundation. Abbot Samson, of Bury, was very wise in commuting reap-silver and other such dues, and putting them on a firmer business basis. Jocelin, it is true, tells us how the more conservative monks grumbled at this sale of past privileges and dignities; yet even the most impenetrable must have seen the advantage of commuting that hollow farce of fetching eels from Southery. The townsfolk had now increasingly more profitable occupations than servile labour. They could afford to pay richly, and were glad to pay, for every new liberty that they could purchase. So all wise lords saw; but all were not wise; and in town evolution circumstances perhaps played a greater part than wisdom; at any rate on the lord's side. We must distinguish here very clearly, however, between the spiritual lords—bishops and abbots and so forth—and the temporal. Not only were the spiritual more naturally conservative in their disposition, but in many cases they were bound by laws which made any transfer or sale of rights difficult. The bishop at his consecration took an oath not to diminish the revenues of his see. The abbot, even without any such definite oath, was under equally definite legal pledge. Moreover, the Churchman had nearly always a more powerful and consistent policy than the lay baron. Thus, "almost to a man they [the great prelates] offered resistance to the municipal movement, which at times developed into an open struggle" (Pirenne, p. 55). The whole medieval history of Lynn centres round its attempt to escape from the power of its lord, the Bishop of Norwich. In the Middle Ages the town was always known as Bishop's Lynn; it was only Henry VIII who, by a forced exchange of properties, turned it into King's Lynn. In the same way at St Albans, Reading, Dunstable, Burton and Bury St Edmunds, we find the citizens struggling from generation to generation to escape from the lordship of their abbot, or at least to gain more favourable terms by purchase or encroachment. At Bury the struggle led to bloodshed in 1381; but the reprisals for that bloodshed were so stern that this final revolt left the citizens as helpless as the men of St Albans. Those last two stories are told in most picturesque detail by Mrs J. R. Green in the first volume of her *Town*

Life in the Fifteenth Century, and by J. A. Froude in his *Short Studies*.

To turn now to the secular barons. These were constantly running into debt, especially from the Crusades onwards. Therefore we find towns on their estates steadily buying fresh liberties. The lords thus profited doubly. Each got a handsome sum in hand for granting his charter, and he profited steadily by the increasing prosperity of his townsfolk, which enabled them to bid high for fresh liberties, piece by piece. The most fortunate municipalities, however, were those which grew up on royal estates. The king's lordship made the freëst towns: from the very first these enjoyed the rights and privileges of "ancient demesne". The king's liberties thus protected his immediate tenants. Another consideration is that kings were comparatively unmeddling. They were remote; they were too busy and too great to worry so much about details as the baron or knight under whose nose the villagers might be living. Thirdly, the king's protection was far more efficient than any other for curtailing the often abusive power of neighbouring barons or county sheriffs; and, lastly, the king was habitually more deeply in debt than the average baron, and therefore more willing to sell liberties for cash.

An admirable concrete instance of such payments comes from Leicester, whose earl was one of the greatest barons in England, about 1110. He, like other Norman earls, had introduced the custom, much resented by the conquered Saxons, of trial by battle, even in a large number of civil cases. At Leicester two kinsmen had disputed a piece of land. There was no alternative (unless either was willing to yield altogether what he believed to be a just claim), but to fight it out. They fought (says the report) from prime (6 o'clock) "to noon, and longer"; until at last one, pressing upon his opponent, drove him to the edge of a ditch. Then, at that point, with a sportsmanlike impulse, he warned his enemy of his danger; at which "such a clamour and a tumult" arose from the bystanders that the lord heard it in his castle and enquired its meaning. The result was that the burgesses, "moved with pity", agreed to give a yearly tribute of 3*d.* from each house which was assessed as a tenement, in order to purchase reversal to the old English custom of clearing such cases before a jury of 24 sworn men.

Here, again, we may turn for similar evidence from Cambridge which has been so admirably studied in detail by F. W. Maitland in his *Towship and Borough.* In 1186 it bought from the king its *Firma Burgi*; this " borough farm " was one of the first liberties to be bought by nearly every town. It meant that, instead of a variety of urban dues which the lord's bailiff would have the right of collecting from house to house, the citizens should henceforth pay by agreement a yearly lump sum, and be left to their own devices for the collection of it. Thus one of the most vexatious and dangerous forms of lordly interference was removed. Then came a series of liberties under John's charter of 1201; Cambridge bought itself free of " New Year's gifts " and " Scot-ales ", exactions by the sheriff. The latter supplies an admirable instance of official oppression. " Scot-ales " were originally in civil life what " Church-ales " were in ecclesiastical. But under the sheriff's management they changed from a friendly and beneficent feast into a burdensome tax; he insisted upon collecting contributions, and there was nobody sufficiently strong to control his management of them; thus the system forms a subject of grave complaint, until it eventually dies out. Next, the town got its " Gild Merchant " —that is its trade union of all who bought and sold on a sufficiently important scale. Probably at Cambridge, as often elsewhere, this Gild included all the burgesses. None had citizen rights but those who belonged to the Merchant Gild; and a fresh step in liberty was freedom of toll for this Gild on all royal lands. Then came the town's own rights of justice; no longer trial by battle, but by compurgation. Next came the grants from King Henry III, including the right of reprisals; which, however, was reciprocal and valid only in relation to other boroughs. The king, herein, " did not grant an absolute exemption to the townsfolk of Cambridge. The man of Cambridge and his goods are to be free from arrest for the debt owed by another unless that other is solvent and the Cambridge burgesses in their court have made default in justice: so, if the Cambridge court has 'denied right' to a man of Huntingdon, it will still be imprudent for any man of Cambridge to visit the neighbouring town. Not until 1275 was an end put to this system of intermunicipal reprisals, and long after that the old principle was still enforced against foreigners." By 1256 the town had obtained the right to elect its own coroners; and, by a coincidence, that same year gave the city of Norwich independence of the sheriffs, and freedom of managing its own taxation and its own borough courts for everything but felony. Cambridge and Norwich, then, are now practically free from all interference from the shire officers. In 1313 the Cambridge burgesses obtained the right of bequeathing lands or tenements within the borough as though they were chattels; a right most important in those ages when land could not be transferred except through complicated legal fictions, with proportionate want of security. At the Peasants' Revolt, the townsfolk joined hands with the rioters and avenged the many ancient grudges they had nursed against the scholars; among other outrages, they burned most of the university documents. Naturally, the reaction in 1382 was highly unfavourable. The *Firma Burgi* was increased by the king, and the profitable "assizes"—that is, rights of controlling the market and taking fines for violation of regulations concerning bread, wine, beer, weights and measures—were transferred from the townsfolk to the university. Thenceforward there was practically no change until Elizabeth in 1589 granted the citizens a secure title to Sturbridge Fair, over which they had exercised practical rights of ownership for 300 years. This last is a very interesting case, as showing how often towns earned their liberties by gradual and natural encroachment. Here again I may quote textually from Maitland. This of Sturbridge was "'by far the largest and most famous fair in all England', which was held in the fields of Cambridge. Seemingly their title was of this sort: A fair had been granted by John to the Lepers' Hospital, which stood in the remotest corner of the territory of Cambridge, where its chapel may be seen to this day. But that hospital had been founded and endowed by the community of the town; and the community claimed to be its patron. Then we may suppose that, as leprosy became much rarer than it had been in the twelfth century, and the hospital was not required, the burgesses began to regard themselves as entitled to the profits of the fair. From Elizabeth they obtained the statement that the fair had been theirs from time immemorial and a grant which would set the question at rest for all time to come."

At this stage we may profitably change our point of view. Hitherto we have regarded urban development almost exclusively from the side of the citizens. We see in these towns the force of the future, the small seed destined to grow and grow until the townsman has become the strongest political power in the State; a little collective nucleus struggling to its own proper development against feudal disorder and individualism, against ecclesiastical conservatism and against royal despotism. There is, however, another side to this. Though much of this town development was unselfish, an instinctive expression of man's social impulses, yet much also betrays man's anti-social impulses; the instinct of rivalry and exclusiveness, and therefore of pugnacity, which we all inherit side by side with our higher social qualities. Cambridge had been born, we may say, in monopoly, in the invidious possibilities forbidding men to trade at any landing place but this. That Cambridge right of reprisals, again, was an anti-social manifestation; and here, finally, we see Cambridge gain one of its most profitable rights by downright encroachment upon the Lepers' Hospital. Moreover, the Merchant Gild, here as in all other towns, like the Craft Gilds which followed by later development, though for their own members they were highly social and beneficent institutions, were often anything but socially inclined towards outsiders.

The Gild is a prehistoric institution; one might even say prehuman, for we see it among all more or less sociable animals. Sheep in a thunderstorm instinctively congregate together under the same tree. Bird-watchers know very well how often rooks or swallows may be seen banded together to drive a hawk out of their purlieus. But, side by side with this natural instinct for protection through unity, the medieval Gild was moulded also by outside forces. The first movement may well have come from pure inward impulse, but certainly that impulse was controlled by lordship from without. True, it was to the citizens' interest to form a trade union; but it was also to the lord's interest that they should do so, and thus give him a definite body to bargain with; security in collective bargaining is one of the main factors of civilization, as we see around us every day of our lives. Therefore, side by side with the citizens' "We will combine" worked the lord's "You shall combine; for otherwise I don't know how to deal securely with you."

In the fourteenth century there were three distinct types of Gild. First the social-religious, answering to the modern benefit societies. The members paid certain fees; they worshipped together at a certain church, or a certain altar of that church. The officers were elected yearly, and the audit of accounts was accompanied by ale-drinking. In such Gilds the money was spent partly on Masses and wax tapers for the services; partly on help for the sick and poor of the Gild; again, for the ale at the yearly audit; and, lastly, sometimes they had sufficient balance to help churches or bridges or the building of town walls. The rules demanded good behaviour—for instance, no member might turn up bare-legged at the meeting—and obedience to the officers. Breach of the rules was punished by fines, or sometimes even with the rod. They were naturally concerned also with the reconciliation of members who might be at variance. For instance: "Hugh of the Solar having struck Roger Alditch in the market of Boston, and the latter having struck the former, both were fined a barrel of beer by the Community of the [Merchant] Gild [of Leicester]."

The next, and perhaps historically earliest, form was the Gild Merchant, for the mutual protection of members, and for the regulation of trade. Such Gilds always rested on a monopoly; no "foreigner" might buy or sell wholesale except from or to its members. At Derby, for instance, a jury convened by royal commission in 1330 reports: "by reason of this Gild the custom has prevailed among them that, if anyone bring neats' leather, wool, or wool-fells into the said town to sell, and one of the said Gild places his foot upon the thing brought, and sets a price for which he would like to buy it, no one but a member of the said society will dare buy it, nor will he to whom it belongs dare sell it to anyone save a member of the said society, nor for a higher price than that which the member of the said society offers. And they [the jurors] say that the profit arising therefrom does not accrue to the advantage of the community of the borough, but only to the advantage of those who are of the said society." The corollary of this was, that only Gildsmen had shops: the rest could sell or buy only in the market; and outsiders paid heavy tolls when they brought goods to market. But within its own limitations the Gild system aimed at absolute fairness. It ruled that everything should go to market and be offered to all buyers, until the ringing of a bell closed business for the day. Only then might the remainder be bought up for retail trade; and even at that point, none but "honest profit" was to be made. At Würzburg (and by a similar London regulation) when a boat brought a cargo of coal, this could be sold in retail only during the first 8 days, each family being entitled to no more than 50 basketfuls. The remaining cargo might be sold wholesale, but the retailer was allowed to raise a "decent" profit only, the "indecent" or dishonest profit being strictly forbidden. Hence the guilt of "forestalling" and of "regrating" (otherwise "engrossing"). To forestall was to buy the goods up before they had been offered in open market. To regrate or engross was to buy wholesale in order to create a "corner" and gain retail profits. Thus, we have such regulations as the Statute of Kilkenny made for all Irish ports (1367). "It ordered that the mayor, sovereign, or other chief officer of the town should call before him two of the most discreet men of the place, as well as the merchant to whom the said wares belonged, and the sailors of his ship. The merchant and the sailors were to state, on oath, the first cost of the goods, and the expenses of transportation. Then the mayor or chief officer of the town, and the two discreet men, were to name a price at which the wares must be sold." The next natural step was towards municipal trading, the so-called "common town bargains". These were cargoes purchased by certain civic officials in the name of the town, and then distributed in shares among the merchant burgesses, no one being allowed to buy wares landed in the port, unless the municipal authorities refused to purchase them. This seems to have been quite a common practice in England, Ireland, Wales and Scotland. That was an obvious way of meeting oppressive trusts: it may be compared with the present-day proposal to nationalize coal, banks, and all key industries. There is much to be learned from the medieval gild by social students who can avoid the extremes of indiscriminate admiration and indiscriminate blame.

Thirdly come the Craft Gilds, which began to grow up in the thirteenth century, often having the same members as the Gild Merchant. In their way they had also the same objects, to maintain trade interests and to keep up the standard of work. They only differed, first in that they admitted only the special trades—the tailors, saddlers, etc., each forming one gild—and, secondly, that they were therefore to a certain extent more democratic, although this quality has often been exaggerated. We often find them including all the members of the Gild Merchant, and thus in time superseding it. Then, after this decentralization, there often came a process of centralized action, and the heads of the respective Craft Gilds became the Common Council of the town.

The advantages of these Gilds were obvious. First, they protected trade in a rude society; secondly, they settled the qualities of workmanship; and, thirdly, they had great social qualities. But at the best of times they did not work without considerable friction. That report from the Derby jury to the commission of 1330 complains that the usages of the Gild Merchant "redound to the injury, oppression and pauperization of the people". Moreover, at later times, when the system had become conservative, it caused unspeakable stagnation, especially in its absolute forms in France before the Revolution. And, finally, though its principle was based on sociability, that was a sociability strictly limited; the Gildman loved his friend, but fought his enemy. A Derby charter of 1204, ratified in 1330, provided *inter alia* "that no one should dye cloth within ten leagues of Derby, except in Derby and in the liberty of the Borough of Nottingham". When, about 1550, Bishop Voysey of Exeter tried to transplant the manufacture of kerseys from thence to his own native town of Sutton Coldfield, Bishop Godwin denounced this as a "horrible sacrilege", which God could not bless.

Thus the study of English town life, like that of early Roman history, shows the people learning self-government through a series of petty quarrels. It was a great advance to have a system of representation, yet that was rudimentary; offices were often forced upon unwilling recipients. Even membership of Parliament was frequently avoided wherever possible. Hence, though medieval town life was a step forward in freedom, in England it never got beyond the oligarchic stage; and on the Continent, whenever it became truly democratic, as for a short time in North Italy and the Low Countries, there was a rapid "fascist" reaction. The town burgesses in England always formed an oligarchy. As Maitland puts it, *liberty* and *franchise* in the Middle Ages meant too often liberty to oppress someone else. Lord Acton, again, draws this distinction between medieval liberty and modern, that the former depends upon property. Thus, even at the end of our period, we must beware of supposing that the town is as definite and vertebrate, so to speak, as a modern borough. Maitland puts this clearly in his account of the Sturbridge incident: "The Fair was their [the townsmen's] Fair, and they (each for himself) meant to make profit thereout. The Town in its modern sense—the Town which has rights and duties, the Town which owes and is owed money, the Town which can make a contract even with one of the townsmen, the Town which can be landlord or tenant, the Town with which the treasurer can keep an account, slowly struggles into life."

Such is the growth of a fairly ordinary country town, exceptional only in the slowly growing reputation and power of its university. Let us pass on now to consider London, incontestably the capital already in those days, yet with scarcely more inhabitants, even at the end of our period, than modern Cambridge has. How did the city of Chaucer and Gower and *Piers Plowman* differ from other great cities of that time or of our own age?

London was one of the few English towns in which there was a really considerable foreign element. England as a rule was insular: London could be called cosmopolitan; not, it is true, in the sense that Venice and Bruges and Florence were, but still enough to give a great stimulus to English life. Especially conspicuous here were the merchant vintners of Gascony, from whom Chaucer sprang. The London records are full of foreign names until the middle of the fourteenth century; but when we put our own metropolis side by side with that of many cities on the Continent it shrinks in comparison. Certainly its population was far inferior to that of the greatest, such as Milan or Bruges or Paris. Again, we were far behind some of those other cities in the organization of trade. At Zwin, for instance, the port of Bruges, there was a regular packet service to Genoa and back as early as the fourteenth century. London never had anything of the kind. In buildings, again, with the exception of the Tower and St Paul's Cathedral, and Holy Trinity Priory, and Westminster Abbey and Palace, it could scarcely compare with any great Continental city: certainly not with the semi-oriental splendour of Venice, or with a royal palace like the Ste-Chapelle, or with Cloth Halls such as those of Ypres and Bruges. Its few stone houses were not comparable to those of the Cologne merchants which still survive; nor again had it that republican spirit which distinguished some of its Continental rivals: cities which could make war upon kings themselves. Even in its width of seafaring life London was only in the second rank. Chaucer's model Shipman knew only the coasts from Gothland (Jutland) to Finisterre. We did generally command the narrow seas, but Henry VII was the first who gave real breadth to our maritime energies.

In pre-Conquest days a man who had been thrice oversea in his own ship acquired thereby the status of a thane. Our merchants, therefore, could not compare with the greatest of the Baltic ports or Genoa or Venice: Marco Polo, the Venetian traveller, was only one representative of a very large class. The Florentine merchants published guides for their agents which have handed down for us to the present day the rate of exchange in London, together with lists of monasteries where wool was to be had. Again, when we turn from trade to the mind, we must confess that London was not a very intellectual capital. When Fitzstephen wrote [1190] there were only three regular schools—St Paul's, St Martin's le Grand, and St Mary's le Bow—though occasionally the Church allowed other masters to teach when they were distinguished enough. In 1446 this was found insufficient, and two new schools were authorized, at St Dunstan's in the East and St Anthony's Hospital. Yet at the same time strict measures were taken against unauthorized teachers. Evidently the demand far exceeded the supply. Next year four London rectors of other churches petitioned Henry VI for leave to set up schools in their parishes. Permission was granted, and one set up a school; of the others no trace can be found. It is probable that they were nipped in the bud by monopolists. There was no London University until just a hundred years ago. Even Oxford, which was among the most distinguished in Europe, invented nothing really comparable to that book market, minutely regularized, which had grown up at Bologna and Paris, and which Oxford imitated in their wake. Again, in a city like Florence the literary and artistic activity permeated the whole population: wealthy young citizens and nobles vied with each other in poetry and song. Cologne and Mainz and Bruges, the earliest homes of printing, with Ghent, the great weaving centre, far surpassed us in mechanical activity. Except for the distinction of our chroniclers, some of whom were among the greatest—and Matthew Paris may probably be counted greatest of all in Europe—book-learning was low among us compared with Italy and France. When Boccaccio comes to mention us in his Latin poem, he writes: "Hispanus et Gallus studiis tardusque Britannus." Certainly those private letters which have survived in English, written by nobles and squires and merchants and clergy, contrast most unfavourably with French and Italian and German contemporaries, not only in literary style but in uniformity of grammar and spelling. Medieval London, like modern, was greater as a practical than as an intellectual school.

Moreover, it needs to be repeated that the immediate political influence of our cities, even including the metropolis, was not comparable to that of some on the Continent. The Lombard cities and those of the Low Countries were at times almost independent states, showing all the bitter nationalism and internecine wars against each other which are sometimes imagined to be peculiar to post-Reformation society; war, moreover, not only with each other, but sometimes with emperor, king or pope. Ghent, when blockaded by her own count in alliance with the King of France, was strong enough to take the city gates defiantly off their hinges for two years: let those come in who dared! Paris University, again—not merely the city but this mere trade union of masters—became in the later Middle Ages one of the Great Powers of Europe in politics. She was the mainspring of that Conciliar Movement of the fifteenth century which for a short time introduced a sort of Whig constitutionalism into the despotic papal State. Yet though London on all these points was manifestly inferior to the greatest of the Continental cities, the very inferiority of our towns was in one respect a political advantage. Our cities were not abnormally developed to the detriment of central authority. They grew only by slow evolution, under efficient discipline from the royal executive. Thus, while in detail they worked out their own liberties surely and solidly, so also by expansion they worked to promote the national liberties. A tyrant could not neutralize the English towns by appealing to their jealousies and their ingrained hatred of each other; London did not hate Bristol or Norwich or York as Florence hated Pisa. The English towns were just moderate-sized areas of local government, and therefore moderate schools of political capacity. Their general interest was in favour of good government for the whole country; while at home, within their own walls, the citizens learned daily the habits of self-control, of give-and-take, which make good government possible. Thus, in England, where the cities were governed with the least bloodshed, least quarrels and fewest revolutions, they played politically the least brilliant part. Yet they played perhaps a more solid and enduring part than even in Italy. Wherever a great cause was to be fought for, the towns in general were on the side that had the future before it: under Henry III they backed De Montfort; in the Wars of the Roses they backed the Yorkist party. For any cause of good government their support was perhaps all the more effective in the aggregate, because their individual pretensions were so much smaller than those of the Italian cities. And these qualities they brought into the councils of the nation, all the more certainly because the whole movement was so gradual and so impersonal. Freeman justly remarks that, if the town of Exeter had had a brilliant political history, then the political history of the English nation would have been less brilliant than it has been.

Here, however, some exception must be made for London. Its political importance came out perhaps more conspicuously in revulsion from Richard II's attack on it. At first, we see the king making and unmaking mayors as he chooses, supporting one city faction against another; then comes the reaction, and we see the Merciless Parliament beheading Nicholas Brembre, Richard's appointed mayor, for illegalities committed during his office. Even the monk Walsingham, who had no sympathy with the Londoners bears testimony to their formidable character. He writes: "They were of all people almost the most proud, arrogant, and greedy, disbelieving in God, disbelieving in ancient customs": and he goes on to say how, to break their spirit, Richard II had to get together a considerable army of professional soldiers. Froissart, again, who knew the great cities of the Low Countries very well, wrote: "Where the men of London are at accord and fully agreed, no man dares gainsay them. They are of more weight than all the rest of England; nor dares any man drive them to bay; for they are most mighty in wealth and in men."

The effect of this was that no king prospered in English history who had made enemies of the Londoners. Richard II's fall may be said to have begun with that quarrel; and from quite early days the Londoners had claimed to speak for the whole kingdom. For instance, in Magna Carta London is the only town mentioned or provided for. The citizens there claim from the king certain liberties, just as the barons do. They are a sort of Fourth Estate, as the Trade Unions are in modern English politics; and, from much earlier times still, they had taken a very prominent part in royal elections. They had the boldness to choose Edmund Ironside when the Witan chose Cnut. There they had absolutely no constitutional right; London was simply a city like the rest; but they asserted their practical right. Later again, they elected Stephen before the barons had met at Winchester to choose him; and J. R. Green brings out rightly the significance of this gesture: for we must remember that those were days before formally constituted parliaments, and before England was largely populated; so that this assembly which could be gathered in a few minutes at the western end of the London market-place, within the walls, would probably far exceed in number and intelligence, as well as in wealth and military power, any assembly likely to be gathered elsewhere in England at the time.

But, though London stood above the other cities of England almost as incontestably as in the present day, yet it was still in full touch with country life. The Middle Ages produced no revolted cockney like Keats, Blake, Turner and Ruskin; country and town joined each other naturally and harmoniously. Here, as at Cambridge and elsewhere, the citizen was often an agriculturalist. Chaucer, dwelling in the great tower of Aldgate, had literally only a step from his own door to the fields and the daisies. Little as we may wish to go back into anything like the totality of medieval life, this will always stand in history as a reproach to many of our modern failures. There is a world of social significance in the fact that, when a rich modern suburban house invites a bevy of London slum girls to a day in its own meadow and paddock, the strangers imagine the daisies and buttercups to have been planted there. Medieval London, even at the full of its development, had that picturesqueness and freshness and simplicity, those relics of the self-sufficing theory of the village with all its necessities made and consumed on the spot, which Ruskin shows us in that magical description of old Abbeville in his *Praeterita* (ch. IX).

25. HOME LIFE

Hitherto, we have regarded the town mainly on its constitutional side. Let us now look at its daily life; and here again Cambridge will give us a fairly typical country borough before we come to London.

We must take care to enter before dark, or we shall find the Trumpington and the Barnwell Gates closed in our faces. Cambridge, it is true, never had town walls, but only a ditch and palisade which may still be traced in the lay-out of its streets, and which was crossed by two gated bridges. Here is an admirable example of the superior orderliness of English life, both civil and religious, as compared with any district of equal extent on the Continent of Europe. I have already suggested that this comparative order is due to the effective though slow fusion between Normans and Saxons, and to the fact that we have never been seriously invaded since those days. But, whatever the cause, the fortunate superiority is in itself unquestionable. In a letter received from the late Dom Ursmer Berlière not long before his death, he alluded casually to the greater orderliness of English Church life as a thing that needed no proof. In the civil domain it suffices to consider that Lynn was scarcely better defended than Cambridge, though it was perhaps the richest town in England per head of population in the Middle Ages, somewhat analogous to Frankfurt a/M. in modern Germany, or Hartford in America. Lynn was originally defended only by its great river on one side and a ditch with two gates on the other. It is true that, at the end of the thirteenth century, the citizens began building a wall, which within the next two generations grew to cover perhaps one-third of the circuit; but there the building stopped and was never resumed. On the other hand, in Rhineland, or on the Neckar and Main, elaborate fortifications still survive round villages which could scarcely, or never, have attained to urban rank even in medieval England; walls at least as high and strong as those of York and Chester. For in Germany, where feudalism remained a political force down to the Reformation and beyond, as Götz von Berlichingen's autobiography shows us, any mere "free knight" of the Empire needed only to send a letter of defiance in order to justify his making war against another noble or city; hence the elaborate defensive precautions which were needed to protect the peaceful trader. With us, except during the wars of Stephen's anarchy, nothing of the kind was needed, not even during the Wars of the Roses.

We come in, then, by the Trumpington Gate, and may put up at the signs of inns which still exist, The Black Bull, or The Blue Boar, or The Red Lion. Two explanations have been given for these inn signs, apart of course from the fact that there was no law, nor apparently even custom, to prevent a host from choosing after his own fancy. In some cases the lord and his retinue would frequent one inn rather than another, and his shield might be seen hanging out at the door or on the balcony; or, again, the lord might actually allow his steward during his absence to entertain for payment at his town house. When we say "lord", it must be remembered that each town had originally been as definitely the property of some landlord, lay or ecclesiastical, as the man's own park was; so that he retained rights and influence over it, if only moral, even when it had come to so much fullness of municipal liberty as towns ever did reach in the Middle Ages.

We go to our inn, then, and retire to bed soon after curfew, unless we prefer to sit awhile drinking with others over the embers of the fire in the hall. There is little temptation to go out after dark; and indeed, on the other hand, there may be considerable danger. Eavesdroppers and night-walkers, men who prowled on the chance of robbery or manslaughter, are constant objects of medieval town legislation. At Oxford, for instance, the penalty for habitual night-walking was twice that of shooting an arrow at the proctor with intent to wound him. If we are rich enough, we shall have brought our bedding with us on our sumpter-beasts; otherwise, we may commend ourselves to sleep as Gascoigne did, with pious reflections on our Last Rest:

The hungry fleas which friske so freshe, to wormes I can compare,
Which greedily shall gnaw my fleshe, and leave the bones ful bare.[1]

We shall wake up to a ringing of bells, bells of all kinds. This is the "Ile Sonnante" of Rabelais. Of our thirteen parish churches at Cambridge three or four will doubtless have "morrow-Mass" at dawn, for travellers or early working folk. Then there is the service of prime at all the conventual establishments: Dominicans, Franciscans, Augustinians and Carmelites, with more distant bells from St Rhadegund's Nunnery, and more distant still over Midsummer Common from Barnwell Priory; and possibly a morrow-Mass at Chesterton just beyond. John Major, the Scottish historian, who studied for a while at Cambridge, recalls in a memorable passage the sweet sound of her bells over the water; and the numerous London churches fostered bell-ringers who were proud of their art. Moreover, in great towns like Coventry there was also a special town bell for the opening of the market, or for early work: "the bell called *daybell*". In most cases, however, the church bell was a sufficient guide.

To market nearly everybody would go for a few minutes at least, as they do in the smaller towns of Italy to the present day. This was the main commercial focus of the town. Shops were neither large nor numerous. An enquiry of 1301 gives us an exact list from Colchester, a considerably larger town than Cambridge. There were 31 shoemakers, tanners, and leather-sellers, a fact which may remind us that Colchester is not far from the edge of the great Essex forest, part of which still survives round Epping. Smiths were 10, weavers 8, butchers 8, bakers 7, carpenters 5, mercers 13. The enquiry gives in each case an inventory of the contents of the mercers' shops. They were nearly always the same—gloves, belts, leather-purses, needle-cases and other small ware. One, however, a considerable capitalist, possessed a good deal of cloth and silk. Another had a stock of verdigris and quicksilver, articles which entered into very many medieval ointments or lotions.[2] In the early part of our period there would be nothing to distinguish a shop from an ordinary dwelling house, the goods being sold either in the street or in the dwelling room. Later shops, however, were of a type that still survives here and there, built of wood with shutters outside, which could be let down into the street so as to form a table for the exhibition of wares, and a little penthouse roof to shelter this table. By this time the whole lower storey was often occupied by the shop, the upper storey containing the hall and bower, or sometimes several bedrooms. At that stage of development the shop itself (as again in modern Italy) would often be let by the owner, whose family would occupy nothing but the upper storey, the "solar", as Chaucer calls it. Men of the same trade or craft commonly congregated together; we still see this at York in the Shambles, and nearly every town had its Mercers' Row. In London, the "cooks" (i.e. restaurant-keepers) were mostly on Thames-side; at Cambridge they gave their name to Petty Cury (i.e. "Little Cookery"). Most of the scenes that would interest us in the town would be commercial or quasi-commercial. This is so even with the churches. Wool might be found stacked in the nave of a church at Southampton, and we have seen how a Devon parson even brewed in the church. Again, at Cambridge as elsewhere, booths were often erected in the churchyards, and fairs might be held there. These entailed frequent quarrels, and both there and at Bury St Edmunds we find churchyards polluted by bloodshed. Gallows, the stocks, the pillory, the cucking-stool and the penal tumbril, which form conspicuous objects in streets or the market-place, are kept there as sanctions for the municipal and commercial laws. The gallows are mainly for theft, the others for breach of market rules, unfair trading or downright fraud. This may be illustrated by a few London scenes. A man is guilty of selling corrupt wine, and the City court decides "that the said John Penrose shall drink a draught of the same wine which he sold to the common people; and the remainder of such wine shall then be poured on the head of the same John; and that he shall forswear the calling of a vintner in the city of London for ever, unless he can obtain the favour of our Lord the King as to the same". Next year, John Russell, at Billingsgate, "exposed 37 pigeons for sale, putrid, rotten, stinking, and abominable to the human race, to the scandal, contempt and disgrace of all the City. And the said John Russell says that the same pigeons are good and proper for sale to mankind, and he offers to prove the same, etc. And hereupon, two pie-bakers, being sworn to inspect and examine whether the said pigeons are good and proper or not, say upon their oath that the said pigeons are not good or wholesome for mankind, but rather to the corruption of man. Therefore he is to have judgment of the pillory, and the said pigeons are to be burnt beneath the pillory, and the cause of his punishment is to be there proclaimed."[3]

At Cambridge, to take a few scenes almost at random, we find criminals running for sanctuary to the church, sometimes as the final goal of a wild hue and cry and a breathless chase down the street. Then, the burning of heretical books, sometimes even of heretical persons; and in 1441 we might see duly exposed one quarter of the body of a priest who had been accused of necromantic attempts on the king's life. Very common presentments are those which testify to terrible disorder and filth in the streets—dung heaps are as ubiquitous here as at Bury St Edmunds, though a great advance was made in 1401 by the enactment that such heaps should be cleared every week. Again, trunks and stocks of trees lying about, signs projecting to the danger of men's heads as they walked, neglect to pave one's own part of the road; and, worst of all, "certain noxious open gutters made by the Masters of Michaelhouse and Gonville Hall, which ran from those colleges to the High Street, through which many masters and scholars had access to the schools of the University", gutters which "gave out an abominable stench, and so corrupted the air that many masters and scholars passing fell sick thereof"; quite apart, we may suppose, from their noxious effects on the actual inmates of Michaelhouse and Gonville Hall. This was a glaring case which brought down royal interference; and it is not insignificant that the first Urban Sanitary Act in English history, that of

1388, was passed by a parliament held at Cambridge, and preceded by active measures to make the town presentable for this august assembly. Swine ran about the streets and rooted amid its garbage: only in a few model cities like London was this forbidden: "he who will nourish a pig, let him nourish it in his own house"; swine that run wild in London may be slain. Fevers, consequently, were almost endemic; St John Fisher, in his sermon before Henry VII, described how they had decimated Cambridge University. Less than a generation after this, in 1524, Erasmus wrote that letter to Wolsey's physician, his friend, which is too briefly summarized in the *Letters and Papers of Henry VIII.* "I often wonder and grieve to think why Britain has now been afflicted so many years with chronic pestilence, especially the Sweating Sickness, a disease which seems almost peculiar to that land. We read that a city was once freed from long-standing pestilence by changing the buildings at the advice of a philosopher. Unless I am mistaken, England might be freed in the same way. First, they never consider towards which quarter of the heaven their windows or doors look. Next, their halls are almost always so constructed that no air can be carried through them, as Galen earnestly warns us. Again, a great part of their walls is transparent with panes of glass, which so admit light as to exclude wind, and yet through their crevices they admit that thin-drawn air, sometimes somewhat pestilent, which is long stagnant there. Again, almost all the floors are of clay and rushes from the marshes, so carelessly renewed that the foundation sometimes remains for twenty years, harbouring there below spittle and vomit and urine of dogs and men, beer that hath been cast forth and remnants of fishes and other filth unnamable. Hence, with the changes of weather, a vapour exhales which in my judgment is far from wholesome for the human body. Add that England is not only completely surrounded by sea, but is also marshy in some parts and intersected by salt rivers, to say nothing meanwhile of the salt fish* in which the multitude take wonderful pleasure. I feel certain that the island would be far more healthy if they gave up the use of rushes; again, if their bed-

* *Salsamentis*: see Erasmus's *Ichthyophagia, passim.*

rooms were to be built so as to be open to the air on two or three sides, with all glass windows so constructed as to be fully opened or fully shut, and so shut as not to admit the entrance of noxious draughts through the gaping crevices: for, even as it is sometimes wholesome to admit God's air, so it is sometimes wholesome to exclude it. The common herd scoffs at any one who is offended by the cloudy heavens. I myself, thirty years ago, if I had entered a bedroom which no man had occupied for some months, began immediately to suffer from fever.† It would help also if the multitude could be persuaded to a sparer diet and more moderate use of salt meat; and, again, if public opinion required of the officials that the streets should be less defiled with filth and urine, and that the roads in the neighbourhood should be cared for. You will laugh, I know, at my idleness which allows me to trouble myself about such things. I feel favourably towards the land which gave me hospitality for so long time, and in which I would gladly end the rest of my life, if that be possible. I do not doubt that you, in your prudence, are better informed; yet I wished to advise that, if my judgment be consonant to your own, you should persuade the great folk of these things: for, in past time, Kings were wont to care for such."[4]

The very tone of this letter shows us that we listen here not to the mere satirist, gloating over his prey, but to the observant scholar and traveller, writing from painful experience. Wolsey's biographer describes his master's custom, when going to Westminster Hall, of "holding in his hand a very fair orange, whereof the meat or substance within was taken out, and filled up again with the part of a sponge, wherein was vinegar, and other confections against the pestilent airs; the which he most commonly smelt unto, passing among the press, or else when he was pestered with many suitors". His royal master, in 1526, ordained "for the better avoydyng of corruption and all uncleannesse out of the King's house, which doth ingender of infection, and is very noisome and displeasant unto

† I.e. rise of temperature: Martial uses this word *febricitare* of the common "cold".

all the noblemen and others repaireing unto the same" "that the three master cookes of the kitchen shall have everie of them by way of reward yearly twenty marks, to the intent they shall provide and sufficiently furnish the said kitchens of such scolyons as shall not goe naked or in garments of such vilenesse as they now doe, and have been accustomed to doe, nor lie in the nights and dayes in the kitchens or ground by the fireside; but that they of the said money may be found with honest and whole course garments, without such uncleannesse as may be the annoyance of those by whom they shall passe".[5] Almost equally significant is the ordinance for the royal barber: "This barbour shall have, every Satyrday at nyght, if it please the Kinge to cleanse his head, legges, or feet, and for his shaving, two loves, one picher wine. And the ussher of chambre ought to testyfye if this is necessaryly dispended or not."[6] It must also be borne in mind that, even at this date, the pocket-handkerchief was almost unknown, and the sneezing noble might shift as even the peasant is learning not to shift nowadays. Erasmus, as we see by the apologetic tone of his letter to a physician, was before his age in the importance which he attributed to health of body. We find it natural that St Bernard should scout the fear of fever: "The holy fathers our ancestors sought for damp and narrow valleys in which to found their monasteries, in order that monks, being often ill and having death before their eyes, might not feel themselves to be in possession of any certain lease of life." But it is startling to find that his great opponent, the comparatively rationalistic Abailard, took much the same view; and it is a tribute to the sturdy common sense of Bishop Grosseteste that he dissented from them both, believing in the maxim *mens sana in corpore sano*.

This question, however, has brought us away from the country town, Cambridge, to a London which was then as definitely our capital as now, though with no more than about 50,000 inhabitants. It is true that the Venetian ambassador in Henry VII's reign gave, as a rough estimate, that London had about the same population as the Florence of that day, but this must be one of his many exaggerations, unless Florence was far less populous than we have every reason to believe. To see medieval London we must imagine a clear-flowing river; an undulating site; a ring of walls; and, at the very gates, gardens and fields and moors. The name of Moorgate tells its own tale. Northward rose the hills of Hampstead and Highgate, mostly clad in bare heath; on the south the wooded slopes of Sydenham and Norwood; and beyond all this a more thickly wooded country, especially in the direction of Epping and Harrow; Epping Forest was continuous almost as far as Bishop's Stortford. All this was almost visible from London streets; those streets which William Morris, judging merely as an artist, has celebrated as "London small and white and clean". Very clean, at least to the outward eye, was London then in comparison with the modern city. Medieval builders knew very well that one of the best preservatives of stone or timber is lime-wash. Therefore, not only were the houses whitewashed or painted, but often the greatest buildings. In Henry III's Account Rolls we find the expense of prolonging the gutters of the White Tower of London, in order that the rain might not drip down the walls and disfigure them. A London clean, then, yet in its way almost as busy-looking as at present. Narrow streets, open shops with projecting walls and penthouses, and hanging signs, and noises as multitudinous to the ear as those picturesque irregularities to the eye—the sawing and scraping of the carpenter, the tick-tack of the weaver's shuttle, the tap of the coppersmith, and the blacksmith's ringing anvil. There will be much singing of folk at work. Chaucer's younger contemporary, Hoccleve, complains of the ordinary artisan's freedom in this respect, in comparison with his own sedentary and silent labour as a scribe in the royal office of the Privy Seal at Westminster. Above all, in the busiest parts, such as the market of Cheapside, we should hear the stentorian, brazen voices of masters, mistresses or apprentices inviting us to buy their wares. We see this plainly in *Piers Plowman*:

Cooks to their knaves cried "Hot pies, hot!
Good griskin and geese—go dine, go!" [*pork*

Taverners unto them told the same tale—
White wine of Oseye, and red wine of Gascoyne,
Of the Rhine, and of Rochelle, the roast meat to digest.

And if we look into one of these taverns, especially one of the side-street taverns for the poor, there we have Langland's unforgettable picture of the miscellaneous company—mostly handi-workers and women of the lowest classes, but with an unclerical priest among them, and a hermit—sitting and soaking their ale in an atmosphere that you could cut with a knife. That was one side of medieval London—the side that the author of *Piers Plowman* knew, perhaps, best, but which was not unknown to Chaucer also.

In the streets, we should see many picturesque Gild liveries, such as Chaucer mentions in his Prologue; and, even apart from these, we should be interested in the trade uniforms, one of which (the butcher's slop) still survives among us. Then, again, the liveries worn by barons' or knights' retainers, and the costume of the clergy, would add a note of colour. In the Middle Ages there were only two definite requirements for clerical costume. In the first place the outer garment must be long—almost to the ankles—and buttoned or fastened the whole way down: in other words, here was the ancestor of the modern cassock. The colour, however, was at the wearer's choice, except that the three most expensive and fashionable were forbidden—red, green and striped or parti-coloured.

The town meetings were mainly held in the open air. In one London record we have a very vivid picture of the folkmoot at St Paul's Cross, with its voting by cries of "ya, ya" or "nay, nay, nay".[7] Here, again, is another scene from 1388. "William Wottone, Alderman . . . went to the Shambles of St Nicholas in London, and seeing divers pieces of meat lying for sale at the shambles there of Richard Bole, butcher, asked the said Richard at what price he sold the same; to which he made answer, that four shillings was the price. Whereupon the Alderman said that the meat was too dear; to which the said Richard made reply;—'I do verily believe that the meat is too dear for thee; who, I suppose, never bought as much meat as that for thine own use.' And thereupon, the said Richard immediately observing that William aforesaid was wearing a hood of the Alderman's pattern, and so knowing thereby that he was an Alderman, he further said to him,—'Art thou an Alderman?' to which the other answered—'Yea; why askest thou?' whereupon he said,—'It is a good thing for thee and thy fellows, the Aldermen, to be so wise and wary, who make but light of riding on the pavement, as some among ye have been doing.' For which words so uttered, . . . after due consideration had upon the matter, because that the same words were expressly uttered in disparagement of our Lord the King, as well as to the scandal and dishonour of the said Mayor, Sheriffs, and Aldermen, and all other the officers of the city aforesaid, it was adjudged that the said Richard should be imprisoned in Neugate for the next half year; and that, on his leaving prison, with his head uncovered, and bare legs and feet, he should carry in his hand a wax torch, weighing one pound, and lighted, from Neugate through the Shambles aforesaid, and so straight through Chepe as far as St Laurence Lane, and through that lane to the Chapel of the Guildhall, and there make offering of the same unless he should meet with increased favour in the meantime. Afterwards however, on the same day, as well at the instance of the Archbishop of Armagh, Primate of Ireland, who entreated the Mayor and Aldermen in behalf of the same Richard, as at the entreaty of the reputable men of the said trade of butchers, the imprisonment for half a year was remitted unto him; on the understanding that on the same day he was to be taken back to Neugate aforesaid, etc., and there make offering of the same; which done, he was to be released."[8]

Then, as now, political life was not always a clean job. Men not infrequently needed compulsion to sit in parliament; and it was common to prescribe pecuniary sanctions for refusal of civic office. In the fifteenth-century poem *How the Wise Man taught his Son,* the father says:

And sonne, also I warne thee,
Desire noon office for to beere,
For than it wole noon other fee,
Thou muste thi neighboris displese and dere,

Or ellis thou muste thi silf forswere,
And do not as thin office wolde.[9]

If we look into one of the better houses, we shall find the type which still survives at Alfriston Vicarage and in a few others of fourteenth-century date. In nearly every case it is the carpenter who builds it; stone is too expensive for anyone but aristocrats or great ecclesiastics or Jews; sometimes a house in a small town is described as "The Stone House". Even brick is unusual until quite the end of our period. Miss Abram quotes a typical example. "In 1483, a man at Gloucester agreed to build a house forty-seven feet by fifteen, and eighteen feet high, of 'standard werke', and 'all the timber of oak', for £14." Hence frequent fires. In London a city regulation insisted on stone party-walls between house and house, in order to limit these; and in towns each parish had great poles with hooks for pulling down the blazing house before it could kindle its neighbours; such a hook survives in St Benet's Church in Cambridge.

The furniture we shall find to be very scanty. Here is an inventory of one of the wealthiest at Colchester, at the end of the thirteenth century. The citizen had a trestle-table; this was the ordinary arrangement, so that the boards could be put away in a corner except at meal-times; it was a distinctive note of Chaucer's Franklin's great hospitality that he had a "table dormant" in his hall. Nothing in the way of chairs; some sort of settles or stools was doubtless taken for granted and not inventoried. Two silver spoons, a cup, a table-cloth and two towels, a brass cauldron, a brass dish, washing-basin and ewer, trivet, and iron candlestick, two beds, two gowns, a mantle, one piece of russet cloth (for making up into clothes some day); three pounds of wool, two barrels. So much for the household furniture.[10] The man was a butcher, and thus he possessed pickling tubs, meat, fat, corn, hay and a cart. The purely household furniture is priced at £2. 5*s.* 5*d.*, his stock-in-trade at nearly £3. This we must multiply by 40 or a little more. If this seems almost incredibly meagre, we must remember that the inventory was for taxation purposes, and no doubt all was not confessed, while that which was confessed was considerably underestimated. The general impression of scantiness, however, is entirely borne out by contemporary wills and inventories, which survive in considerable numbers.* The richer folk had hangings for their rooms, which might run to considerable expense, and feather-beds with valuable quilts. Even kings and popes had no easy-chairs, but would often sit on their beds to receive ambassadors. Still, when all has been reckoned, these things were not only primitive according to our modern ideas, but comfortless and insanitary. The fork was not yet invented for meals; handkerchiefs were almost unknown; folk ordinarily slept either naked or in their day-clothes, and the rushes on the hall floor were changed quarterly or yearly. Even in highly civilized Florence, and at the middle of the fourteenth century, when the artist Cennino Cennini gives a recipe for particularly fine plaster to be made from calcined chicken-bones, he advises us to seek the oldest and driest chicken-bones we can find lying about the floor.[11] Add to this that dogs and animals were freely admitted, and that the servants would often sleep in the hall unencumbered by any table dormant.

As Cutts points out, many of the Colchester citizens had only one living room which served all purposes. Fever was as great an enemy as fire. One of the things, however, which would pinch us most immediately would be the cold; in rooms with ill-fitting doors and windows, which in the majority of cases were unglazed, so that there was no alternative between darkness and open air. The fire burned commonly in a brazier in the middle of the hall, the smoke escaping as best it could through the roof; but here again, in a great town like London, there was provision for stone chimneys. In Montaigne's *Voyages*, when he goes to Switzerland, he notes with a special emphasis how the rooms are so well warmed with porcelain stoves that one actually takes off one's hat and one's furs when sitting indoors![12] In mid-sixteenth-century France, as in England, warm clothes were needed even more indoors than in walking abroad. Molière's plays and Thomas Ellwood's autobiography show how regular it was to wear one's hat indoors,

* See, for instance, wills of wealthy clergy in E. L. Cutts's *Parish Priests and People*, pp. 174ff.

even in the seventeenth century. To quote again from Miss Abram (fifteenth century, p. 178): "In some towns windows, doors, lattices and locks were regarded as tenants' fixtures." "Carpets are seldom mentioned in wills and inventories until the close of the fifteenth century. Henry VII had one in his bedchamber, but some of his rooms were strewn with rushes or straw" (p. 182). "It is probable that, as civilization advanced, reception-rooms were used more frequently, and bedrooms less frequently, for the purposes of hospitality. Nevertheless, we have come across two cases of men of good social standing (a canon of Wells, 1492, and a Sergeant at Law, 1500) who had beds in their parlours. . . . In one of Hoccleve's poems, *Jereslaus's Wife*, an earl and countess, their daughter and her governess, all slept in the same room" (p. 175). Again (p. 185): "A point which has struck us very forcibly in reading descriptions of medieval houses, and at which we have already hinted, is the small number of bedrooms possessed even by people who were not too poor to pay a fairly high rent."

Artificial light, again, was extremely expensive. In its cheapest form it was a dim cresset of oil or a rushlight of mutton-fat; and, winter fodder being so rare, the result was that a pound of fat cost four times as much as a pound of lean meat. There was thus a great temptation to sit up by the embers of the fire and drink into the night. Fitzherbert attacks this from the business point of view. "One thinge I wyl advise the to remembre, and specially in wynter-tyme, whan thou sytteste by the fyre, and hast supped, to consyder in thy mynde, whether the warkes, that thou, thy wyfe, and they servantes shall do, be more avauntage to the than the fyre, and candell-lyghte, meate and drynke that they shall spende, and if it be more avantage, than syt styll: and if it be not, than go to thy bedde and slepe, and be uppe betyme, and breake thy faste before day, that thou mayste be all the shorte wynters day about thy busynes."[13]

Thus to the very end there were glaring contrasts between the cloths of gold and brocade of the greatest folk, the elaborate art lavished on all their buildings, their furniture and even the commonest domestic articles, their extraordinarily ceremonious manners (duly noted by the Venetian envoy in Henry VII's reign), and those other things in the background which strike us as strangely uncultivated, even when we have made fullest allowance for the true gentility which may underlie a rough exterior. The meals, again, showed the same contrasts. Here, for instance, is an extract from the famous *Northumberland Household Book,* regulating the castles of perhaps the greatest baron in England at the beginning of the sixteenth century:[14]

> "BRAIKFASTIS for my lorde and my lady. FURST a Loof of Brede in Trenchors* ij Manchetts [small loaves] j Quart of Bere a Quart of Wyne half a Chyne of Muton or ells a Chyne of Beif Boilid.
>
> "BRAIKFASTIS for my Lorde Percy [aged 10] and Mr Thomas Percy. ITEM Half a Loif of household Breide. A Manchett j Potell [4 pints] of Bere a Chekynge or ellse iij Mutton Bonys boyled.
>
> "BRAIKFASTIS for the Nurcy for my Lady Margaret and Mr Yngram Percy. ITEM a Manchet j Quarte of Bere and iij Muton Bonys boiled.
>
> "BRAIKFASTS for my Ladys Gentylwomen. ITEM a loif of Household Breid a Pottell of Beire and iiij Muton Bonys boyled or ells a Pece of Beif Boilid.
>
> "BRAIKFASTS for my Lords Breder his Hede Officers of Houshold and Counsaill. ITEM ij. Loofs of Houshold Briede a Manchet a Gallon of Bere ij Muton Bonys and ij Peces of Beif Boilid."

The Percy meals were the same in Lent, except that (1) it was only the children who then breakfasted daily; the rest, only four times a week; (2) fish was substituted for flesh; e.g. the nurse and the babies had a piece of salt fish, a dish of sprats, or three white herring. This was extremely cheap—the nurse's and children's breakfasts together cost only about 1*s.* 6*d.* of

* Trenchers were slices of bread which our ancestors used as plates, eating their meals upon them and leaving them as remnants for the poor or for their dogs.

modern money. If the amount of beer seems startling, we must remember in the first place that our ancestors were under no temptation to drink water. It was only in a few towns of the later Middle Ages, and then almost entirely through the monasteries or friaries, that aqueducts were brought in. Again, practically no hot drinks were known, except alcoholic or medicinal. Thus ale and beer not only supplied very considerable calories from the strictly dietetic point of view, but comforted the stomach after the fashion of modern tea and coffee. The monastic allowance, where we find it specified, is seldom less than a gallon of ale a day. A priceless record from Coventry in 1520, which gives both the population of the city and its consumption of malt and wheat, points to a consumption of a quart of ale per diem per soul, man, woman and child. Thus, the men's average would run at least to two quarts. Side by side with this rough Gargantuan plenty we find at exceptional times the greatest extravagances, especially in so-called "subtleties", many specimens of which, at the Bishop of Ely's installation feast in 1478, I have printed in *Life in the Middle Ages* (III, 150). The records of the Percies and the Pastons show how it was quite common for young married couples to live, often for many years, in the house of one of the parents. A Chancery petition of about 1475 shows an action brought by Thomas Alexander, Gentleman, against the executors of John Jeny "for breach of agreement to provide complainant with meat, drink, and lodging if he married Agnes, daughter of the said deceased [John Jeny]".[15] Marriages were generally, in the main, business contracts, the French *mariage de convenance*; which, however, as P. G. Hamerton shows us from his experience in modern France, results very often in a healthy and pleasant *camaraderie* between husband and wife. The Church law of prohibited degrees, though less inconvenient in town than in village, where perhaps half the population stood in prohibited kinship to each other, did nevertheless bring a good deal of uncertainty into married life. Miss Abram points out how "on one occasion, in May 1357, no less than fifty men and as many women received dispensations to remain in marriages so contracted, because they had acted in ignorance. It was apparently not very difficult to obtain dispensations: in 1413 the Pope granted his nuncio a faculty to permit any men or women related in the third degree only, or in the third and fourth, or in the fourth and fifth, to marry; and to allow a hundred persons so related to remain in marriages already contracted, and to declare their children legitimate."[16] In the matter of wardship, by which the marriage of wealthy young heirs was often sold, townsfolk had a great advantage on the feudal nobility. In many towns, unless the parents had appointed definite guardians by will, the mayor and aldermen took charge of boys and girls during their minority, and were allowed a good percentage of the profits received from the estate which they administered, but rendered business accounts when the time of majority came. One case recorded in Riley's *Memorials of London* shows that a ward, left with £300, found himself, after 13 years' minority, possessed of £580. 1*s.* 4*d.*, even after all expenses of food and maintenance had been paid, through the good management of his guardian, who had traded with the money at an interest of 4*s.* in the pound, half of which he had kept for himself. "Some boroughs also provided legal aid for widows and orphans: at Hereford, the bailiff and steward were ordered to help them at all times, both in court and out of it, if any wrong or injustice were done to them."[17]

After all these prosaic details, necessary enough in themselves, we cannot leave medieval London without recalling two poetic testimonies. The Scottish poet Dunbar, writing at a time of bitter warfare between the two countries, was such a true Chaucerian that he could not but admire Chaucer's city.

Above all rivers, thy river hath renown;
Whose beryl streamës, pleasant and preclare,
Under thy lusty wallës runneth down;
Where many a swan doth swim with wingës fair!
Where many a barge doth sail and row with oar!
Where many a ship doth rest with top-royal!
O town of towns, pattern and not compare!
London! Thou art the flower of cities all!

Upon thy lusty Bridge of pillars white
Beën merchants full royal to behold!
Upon thy streets goeth many a seemly knight,
In velvet gownës and in chains of gold!
By Julius Caesar, *thy Tower founded of old,*
May be the House of Mars *victorial;*
Whose artillery with tongue may not be told!
London! Thou art the flower of cities all!

Strong be thy wallë that about thee stands!
Wise be the people that within thee dwells!
Fresh is thy river, with his lusty strands!
Blithe be thy kirks, well-sounding be thy bells!
Rich be thy merchants, in substance that excels!
Fair be their wives, right lovesome, white and small!
Clear be thy virgins lusty under kells! [*caps*
London! Thou art the flower of cities all!

Side by side with this, we have William Morris's picture, where he bids us dream of

London, small and white and clean,
The clear Thames bordered by its gardens green;
Think that, below bridge, the green lapping waves
Smite some few keels that bear Levantine staves
Cut from the yew wood on the burnt-up hill,
And pointed jars that Greek hands toiled to fill,
And treasured scanty spice from some far sea,
Florence gold cloth, and Ypres napery,
And cloth of Bruges, and hogsheads of Guienne,
While nigh the thronged wharf Geoffrey Chaucer's pen
Moves over bills of lading. . . .

26. TRADE AND TRAVEL

England during nearly all our period was quite in the second class as a trading country. The fullest trade in Europe was carried on by the cities of North Italy, the Rhineland and the Baltic and the Low Countries. So far as England is concerned, the early beginnings of travel and trade are best illustrated by the lives of Saewulf and St Godric of Finchale. Both of these sea-adventurers plunged finally into the great spiritual adventure of their time, the strict monastic life.

Saewulf was a merchant who chose for his confessor the saintly Bishop of Worcester, Wulfstan. The bishop tried to "convert" him; Saewulf shrank from taking the vow, but Wulfstan prophesied that he would do so before he died. Six years after Wulfstan's death, Saewulf undertook a penitent pilgrimage to Jerusalem, deliberately choosing the most adventurous route, as one "conscious of his own unworthiness". He was wrecked near Bari; when he started again, it took him thirteen weeks to reach Jaffa. Here he landed at once; next day a hurricane destroyed, before his eyes, 23 of the 30 great ships in the harbour. He saw and worshipped at all the holy places; then, through many dangers from Mohammedan fleets and pirates, he reached Constantinople safely after a voyage of four months from Jaffa. Some years later we find him a monk at Malmesbury.

At Finchdale, near Durham, there died in 1170 a hermit named Godric who had lived very many years, perhaps as many as forty, in fasting, cold, and prayer. One of the Durham monks took every opportunity of haunting his company, and jotted down many of his words and many particulars of his life on the evenings (as he assures us) of the very days on which he had heard them.[1] He writes: "This holy man's father was named Ailward, and his mother Edwenna; both of slender rank and wealth, but abundant in righteousness and virtue.

They were born in Norfolk, and had long lived in the township called Walpole. . . . When the boy had passed his childish years quietly at home, then, as he began to grow to manhood, he began to follow more prudent ways of life, and to learn carefully and persistently the teachings of worldly forethought. Wherefore he chose not to follow the life of a husbandman, but rather to study, learn, and exercise the rudiments of more subtle conceptions. For this reason, aspiring to the merchant's trade, he began to follow the chapman's way of life, first learning how to gain in small bargains and things of insignificant price; and thence, while yet a youth, his mind advanced little by little to buy and sell and gain from things of greater expense. For, in his beginnings, he was wont to wander with small wares around the villages and farmsteads of his own neighbourhood; but, in process of time, he gradually associated himself by compact with city merchants. Hence, within a brief space of time, the youth who had trudged for many weary hours from village to village, from farm to farm, did so profit by his increase of age and wisdom as to travel with associates of his own age through towns and boroughs, fortresses and cities, to fairs and to all the various booths of the market-place, in pursuit of his public chaffer. He went along the highway, neither puffed up by the good testimony of his conscience nor downcast in the nobler part of his soul by the reproach of poverty. . . . At first, he lived as a chapman for four years in Lincolnshire, going on foot and carrying the smallest wares; next he travelled abroad, first to St Andrews in Scotland and then for the first time to Rome. On his return, having formed a familiar friendship with certain other young men who were eager for merchandise, he began to launch upon bolder courses, and to coast frequently by sea to the foreign lands that lay around him. Thus, sailing often to and fro between Scotland and Britain [Brittany?], he traded in many divers wares and, amid these occupations, learned much worldly wisdom. . . . He fell into many perils of the sea, yet by God's mercy he was never wrecked; for He who had upheld St Peter as he walked upon the waves, by that same strong right arm kept this His chosen vessel from all misfortune amid these perils. Thus, having learned by frequent experience his wretchedness amid such dangers, he began to worship certain of the saints with more ardent zeal, venerating and calling upon their shrines, and giving himself up by whole-hearted service to those holy names. In such invocations his prayers were oftentimes answered by prompt consolation; some of which prayers he learned from his fellows with whom he shared these frequent perils; others he collected from faithful hearsay; others again from the custom of the place, for he saw and visited such holy places with frequent assiduity. Thus as he aspired ever higher and higher, and yearned upward with his whole heart, at length his great labours and cares bore much fruit of worldly gain. For he laboured not only as a merchant but also as a shipman . . . to Denmark and Flanders and Scotland; in all which lands he found certain rare, and therefore more precious, wares, which he carried to other parts wherein he knew them to be least familiar, and therefore coveted by the inhabitants beyond the price of gold itself; wherefore he exchanged these wares for others coveted by men of other lands; and thus he chaffered most freely and assiduously. Hence he made great profit in all his bargains, and gathered much wealth in the sweat of his brow; for he sold dear in one place the wares which he had bought elsewhere at a small price. Then he purchased the half of a merchant ship with certain of his partners in the trade; and again by his prudence he bought the fourth part of another ship. At length, by his skill in navigation, wherein he excelled all his fellows, he earned promotion to the post of steersman. . . . For he was vigorous and strenuous in mind, whole of limb and strong in body. He was of middle stature, broad-shouldered and deep-chested, with a long face, grey eyes most clear and piercing, bushy brows, a broad forehead, long and open nostrils, a nose of comely curve, and a pointed chin. His beard was thick, and longer than the ordinary, his mouth well shaped, with lips of moderate thickness; in youth his hair was black, in age as white as snow; his neck was short and thick, knotted with veins and sinews; his legs were somewhat slender, his instep high, his knees hardened and horny with frequent kneeling; his whole skin rough beyond the ordinary, until all this roughness was softened by old age. . . . In labour he was strenuous and assiduous above all men; and, when by chance his bodily strength proved insufficient, he compassed his ends with great ease by the skill which his daily labours had given, and by a prudence born of long experience. . . . He knew, from the aspect of sea and stars, how to foretell fair or foul weather. In his various voyages he visited many saints' shrines, to whose protection he was wont most devoutly to commend himself; more especially the church of St Andrew in Scotland, where he most frequently made and paid his vows. On the way thither, he oftentimes touched at the island of Lindisfarne, wherein St Cuthbert had been bishop, and at the island of Farne, where that saint had lived as an anchorite, and where St Godric (as he himself would tell afterwards) would meditate on the saint's life with abundant tears. Thence he began to yearn for solitude, and to hold his merchandise in less esteem than heretofore. . . . And now he had lived sixteen years as a merchant, and began to think of spending on charity, to God's honour and service, the goods which he had so laboriously acquired. He therefore took the cross as a pilgrim to Jerusalem; and, having visited the Holy Sepulchre, he came back to England by way of St James [of Compostella]."

Here, then, is an English merchant-adventurer, splendidly endowed by nature for his job, but restricted by the smallness of his ship and the simple navigation of those days. His limits were "Denmark and Flanders and Scotland"; to Rome and Jerusalem and Compostela he went by the ordinary pilgrims' ways, like any other man. Even Chaucer's Shipman of two centuries later, that weather-beaten master of his trade, knew only from Jutland to Cape Finisterre in Portugal; or, possibly, even the less distant Finistère in France. For the great adventurers of the Middle Ages we must go to Italy and Flanders, where commerce and manufactures were incomparably more developed than in Britain. It was through travellers from those countries, whether for religion or for gain, that the Far East became better known between 1250 and 1350 than at any other period until after the Reformation. And the pioneers of this movement were Franciscan friars; the missionary showed the way to the trader.

Similarly, before that date the Crusades had increased enormously the importance of the Mediterranean merchants and sailors, who carried troops and munitions oversea, built siege machines for the Crusaders, and often fought as well or better than the soldiers. Moreover, they were better organized and disciplined. Making all allowance for the enormous gulf between theory and practice in the Middle Ages, there is great significance in the sea-laws, which were decreed by our Richard I for that fleet which sailed from Gascony in 1190. These ran: "Know ye that we, by common counsel of men of worth, have made the rules of justice written here below. He who on shipboard shall kill a man, let him be bound to the corpse and cast into the sea; if he kill him on land, let him be bound to the corpse and buried in the earth. If any be convicted by lawful witnesses of having drawn his knife to smite another, or if he have wounded him to the blood, let him lose his hand. If, however, he have only smitten him with his hand, without effusion of blood, let him be thrice plunged into the sea. If any man speak opprobrious or despiteful words, or invoke God's hatred against another, let him give an ounce of silver for every such offence. If a thief be convicted of theft, let his head be shaven as though for the ordeal by battle, and let boiling pitch be poured on his head, and the feathers of a feather-bed be shaken over his head, that he be known for what he is; and, at the first place at which the ship may touch, let him be cast forth." This, being a war-code, was of special stringency; doubtless it was seldom enforced with literal strictness; but it expressed the king's determination to maintain far sterner discipline on board ship than any land forces ever reached in those days.* And we have sea-codes, some perhaps earlier than this, which testify to the efficiency aimed at, and to some extent obtained by the best sea-traders. The Laws of Oléron, which date

* Joinville (§ 644) gives us a glimpse of Crusaders' naval discipline; thieves and similar offenders were banished to the cock-boat, which was towed behind the ship.

at least from 1266, were accepted by Western France, Flanders and Holland, England, Castile, and most of the Baltic cities. Very similar were the Laws of Wisby, of Jutland, and the code of "the Consulate of the Sea" in the Mediterranean, with other derivative codes which were carefully recorded, for the use of medieval English law-courts, in the *Black Book of the Admiralty*. These laws prescribe severe, but only reasonably severe, punishments for indiscipline or crime on the sailors' part; they protect the men, on the other hand, from unfair treatment; and they regulate the conflicting interests of the captain and the merchants, whose cargoes or whose persons he is carrying, in almost modern detail; they are evidently the fruit of centuries of experience.

Another definite step forward in civilization may be found in the institution of "consuls" at different ports, and the consequent agreements, verbal at first but afterwards written, for the guidance of such consuls and the fellow-countrymen whose interests it was their duty to guard. The earliest of these written agreements dates from 1184; and, as time went on, we find these commercial relations between Christian and Mussulman often regulated on higher principles than were yet recognized by feudal law at home. In 1270, for instance, the principle of reprisals was repudiated; again, the right of wreckage was abolished here centuries before it was abolished in Europe. Moreover, freedom of worship was allowed to these Christian traders in Mohammedan ports. Numerous documents testify to the commercial peace which often reigned between these political enemies, even in the thick of the Crusades. Indeed, this was one great difficulty both in Church and in State. We find popes and princes legislating against the supply of war material from Mediterranean ports to Saracen enemies; but Venice and Genoa and the Spanish ports drove a busy clandestine trade in these articles. After Saladin's victories, commerce became still busier between West and East. Not even a Pope like Innocent III could seriously check it; while the rulers of Aragon and Venice and Genoa were not always serious in their professed steps against this "blasphemous trade". After all, if the Italians had really cut off commercial intercourse with the infidel, either in ordinary articles or in war materials, their places would probably have been taken by Flemings or Baltic smugglers. Thus, in spite of the plainer and plainer proof that such commerce prolonged Mohammedan resistance and thwarted Crusading energies, the hope of gain steadily counteracted national or religious emnities.[2] In 1250 there was a "street of the English" at Acre; and most of the great maritime cities of the Mediterranean had their "street" in the main Syrian ports. Chronic piracies and frequent international wars had to be reckoned with; but so great was the pilgrim's spiritual and the trader's worldly gain that intercourse grew in proportion with general prosperity. Indeed, war itself provided one lucrative article of commerce; Narbonne, for instance, had a slave-market at a regular tariff: two slaves there cost as much as a mule, two mules as much as a horse. Two prelates in England, Lanfranc of Canterbury and Wulfstan of Worcester, share the credit of having put a stop to the selling of native slaves to the Irish. But in Southern France and Italy the slave-trade continued all through the Middle Ages, and the milder servitude of villenage was justified on moral and economic grounds by orthodox medieval philosophers; Wyclif alone has been marked as an exception to this general rule. No Pope or Church Council fulminated against slavery; the Archbishop of Narbonne, in 1149, left his Saracen slaves by will to the Bishop of Béziers; and, in 1251, another Archbishop of Narbonne complained that the viscount had withheld from him his rightful profits on two slave-markets, to the amount of 2,500 sols, or about £15,000 in modern purchasing power.

In the later Middle Ages, Flanders and the North German Hansa were of most importance for English trade. This great corporation had its depots, with extra-territorial privileges, in many great towns: the Steelyard in London; smaller factories, under the control of the captain of this London Steelyard, in Lynn, Boston, York, Bristol, Ipswich, Norwich, Yarmouth, and Hull. In the later fifteenth century, English and Hansa interests conflicted very definitely; there was much rivalry, friction, and complicated negotiations, in the course of which we find the Germans writing: "The English, after their fashion, gave us many soft words": that chapter of history is admirably told by Mr Postan.[3] The *Libelle of English Policye,* and Henry VII's business-like efforts to strengthen our fleet, are familiar to all readers of history. For the present purpose, it is more important to bring out the adventurous side of this subject. St Godric's life shows admirably on the one hand the physical qualities required by the medieval merchants, and on the other, their daring and resourcefulness not only in speculation, but in the carrying out of plans. Whenever a merchant worked thus for himself, he was not the equivalent of the modern bald man sitting in a counting-house, but essentially a merchant-adventurer, ready in many cases not only to meet the buccaneer or pirate in self-defence, but even to do a little buccaneering on his own account.

From trade now we may pass to travel. Though the difficulties may very easily be exaggerated, they were unquestionably very great. Commonly the roads were only tracks, though in great cities abroad the towns were paved. Consequently, except along the main roads, wagons were seldom used except from the field to the barn. Otherwise transportation was by lighter carts or on the backs of the beasts. Moreover, such as they were, these tracks were ill kept. The city streets might be encumbered with blocks or trunks or branches, and in the road itself there were often pits. One of the fifteenth-century statutes of the city of Coventry runs: "Also that no man from henceforth dig clay upon Cheylesmore Green, nor in the highway betwixt Summerleaze Butts and Spon market, upon pain of 40*d*."[4] Similar reference may be found elsewhere; and Mrs Green, in her *Town Life* (II, 31) tells a tragic story to this effect. "In 1499 a glover from Leighton Buzzard travelled with his wares to Aylesbury for the market before Christmas Day. It happened that an Aylesbury miller, Richard Boose, finding that his mill needed repairs, sent a couple of servants to dig clay 'called Ramming clay' for him on the highway, and was in no way dismayed because the digging of this clay made a great pit in the middle of the road ten feet wide, eight feet broad, and eight feet deep, which was quickly filled with water by the winter rains. But the unhappy glover, making his way from the town in the dusk, with his horse laden with paniers full of gloves, straightway fell into the pit, and man and horse were drowned. The miller was charged with his death, but was acquitted by the court on the ground that he had had no malicious intent, and had only dug the pit to repair his mill, and because he really did not know of any other place to get the kind of clay he wanted save the highroad."

An average day's journey was from 20 to 25 miles, though sometimes we find surprising feats of travel. The ordinary rate may be seen in a Fellow of Merton, Oxford, who visited the Pope on business at Avignon in 1331. He and his servant, carrying their bedding with them on the third horse, took 34 days on the journey. But this included a good many stops; and the return journey from Avignon to Wissant took only 14 days. There were evidently regular and traditional stages, as in more modern posting days: this man made 18 stages from London to Lyons, and Sir Richard Guildeforde in 1504 made 17. Each time they made an offering after their safe-crossing of the Channel; at Canterbury, homewards, "four pence sterling"; but at Calais, outwards, only 1*d.* to the Church of St Nicholas, so dear to Ruskin in our own day.* One of their horses "died through the tempest"—a loss of 9*s.*—and the passage from Wissant to Dover cost 3*s.* 6*d.*[5] A century and a half later, the *Northumberland Household Book* prescribes: "Whensoever any of his Lordeship Servauntes be comaunded to ride on message in Winter . . . that every of theym be allowed for the tyme for his being furth in his jornay . . . ij*d* for every meall and *ob* [½d]for every his baiting; and for his Hors every day and night of his saide jornay iiij*d*,*viz.* a penny for his baiting ande iij*d* at night for his provounder. The whiche is in all for a Man and his Hors in the Daie in Winter

* In some sort, it is the epitome of all that makes the Continent of Europe interesting, as opposed to new countries. . . . That Calais tower has an infinite symbolism in it, all the more striking because usually seen in contrast with English scenes expressive of feelings exactly the reverse of these." (*Modern Painters,* IV, Pt. v, ch. i, § 2.)

viij*d* if it be Etting-Daye; and, if it be Fasting-Daie, than ij*d* to be abated; the which is vj*d* on a Fasting-Day."[6] In summer, the man's expenses are the same, but the horse's only 1½*d.*: total 5½*d.* per eating-day and 3½*d.* per fast-day. The halfpenny for the man's "baiting" is mysterious; we must probably read it as "lodging", but it is not counted in the addition either of the winter or of the summer total. The Lestrange accounts of half a century earlier give much the same prices (*Archaeologia*, XXV, 411ff.).

By sea, things went naturally less smoothly. When Eustache Deschamps, Chaucer's friend and fellow-poet, crossed the Channel, he described the little ship as "a perilous horse to ride"; and dangerous or fatal passages were matters of common history. Froissart tells us how Sir Hervé de Léon "took the sea [at Southampton] to the intent to arrive at Harfleur; but a storm took him on the sea which endured fifteen days, and lost his horse, which were cast into the sea, and Sir Hervé of Léon was so sore troubled that he had never health after."[7] King John of France, a few years later, took eleven days to cross the Channel; and Edward III had one passage so painful that he was reduced to explain it by the arts of foreign "necromancers and wizards". This gives emphasis to a case registered by Blount in his *Antient Tenures* (pp. 61, 63). There he recounts how, under Endward I: "Solomon Attefeld holds land at Keperland and Atterton in the county of Kent on serjeanty, to wit that, whensoever the Lord King may wish to cross the sea, the said Solomon and his heirs are bound to cross with him to hold his head on the sea, if need be." On another roll the usual ports of crossing are specified: Dover and Whitsond—i.e. Wissant by Calais. Here, again, are extracts from a fifteenth-century poem on the pilgrimage to St James of Compostela:

Men may leve alle gamys,
That saylen to seynt Jamys!
Ffor many a man hit gramys, [*grieves*
When they begyn to sayle.

Ffor when they have take the see
At Sandwyche, or at Wynchylsee.
At Brystow, or where that hit bee.
Theyr hertes begyn to fayle.

. . .

A boy or tweyn anone up styen [climb
And overthwart the sayle-yerde lyen;—
"Y how! taylia!" the remenaunt cryen,
And pulle with alle theyr myght.
"Bestowe the boote, Bote-swayne, anon, [stow
That our pylgryms may pley theron;
For som ar lyke to cowgh and grone
Or hit be full mydnyght."

"Hale the bowelyne! now, vere the shete!—
Cooke, make ready anoon our mete,
Our pylgryms have no lust to ete,
I pray god yeve hem rest!"
"Go to the helm! what, howe! no nere? [nearer
Steward, felow! A pot of bere!"
"Ye shalle have, sir, with good chere,
Anon alle of the best."

"Y howe! trussa! hale in the brayles! [ropes
Thow halyst nat, be god, thow fayles! [slackest
O se howe welle owre good shyp sayles!"
And thus they say among.
"Hale in the wartake!" "hit shal be done." [rope
"Steward! cover the boorde anone,
And set bred and salt therone,
And tary nat to long."

Then cometh oone and seyth, "be mery;
Ye shall have a storme or a pery." [squall
"Holde thow thy pese! thow canst no whery, [curse?
Thow medlyst wondyr sore."

Thys mene whyle the pylgryms ly,
And have theyr bowlys fast theym by,
And cry aftyr hote maluesy, [*Malmsey*
Their helthe for to restore.

And some wold have a saltyd tost,
Ffor they myght ete neyther sode ne rost; [*boiled nor roast*
A man myght sone pay for theyr cost,
As for oo day or twayne.
Some layde theyr bookys on theyr kne,
And rad so long they myght nat se;—
"Allas! myne hede wolle cleve on thre!"
Thus seyth another certayne.[8]

From about the same date, we have evidence from a Travellers' Guide. A little work of *Dialogues in French and English* was printed by Caxton about 1483. He took the French portion from a French-Flemish phrase-book compiled at Bruges, probably in the first half of the fourteenth century: this he printed side by side with an English translation of his own for the use of travellers: we may take this as a sample.

"Yf ye owe ony pylgremages, so pay them hastely. Whan ye be mevyd* for to goo your viage, and ye knowe not the waye, so axe it thus, in comending the peple to god: 'To god, goode pepel; I goo to Saynt James, ([or], to our lady of boloyne). At whiche gate shall I goo out, and at whiche hande shall I take my way?' 'On the right hande, whan ye come to a brigge, so go ther over; ye shall fynde a lytill waye on the lyfte honde, whiche shall brynge you in a contre there shall ye see upon a chirche two hye steples; fro thens shall [y]e have but four myle unto your loggyng. There shall ye be well easyd for your money, and ye shall have a good Jorne†.'

"'Dame, god be here!' 'Felaw, ye be welcome.' 'May I have a bedde here withinne?—May I here be logged?' 'Ye, well and clenly, alle‡ were ye twelve, alle on horse-

* moved. † journey. ‡ even though.

back.' 'Nay, but we thre. Is there to ete here within?' 'Ye§, ynough, god be thanked.' 'Brynge it to us. Gyve heye to the hors, and strawe them well; but that they be watred.'

"'Dame what owe we? We have ben well easyd. We shall rekene to morrow, and shall paye also, that ye shall hold you plesid. Brynge us to slepe; we ben wery.' 'Well, I goo, ye shall reste. Jenette, lyghte the candell; and lede them ther above in the solere|| tofore; and bere them hoot watre for to wasshe their feet; and covere them with quysshons¶, se that the stable be well shette**.'

"'Dame, may men goo by ship from hens to boloyne?' 'Ye, now ther is a shippe redy ful of peple. God wel them conduyte††! God brynge them in savete!'"

Of travel in the modern aesthetic sense there was little in the English Middle Ages. Men went abroad to fight, as Chaucer's model knight did, or on business, like Chaucer himself, or on pilgrimages, in virtue whereof (as *Piers Plowman* cynically assures us) "they had leave to lie all their life after". The greatest of these liars (as we shall see later) was Sir John Maundeville. Although this man does really seem to have had some connection with St Albans (his name is scratched in a contemporary or subcontemporary hand on that pillar of the abbey church which has also a painted inscription concerning him), yet he cannot be trusted in any one of his assertions: modern students have left scarcely one shred of his *Travels* which is not demonstrably stolen from earlier and more veracious travellers. Those others do show, however, the extent to which a few friars or knights interested themselves in the natural or social peculiarities of foreign countries; and, even among those whose main interest was business, Marco Polo shows a lively and scientific curiosity which may bear comparison with Darwin's *Voyage of the Beagle*. Chaucer, too, though his work in Italy was that of ambassador and commercial negotiator, made such use of his opportunities that we may fairly dwell a little on his travels there as a matter not

§ yea. || upper room. ¶ cushions; i.e. quilts.
** shut. †† conduct.

merely of personal but of deeper social interest. It marks the first definite and visible stage of Italian influence over English thought. Little as Chaucer's successors imitated him on that particular point, it is from this time that we must begin the English Renaissance, in its first glimmerings of dawn.

Italy was to Chaucer both what Europe is to a modern American, and what America is to a modern European. On the one hand, he found in Lombardy and Tuscany, even more than at Bruges, newer methods in trade and industry, and incomparably vaster business buildings, than even in his native London. On the other, he found in Italy what so delighted Ruskin at his first landing under Calais tower: here "the links are unbroken between the past and present; and, in such use as they can serve for, the grey-headed wrecks are suffered to stay with men". Crossing by Mont-Cenis, as he probably did, he would find at Susa (or, if by the Great St Bernard, still more definitely at Aosta) what Virgil had sung as one of the glories of his native land, the living rivers that flowed under the hoary walls—*fluminaque antiquos subterlabentia muros.* Again, Florence was by that time, what in earlier days Paris and the Ile-de-France had been, the great home of modern art. Here, to take only one example, he would see Giotto's Campanile almost as it emerged from the hands of the builders; and at Pavia the palace of the Visconti boasted a specially famous series of Griselda pictures on its walls, which he must have heard of if he did not actually see them. And, lastly, there was the stimulus of song. In the Italian tongue, each word has on an average four times as many possible rhymes as in English; and Italian open-air life lends itself with equal superiority to evening song, when the day's work is done. Chaucer's England was probably more a land of peasant song than any parts nowadays except Wales and the West Riding; but the mass of song in Italy would be as much greater than ours as the mass of picturesque incidents in mountain-country is, by demonstrable calculation, greater than in the lowlands. It was upon this mass of popular *stornelli* and *rispetti* that Boccaccio modelled his own *ottava rima,* which so strongly influenced Chaucer's seven-line stanza, borrowed itself from the French of Machault. The autobiography of Brother Salimbene of Parma, a writer roughly contemporary with Chaucer's grandfather, is crowded with descriptions of this good friar's musical friends; Brother Vita, who sang so sweetly that a nun leapt from her convent window to join him; Brother Henry of Pisa, the great hymn-writer, who borrowed the air of one of his masterpieces from a servant-maid whom he once heard tripping across the cathedral from door to door, and singing as she went "And if thou carest not for me, I will care no more for thee"—*E se tu non cura da me, Io non curarò da te!* If not already before St Francis's time most certainly afterwards, Italy was "a nest of singing-birds" even beyond Elizabethan England. Nor must we look upon Chaucer as merely passive here. Poetry, like life of any kind, is contagious. Salimbene tells us how Brother Vita would amuse himself with provoking the nightingales to alternate song and response. Our own poet, like his then master Boccaccio, would not disdain to sing in direct rivalry with the hundreds of untaught nightingales whom he heard around him. Landor, in one of his best known poems, hailed the young Browning, at that time scarcely known, as the most observant man who had trodden the English lanes since Chaucer; and he went on to prophesy still greater triumphs from Browning's long sojourn in Italy, amid the magic of the South; amid the cliffs and groves of Sorrento and Amalfi, where

The siren waits thee, singing song for song.

That siren, that emulation, Chaucer found from his much briefer, yet not less momentous, Italian journeys.

27. JUST PRICE AND USURY

This subject is so characteristic of the difference between medieval and modern life, for good or for evil, that we must dwell upon it at some length.[1]

Until the middle of our period there was very little capitalism in England. There was plenty in Florence and Venice, Cologne and Lübeck, Ghent and Bruges; there we already find merchants of the modern type, risking their own money and other men's lives. In England, for some time after the Conquest, most men risked not only their money but their life. In London, however, and Bristol and a few other towns, there was the beginning of capitalism. It was marked at first mainly among the great foreign merchants who traded with us; Lombards, or men of the Hansa or Flemings; and, with capitalism, came an intensification of the problem of usury, of lending money out at interest. Here, as in so many other ways, the Church did indeed guide, but less definitely and less widely than is often represented: certainly less than her position and her lofty exclusivist pretensions would warrant. The problem of trade morality scarcely existed in the days when the first apostolic Christian community had all things in common; when there were no church buildings and only a fluid hierarchical organization. Even in the succeeding generations, it is natural to find the Christian Fathers either ignoring or reprobating trade, just as they ignored or reprobated the decoration of churches with images. At a far later time, in the Middle Ages proper, Pirenne points out that "the Church, the most powerful landowner of the time", adopted "towards commerce an attitude not merely passive but actively hostile"; "the needs of the bourgeoisie . . . ran counter to all the interests and ideas of a society dominated materially by the owners of large landed property, and spiritually by the Church, whose aversion to trade was unconquerable" (48-51). For it was inevitable that the conviction of the overwhelming importance of a choice between eternal salvation and eternal damnation should very deeply colour the early Christian theories of industry and commerce.[2] Roman imperial law had treated bargaining as a bald matter of competition: sell as dear and buy as cheaply as you can; all is fair, short of actual cheating. But medieval Church law (and State law as influenced by it) went not so much on the principle "each look after himself", as upon "each look after his neighbour"; "do unto others as ye would they should do unto you". At first, this was taken in a very extreme sense. Sir William Ashley quotes very strong sayings from Tertullian, Jerome and St Augustine: this last even pleads: "Business is in itself an evil, for it turns men from seeking true rest, which is God." Still more interesting, perhaps, is a passage attributed to St John Chrysostom which Sir William does not quote, but which was incorporated in Canon Law by Gratian (*Decretum*, Par. 1, dist. 88, cap. 11): "Whosoever buyeth a thing, not that he may sell it whole and unchanged, but that it may be a material for fashioning something, he is no merchant. But the man who buyeth it in order that he may gain by selling it again unchanged and as he bought it, that man is of the buyers and sellers who are cast forth from God's temple." In other words, you may buy raw material for your work; but to buy the finished article for trade is sinful, and only one degree better than usury. This, after all, follows logically from St Paul; if no Christian may go to law with his fellow-Christian, then there can be no extensive trade between Christian and Christian. But the Church gradually receded from this impossible position; prohibition gave way to regulation, and there grew up the theory of the Just Price; i.e. a price which enables the seller just to keep up that household which his state of life, whatever it may be, does on the average require. Anything beyond that is sinful superfluity; and any trade which brings a man more than that is unlawful trade. Such was the ideal of the whole later Middle Ages; an ideal, it may be freely confessed, which we did wrong ever to lose sight of altogether. To divorce political economy from ethics is as unscientific as the divorce between any other two sciences.

Thus, in the later Middle Ages, the original crude prohibitions gave way to the notion of the just price as formulated, for instance, by St Thomas Aquinas. With him trade is not sinful in itself, but only dangerous, as tempting to sin. A man has the right of selling things dear enough to keep himself and his family in what may be looked upon as reasonable comfort, or even in the dignity required by his position in life. So far he has a right, but no farther. To sell dearer than this is profiteering. Aquinas's sense of the necessary moral limitations, and therefore of the moral danger, is best expressed in his own words.[3] Learned as he was, he knew that Canon Law had incorporated St John Chrysostom's doctrine. He had to face the fact that this doctrine was reinforced by that Holy Writ which (as we shall see later on) he was bound to accept as final, either in its literal or in its allegorical sense. Christ, he knew, had driven the traders from the Temple. He begins, therefore, by pointing out that there is such a thing as trading for the public good, " to provide a house or a city with the necessities of life ", which may be distinguished from trading " not for the necessities of life but for the sake of gain ". He continues : " The first kind of exchange is laudable, since it serveth natural necessity; but the second is justly blamed, because, in itself, it serves the greed for gain which knows no limit, but tends to infinity. Therefore trading, considered in itself, has a certain baseness [turpitudinem], in that it does not imply, in its nature, an honourable or necessary end. Nevertheless it does not by its nature imply anything vicious or contrary to virtue; wherefore nothing prevents gain from being directed to some necessary or even honourable end, and thus becoming lawful."

This is admirable; but the rock upon which it split was the difficulty of practical application. It supplies a rule for the confessional, but not for business dealings between man and man. We have seen how the Church was willing to go on for four centuries, at least, in reliance upon that word *sanior* as a crucial term of law, yet without ever arriving at a clear conception of this *sanitas*, this " soundness "—how, indeed even on the very verge of the Reformation, the most elaborate practical definition of that crucial word merited the ancient sarcasm *Ignotum per ignotius.* If this was so in the case of a word which, to a resolute legislator, need have offered no more difficulty of practical definition, in view of probable or certain contingencies, than the difficulties which face our framers of rules for cricket and golf clubs, then how much less can we expect a successful practical definition of that word *just*, with all its elusive implications? Therefore medieval practice fell far short of St Thomas's ideal.[4] While the Gild system aimed at enforcing the Just Price, it brought other injustices in its train; Gild morality, at the best, was that of loving your friend within and ignoring, if not hating, your rival outside. Corresponding attempts to regulate wages (as we know from the Statutes of Labourers) were similarly two-edged.

On these principles, the problem of usury necessarily emerged and became the burning question in medieval political economy. In earlier Canon Law we find just the crude repudiation of all usury, as in the Bible. Moreover, this "usury" is originally defined as "any taking of money beyond the capital lent". Indeed, canonists forbid not only the taking but even the expectation of any gain in money; and, further still, even any hope in the lender's mind that he will get favour or any other worldly profit by his loan! As society developed, that doctrine became obviously untenable; but the modifications subsequently made were so piecemeal and, in some of the most important cases, so unofficial, that this remained one of the thorniest subjects for confessors almost into the lifetime of living men—so much so, that about 1830 the difficulty was met by orders from Rome forbidding priests to make enquiries in the confessional as to the penitent's investments.

Two things, it would seem, hampered the medieval Church in solving thoroughly this problem of economic relations. In the first place, we have already seen how the principle of serfdom was ingrained in medieval society, and with it the principle of God-ordained distinctions of classes; not absolutely watertight, of course, but so strong that it was dangerous to neglect an order which was so evidently providential. "To remain in that state in which he was born and faithfully to fulfil the obligations which it entailed, such was the counsel which the Church gave to every Christian."[5] Therefore, in spite of egalitarian pronouncements here and there (as when, in *Piers Plowman*, we are reminded that a churl's bones in the graveyard are hard to distinguish from those of a knight), no real approach to socialism was possible. We find only sudden and fleeting Bolshevik convulsions, of which the most important was the revolt of the peasants of the Flemish sea-board in the early fourteenth century, and next that of our own John Ball in 1381, with his "When Adam delvéd and Eve span, who was then the gentleman?" That, then, was the first difficulty; and the second was that this insistent problem of usury seldom led the *official* Church to pay serious attention even to the most obvious rules of political economy; for, though St Thomas was a saint and a genius, his work was unofficial. Thus, while the ecclesiastical prohibition of usury rested originally on a narrowly literal interpretation of Old Testament texts, just as the medieval Sabbatarianism did, yet, in so far as the Church abandoned this crude prohibition, the change came less from a general survey of the whole philosophical question than by successive modifications, introduced under pressure of the laws of natural justice and human nature.

The real justification of usury is in that extension of industry and trade which we call the capitalist system. This scarcely existed as yet in the England of 1300. Under capitalism, usury helps in further production. The man who has £10 to spare, instead of keeping it barren in a chest, lends it to some commercial undertaking, either directly, as by taking shares in a railway company, or indirectly through his bank. That money goes to buy more raw material and pay more workmen, and so to increase not only the lender's private funds, but also the world's production and wealth and general comfort. If, on the other hand, £10 is lent to a peasant farmer who is approaching bankruptcy because, for one reason or another, he is unable to keep pace with his competitors—that is, to a man whose only object and whose only possibility is simply to keep himself and his family on the little farm, and drive the wolf from the door, and who will perhaps produce less than a younger or more energetic competitor who would come in when he was turned out—in such a case, from the purely productive point of view, it is probably better that the man and his family should go to the workhouse; so that, although there are far stronger charitable reasons for my lending him money, there is far less reason in political economy than in my entrusting it to the bank. Moreover, if we consider charitable reasons alone, of course I ought to lend to the man gratis or at an almost nominal rate of interest; and yet (still speaking from the purely commercial point of view) I cannot justify my own risk in lending to him except by charging him something even higher than the ordinary rate of interest, in proportion to the feebleness of the security that he can offer me. Therefore the natural tendency in human nature is for those who lend on usury to the poor, in so far as they are business folk at all, to charge high rates and steel their hearts against all compassion. This, then, was a problem far more frequent under medieval economic conditions than even at present. The village population, which is so exceptional with us, was normal between the Conquest and the Reformation. We may almost say that everything then was on a village scale. Moreover, even the town of the Middle Ages was, as we have seen, in one sense more parochial than the modern village, since to a very great extent it aimed at being self-sufficing. Whereas the modern villager shops a good deal in the town, the medieval villager went comparatively seldom to the market or fair unless he lived close by; and, even then, it was often simply for barter and not for money exchange. Moreover, in many cases, even in the towns, craftsmen bought their own materials and sold their own wares : thus the shopkeeping class was only beginning to come into existence. Therefore the law of bargaining was not that which has naturally grown up among enormously greater populations with enormously wider exchange of articles; it was not the old Roman law of *caveat emptor,* bidding each man look after himself, but a system of Gild supervision. The craftsman, again, having chosen his craft and gone through it to the final stage, was thenceforward sealed to it. He must abide by his choice; so that it was natural for those of the same craft to dwell together in the same street; whenever we can trace the street names of medieval towns, about half of them describe the occupations of the in-dwellers. Even of the town merchant, Ashley can write: "His capital was small. He dealt directly with the customer, and between himself and the one or two boys whom he might employ there was no social gulf." That has already been suggested by the inventories of Colchester traders quoted in Chapter XXV. Already, however, the immense trade impulse on the Continent, from the Crusades onwards, began to demand serious revision of the original Christian teaching on usury; and the problem was taken up by the Schoolmen, of whom again we may take St Thomas Aquinas as typical.

It was recognized as a matter of common sense that a loan was a contract, and that a breach of contract might justify the claim for damages. Thus St Thomas grants the legitimacy of interest for *damnum emergens,* e.g. for the actual loss which the lender may suffer if the borrower fails to repay within the stipulated time. He refuses, however, to allow interest for *lucrum cessans*; for the cessation of (potential) gain. The lender may, indeed, plead truly, as a matter of fact: "During the year for which I lent you this £10, I lost what I might have gained by lending it or employing it elsewhere." To that, St Thomas replies: "True; but why should not your gains cease, in ethics, during this time when you yourself were taking no trouble to work for it?" It will be seen, therefore, that these refinements, though tending in the right direction of philosophic definition, lent themselves to legal fictions, the worst of which was that of a sham contract. In the least objectionable forms of such fictions, the lender would stipulate upon an extremely early date for repayment, beyond which date—so soon as to be practically impossible for the borrower—interest might legally be charged on the admitted principle of *damnum emergens.* In some cases of this kind, the interest under these semi-fraudulent contracts was 5 per cent. per month; that is, 60 per cent. per year, *pro recompensatione damnorum*—and this at a time when the civil law prohibited Jews from charging more than 43 per cent.! Gradually, then, such contracts were softened down into something less grossly unfair, and therefore more customary. In these cases, by the natural working of opposite interests in bargaining, the period of freedom was slightly lengthened and the interest after that free period was considerably reduced. Then, by a similar operation of conflicting interests, a concordat was arrived at by which the excuse of the free period was dropped altogether; interest was now charged from the very first day of the loan, but usually at a far more reasonable rate. This, however, was a definite breach of the theory of Canon Law. Strictly, it was illegal all through the Middle Ages; but in England as elsewhere it was recognized by the civil courts.

Here, as in so many other worldly compromises, the Court of Rome took the lead, not from any essential spirit of injustice, but simply because it was the greatest business organization in Europe, with strongest traditions and widest grasp. Matthew Paris records the complaints of Bishop Grosseteste on his death-bed against Innocent IV (1253).[6] Matthew, it is true, monk though he was, was a severe critic of the Popes; but for the essentials of his picture we have plenty of corroborative evidence. "Though many other popes have afflicted the Church, this one hath oppressed her with a more grievous servitude, and hath multiplied injustices. For the Caursins are manifest usurers; and they have been cast forth from France (for this plague was then unknown in England) by holy fathers and teachers whom we have seen and known personally. . . . Notwithstanding, this Pope hath raised them up and protected them in their high place; and, if any man speak against them, he is wearied with loss and labour, as we have seen in the case of Bishop Roger of London. The whole world knoweth that usury is held in detestation in the Old and New Testament, and is forbidden by God. Yet now the lord Pope's merchants or money-changers practise their usury publicly in London, to the disgust of the Jews. They plot divers and grievous machinations against men of Holy Church, and especially Religious, compelling men under pressure of penury to lie, and to append their signs-manual to false deeds; which is as it were to commit idolatry and to renounce Truth, which is God. . . . And if, by chance, thou wilt pay the papal usurer the principal of the money, which thou hast now in thy possession, within a month or less [of the day of borrowing], he will not accept it unless thou pay him the whole hundred pounds. This is worse than a Jew's conditions; for the Jew will receive the principal courteously whensoever thou shalt return it, with only so much interest as is proportionate to the time for which thou hast had it in hand." Elsewhere, Matthew writes in his own name: "From that time forward [1229] the land [of England] has never lacked certain Ultramontanes, who style themselves merchants; most impious usurers, who seek nothing else than to ensnare those men in especial whom the Roman Court is pressing for money."[7] Another Benedictine chronicler, Oxenedes, bitterly resents the fact that "usury, which is forbidden in both Testaments, is now practised almost as a lawful trade by those usurers of the Roman Pontiff who are called 'merchants'". Under the year 1258 he writes again: "The plague of usury . . . did so ensnare the English religious houses, that there was no conventual house, nor cathedral, nor any so modest foundation but that it was involved in so many debts as made it despair of acquittance at any time."[8] This systematic protection of usurers was imposed upon the Popes by their own rapidly growing practice of selling the richest offices in the Church; for such was the practical effect of demanding from bishops or abbots a whole year's income in advance ("first-fruits", "annates") as a condition of papal institution. One of the greatest of our English archbishops, Pecham, was a Franciscan of those earlier days when St Francis's renunciation of worldly goods was still taken seriously. He accepted the spiritual office, and, in fact, did much for the sadly needed reforms in his diocese and province; but how was he to pay the "Pope's merchants" such a sum of ready money as an earl would not have found it easy to raise? In 1279 he wrote.[9] "To the most holy Father and lord in Christ Nicholas, by divine providence supreme pontiff of the holy Roman Church, his poor little brother John, priest of Canterbury, sendeth greeting, falling down with all reverence and kissing his holy feet.

. . . There hath lately reached me a letter of execution, horrible to see and terrible to hear, whereof the final purpose is this: that unless, within a month from the feast of Michaelmas next coming, I pay fully and completely to the merchants of Lucca, from whom I borrowed at the Court of Rome, the sum of a hundred marks for a hundred pounds [which I am to pay at the end of the term] I shall be forthwith involved in the sentence of excommunication, and shall be denounced as excommunicate in my own and other cathedral churches, with bell, book and candle, on every Sunday and holy-day. . . . And this although, according to the contract which I signed, I might have secured freedom to myself and my church for an indefinite time, so long as I paid the damages and interest to the aforesaid merchants, in consideration of the losses they would incur by my delay. . . . Therefore, most holy Father, may it please your most merciful Holiness to reach me the right hand of succour and to revoke this cruel letter . . . otherwise, I see no other refuge but either to leave this prelacy committed to me, to disperse my household or flock, and to depart as an exile into some distant land, where I may lurk alone in some monastery and bear this anathema with humility until, as God shall give occasion, I shall have succeeded in satisfying the aforesaid merchants from the revenues of my see, in proportion as they can be raised from time to time; or, again, to borrow further from these merchants, and as a borrower, to fawn upon them and bear with patience their base speech (though, by your Holiness's special mandate, it would be my duty to take strong measures against such lenders), since in these days no other men can be found in England who have money enough, nor, in the face of the present change and clipping of coinage, could I borrow elsewhere [than from these merchants of Lucca]." If great prelates ceased to complain with this freedom of speech, it was not because the abuse ceased, but because it became chronic and hopelessly ineradicable. It became so much a part of the ordinary rich merchant's work that it was finally registered under an apparently innocent name. The word *chevisance* originally meant any kind of bargain or mercantile exchange; but by Chaucer's time it had come to mean "usury", carried on under the current bootlegging system. Here, again, we may detect one of our poet's quiet touches of satire. How should the average modern reader suspect all that underlies that couplet about the merchant?

So estatly was he of his governaunce
With his bargaynes and with his chevyssaunce.

But here, as usual, "the moral Gower" bleats out with brutal frankness the things which his friend Chaucer has but hinted without a change of muscle in his countenance. Gower writes, in his *Mirour* (line 7225): "The city usurer keeps on hire his brokers and procurers who search for knights vavasours and squires. . . . Presently that trick will be played which in modern jargon is called the *chevisance* of money." And we have a royal ordinance of 1365 against usurious contracts which "the more subtly to deceive the people, men call exchange or *chevisance*".[10] A little earlier, Benvenuto da Imola writes in his great commentary on Dante: "He who practiseth usury goeth to hell, and he who practiseth it not, tendeth to destitution."[11] For, by this time, whatever the Church might preach, the merchant's interest coincided so exactly with papal practice that a common-sense *modus vivendi* was found; men did not trouble about their fellows' motives for taking interest, so long as they did not in fact take too extortionately. Mr H. G. Richardson, who has made considerable researches on this subject among the royal archives in Paris, kindly supplies me with the following brief facts. In 1312 20 per cent. was the ordinary rate there; but at the Great Fair of Champagne only 15 per cent.: perhaps because the clients were all well-known and solid merchants. In 1333 the officially legalized rate was 20 per cent. In Vermandois (1350) he finds 40 per cent. permitted, and from 1378 onwards many licences were granted for 50 per cent.

Meanwhile a fresh problem had arisen. As trade expanded, and especially by sea, there came in the question of partnerships in trading companies. Here again St Thomas's solution remained classical throughout the Middle Ages. He decided that, although it was sinful to take any interest which represented neither loss nor labour on the lender's part, yet the risks involved in distant trading might justly count as labour. If, therefore, a ship sails to distant parts freighted with the goods of half a dozen lenders at £100 each, these men must take the full risk of loss which is shared by the owner and captain of the ship. If they are content to accept frankly the chance that, after all, ships and goods may have perished; or again that the goods, though brought safely to the foreign land, were sold at a heavy loss, then they are justified in accepting any percentage of gain which may accrue under more fortunate conditions. If, however, they make a contract securing to them (on whatever terms of interest) the final restitution of their full capital in so far as the borrower's means enable him to restore it, then that contract is usurious. The lender has not earned his money by the "labour" of taking his fair share of the risk.* Yet even this concordat dates from only about 1250; moreover, it is in flat contradiction with a papal decree embodied in Canon Law, Gregory IX's Decretal *Naviganti*! † Moreover, even down to the verge of the Reformation moralists may be found ignorant of St Thomas's refinements; men who condemned all taking of interest as usurious and therefore as contrary to express Divine commands. It is interesting, however, to find in our chancery records a case which reposes on a principle common both to *Naviganti* and to St Thomas's doctrine. In about 1470 we find an "Action brought by Robert Whynbarrogh, clerk of the said sheriffs [of Norwich], who contends that certain money was lent by him to the complainant to be employed to his use in the complainant's business, and that he is therefore entitled to a share of the profits arising out of the transactions in which that money was employed, as well as to the repayment of the principal; 'which is usury'".[12]

The last and perhaps most important modification was the permission to buy rent-charges (*census*), from which comes the ordinary German name for interest, "Zins". X, let us say,

* It is not that the philosopher here juggles with the term "labour". We shall see, in a later chapter, how Cambridge boys received a groat for their "labour" of submitting to public fustigation.

† For a full account of this almost incredible episode, see my article in *History* for July 1921.

owns a piece of land from which he derives a yearly rent of £10. *Y* purchases from him for £100 or £150 that rent. In plain words, *Y* invests his £100 or £150 at 10 or $6\frac{2}{3}$ per cent. Thus, such purchases might easily be permitted as non-usurious. If *Y* had every moral right to buy the land outright, why should he not buy the yearly produce of that land? At first, however, it was insisted that the land must actually exist, and that *Y* must actually purchase it, though on the condition that *X* might compel its redemption by repaying the money. Gradually, however, that restriction was abandoned in practice. It was too artificial to maintain itself: men bought and sold rents like any other marketable commodity, and the *census* became a favourite investment for religious bodies.

So much has been written lately concerning the medieval *theory* of Just Price and Usury, with so much neglect of the at least equally important evidence as to *practice,* that it will be profitable here to pursue the subject as illustrated by monastic banking. For, since the monasteries were among the greatest capitalists, this economic loss touched them as it touched the merchants outside. A modern scholar, Professor R. Génestal, has made a detailed study of this movement in twelfth- and thirteenth-century Normandy. where the social conditions resembled our own more closely, perhaps, than anywhere else.[13] He points out that there were two periods: first that of mortgage, and secondly that of rent-charge. In the first, or mortgage period, the borrowers from monasteries were almost always nobles or wealthy folk in temporary need of money. In proof of the thorough business spirit in which the monks regarded these transactions, we have the fact that they constantly show themselves unwilling to be repaid too soon. We therefore find contracts in which the lenders expressly exclude repayment until 2 or 3 years have elapsed, or 6; more often 9, or 15, or 18; oftenest of all, 21. Moreover, by Roman law the mortgager might foreclose after the lapse of 30 years; and, since the monks' usual practice was to lend a sum not exceeding two-thirds of the real value (sometimes even less), it was a great advantage to the lender to prolong to this term. So long as the loan lasted, he received about 15 per cent.; and he had the security of a pledge which could be sold at a higher price than the sum lent. Many of the borrowers are men on the point of starting for the Crusades; no peasant in that position would have lands to pledge: the land belonged to his lord. Moreover, the statistics of these mortgages show us that the loan was seldom below 5 *livres,* and at least half were of 10 *livres* or more. Thus the conclusion is that the mortgage system served only for the rich, and only for men who were borrowing for consumption. Therefore it came under papal prohibition, which did in fact practically kill the system so far as monks were concerned. Thenceforward, though the abbeys still invested heavily and profitably, it was under the *census* system. The rate of interest for such rent-charges during the years covered by Génestal (1150-1300), though high for modern ideas, was a good deal lower than that for mortgages in the earlier years. A table which he has drawn up gives forty-two cases at 10 per cent. and sixty-five at a higher rate, the lowest of all being not quite 7 per cent. The average would thus be from 11 to 12 per cent. And—another contrast—the sums invested under the *census* system are much smaller: the large majority are only 1, 2 or 3 *livres.* Moreover, the borrowers, whenever we can trace them, are people living fairly near the abbey, and often actual tenants. Thus he sums up: "During our first period we have seen that credit is rare and unproductive, open only to lords and generally leading them to ruin; at that time the abbeys are of very small importance for the matter [of credit]; they alone, [and not the borrowers], enrich themselves by the mortgage system. The second period, on the contrary, shows us these same abbeys spreading around the benefits of a credit destined to facilitate production, open to the middle classes and especially to rural folk, who, without overburdening themselves, can thus procure what they need for agricultural improvement. The monasteries are real land-banks, thickly spread over the country; they play a most important economic part, and one which they alone could have played." Yet it was as economists that they played it; banking had grown up as naturally in the monasteries as it grew up among the merchants outside. Henry of Ghent in [1280] does indeed take the old strict view of the census-system as usurious. But such rigorists were swept away by the tide: they were hopelessly out of date. The monks of St Martin-des-Champs had been lending money on exactly the same terms as ordinary bankers as early as about 1070. Lamprecht, in a passage which Lord Acton pencil-marked in his own copy of the book, wrote of " the free and easy way in which business was done at Cluny . . . the bank-business of St André was managed by Jewish financiers in the service of the abbey ". It is to these Jews that we must turn in the next chapter.

It is sometimes asserted, though without documentary proof, that monasteries anticipated the *Mont de Piété* system of gratuitous loans to necessitous folk. Here, for instance, is the plea of Gustav Schnürer, whose voluminous apologetic book, *Kirche und Kultur im Mittelalter*, enjoys a wide circulation in German and French. He writes (II, 188-9): " But especially the monasteries, as the Church had done formerly in the time of decaying Roman [Imperial] money-economy, mitigated much social want by their action as loan-institutions. Since Church teaching forbade the taking of interest, the debtor was protected against usury. They [the monks] lent smaller sums to the peasants, when they came into temporary difficulties through failure of crops; they lent larger sums for pilgrimages, military expeditions, liberation from captivity, and marriages." Schnürer offers no evidence whatever for the one essential point in all this, the *gratuitous* character of such loans; and his assertion is contradicted, on careful inspection, by almost every great monastic chartulary. Génestal, in his monumental study, finds no case of this kind to quote; and readers may find a great deal of evidence to the contrary in the chapter which I have devoted to this subject in the third volume of *Five Centuries of Religion* (ch. XVI). The plea, in fact, is among those which were invented long ago by apologists writing mainly from their imagination, and which have since been repeated from book to book without verification. Anti-clerical legends of that same imaginary class, such as " the Walled-up Nun " and " the Indulgence as an Official Licence for Sin ", have long disappeared from the pages of all respectable writers; and it is high time that apologists on the other side should cease to repeat without verification these sweeping assertions of extreme social importance.

Monts de Piété did indeed grow up in the great Continental cities towards the end of our period, and mainly from the impulse given by Churchmen; but they testify especially to the growth of civic activities in social service. As early as 1251 we find in the *Calendar of Papal Letters* (I, 267): " [Papal] confirmation to the Bishops of Bath and Wells and Salisbury of the ordinance by which many burgesses of cities and places in England have set aside a certain sum of money to be lent to the poor without interest, by trustworthy persons, that they may not be oppressed or devoured by usury, with mandate to the same not to allow any interference with the said ordinance." But there is little trace of this system in later generations: nothing resembling the scale on which it was worked in Florence or Siena. English universities, again, adopted the system which was worked at Paris and elsewhere, of " chests " for gratuitous loans. Some benefactor first left a sum of money as foundation; this was kept in a chest under official custody, and loans were made from it without interest. But to the real poor these were useless; for the invariable rule of the " chest " was that the borrower should deposit a pledge of equivalent value. These " chests ", therefore, met only the difficulty which we have already seen in a previous chapter, that any one who was away from home in the Middle Ages, like a modern traveller in some distant land, might well be in dire momentary need of money, despite his fundamental solvency or even his great wealth.

28. THE GHETTO (1)

The Jews have grown to embody, if indeed they did not embody from the first, an element very important in society, but, in its crudest form, definitely antagonistic to the cruder forms of other equally important elements. We cannot think of them in the Middle Ages apart from what they were in the Old Testament and what they are to-day.

He was a Jew by birth who said He was come to bring " not peace, but division "; or (to quote from St Matthew) " not peace, but a sword ". We ourselves, however unconsciously, are constantly implying the same thing when we say of any man that he is " in deadly earnest " : the living flame within this person may have deadly reactions outside. In proportion as one man is determined to follow his own conscience—in proportion as he is wholly possessed by the greatness of any cause which he espouses—in that same proportion must he risk collision with others equally resolute, equally conscientious, yet diverging certainly to some extent (given the endless variety of human character), and possibly diverging in some of the most essential respects. This is nowhere seen more clearly, perhaps, than in the history of Christianity and Judaism in their mutual relations. Here we see exemplified those words of Christ which follow : " The father shall be divided against the son, and the son against the father; the mother against the daughter, and the daughter against the mother." Yet Christ proclaimed emphatically that His mission was not to destroy the Jewish law, but to fulfil it. The whole of the Epistle to the Hebrews is one continuous argument in that sense. Perhaps the most important tenet which Christianity inherited from Judaism was its fundamental doctrine of the Unity of God and the Goodness of God. The first words of the Lord's Prayer are an echo from the Psalmist : " Like as a father pitieth his children, so the Lord pitieth them that fear him." All the earliest Christians were

Jews; and, when Gallio treated the contention between them and their unconverted brethren as a mere difference between Tweedledum and Tweedledee, he only anticipated the confusion which seems evident in the mind of so keen an observer as Juvenal, two generations later. Yet in this field, very soon, we find father divided against son, mother against daughter; and the blackest chapter in Christian history is that of the relations between Church and Synagogue.

The key to this mystery, in so far as it can be explained in a few words, lies in two facts: the Jew was exclusive, and the Jew was proselytizing, from the earliest stages of history at which we can see him distinctly. And that history shows very clearly how false it is to suppose that the exclusive spirit and the proselytizing spirit are mutually exclusive. To the Jew, Jehovah was the God of Israel; other races, the Gentiles, were outside the Almighty's Covenant: "to Abraham and his seed were the promises made." None of the other religions within the vast compass of the Roman Empire seems to have rested on such an exclusivist foundation. Next, when a succession of cruel conquests broke up and dispersed the Jews—the Babylonian captivity, the fight against Antiochus Epiphanes and those later wars against Rome—then the Hebrew, in his dispersion, became a proselytizer. That is what pagan observers noticed most definitely in him during the first few generations of the Empire. The actual seed of Abraham was dispersed, but the promise made to Abraham might now be claimed by all who could be persuaded to accept circumcision and the Mosaic Law. Thus in the reception of converts Judaism was far from exclusive; the Pharisees "compassed sea and land to make one proselyte". But, within the fold, there still remained the old exclusivist doctrine of salvation: the uncircumcized were outside the Covenant. When once we have grasped these two points clearly, we may see why the Jews were unpopular in the Roman Empire, quite apart from their rivalry with Christianity. To Horace, the Jew is the boorish unsociable fellow who, if you are not a fellow-Jew, takes a positive pleasure in misdirecting you on your road. To Tacitus, he is an enemy of the human race. For in fact he was intensely clannish; Jew helped fellow-Jew in a way that often put others to shame: but the other side to that picture was his comparative want of fellow-feeling towards the Gentile. We all know by experience what extreme clannishness leads to. He who ignores outsiders is naturally ignored himself; the great world gives him the cold-shoulder. He becomes very sensible of this, and that exaggerates his exclusiveness; an inferiority-complex comes in to re-inforce his pre-existent superiority-complex; and the two grow and grow together. Thus the Jew's injustice to outsiders, and the Gentile's injustice to the Jews, have acted and reacted upon each other for eighteen centuries; and thus the Jew's intense sense of unity, within his own comparatively narrow compass, has been like a particle of grit in the eye of the great world outside.

From the Synagogue, let us now pass to the Church. Christianity, absorbing so much as it did from every strand of thought in the Roman Empire, took over from Judaism not only its trust in One Good and Almighty God but also its combination of exclusiveness and proselytism. What Gibbon calls "the inflexible and intolerant zeal" of early Christianity came into collision with the inflexible and intolerant zeal of ancient Judaism; and the result, when once Christianity had obtained State recognition with State force at the back of it, was a long and terrible conflict. The whole of Western Europe was now dominated by a new creed even more exclusivist and proselytizing than the old Judaism against which it must needs fight. On the first of these points the motto of the orthodox ran *extra ecclesiam nulla salus*. This was taken literally; nobody explained then (as so many explain now) that *extra* in Latin does not mean *outside*, that *ecclesiam* does not mean *Church*, that *nulla* does not mean *no*, nor *salus* salvation. On the second point, even the crudest physical force was too often applied; and men grew accustomed to interpret that Gospel parable, with its "compel them to come in", not only in the tyrannical sense in which St Augustine had expounded it in the heat of that semi-religious, semi-political civil war between Catholic and Donatist, but with even cruder intolerance.

We have no evidence for pre-Conquest Jews settled in

England.[1] William of Malmesbury tells us explicitly that the Conqueror brought them in from Rouen. His motive seems plain; he would thus be able to collect his feudal dues, scattered all over the country, not in kind but in coin, and the Jews were the most natural financial agents. For in France they had already been long compelled to specialize in this field. Until the ninth century, they had been comparatively free, though we naturally find a series of ecclesiastical and civil rules which put them at a definite disadvantage against the Christian majority; and there were frequent clashes of the kind that might be expected among those undisciplined populations. Forced baptisms occurred fairly frequently, and Christian-Jewish marriages were forbidden; yet Jews might possess lands, and were prosperous traders. Charlemagne had taken them under his protection; so had his son Louis the Pious. Churchmen of the ninth century complained of their popularity and influence, as physicians and especially as merchants, but not yet as usurers. However, with the decay of royal power and the growth of feudalism, the robber-nobles had been tempted to flay the Jew even more than the peasant. Again, when Christian society began to organize its trade under the Gild system, here also the Jew was an alien and unwelcome element. The eleventh century was marked by massacres, for which excuses were found in an asserted league between the Jews and the Muslim conquerors of Jerusalem. In 1065 Pope Alexander II tried to protect them from massacre; and, to the very end of the Middle Ages, no Pope countenanced such bloodshed. Thus, although the worst cruelties came only with the Crusades and with the later legends of ritual murder, the French Jews were already under severe disabilities when William brought them over: they were practically compelled to specialize in finance. They were not numerous, but they were widely distributed; even in villages a Jew or two might well be found, yet, apart from Paris, it is doubtful whether any town had more than a hundred Jewish households. This state of things was repeated in England: the Jews became widely scattered financiers, especially in the royal service.

For they were the king's men, and, in process of time, became practically the king's chattels. Pollock and Maitland[2] describe one of the two main ideas that our law in later time has about the Jew. "He, with all that he has, belongs to the king. Bracton puts the same thought in these words: 'The Jew can have nothing that is his own, for whatever he acquires, he acquires, not for himself, but for the king; for the Jews live not for themselves but for others.' The other main idea is one which will not seem strange to us after what we have said of villeinage. This servility is a relative servility; in relation to all men save the king the Jew is free. He will require some special treatment, for if he is to be here at all and do any good, he must be allowed to do things that are forbidden to Christians, notably to take interest on money lent; and courts of justice must pay some regard to his religion; for example, must suffer him to swear upon the Pentateuch instead of the Gospels; but in general, if his royal master's interests are not concerned, he is to be dealt with as though he were a Gentile. A third principle is accepted—the Jews themselves would strongly desire its acceptance—namely that when the interests of neither the king nor any other Gentile are concerned the Jews may arrange their own affairs and settle their own disputes in their own way and by their own Hebrew law." Again: "The Jew's relation to the king is very much like the villein's relation to his lord." Yet, for several generations, this subjection was scarcely more unfavourable in practice, apart from exceptional exercises of tyranny, than that of the villein. Mr Joseph Jacobs sums up judicially the legal (as apart from religious and social) status which Jews had acquired in England at the end of the twelfth century.[3] He writes: "They could not be regarded as aliens any more than could the Norman nobles with whom they had originally come over; besides, alienage could not become hereditary. . . . They were not heretics, since their right to exist was recognized by the Church. They were usurers for the most part, and their property, like that of all usurers, escheated to the king at their demise. But, on the other hand, their usurious debts could be recovered at law, whereas the Christian usurer could not recover more than his original loan. They were in direct relation to the king and his courts; but this did not imply any arbitrary power of the king to tax them or to take their money without repayment, as is frequently exemplified in the Pipe-Rolls. The aids, reliefs, fines and amercements demanded from them were no other than those asked from the rest of the king's subjects, though the amount contributed by the Jews may have been larger. They were the king's 'men', it is true, but no more than the barons of the time; and they had the special privilege of the baronial rank, and could move from place to place and settle anywhere without restriction. It will be seen how this privilege was afterward taken away from them. Altogether, the status of the English Jews, who partook of the nature of baron, alien, heretic and usurer, was peculiar; but, on the whole, their lot was not an unfavourable one."

Yet, before the end of the century, very unfavourable changes came. The Jews were no longer so useful to kings and great nobles and even popes. As usurers, they had rivals in the southern Frenchmen ("Caursins", i.e. men of Cahors) and, presently, in those Italian merchants who gave their name and character to our Lombard Street. The rise of the English Gilds increased that rivalry; kings and great men could now borrow on usury from English "merchants". In 1186, the Jews had been assessed, for personal property, at one-fourth the value of the whole country; and, about the same time, Aaron of Lincoln alone had left £15,000 worth of debts owing to him from barons throughout the country.[4] A single Jew of Gloucester, in 1170, had financed Strongbow's conquest of Ireland. Yet in 1255, when Henry III pawned the whole "Judaismus" of England to Richard of Cornwall, it was for only 5000 marks. Not only in usury, but in other ways the Jews were losing ground heavily through consecutive legal restrictions.[5] For, though trade was permitted to them, yet the Gilds were already securing a monopoly of skilled labour, and the Gilds Merchant monopolized the markets. In 1253 Jews were in a manner bound to the soil, like the serf their legal analogue; it was enacted that they might dwell only in one of the 25 towns which possessed an "archa" [chest] for the preservation of their documents and money contracts. In 1269 they were forbidden to claim the landed property which might revert to them by the non-payment of a mortgage; and in 1271, to hold land of any kind. In 1275, the *Statutum de Judaismo* restrained them still further, and forbade their lending on usury. In 1278 there was a great outcry against coin-clipping; 293 Jews were executed in London, and it is quite possible that all were guilty. For, as Mr Jacobs truly observes, "by depriving the Jews of a resort to usury, Edward was practically preventing them from earning a living at all under the conditions of life then existing in feudal England; and in principle the 'Statute of Judaism' expelled them fifteen years before the final expulsion".[6]

For, all this while, the natural and insistent pressure of religious intolerance was increasing. The ordinary manners of that age made no allowance for the co-existence, under one and the same State, of two creeds in deadly earnest. Christian and Muslim and Jew might enjoy equal rights in Sicily; but that was under the infidel Frederick II. Elsewhere, the great churches consecrated intolerance in the statuary of their portals, where the crowned Church bore on one side her triumphant banner and, on the other, a corresponding niche showed the Synagogue with head bent, bandaged eyes, and a staff breaking in her hands.

In Norman times, this difficulty had always existed in the background. William of Malmesbury, in his history of Rufus's reign, relates how "the Jews gave proofs of their insolence towards God. At one time, at Rouen, they endeavoured to prevail, by means of presents, on some converted Jews to return to Judaism; at another, in London, entering into controversy with our bishops; because the king (in jest, as I suppose) had said that if they mastered the Christians in open argument he would become one of their sect. The question therefore was agitated with much apprehension on the part of the bishop and clergy, fearful, through pious anxiety, for the Christian faith. From this contest, however, the Jews reaped nothing but confusion; though they used repeatedly to boast that they were vanquished not by argument but by power."[7] Again, Mr Jacobs recounts how Henry II "was indeed accused by the contemporary chroniclers of unduly favouring those 'enemies of Christ'. They lived on excellent terms with their neighbours, including the clergy; they entered churches freely, and took refuge in the abbeys in times of commotion. There is even a record of two Cistercian monks having been converted to Judaism; and there is evidence that the Jews freely criticized the more assailable sides of Catholicism, the performing of miracles and the worship of images. Meanwhile they themselves lived in ostentatious opulence in houses resembling palaces, and helped to build a large number of the abbeys and monasteries of the country. By the end of Henry's reign they had incurred the ill-will of the upper classes with whom they mostly came in contact."[8]

Moreover, religious causes became increasingly operative. In 1198, Innocent III commanded Richard of Cornwall, with all other Christian princes, to compel remission of all usury demanded by Jews from Christians. In 1205, he laid down the principle that all Jews were doomed to perpetual servitude because they had crucified Jesus. Thus St Thomas Aquinas is on unassailable ground when he decides that, "since the Jews are the slaves of the Church, she can dispose of their possessions".[9] In 1215 Innocent imposed upon their garments a perpetual badge of infamy; and Archbishop Langton enforced this in England (1218). In 1222 a deacon was burned at the stake for having apostatized and married a Jewess; but there is no record of punishment for the few earlier apostasies to Judaism. Presently came in the horrible fiction of ritual murder. The legend of St Hugh of Lincoln, told in Chaucer's Tale of the Prioress, dates from 1256; this fiction brought death to 18 Jews who refused to plead, and long imprisonment for 73 others. An even earlier story of martyrdom is that of "St William" of Norwich. Religion was pleaded also in excuse for many odious regulations, as Pollock and Maitland remind us.[10] "They were to fast in Lent; they were to wear distinctive badges upon their garments; they were not to keep Christian servants or have intercourse with Christian women; they were not to enter the churches; they were to acquire no more schools or synagogues than they already possessed." The same authors, in their section on the marriage law, write: "We have to suppose a marriage between two infidels and that one of them is converted to Christianity. In such a case the Christian is not bound to cohabit with the infidel consort, and if the infidel chooses to go off, the marriage can be dissolved and the Christian will be free to marry again. . . . It is probable that in their dealings with Jews the English courts accorded this privilege to the faithful. In 1234 a Jewish widow was refused her dower on the ground that her husband had been converted and that she had refused to adhere to him and be converted with him."[11] The annals of Cambridge supply a somewhat similar case, except that the operative factor here is not Church law but feudal custom, working upon the principle that the Jew is a sort of serf to the king. In 1169 "La Countesse, the Jewess of Cambridge, and her sons and the Jews of Lincoln, paid the king a fine of 7 marks of gold [i.e. £42, roughly equivalent to £1700 modern] for a Jewess of Lincoln, whom a son of La Countesse had married without the king's licence."[12] Another Cambridgeshire document of 1241 shows royal commissioners appointed for distraining the Jews who had not yet paid their tallage, and to seize the wives and children of recalcitrants.[13]

In 1232 Henry III founded a *Domus Conversorum* in London for converted Jews; yet, until 1280, the kings still followed the example of their forefathers and claimed all the property of such a convert, in virtue of their royal ownership over that "chattel". In 1235 Henry issued a proclamation prohibiting Christian nurses from serving Jews. This prohibition would be natural enough in any case, considering the normal relations of Church and Synagogue; but it derives further significance from a letter of Innocent III, incorporated in Canon Law, which rehearses how Jews would compel Christian nurses, for the three days succeeding their Easter Communion, to spill their milk, lest the nursling should receive contamination from the consecrated Host. This gives us an illustration not only of the usual orthodox custom of communicating only once a year, but also of the materialism to which the doctrine tempted Jewish thought; a materialism no less crude than that to which orthodox writers testify for popular thought within their own camp. In 1282, Archbishop Pecham closed all the synagogues in Canterbury diocese; and the Dominicans obtained a writ from Edward I compelling Jews to listen to conversion-sermons. Nor was the intolerance on one side only. As Mr Jacobs confesses:[14] "The Jews had throughout been careless in showing their contempt for certain aspects of Christianity. One had seized the cross carried in front of a procession at the University of Oxford in 1268, and in 1274 a Jew was burned for blasphemy at Norwich. Edward had accordingly issued a proclamation declaring any Jew found guilty of blasphemy to be liable to the death penalty. At the end of 1286 Pope Honorious IV addressed a special rescript to the archbishops of York and Canterbury, pointing out the evil effects on the religious life of England of free intercourse with the perfidious Jews, who studied the Talmud and its abominations, enticed the faithful to apostasy, caused their Christian servants to work on Sundays and holidays, and generally brought the Christian faith into disrepute. On this account he called upon the English State and Church to do their utmost to prevent such pernicious intercourse." Next year, the Synod of Exeter "repeated the ordinary Church laws against commensality between Jews and Christians, and against Jews holding public office, or having Christian servants, or appearing in public at Easter; forbidding Jewish physicians to practise", and prohibiting the erection of new synagogues. Edward I, as a loyal son of the Church, followed this up logically in action. He immediately expelled the Jews from his duchy of Gascony; and "on his return to England (July 18, 1290) he issued writs to the sheriffs of all the English counties ordering them to enforce a decree to the effect that all Jews should leave England before All Saints' Day of that year. They were allowed to carry their portable property; but their houses escheated to the king, except in the case of a few favoured persons who were allowed to sell theirs before they left. Some of them were robbed by the captains who undertook to transport them to Witsand; others were drowned on their way to France. Of the 16,000 who left, about one-tenth went to

Flanders, their passage being paid by the king; and a number are found a short time later in the Paris Jewry. The king's booty was not of great amount, for the total rental of the houses which fell into his hands was not more than £130, and the debts owed to the Jews, of which he could collect only the principal, did not exceed £9000. Parliament was said to have voted one-tenth of the tithes and one-fifteenth of the personal property in gratitude for the expulsion, but this merely represents contemporary prejudice. Edward's act was not an act of grace to the nation; as has been seen, no alternative was left to him. The Church would not allow the Jews to become an integral part of the English nation, and they therefore had to leave the country." On two earlier occasions, in 1254 and 1255, they themselves had pleaded to be allowed to leave the kingdom before the last penny had been forced from them. Pollock and Maitland sum up judicially here: "The system could not work well; it oppressed both Jew and Englishman. Despised and disliked the once chosen people would always have been, in a society of medieval Christians; perhaps they would have been accused of crucifying children and occasionally massacred; but they would not have been so persistently hated as they were, had they not been made the engines of royal indigence. From the middle of the thirteenth century onwards the king was compelled to rob them of their privileges, to forbid them to hold land, to forbid them even to take interest. This last prohibition could not be carried into effect; there was little or nothing that the Jews could profitably do if they were cut off from lending money. Their expulsion in 1290 looks like the only possible solution of a difficult problem."[15] St Louis, in 1254, had already banished nearly all from his own lands; in 1306, Philip IV added plunder to expulsion; in 1321, excuses for a pogrom were found in the accusation that they poisoned fountains in order to infect the population with leprosy. In 1321, Pope John XXII would have expelled them from Rome, but Robert of Anjou intervened in their favour. All these points are rehearsed in a plain-spoken article of *The Catholic Encyclopaedia* (VIII, 394), which adds that in Germany their sufferings were still greater. Their quasi-imprisonment in the Ghettos of Rome and other cities is well known. It is pleaded that this measure had its welcome side of affording them some protection from casual mob-violence; yet that, however true, is a two-edged plea. The Ghetto was in fact something of a precedent for the modern Nazi "protective arrest".

29. THE GHETTO (2)

We must not forget how much of this had sprung originally from the Jew's own pride in his creed, and the tenacity with which he had held to the exclusivist principle "Outside the Covenant, no salvation". We must bear in mind the offence given by a minority of these pariahs in their wealth and ostentation, and their sacrilegious holding of Church vessels and ornaments to pledge. Far-seeing statesmen, also, must have foreseen what Pollock and Maitland point out in their survey: "Many an ancient tie between men—the tie of kinship, the tie of homage—is being dissolved or transmuted by the touch of Jewish gold; land is being brought to market and feudal rights are being capitalized." The modern historian may welcome that change; but we cannot blame our ancestors for seeing it with other eyes. But this influence was only indirect; we must not accept the legend that the Jew ordinarily exercised secret and immediate political power in the Middle Ages. As Dr J. W. Parkes has pointed out, Kipling rests upon a misapprehension of the actual facts in his story of the Jews who decided that Magna Carta should be signed. For money (as he points out) means power only when its owner either can give or withhold it at his own choice; but, as the Jew had no power to withhold, he could exercise no power by giving. Nor could he conceal the amount of his money; for he could not claim payment for any debt that was not registered in the treasury of that prince whose chattel he was; our own Star Chamber very likely took its name from such documents (in Hebrew, *Sh'tars*) of which a good number have survived.

Lastly, the Jewish usurer was often made a scapegoat for the rest. There is great significance in the petition of the lesser barons in 1258 against their greater brethren who were swallowing them up.[1] "*Item*, they beg for a remedy in this matter; *viz.* that Jews sometimes transfer their debts and lands which they hold in pledge to barons and to the greater folk of the kingdom, who by that occasion enter into the estates of the lesser [land-owners]: and although the debtors are ready to pay the aforesaid debt with usury, the aforesaid magnates prolong the business, in order that by some means the said lands and tenements may remain in their own hands, saying that they cannot dispense, and know not how to dispense, with the Jew to whom the debt was owing; and they constantly delay the repayment of the said money, so that by reason of death or of some other chance there is evident and manifest peril of imminent loss of inheritance for those who had possessed the aforesaid holdings. *Item*, they [the lesser barons] seek remedy in the matter of Christian usurers, as for instance concerning the Caursins who dwell in London, seeing that it would seem contrary to the Christian religion to maintain or foster any men of that sort, especially from the time that they have adopted the name of Christians. Moreover, through these men's usuries many folk are impoverished and ruined; and also they get and buy many merchandises coming to London, both by water and by land, to the grievous detriment of the merchants and all the folk of the said city, and to the great loss of our Lord King." From this very document it transpires that the worst sinners of all were the Caursins, nominal Christians; and we have seen how Matthew Paris describes the Caursin victory, with papal alliance and papal help, over the Bishop of London's well-meaning attempt to banish usury from his own metropolis.[2]

Moreover, offensive as Jewish pride might have been, there was sometimes excuse for it. By the confession of their most orthodox adversaries, the Christians might well have profited by their example in two most important respects. First, their care for their poor, which Christian moralists cite to shame their own brethren. Certainly those niggardly monastic prescriptions with regard to gleaning, printed on p. 479 of my *Medieval Village*, contrast strongly with the medieval Hebrew law, which runs: "If a man put a basket beneath the vine while he was gathering the grapes, such a one is a robber of the poor. From what time are all men permitted to glean from the field? After the last of the poor have gone. And to take grape-gleanings and defective clusters? After the poor have gone into the vineyard and returned. . . . If a man would keep aught back [for his own poor kinsfolk] he should take away half and give half [to the poor that come to him]. . . . A poor man that is journeying from place to place should be given not less than one loaf. . . . If he spends the night [in such a place] he should be given what is needful to support him for the night. If he stays over the Sabbath he should be given food enough for three meals. If a man has food enough for two meals he may not take aught from the [Paupers'] Dish; and, if enough for fourteen meals he may not take aught from the [Poor] Fund." Secondly, by the acknowledgment of Christian Writers again, the ordinary Jew put the ordinary Churchman to shame by a far better knowledge of his own sacred Scriptures.

The Jews were in those days, as now, patient observers, and unwearied in pursuit of their own lines of thought. As translators, and as theoretical scientists, they did much to bring Greek and Arab culture into the West. The Bishop of Paris might seek out and burn their sacred books; but he could not destroy their influence in his own university. As practising physicians, they were then as now in the front rank. And, finally, they represented, and knew themselves to represent, an older civilization than that of their rivals. They had generations of culture behind them in the days when Tacitus studied Germany as the home of the noble savage, and painted simple German virtues with the object of rebuking his own over-sophisticated society of Rome. The Jew, therefore, felt towards his rivals much as the Muslim did. Prince Ousâma, in his precious autobiography, shows his scorn of these "Frankish" knights and their women, as of half-educated schoolboys and schoolgirls. He is disgusted not only at their cruel sport with old women, but with other points betraying imperfect civilization. And, while the "Frank" was not ashamed to strike his womenkind, and definite prescriptions for wife-beating stood in his Canon Law (as we shall see in a later chapter), Judaism did at least legislate against this. A medieval regulation runs: "The cry of the daughters of our people has been heard concerning the sons of Israel who raise their hands to strike their wives. Yet who has given a husband the authority to beat his wife? Is he not rather forbidden to strike any person in Israel? Nevertheless have we heard of cases where Jewish women complained regarding their treatment before the Communities, and no action was taken on their behalf. We have therefore decreed that any Jew may be compelled, on application of his wife or one of her near relatives, to undertake by a *herem* not to beat his wife in anger or cruelty or so as to disgrace her, for that is against Jewish practice. If anyone will stubbornly refuse to obey our words, the Court of the place to which the wife or her relatives will bring complaint, shall assign her maintenance according to her station and according to the custom of the place where she dwells. They shall fix her alimony as though her husband were away on a distant journey."[3]

This chapter cannot be complete without some contemporary picture of the great massacres. The greatest of all, at York, was engineered by a group of the lesser nobility who were heavily indebted to these usurers, and who in fact battened on their spoil. That of Lynn affords a juster instance, since, even through the natural bias of a Churchman, we have here the story of an unusually honest chronicler who tries to see both sides: William, the Austin canon of Newburgh.[4] King's Lynn (as it has been ever since Henry VIII) was Bishop's Lynn all through the Middle Ages. William has just been relating the outbreak and massacre at Richard's coronation; and he adds that the zeal of the Londoners has "risen in its vehemence to white-heat, not indeed sincerely (that is, merely for faith's sake), but either in envy of the Jews' prosperity or as gaping after their fortunes. Bold and covetous men thought to do God service if they despoiled or destroyed folk who rebelled against Christ; and they wrought with cheerful fury, hindered by little or no scruples of conscience, the business of their own greed; a thing which God's justice was far from approving, though He had aptly ordained it, in order that He might by this means restrain the insolence of that perfidious race, and put a bridle upon blasphemous tongues. In the city called Lynn, illustrious for its trade and commerce, where very many of this race dwelt, and where they were fierce in their multitude and their great wealth and the King's protection, the first movement against them, as hath been reported to me, arose on this occasion. It chanced that one of their superstition was converted to the Christian faith; wherefore they, thirsting for his blood as that of a deserter and transgressor, sought occasion to wreak their malice upon him. One day, as he passed by, they caught up their arms and fell upon him: but he took refuge in the church hard by.* Yet their madness ceased not there, but they began with pertinacious fury and assault to besiege that very church, in order that they might break the doors and drag the fugitive out to punishment. A vast clamour arose from those who were within the church; with resounding cries they called for Christian help. Their noise and report kindled to clamour the Christian folk who were hard-by; and, at that news, those who were far off ran to arms. The Lynn citizens, for fear of the king, acted more remissly; but the young foreigners,* who had come thither in multitude for the sake of trade, rushed bravely upon those proud fighters. These, then, quitted the siege of the church and, unable to sustain the Christian assault, they took to flight. Some were slain as they fled; their houses were stormed and plundered by the Christians and given up to avenging flames; and very many Jews stained the fire or their foemen's sword with their blood. Next day there came a certain distinguished Jewish physician, whom even the Christians had honoured and befriended for the sake of his skill and his modesty. This man lamented the slaughter of his friends in somewhat immoderate terms; and, as though he prophesied vengeance, he awoke the still breathing fury [of the Christians]. They, therefore, seized him forthwith and made him, then and there, the latest victim of Jewish madness. The young foreigners, laden with booty, took to their ships, and sailed thence with all speed, lest perchance they should be submitted to question by the royal servants. The Lynn folk, when they

Jews' Lane at Lynn was at one corner of the greater market-place, and some 200 yards from the church of St Nicholas.

* *Peregrini juvenes*: the men of Ely and Wisbech and Boston would be "foreigners" in Lynn parlance.

were called to account by the king's officers, cast the blame upon the departed foreigners."

Shortly afterwards (writes William) there was a great Lenten tide fair at Stamford, thronged now more than ever by young men bound for the Crusade. These men, "being indignant that the enemies of Christ's Cross who dwelt at Stamford should possess so much, while they themselves lacked for the cost of this great journey, thought fit to extort from them, as unjust possessors, that which they might apply to the needs of the pilgrimage which they had undertaken. Therefore, thinking to serve Christ if they assaulted these men whose goods they coveted, they rushed boldly upon them, without opposition to this great adventure either from the Stamford folk or from those who had come for the fair; nay, even with help from some of them. Some of the Jews were slain, the rest were received into the [royal] castle and escaped with difficulty. Their houses were plundered, and a great wealth of money stolen. The robbers went away with the gain of their work, and none was brought to judgment for public discipline on that account. But one most audacious youth, John by name, passed on to Northampton, where he left part of his money with a man who, inflamed himself with greed for the same, slew him secretly and cast his body forth from the city by night. It was found and by chance recognized by some, while the greedy murderer fled secretly. Soon old women began to dream, and fallacious signs of miracles appeared there so that simple folk attributed to him the merit of a martyr, honouring the dead man's sepulchre with solemn watchings and gifts. Roused by the report, the foolish herd began to flock thither first from the neighbouring parts and then, in their devout curiosity, even from divers provinces; and no man came empty-handed to his sepulchre, since they desired either to see the miracles of this new martyr or to gain his spiritual help. The prudent did indeed laugh at this; yet it was grateful to the clergy, for the sake of the profits that flowed from that superstition. The matter was referred to the bishop, a man of excellent virtue, who, coming to the place in the spirit of fortitude, profaned the shrine of this false martyr, who had been exalted by the zeal of simple and covetous folk, and, with his pontifical authority, forbade under formal anathema this superstitious veneration of the dead man. Thus, by the pious and efficacious work of a good pastor, all that operation of the deceiving spirit was extinguished and brought to nought."

Our chronicler then goes on to relate the similar illegalities at Lincoln (where, however, the royal officers brought fairly prompt protection) and at York, where the tragedy was darkest of all. There, the Jews "had built in the midst of the city, at most profuse expense, houses of great size, comparable to royal palaces. . . . Therefore very many men of that province had conspired against them, not suffering that these men should be rich while they themselves were in want; and, without any scruple of Christan conscience, thirsting for the unbelievers' blood in greed for robbery." The Jews took refuge in the royal castle, where they were besieged by a furious mob under the leadership of an ex-Premonstratensian hermit and some others of the clergy. These men "thought to render great service to God by ridding the earth of this people that rebelleth against the Lord, their darkened minds being blind to that which is written in the person of David (nay, in that of our Lord, since it is said in our Saviour's person) *God shall let me see over mine enemies: slay them not, lest at any time my people forget* (Ps. lviii. *Vulg*.). . . . Thus the Jews ought indeed to live among Christians for our profit, but, by reason of their iniquity, to be our servants." The defence of the castle seemed at last hopeless, and that which followed must be told, here again, in the very words of this enlightened ecclesiastic. "There was there a certain elder (according to the letter, which killeth), a most famous teacher of law, who, as is said, had come from beyond the sea to teach the English Jews. He was honoured by all, and all obeyed him as one of the prophets. When therefore they asked his counsel at this time, he answered: 'God, to whom we must not say "why doest thou thus?" commandeth us now to die for His law. And lo, death is at our door, as ye see, unless perchance (which God forbid!) by reason of the brief space of this life ye think fit to desert our Holy Law, and choose (which to good and manly souls is harder than any death) to live as apostates, in the utmost disgrace, at the mercy of impious enemies. Since therefore we ought to prefer a glorious death to a life of deepest shame, we must choose the most honourable and easiest kind of death; for, if we fall into their hands, we shall die in mockery at their arbitrary choice. Therefore, since our Creator Himself doth now ask again for that life which He gave us, let us render it willingly and devoutly back with our own hands, nor let us await the ministration of our enemies' cruelty to restore that which God doth demand. For many of our race, in their divers tribulations, are known to have wrought in this praiseworthy fashion, supplying us beforehand with the example of a most decorous choice.' When he had thus spoken, very many embraced his fatal counsel; yet to some this seemed a hard saying.* Then said this elder: 'Let those who accept not so good and pious a counsel sit apart, as cut off from this holy community; for to us this mortal life is already worthless in comparison with our love for our Law.' Then, at the will of this most crazy elder, lest their foes should enrich themselves with the spoils, their precious garments were burned under the eyes of all, while the much-prized vessels, and whatsoever else could not be consumed with fire, were rendered worthless by subtle and shameful defilement. This done, they set fire to the roof; yet this, with its too solid materials, burned but slowly. While this horrible business was in progress, the elder prepared for sacrifice in rebuke to those also who had separated themselves for love of their own lives. So, when that man, grown old in evil days, directed that those also who had separated themselves for love of their own wives and children, then that most renowned Joce cut with his keenest knife the throat of his own beloved wife Anna, nor did he spare his own children also. When the other men in turn had done thus, that most unhappy elder slaughtered Joce,

* Compare Joinville's frank words describing defeat and capture at the battle of Mansourah: "Then spake a cellarer of mine . . . 'My counsel is that we should let ourselves be slain [rather than yield to these infidels]; thus we shall all go to Paradise.' But we believed him not" (c. LXIII, § 319).

as being more honourable than the rest. Soon all were slain, together with their master in error, and the tower began to burn within with that fire which, as we have said, had been set to it." The others climbed to the battlements of the tower, cast down to the besiegers the bodies of their fellows, and pleaded for baptism: "Vexation maketh us to understand [Isaiah xxviii. 19] and we acknowledge the truth of Christianity." The mob promised them their lives: but "no sooner had they come forth than, although they constantly demanded baptism, these butchers most cruelly slew them. I myself would unhesitatingly affirm concerning these whom that beastly cruelty thus sacrificed, that if there was no falsity in their petition for holy baptism, then they were in no wise defrauded thereof; in their own blood were they baptized.* But, whether it were falsely or truly that they sought the sacred font, we cannot excuse that execrable cruelty of their butchers. Beyond all doubt these men's first crime is that, without any orderly power, they presumed to shed men's blood like water. The second was, that their rage was rather in envy and malice than in righteous zeal; their third, that they grudged the Jews the Christian grace which these implored; and the fourth, that with a lie they betrayed these poor wretches to come forth to sacrifice. At that time, the whole city was indeed horrible and foul to behold, with so many miserable bodies that lay unburied all around the castle." The mob broke into the cathedral, compelled the clergy to surrender those Jews' bonds which were stored there for safety, and burned them in the midst of the minister. Yet, concludes William, "even unto this day no man hath been sentenced to death for that slaughter of the Jews". The only orthodox victim, in fact, during this whole uproar and siege, was the hermit who in his white robes was always there with religious encouragement. "It was said that on those siege-days, before he went forth to the bloody work, he offered at daybreak the Bloodless Sacrifice; for he was a priest, and had so far persuaded his own blinded mind, as he sought to persuade others, that this work was a holy business." As he helped to move the battering-tower up to the walls, a

* See later in Chapter XXXII.

stone from above crushed him to the earth; and William records this as a just punishment upon a priestly warrior.

A later monastic chronicler, Knighton of Leicester, while he rejoices over the deed, admits likewise the impurity of the motives. He writes how " the zeal of the Christians conspired against the Jews in England, not indeed sincerely, for faith's sake, but either in envy of their prosperity or as gaping after their fortune, a thing which God's justice was far from approving but which He aptly ordained in order that, by this means, He might restrain the insolence of this perfidious race. Beyond those things which the Jews had suffered in their goods and their persons at Lincoln and Lynn, at York also, after a long siege and affliction, the Rabbi, the Master of the Jews, cut the veins of four hundred Jews and then his own, and cut the throat of his wife." He goes on to comment, almost in Newburgh's words, on the false miracles at Northampton.[5]

30. JUSTICE AND POLICE

We cannot do better than begin here with Professor Petit-Dutaillis,[1] whose labours on English constitutional history have done so much to complement the great work of Stubbs. He writes: "Thanks to Henry II who, we are told, was capable of legal innovation, and to his advisers who understood the principles of Roman Law and knew its technicalities, the English monarchy was the only lay power in Western Europe to establish a common-law by the beginning of the thirteenth century. In France and Germany local custom still prevailed. The characteristic of royal justice in England was that it held local custom as of little account, and that, through its system of assizes and writs, it established a procedure and a jurisprudence of general application which was, on the whole, favourable to a free middle class and hostile to the seignorial spirit. We might well add 'hostile to the clerical spirit'; for Henry II sought to limit ecclesiastical jurisdiction and to make certain that criminous clerks were punished. The constitutions of Clarendon formed an important and significant part of his legislation." It is true that Henry's advisers were nearly all clerics; so that, as Pollock and Maitland note with felicitous irony, "it is by popish clergymen that our Common Law is converted from a rude mass of customs into an articulate system; and when the popish clergymen, yielding at length to the pope's commands, no longer sit as the principal justices of the King's Court, the creative age of our medieval law is over".[2] This, however, must be read in the light of the clerical monopoly over all English schools in those days, from the lowest to the highest; so that any man who could even read was presumed by law to be a clergyman. Even so, there is no certainty as to the clerical status of Glanvill, who was one of the greatest of these lawyers; and in Italy, where the clerical monopoly did not exist, the greatest lawyers were commonly laymen. With us, it was at Henry's command that these bishop-lawyers worked, and against the will of the Popes, who recognized clearly that such royal ministers were but unclerical clerics, and that the Church was losing through their services, however indirectly, as much as the State was gaining. In this particular matter the popish clergymen were loyal servants to our king, and disobedient to their pontiff.

Next to the Common Law, we owe most, perhaps, to the Jury system. Here again, as Petit-Dutaillis points out, Henry II was the great initiator. "It was an institution of Frankish origin; the Frankish kings employed the jury to discover criminals and false officials; William the Conqueror introduced the jury to England and used it in the compilation of Domesday Book; but before the reign of Henry II it had been more frequently used for administrative purposes than judicial. Henry II did not cease to use it for obtaining information, but he must have the credit for making it a smoothly-working judicial institution. . . . In using the elected jury in this way the English kings were sowing seeds of a representative system in their counties."

The administration of this Common Law in England, supported by the Jury, was based upon two territorial divisions; the Shire and its subdivision, the Hundred. The Hundred Court sat monthly, and dealt with minor cases; it was presided over by the deputy of the Sheriff. From the twelfth century onwards it lost much of its importance, in proportion as the King's Court of Westminster centralized at the expense of the local courts. In the Shire, the royal representative was the Sheriff (Shire-reeve) in judicial as in fiscal and military affairs. Twice a year, he held a court also in each Hundred, at which the main business was the maintenance and proper working of the Tithing System. From before the Conquest, justice had been secured partly through the division of each *township* (to use a convenient word which covers both *town* and *village*) into tithings, or groups of ten men. These ten were responsible for each other, and were legally represented by one of the group, who was called *tithing-man* or *capital pledge*, the system itself being termed *frankpledge*. We have already seen a similar principle of mutual responsibility imposed upon the Hundred in cases of murder (Chapter v) and its utility for the maintenance of order in smaller areas is obvious. Like everything else in those days, the system was far less regular in many districts than theory demanded; but its operation at Norwich, where it was perhaps exceptionally efficient, has been worked out by Mr W. Hudson with his usual patience and clearness.* In that city "the total number of tithings was about 160. In modern language, the city of Norwich in the thirteenth and fourteenth centuries was organized into 12 (or finally 10) police districts, containing 160 police associations." Each capital pledge was bound to report the misdoings of his own group, and was fined for concealment. Here, for instance, is the beginning of the Leet Court Roll for 1288.[3] "The capital pledges, namely [list of 12 names for one subleet, of which there were then 11 in Norwich], present on their oath that Ernald de Castro wounded Hugh de Bromholm and drew blood from him contrary to the peace, Likewise they present that Nicholas le Jay wounded a certain clerk, a stranger, and cut off two fingers of the said clerk and the hue was raised there and the said Nicholas was taken and imprisoned at the suit of Hugh de Bromholm, constable of the aforesaid leet; and Ernald and others escaped. . . . Concerning those who sell and buy corn, they present that Robert Gerveys buys corn before it comes to the market, whereby the Bailiffs, etc. [i.e. lose their custom]. . . . They present that all the alewives sell two gallons at one penny and two gallons at one penny halfpenny [*sic*]. . . . All [the jurors] are in mercy" [i.e. are amerced for concealment].

The Shire was concerned with major criminal and Crown pleas; but the Sheriff dealt with criminal cases twice a year in the Hundred Courts, that is, in the neighbourhood where the crime had been committed and evidence was most easily obtained. Gradually the Crown took to itself all criminal jurisdiction (whether directly or by delegation) and the manor, on the other hand, took to itself most of the minor jurisdiction. On the manor were held two courts: the Court Leet for police, and the Court Baron for civil cases, such as ownership of land.

* *Records of the City of Norwich*, I, cxxxiv.

At Norwich, as we have seen, it was the Court Leet which dealt with the Frankpledge system. The offences presented "were very numerous, and embraced nearly the whole field of local jurisdiction. Even murder, manslaughter, or death by accident might be presented, but they were not decided by the court. The main presentments were for theft (if serious, this was reserved for a higher court), assaults, raising the hue and cry wrongfully, or without due cause, nuisances of all sorts, market and trade offences (forestalling, regrating, etc.)." By far the commonest offence, here and in other towns, was breach of the assize of ale. For bread and for ale, Government had a fixed tariff, varying according to the price of corn. Mr Hudson notes how at Norwich, as elsewhere, "almost every housewife of the leading families brewed ale and sold it to her neighbours, and invariably charged more than the fixed price. The authorities evidently expected and wished this course to be taken; for these ladies were regularly presented and amerced every year for the same offence, paid their amercements and went away to go through the same process in the future as in the past. Much the same course was pursued by other trades and occupations. Fishmongers, tanners, poulterers, cooks, etc., are fined wholesale year after year for breaking every by-law that concerned their business. In short, instead of a trader (as now) taking out a licence to do his business on certain conditions which he is expected to keep, he was bound by conditions which he was expected to break and afterwards fined for the breach. The same financial result was attained or aimed at by a different method."[4] For the judicial system in English cities had not emerged very far beyond that rudimentary stage of sanctions which is displayed by the present League of Nations. By law, that is, in theory, repetition of the offence should have increased the severity of the fine in proportion to its frequency; but, in fact, the wholesale offender enjoyed a reduction in virtue of his larger business, if indeed he did not escape altogether. For medieval justice, from the king's or pope's court down to that of the manor, was, by the universal testimony of contemporaries, stained by open venality. The judge who steadily refuses "gifts" is extolled as a marvel; that, in fact, is one of St

Thomas More's claims to sanctity. In *Piers Plowman* "Lady Meed" (that is, the Almighty Dollar) rules the king's courts; and, in the cities, mayors wink at the misdoings of wealthy and unscrupulous capitalists. Moreover, this venality infected even the field in which the Church boasted herself as most uncompromising: even that matrimony which she had erected into one of the Seven Sacraments. Here, again, we shall see in a later chapter that Langland is a witness, with unexceptionable colleagues both before and after him, down to Erasmus on the verge of the Reformation. Moreover, the most unimpeachable statistics from our city archives show clearly what went on behind the scenes. At Norwich, the roll of 1289 shows us what fines were adjudged, and what were collected. The former total was £72. 18*s.* 10*d.*; moreover, this, by strict law, should have been very much higher. Yet, even of this mild and diminished total, all that the collectors could account for, after considerable delay, was £ 17. 0*s.* 2*d.* "Some are excused by the Bailiffs without reason assigned; some 'at the instance' of certain great people wishing to do a good turn for a friend. Again, others make a bargain with the collector, thus expressed, as for instance, 'john de Swaffham is not in tithing. Amercement 2*s.* He paid 6*d.* the rest is excused. He is quit.' Sometimes an entry is marked 'vad', i.e. *vadiat,* or *vadiatur,* he gives a pledge, or, it is pledged. The Collector had seized a jug, or basin, or chair. But by far the larger number of entries are marked 'd', i.e. *debet,* he owes it."[5] All our civic records tell much the same tale. Here, for instance, is a case quoted by Miss Abram (p. 263): "John Bristowe of Reading was ordered to pay a fine of four thousand tiles, because he had been rebellious to the Mayor, but he was let off three thousand of them on the spot; and sometimes offenders were allowed to go unpunished because they were too poor to pay a fine: the idea of imprisonment as an alternative did not find favour because it entailed a good deal of trouble and expense on the community."

Let us now take a wider survey of "the King's Peace" in England. Every township had one or two constables. At Norwich, one of the greatest cities in the land, there was one constable to every hundred able-bodied men on the muster-rolls, with subordinate officers under him, *vinteners,* or captains of twenty, and *decennars,* captains of ten. What sort of peace those constables were bound to keep may be read in the royal writs of 1252-3 for Watch and Ward. This enacts: "(1) That watches be held in the several townships as hath been wont, and by honest and able men. (2) That the hue and cry be followed according to the ancient use, so that all who neglect and refuse to follow it up shall be taken into custody as abettors of the wrongdoers, and shall be delivered up to the Sheriff. Moreover, in every township, let four or six men be chosen according to its size, to follow the hue and cry hastily and swiftly, and to pursue the wrongdoers, if need be, with bows and arrows and other light arms, which should be provided at the common cost of the township and remain ever for the use thereof. And to this end let two free and lawful men be chosen from the most powerful in each hundred who shall oversee the work and see that the aforesaid watches and pursuits be rightly carried out. (3) That no stranger abide in the township except by day, and that he depart while it is yet daylight. (4) That no stranger be harboured in county townships beyond one day, or two at most, save only in time of harvest, unless his host be willing to answer for him. . . . (5) That the mayor and bailiffs of all cities and boroughs be bidden that, if any merchant or stranger bearing money do show them the said money and beg for safe conduct, then they must so conduct him through the evil passes and doubtful ways; and if he lose aught for default of such conduct or under their conduct, then let him be indemnified by the inhabitants of the said borough or city." This system was extended and consolidated in 1285, by an ordinance which fixed for the rest of the Middle Ages the form taken by our constabulary and militia; it gave us a nation organized for the double purpose of soldiery and police.

With all this, though England was more orderly than other great states, yet the coroners' rolls show manslaughter in enormous preponderance over death by accident. It is impossible to judge, at this distance, whether most of these cases would pass for wilful murder at the present day; but the statistics seem to point to at least ten times as many definite murders, per head of population, and possibly even twice or thrice that proportion. Certainly the manslayer and the thief —for grave theft was, in law, no less a hanging matter—had in those days far greater chances of escape. The rolls recount, with wearisome iteration, that "he has fled, and has left no chattels" for confiscation; or, again, he has taken sanctuary and abjured the realm.

It is a prehistoric and universal principle that the burden of defence should rest upon all able-bodied males. The decadence of ancient Rome, even in art and literature, synchronized with those generations which accustomed themselves to be defended by hired troops, and even to a great extent fed and amused at the public expense. France in the fourteenth century had let this principle slip; musters were indeed commanded sometimes, but only as an oblique form of taxation; the man was allowed, and even encouraged, to buy himself off; we may say more, royal officials might even compel him to choose redemption instead of personal service. Under St Louis himself, when the inhabitants of three villages in the South maintained (with perfect justice), that they would not pay this time for substitutes but come in person at the royal call for a levy of defence against the Spaniards, then the *viguier* of Béziers settled the dispute with one level volley: "March to the bridge of Vidorle or don't march, just as you please. I intend to get £12. 10*s.* from you. You bloody peasants, whether you will or whether you won't, you shall pay all the same!"—*O rustici sanguinolenti, vos dabitis, velitis vel non.*[6] Matters were very different in England, where the Fyrd, the Anglo-Saxon militia system, was reorganized by Henry II and again by Edward I.[7] By the latter's "Statute of Winchester", every able-bodied man was bound not only to possess arms on a scale proportionate to his wealth, but also to learn their use. For Edward was determined to wed practice with theory: he had learned from his Welsh enemies that the longbow, already a well-known weapon among his own subjects, was far superior in battle to the crossbow: therefore he gradually set about training a large force of archers. Falkirk (1298) was the first important battle in which the archery was used in scientific combination with cavalry. Bannockburn (1314) was the last in which the English repeated the old blunder of relying on mounted knights and men-at-arms, and allowing the infantry to act as a more or less disordered mass. Mr Hudson has printed from the Norwich archives lists of armed citizens between 1355 and 1370 which show that the city provided and reviewed a somewhat larger proportion than would be furnished by the modern system of conscription on the Continent. Many of these men, of course, turned out with no more than the minimum requirement of club and knife. The next step was to add a sword or an axe to those primitive weapons; and so on, through the archers, to the numerous "half-armed men", who had in addition to their offensive weapons a plated doublet with visor and iron gauntlets; and finally the "fully-armed", who had in addition a shirt of mail under the doublet, with neck-piece and arm-plates, and who boasted each a total equipment which must have cost some £50 or £60 of modern money.

These archers of Norwich were evidently of the upper class, men accustomed to shoot at game, which, in the advanced Eastern Countries, would be comparatively rare. But, for the army in general, the great majority of archers were recruited from forest districts such as Charnwood or Cheshire and the borderland of Wales; while the "knife-men" came mainly from hilly districts like Wales and Cornwall. Under this system, in 1346, while our armies were winning Crécy in France, and the Scots attempted to take us at a disadvantage in the rear, they received one of the most crushing defeats in their history. Again, a threatened invasion in 1360 called out all men from sixteen to sixty; many clergy fought in person, and others hired substitutes. These facts have far greater importance than has commonly been assigned to them. We may feel that war, even at its best, is thoroughly unworthy of our present civilization; yet, just as it takes two to make a quarrel, so also it takes both sides to maintain peace; and, when the fire is once kindled, it is better to be victor than vanquished. Moreover, when we consider that war, even in the fourteenth century, was by no means a mere matter of brute force but required also much force of character and intellect, it is difficult to escape the conclusion that, on the whole, in the long perspective of history, victory has gone to the side best fitted to survive. In that great struggle between medieval England and France, no doubt both sides were morally in the wrong; but, in the events themselves, certain points are beyond dispute. In the first place, the English waged war with greater national cohesion; in our armies, it was possible for a man to rise from the ranks to the highest commands. In France, on the other hand, the nobles and their feudal levies controlled all; and where the citizen militias were brought in, as at Crécy, these were a disorganized rabble destined merely for slaughter. Though Du Guesclin was the greatest general produced on either side, his first important victory was due to the lucky chance that a prince of the blood had sufficient good sense to hand over his command to him for that day; and it was part of his greatness that he clearly recognized the superiority of the English system. Siméon Luce writes truly: "Such seems to have been the opinion of Bertrand du Guesclin, the most renowned captain of the Middle Ages, who never fought a great pitched battle against a real English army if he could possibly help it. At Cocherel his adversaries were mostly Gascons; and at Pontvallain he crushed Knolles's rear-guard by one of those startling marches of which he had the secret; but he was beaten at Auray and Navarette," i.e. in the two great pitched battles in which he met us.[8] We need pursue this side of our subject no farther here, for unquestionably wars and the diplomatic manœuvres which have led to wars have hitherto bulked too large in history.

But two points may here be noted, for their social importance. In the first place, the comparative orderliness of our Peasants' Revolt in 1381, as compared with all similar revolts on the Continent. We must recognize not only the general discipline of the peasant rebels, but also the extent to which it was possible for the Government to bargain with them collectively; the treachery by which that bargain was subsequently broken is irrelevant to the present question. Secondly, we must note (and this is by far the more important point) that the same system which gave us the most efficient army in Europe supplied us also with the most orderly police force, and enabled " the King's Peace " to become a greater reality here than elsewhere. While Dante was describing the Italy of his day as " a hostelry of pain ", our English liberties were growing on from precedent to precedent; and, behind all those ill effects of the Hundred Years' War which cannot be blinked on either side, English civic liberties and the expansion of our trade stand out in startling contrast with the decay of towns and commerce in France. To this we must return in Chapter XXXIX; meanwhile let us look more closely into the working of the medieval militia as a police system.

Let us choose a concrete case for quotation and comment. In 1311 William of Wellington, chaplain of the parish of Yelvertoft, quarrelled with one of his parishioners and killed him with a bludgeon.[9] The jury " say on their oath that they know no man guilty of John's death save the said William of Wellington. He therefore came before the aforesaid coroner and confessed that he had slain the said John; wherefore he abjured the realm of England in the presence of the said four townships brought together [for this purpose]. And the port of Dover was assigned to him." What, then, happened to this William when he " abjured the realm "? We will blink for a moment the fact that, as a priest, he should by theory have been immune from ordinary justice; let us face his position as if he had been an ordinary layman. By this abjuration he saved himself from summary execution; and the coroner might be detained several days before he could come and deal with him. Meanwhile the community would keep watch over the church or other sanctuary in which he had taken refuge. Then, on the coroner's arrival, the criminal's confession was registered and he took his oath to quit the realm within 40 days. Coming to the gate of the church or churchyard, he swore solemnly before the assembled crowd: " Oyez, oyez, oyez! Coroner and other good folk: I, William of Wellington, for the crime of manslaughter which I have committed, will quit this land of England nevermore to return, except by leave of the Kings of

England or their heirs: so help me God and His saints!" The coroner then assigned him a port, and a reasonable time for the journey; from Yelvertoft to Dover it would have been about a week. His bearing during this week was minutely prescribed: never to stray from the high-road, or spend two nights in the same place, to make straight for his port, and to embark without delay. If at Dover he found no vessel ready to sail, then he was bound daily to walk into the sea up to his knees—or, according to stricter authorities, up to his neck—and to take his rest only on the shore, in proof that he was ready in spirit to leave this land which by his crimes he had forfeited. His dress meanwhile was that of a felon condemned to death—a long, loose white tunic, bare feet, and a wooden cross in his hand to mark that he was under protection of Holy Church. English law was glad to have thus rid itself of a villain, and troubled no further; but the records leave us sceptical whether any very large proportion of these unwilling pilgrims actually found their way across the sea. No doubt in some cases, in spite of ecclesiastical protection, they would be waylaid and fallen upon by friends of the murdered man. In many more cases, and probably in the majority, this criminal would see no reason why he should take so much trouble to go to France, where he might meet with no better reception than in England. He would therefore take the earliest opportunity of slipping away from the high-road; thence he would march as a vagrant to some district where he was unknown, and join that class of sturdy beggars or malefactors who bulk so largely in *Piers Plowman*. After all, such men were welcome recruits for the army; and there was generally fighting somewhere. When there was not, as *Piers Plowman* will tell us, the countryside swarmed with discharged and workless soldiers. There is one other alternative: what if William had refused to confess guilt and simply clung to the sanctuary? To judge from the records, at least 50 per cent. did thus refuse; and here both theory and practice leave us uncertain. The law gave him 40 days of grace in any case; yet if, on the expiration of that period, the lay authorities came in and tore him from the altar, they might have to reckon with episcopal excommunication. Therefore the lawyers tried to throw the onus of expulsion upon the bishop or archdeacon through their servants; but we may well excuse the ecclesiastical authorities for shrinking from thus facing a desperate malefactor. Here, therefore, as in so many other cases, the issue was left more or less to chance: *solvitur ambulando.* The village did its best to starve the man out, and meanwhile to watch him night and day. One offender, whose 40 days had expired on August 12th, 1374, held out against this blockade until September 9th, when he fled; then there was a hue and cry of the whole village. Let us suppose that our priest did the same. He might indeed run the gauntlet and make good his escape, leaving his quondam neighbours to prove before the justices that they had done all they could; failing which, they must pay a fine for their negligence. On the other hand, however, a stick or stone might bring him down at close quarters, or an arrow from afar; then in a moment he would be overpowered and beheaded, and that chase would be long remembered for its excitement in Yelvertoft.

So much for the ordinary offender, but in this case of William of Wellington there was a gross irregularity. St Thomas Becket, " the holy blissful martyr ", had by his death consecrated the principle that a felonious cleric might be condemned by clerics alone. Thus the routine was that a clerical homicide or thief, though he might be arrested by layfolk and tried by them, must yet be handed over to the bishop to be finally dealt with. The lay judges took care to pronounce their own decision first; they handed the man over to the bishop as a criminal. But beyond that they had no responsibility, and the bishop commonly admitted him to " compurgation ". By this system the accused presented himself with as many " compurgators " as the bishop chose to specify in virtue of the man's own character and the gravity of his offence. The accused himself then swore solemnly on the Gospels to his innocence, and each of the compurgators swore that to the best of his knowledge the accused had sworn the truth. The records themselves would have suggested very strongly in any case that, human nature being such as it is, and the tendency of every class of society being to stick by its fellow-members, this system of compurgation would lead to a good deal of perjury and give the criminal unfair chances of escape. However, we are not left to mere inferences of that kind; for contemporaries sometimes speak quite plainly, and condemn the system in the strongest terms. The great Oxford Chancellor Gascoigne [1450] took care to leave on record in his own hand, on the register of his university, that the system was often "an occasion of intolerable iniquity". Chaucer's contemporary, Gower, says equally plainly that the clergy are thus judges in their own cause and each shields the other: "My turn to-day; to-morrow thou shalt do the like for me." The Commons were finally obliged to press the king for fresh and more stringent laws to remedy the notorious fact that "upon trust of the privilege of the Church, divers persons have been the more bold to commit murder, rape, robbery, theft, and other mischievous deeds, because they have been continually admitted to the benefit of the clergy as often as they did offend in any of the [aforesaid]".

To go back, then, to William of Wellington. A few years before the date of his trial we find Edward I sending out a general warning to the Bishop of Worcester, "forbidding him to take the purgation of clerks detained in his prison, whose crimes are notorious; but with regard to others he may take such purgation". Therefore we need not wonder that, since William's crime was notorious to the people of Yelvertoft (for the attack was in fact most brutal and unprovoked), they had taken the law into their own hands and dealt with their priest as though he had not been anointed with oil. Less than a century later, as we have seen, the citizens of London took to this as a regular policy, in spite of Church Law.

However, in spite of the enlistment of the whole population in favour of the King's Peace, even comparatively orderly England showed a proportion of manslaughters which would be considered scandalous in modern times. Impulse played a part so far more important than reflection; and the chances of escape were so great. Attentive readers of Chaucer must have noticed that when Harry Bailey, the Host, confesses himself to be "perilous with knife in hand", and deplores his wife's instigations to fight, he reckons as his possible fate not the gallows, but only outlawry:

I wot well she will do me slay some day
Some neighëbour, and thennë go my way. . . .

The fact is that judicial statistics of the Middle Ages show the murderer to have had many more chances of survival than the convicted thief. The Northumberland Roll of 1279 (to choose a typical instance) gives 72 homicides to only 43 accidental deaths. These 72 deaths were brought home to 83 culprits, of whom only 3 are recorded to have been hanged. Of the remainder, 69 escaped altogether, 6 took sanctuary, 2 were never identified, 1 pleaded his clergy, 1 was imprisoned, and 1 was fined.

We cannot altogether omit the Ordeal, although this was formally abrogated by Innocent III and had been waning in popularity from the Conquest onward, except in cases of trial by battle. The ordinary ordeal was one of the many prehistoric customs finally tolerated, and even blessed, by the Church. There was a solemn ritual for the consecration of the fire or the water, as the case might be. In the water ordeal, the accused who sank was safe; if he floated he was condemned. If the ordeal is that of fire, a red hot iron must be carried three paces; the hand is then sealed up for three days, and if at the end a blister as large as half a walnut is found this is fatal; or, again, another ordeal was to plunge the hand and take out an iron from a cauldron of boiling water. Professor Maitland's comment here is suggestive. "We must, however, not forget the psychology of this system. In itself it may seem the height of absurdity sanctioned by the grossest superstition, but there can be little doubt that in fact the ordeal would be a very effective test in a large number of cases. The man who knew himself to be guilty might very well shrink before it came to the actual point, and make a clean breast of it." For the superstition was two-sided; not only did its psychology fortify justice, but it also weakened the criminal proportionately. Among all the marvellous tales circulated in the Middle Ages—and we must always remember that in those tales the supernatural shows itself equally effectively whether coming from God or from the Devil—there is a considerable number dealing with divine justice upon false swearers. A fisherman, for instance, coming away victorious from the ordeal at Cologne in which he had perjured himself, and being asked whether the hot water had not pained him, dipped his hand over the boatside into the water and answered, "I felt it no more than I feel this." Next moment, he withdrew his hand in agony, for the Rhine water had scalded him! So, again, we may still see a statue in the great church of Abbeville which records the miraculous judgment upon the wife of St Gengulfus, parodied in the *Ingoldsby Legends*. Here the saint, suspecting his wife of infidelity, requested her to pick a stone out of a fountain. There also the cold water scalded her, her sin was proclaimed. In an atmosphere of such stories it must often have needed considerable nerve to face the ordeal at all, and in any case the conscious criminal might show his guilt so clearly in his face, even while he performed the necessary acts, that the priest could safely interpret against him those exceedingly elastic tokens which were supposed to show the judgment of God. It must be noted that the ordeal, though it went out of favour in the middle of our period, was revived in the later Middle Ages for the trial of witches.

Trial by battle was imposed upon the unwilling Anglo-Saxons by their Norman conquerors. This was never so definitely condemned by the Church, even in later times, as other ordeals, and indeed it was not blotted from the English Statute Book until the early nineteenth century. The formalities here, civil and ecclesiastical, were more minute than any other cases. When an "appeal of felony" was made, the accuser and accused must originally fight in person, unless youth or maiming introduced an obviously unfair element. The combatants had to swear solemnly to the truth of their cause, and to having no trust in witchcraft. When it is not a question of felony, but only a dispute for ownership of land, substitutes are allowed, and in fact many great folk kept hired champions. The ordinary weapons were evidently traditional—a shield, a pick something like a small ice-axe, and a leather jacket were allowed. The funeral brass of Wyville, Bishop of Salisbury

(1375) bears the figure of the episcopal champion standing in a fortified gateway, which no doubt represents the bishop's successful contest for the ownership of Sherborne Castle; and we find mention of a similar episcopal champion in the Rolls of Swinfield, a Bishop of Hereford (1320). Such a battle might last all day long "until the stars appear". In a criminal case the conquered combatant was hanged or mutilated off-hand.

Perhaps the greatest superiority of English over Continental justice was the absence of torture from the law-courts. Here one of our most emphatic witnesses is Sir John Fortescue, in his comparison between fifteenth-century England and France on this matter. He writes: "My penne is both wearie and ashamed to rehearse the outragiousness of torments devised in this behalfe. . . . But who is so hard harted, which, being once released out of so cruell a Racke, though he bee innocent and faultlesse, would not yet rather accuse himselfe of all kindes of offences, then againe to commit himself to the intollerable crueltie of the torment once proved: and had not rather die at once (seeing death is the end of all miseries) then so often to bee killed, and to sustaine so many hellish furies, painfuller than death it selfe.'"[10] To this freedom from torture (apart from the *peine forte et dure*) there was only one great exception in all our period. When, in 1311, Philip IV of France desired to destroy the Templars, and made Clement V his unwilling accomplice from beginning to end of that bad business, evidence was easily procured against them in France by means of torture. The prisoners were made to confess things so absurd that no modern historian maintains the particular facts, however he may be tempted to believe, for the sake of king or pope, that there must have been some general truth in the accusations. In England, it was found impossible to obtain condemning evidence. Therefore the Pope wrote to Edward: We hear that you forbid torture as contrary to the laws of your land; but no State law can override Canon Law, Our Law; therefore I command you at once to submit those men to torture. He added a threat: You have already imperilled your soul as a favourer of heretics; and with it a bribe: Withdraw your prohibition, and we grant you remission of your sins.

Therefore we find Edward replying that "through reverence for the Holy See" he will give the Inquisition a free hand in England. There is no record that anything more was needed, and that torture was actually applied to these poor wretches in our own country. If not, it is evident that the mere threat of torture was enough, as it well might be: in any case the evidence needed was somehow obtained, and they were condemned. Thus, whether in practice or merely in threat, torture found its way into the English law courts for the first and almost only time until the reign of Mary.

It will be seen, therefore, that this combined military and police system, which was perfected by the Statute of Winchester, was responsible for many of the advantages which England enjoyed in comparison with her neighbour and rival, France. It secured us safety from invasion. During the whole Hundred Years' War, even during the time when we lost command of the seas, the French never did more than burn one or two of our ports and occupy the Isle of Wight for six months. It rendered a large mercenary army unnecessary. When Charles V's ambassador urged upon him that England might be easy to invade, he instanced that Henry VIII had no soldiers of his own beyond his bodyguard of a hundred archers at the Tower. And we shall see that, when Charles VII of France created an army which was finally able to drive out the English invader, that was only at the cost of fixing upon the French people, until the Revolution of 1789, a mercenary army at the sole control of the executive, fed by irresponsible taxation. It was the London trainbands—that is, the more efficient part of the militia—which enabled the parliament to assert our liberties against Charles's professional army in 1642, and it was the militia again which made it possible for Wellington to hold out through the Napoleonic Wars. In the spring of 1914, I had the privilege of discussing these matters with Albert Thomas, right-hand man to the great socialist and pacifist leader Jean Jaurès. He assured me of the loyalty of all socialists to the system of conscription, excepting only the tiny handful who dreamed of a nation completely unarmed. Some fifteen years later, he came to Cambridge as Secretary of the International Labour Bureau at Geneva. I asked him whether the War had done anything to change his mind on that subject. He replied that, on the contrary, it had reinforced his conviction, not only from the military but even more from the social standpoint. "For", he added, "no democracy can afford to leave its military forces at the sole command of the Executive."

This fusion of military and police control did much for the unity of the nation. It favoured the growth of that "Common Law" which is at the base not only of British justice, but of American also: it was in virtue of the Common Law inherited from us that Abraham Lincoln was able to introduce compulsory manhood service in answer to the South. This co-operation of all classes in England prevented the feudal distinctions from stiffening, as in France, into a rigid caste-system. If, in our parliaments, the knights of the shire sat with the burgesses and not with the greater barons, and the lower clergy also were content to disinterest themselves of all parliamentary business except their own taxation, this was due, at least in a great measure, to the natural co-operation of classes in peace and war. Apart from the clergy with their Canon Law, English Common Law became that of all men; the army and the administrators themselves were bound by it, as well as civilians and subjects; the nobles as well as the commonalty. Here, even in the Middle Ages, was equality in the sense of equal legal standing for all freemen. The law crystallized this as part of the same process by which "blue blood" lost the predominance which it kept in some Continental countries. Our kings had been strong enough to enforce primogeniture among their baronage, and to keep to themselves the right of creating new baronages: thus the younger sons became commoners, and the great lords had to work in co-operation with the other elements of society. Hence the growth of a spirit of reasonable compromise, and, as Maitland pointed out, a tradition of local government which has been of the utmost social value in the position which it has assigned to unpaid and unprofessional work for the State, and in the healthy link which it has maintained between local needs and the central government. The king's writ might not run in medieval England quite as it runs to-day. In the fifteenth-century Chancery Petitions we find an Abbot of Westminster complaining that Roger Power of Bletchington "threatened to make the bringer of the king's writ [in the abbot's favour] eat the same"; and, again, Robert Talbot bringing an action against his adversaries for "disworshipping" the king by compelling the servers of one writ to eat it, "both wax and parchment", and treading another underfoot.[11] But Commines points out, even concerning the Wars of the Roses, how far more orderly the English were in their disorders than the people of France.

So much for State law and justice. Papal law (Canon Law), is too wide a subject for treatment in detail without far more space than the present volume can afford. It has already come in incidentally, and will fill the greater part of Chapter LXVI: therefore, at this point, the briefest summary must suffice. In early Christianity we may say that, as in Islam, Church law was the only law. To St Paul, it was preposterous that brother should go to law with brother, and before unbelievers. With Constantine came in the problem of Church and State. Henceforward we find a series of enactments by which the State undertakes to back up by physical force the regulations which had hitherto reposed only on moral force. Imperial statutes gave to the Church the right of holding property, the protection of sanctuary for her buildings, freedom for the clergy from military service, and, finally, the right of condemnation for heresy, with consequent State punishment for any man thus stigmatized (Theodosian Code, A.D. 438). About 450, the Western Emperor, Valentinian III, granted the Pope power to legislate as chief bishop for the whole Western Church; so that, from thenceforth, papal decretals had the force of law within the religious sphere. At first, Popes made very modest use of this new privilege: the time was not yet ripe. But Justinian's codification of Civil Law (529) supplied the model and impetus for a similar movement in the Church. Thus there gradually grew up collections of decrees—imperial, papal, synodal—affecting the Church as such: a *Jus Canonicum* in imitation of the *Jus Civile*. Such collections claimed both religious and civil sanction: " If you break these laws, you will be damned while I shall be saved; meanwhile the State will empower me to fine you and to appropriate your fine." This inextricable mixture of legalism and theology, especially in the age of the barbarian conversions, has already been noted in Chapter III.

At this point, an epoch-making step was taken by a Roman monk, Dionysius Exiguus. His compilation of conciliar decrees and papal decretals [A.D. 500] was so much completer and more orderly than its predecessors, that it was frequently quoted by Popes, and, thus by Charlemagne's time, had attained to such a semi-official status as publications like *Bradshaw* and *Hansard* enjoy at the present day. Considerable additions were made by different canonists, especially between 1080 and 1120; and then came another epoch-making work, Gratian's *Decretum*. Here, again, the author was an Italian monk, and his work is correctly described in its original title, *The Concordance of Discordant Canons*. The arrangement, with all its defects, was far more orderly than in any of his predecessors; and this book became the first volume of the *Corpus Juris Canonici*: yet it is characteristic of medieval want of method even in the most important matters, that it never was official in the strictest sense. At the same time, it was possible for such a learned friar as the author of *Dives and Pauper* to speak of Gratian's *Decretum* as " the chief book of Law Canon "; and a solemn papal commission of 1582 edited the whole *Corpus* without any distinction between Gratian and the rest, and with a papal brief forbidding any alteration in the Text of Gratian.* The rest of the *Corpus* was formed from later papal decretals, formally enregistered and arranged from 1234 onwards at the command of different Popes, and ending with those of John XXII [1317]. From that time forward the great States were becoming too powerful, and the Papacy too insecure on its political foundation, for a policy so provocative of conflict.

* Compare Professor Imbart de la Tour's criticism in other fields: " The façade of the institutions [of the Dark Ages] was ill fitted to hide the internal anarchy which threatened them." (*Rev. Hist.* LXIII, 23.)

Yet this law, with all its defects, was far completer and clearer and more methodical than that of any of the great States. From the clergy of Europe it exacted full obedience; our loyal English Canon Law stood to the *Corpus Juris Canonici* only in the relation of by-law to Statute law. From the laity it demanded, as it still does in its revised code of 1917, obedience above that of the law of the land in case of conflict. Such claims, however, were frequently resisted by the English laity, even before the anti-papal legislation of Edward III; and the total collapse of Canon Law under Henry VIII is well known. His visitors at Oxford, in the year before the Suppression of the Monasteries, forbade the study of Canon Law as part of the advanced policy which moved them to establish three Greek lectureships, beyond the one which Bishop Fox had already founded at Corpus College.

NOTES

These references are in many cases repeated from my own statements in other books, where fuller vouchers and details are given. Unless otherwise stated, they are published by the Cambridge University Press.

Five Cent[uries of Religion], vols. I-III.
[The] Med[ieval] Vill[age].
Ten Medieval Studies.
Social Life [in Britain from the Conquest to the Reformation].
Life in [the] M[iddle] A[ges], vols. I-IV.
Art and [the] Ref[ormation] (Blackwell, Oxford).
Chaucer and his England (Methuen).
[From] St F[rancis] to D[ante] (Duckworth).
Rom[anism] and Truth, 2 vols. (Faith Press, Leighton Buzzard).

The following abbreviations are used:

C.P.L. Calendar of Papal Letters.
E.E.T.S. Early English Text Society.
P.L. Migne, *Patrologia Latina.*
R.S. Rolls Series.
S.S. Surtees Society.

CHAPTER 1 (pp. 17-29)

(1) M. Rostovzef, *Storia Economica e Sociale del Imperio Romano* (1933), 588. (2) *P.L.* LXXVI. 1009 (Bk II, hom. vi). (3) Rostovzef, 591. (4) *Hist. Eccl.* Bk IV, c. 13.

CHAPTER 2 (pp. 30-44)

(1) See M. P. Charlesworth, *The Virtues of a Roman Emperor* (Clarendon Press, 1937). (2) *P.L.* LIX. 42 (1). (3) *Register* of Greg. I, Bk III, letter 61. (4) *Liber de Antiquis Legibus* (1863), 34. (5) Stubbs, *Const. Hist.* I. 135. (6) *Decret. Greg.* Lib. I, tit. vi, c. 22. (7) *Sext. Decret.* Lib. I, tit. vi, c. 9.

CHAPTER 3 (pp. 45-56)

(1) Bede, *Hist. Eccl.* Bk III, c. 25. (2) Readers interested in this subject should consult Bishop G. F. Browne's *Importance of Women in Anglo-Saxon England,* 60ff., and F. H. Thurston's *No Popery,* 147ff., where Browne is corrected on several important points, though others are left unanswered. (3) Lavisse and Rambaud, *Hist. Générale,* I. 296. (4) *P.L.* LXXXIX. 702 (Ep. XII). (5) *Ibid.* 811, 813. Here, for instance, are extracts from Boniface's letter to Pope Zacharias in 742 (Migne, *P.L.* LXXXIX. 746): "Carloman, chief of the Franks, has summoned me and asked me to convoke a synod in that part of the Frankish realm which is in his power. . . . For the Franks, as the elders say, have held no synod for more than 80 years, nor had any archbishop, nor have founded or renewed canonical laws for the Church. Nowadays, among the majority of the cities, the episcopal sees have been given over to the possession of greedy layfolk or adulterine clerks, fornicators and publicans, who enjoy them in secular fashion. . . . If, among these, I find deacons, as they are called, who from their boyhood onward have been always in fornication and adultery, leading their lives continually in all uncleanness, who have come to the diaconate by that token and who now, within the diaconate, keep in their bed four or five concubines or more, yet neither blush nor fear to call themselves deacons and to read the Gospel [at Mass], and who, coming thus in such unchastity to the order of priesthood, persisting in the same sins and adding sin to sin, perform the priestly office and claim the power of interceding for the people, and offering the holy oblations; and in these latest days (what is worse) by the same token they rise from step to step and are ordained and created bishops —if (I say) I find such men among them, I beseech [your Holiness] that I may have your precept and your written authority in judgment upon such things, that the sinners may be convinced and rebuked by your Apostolic answer. Moreover, bishops are found among them who, though they say that they are no fornicators or adulterers, are yet drunken and quarrelsome, or hunters, and men who fight under arms in battle, and shed men's blood with their own hands, whether of heathens or of Christians." (6) See Addis and Arnold, *Catholic Dictionary* (10th ed. revised), 554, and Hefele, *Beiträge.* I have summed up the discussion on this subject on pp. 25ff. of the 20th of my *Medieval Studies* (6*d*.). (7) *P.L.* LXXXIX. 526. (8) *Ibid.* 761. (9) *Ibid.* 951. (10) *Ibid.* 946. (11) *Ibid.* 768. (12) *Register,* Bk II, letter 51; this country was probably Dalmatia.

CHAPTER 4 (pp. 57-70)

(1) Pollock and Maitland, *Hist. Eng. Law* (2nd ed.) I. 67. (2) *Camb. Med. Hist.* II. 647. (3) Lavisse and Rambaud, *Hist. Générale,* II, 48. (4) H. Pirenne, *Econom. and Soc. Hist. of Med. Europe,* 202.

CHAPTER 5 (pp. 71-82)

(1) *De Gestis Regum* (R.S.), II. 304. (2) Stubbs, *Select Charters* (1890), 201 (Bk x, ch. 10). (3) Ed. Lumby (R.S.), II. 165.

CHAPTER 6 (pp. 83-95)

(1) *Documents* (ed. H. Philpott, 1861), 2. (2) *Norfolk Archaeology,* XX. 179; *History Teachers' Miscellany,* I. 165. (3) Wilkins, *Concilia,* I. 287.

CHAPTER 7 (pp. 96-109)

(1) Froissart (Globe ed.), 251. (2) *Babees Book* (E.E.T.S.), introd. xlvi. (3) W. J. Ashley, *Economic History,* vol. I, pt ii, 333. (4) *Miracles of K. Hen. VI* (ed. R. A. Knox and Shane Leslie, 1923), 131. (5) *Eynsham Cartulary* (Oxford Hist. Soc.), II. introd. xx. (6) *Piers Plowman,* B, Prol. 103; II. 93, 95; VI. 107; C, VI. 9. (7) *First Sermon before Ed. VI.* (8) This has been conclusively proved by Mr Geoffrey Baskerville, in his *English Monks and the Suppression of the Monasteries* (Cape, 1937), which for the first time utilizes the vast mass of material among the public records. (9) *Predigten* (ed. F. Pfeiffer), I. 478.

CHAPTER 8 (pp. 110-121)

(1) F. Curschmann, *Hungersnöte im Mittelalter* (Leipzig, 1900), 9, 20, 25-6, 49, 52. (2) *Social Life,* 472. (3) *Five Cent.* I. Appendix XXIII. (4) *Lanercost Chronicle,* 109. (5) *Exempla* (ed. Crane, 1878), 131. (6) *Life in M.A.* I. 90. (7) G. L. Kittredge, in the preface to F. J. Child and H. C. Sargent, *English and Scottish Popular Ballads* (Boston, 1904), p. xviii. There is an interesting article on notices of sport in the Kingston parish accounts in the *Journal of British Master Glass-Painters* for Oct. 1935.

CHAPTER 9 (pp. 122-140)

(1) *Modern Language Review*, Jan. 1907. (2) *P.L.* CIV. 158. (3) *P.L.* CIV. 214; CV. 161; R. L. Poole, *Illust. Hist. Med. Thoughts* (1920), 29. Cardinal Gasquet (*Eve of Ref.* (1900), 303) quotes liberally from *Dives and Pauper* to prove the falsity of the Reformers' belief that "the Church had given occasion to wrong ideas of worship in the minds of the common people, and that the reverence shown to the symbol of our redemption [i.e. the *Cross*] on that occasion [Good Friday] amounted practically to idolatry". He takes the liberty of omitting a passage, *from the same pages of the book from which he quotes*, which gives the lie direct to his apologetics. For the author of *Dives and Pauper* writes, concerning the statutory Church ceremonies relating to the Cross: "And this blyndeth moche people in their redynge [*interpretation*] For they meane [*think*] that al the prayers that holy church maketh to the crosse, that she maketh them to the tre [*wood*] that Christ died on, or els to the crosse in the church, as in that anteme *O crux splendidior.* And so for leudnes [*ignorance*] they ben deceyued, and worshypp creatures as god himself" (Com. 1, c. 4 (ed. Berthelet), f. 15 v°). The Cardinal's quotations from *Dives and Pauper* in his *Parish Life in England* are also very inaccurate. (4) *P.L.* CXLII. 675. (5) *Lives of the Brethren* (translated by Fr J. P. Conway, O.P. 1896), 290. From the recollections of Blessed Cecilia, a Roman nun who had been clothed by St Dominic himself. The saint came one night to her convent in Rome and preached to the sisters from behind the grille. He warned them against the different shapes taken by devils to deceive the elect. "The venerable father had scarcely said the word ere the enemy of mankind came on the scene in the shape of a sparrow, and began to fly through the air, and hopping even on the Sisters' heads, so that they could have handled him had they been so minded, and all this to hinder the preaching. S. Dominic, observing this, called Sister Maximilla, and said: 'Get up and catch him and fetch him here to me.' She got up and, putting out her hand, had no difficulty in seizing hold of him, and handed him out through the window to S. Dominic. S. Dominic held him fast in one hand and commenced plucking off the feathers with the other, saying the while: 'You wretch, you rogue!' When he had plucked him clean of all his feathers amid much laughter from the Brothers and Sisters, and awful shrieks of the sparrow, he pitched him out, saying: 'Fly now if you can, enemy of mankind.' 'You can cry out and trouble us, but you can't hurt us!' . . . And so it came about that he employed for God's glory what the enemy of mankind had from envy done for their hurt and hindrance. The sparrow which flew in that night disappeared, and no one saw whither he went." (6) *L'Église et la Pitié envers les*

Animaux, par la Marquise de Rambures (Paris, Lecoffre; London, Burns and Oates, 1903). (7) *Alphabet of Tales* (E.E.T.S.), 71. (8) See *Five Cent.* I. 107ff. and Appendix XI. (9) *Ibid.* 112ff. (10) *Depositions of Durham* (S.S. 1845), 27. (11) *Calendar of Chancery Petitions,* I. 103, 111, 112, 173. (12) Surtees Society, 1890, 343. (13) See especially pp. 416, 464-5, 506, 540, 549.

CHAPTER 10 (pp. 141-160)

(1) *Élections Épiscopales,* 135. (2) *Hist. Dunelm. Scriptores Tres* (S.S.), 118. (3) A. L. Smith, *Church and State in the M.A.* 18-19. (4) Eadmer, *Vita Anselmi,* Lib. I, c. v, 37. (5) R. W. Church, *St Anselm,* 92-3. (6) Grandisson, *Register,* 586. (7) *Ibid.* 1027. (8) *Piers Plowman,* B, XV. 537; C, XVIII. 260. (9) *Register,* 979. (10) *Gemma Ecclesiastica* (R.S.), II. 325. (11) *Mat. Hist. Thos Becket* (R.S.), VII. 20, 59; cf. III. 44. (12) Ep. 166 (*P.L.* CXCIX. 156).

CHAPTER 11 (pp. 161-165)

(1) The vouchers for all statements in this chapter may be found in the second volume of my *Five Centuries of Religion,* and in Dr R. A. R. Hartridge's *History of Vicarages in the Middle Ages* (C.U. Press, 1930). (2) *Reg. Wykeham,* I. 361ff.

CHAPTER 12 (pp. 166-179)

(1) Rashdall's *Universities* (1st ed.), 701, 704. (2) *Opera* (R.S.), III. 234, 368. (3) Wilkins, *Concilia* (1st ed.), II. 150. (4) E.g. C.P.L. v. 179, 258, 528; VI, *passim.* (5) More's *English Works* (1557), 328; cf. *Reg. Rad. de Salopia* (Somerset Record Soc.), 131; *Reg. Stapeldon,* 179. (6) *Opera* (1703), v. 808; P. S. Allen, *Selections from Erasmus,* 17. (7) *Prologue* to *Vox Clamantis,* Bk, I, l. II; *Mirour de l'Omme,* l. 18,445. (8) *Mirour,* ll. 18,752ff. (9) *Ibid.* l. 20,545. (10) *Ibid.* l. 20,137. (11) *Ibid.* l. 20,861. (12) *Ibid.* ll. 21,113ff. (13) *Vox Clamantis,* Bk IV, ll. 551ff. (14) *Piers Plowman,* B, XIX. 439; XX. 278ff. (15) G. Mollat, *Les Papes d'Avignon* (1912), 234.

CHAPTER 13 (pp. 180-193)

(1) *Decret. Greg.* Lib. III, tit. v, c. 15; cf. c. 5. (2) A. L. Smith, *Church and State in the M.A.* 8. (3) *Reg. Romeyn* (S.S.), I. 91.

(4) *Cal. Chancery Proceedings*, I. 149, 166. (5) Wilkins, *Concilia* (1st ed.), I. 586, 589, 669ff., 693, 704. (6) *Ep. ad Ecgbertum*, § 3. (7) Tyndale's *Answer to More* (Parker Soc. 1850), 75. (8) *Opera* (R.S.), I. 90; II. 341-6. (9) *St Osmund's Register* (R.S.), I. 304ff. (10) More's *English Works* (1557), 561. (11) *Instructions for Parish Priests* (E.E.T.S.), 10. (12) *Rev. Hist.* LXIII (1897), 22-3; LXVII. 12; LXVIII. 23-47. (13) *Times Lit. Sup.* (Dec. 28, 1935), 892. (14) Gasquet, *Parish Life in Med. Eng.* 20; Crump and Jacob, *Legacy of the M.A.* 33. (15) *Instructions for Parish Priests* (E.E.T.S.), 24. (16) *Reg. Romeyn* (S.S.), I. 106. (17) *York Fabric Rolls* (S.S.), 263. (18) Wilkins, *Concilia* (1st ed.), II. 160. (19) Pollock and Maitland, *Hist. Eng. Law*, I. 356; Holdsworth, III. 535. (20) *Hist. Ag. Prices*, I. 683. (21) *Trans. Royal Hist. Soc.* (3rd series), VI. 115. (22) Wilkins, *Concilia* (1st ed.), II. 697. (23) Hartridge, *Vicarages*, 159-61. (24) C. R. Haines, *Dover Priory*, 421, 443, 451. (25) *Oxford Archaeol. Soc. Report*, 1925. (26) *Dives and Pauper*, Com. v, c. 8.

CHAPTER 14 (pp. 199-207)

(1) A certain school of journalist-historians is adopting nowadays the policy of attempting to laugh Lea out of court as an inaccurate and bigoted compiler. This gains some plausibility from the multiplicity and startling nature of his facts, which lend colour to the charge of exaggeration, and from the unfavourable light they cast upon the Roman Church of the Middle Ages, thus suggesting the suspicion of religious prejudice. Yet Lord Acton, the most learned of modern British historians, who claimed that his Roman Catholic faith was dearer to him than his life, testified to Lea's accuracy and general impartiality, with a warmth and expansiveness which he seldom showed to any book, in *The English Historical Review*. The misrepresentation has lately taken such proportions (especially in the third and fourth volumes of the co-operative *History of European Civilization* edited by Mr E. Eyre and sold, though not controlled, by the Oxford University Press) that I have dealt with it in a separate monograph, under the title of *Sectarian History* (72 Kimberley Road, Cambridge, 2*s*. 6*d*. post-free). It is evident that two of the contributors to that history, undertaking to correct Lea on a crucial point of religious history, had not even read the first page of the document to which they professedly appeal. The fact is that Lea's bulky work has never been corrected except on an almost negligible minority of details; and, if he had lived twice as long and been able to read twice as much, he could have doubled the mass of his already overwhelming evidence. (2) A. L. Smith, *Church and State in M.A.* 13. (3) *Ten Medieval Studies*, 141-6. (4) *E.H.R.* XLIV. 444-5, 451, 453; XLV. 93-4, 100, 447, 458. (5) The greatest

evidential force of these visitations lies in their cumulative effect, so long as we do not forget to discount them as we discount all evidence from police reports. I therefore add here a selection of details omitted from my text lest they should be wearisome, yet necessary for any full comprehension of parish life in a rather wild district. (A) The visitors report as follows upon *Clunbury*. The parishioners say that Sir Edward, chaplain [in modern parlance, *curate*] of the parish, doth not serve the parishioners duly, as he should; nay, rather, he stirreth quarrels and contentions among the parishioners, and doth other detestable things, to the scandal of the church. *Item,* that the said Sir Edward was called upon to administer extreme unction to Richard Crowe on his deathbed; yet he expressly refused to do this, and thus the said Richard died without that sacrament by default of the said chaplain. *Item,* that the said Sir Edward absented himself from the church on the feast of Corpus Christi, so that the parishioners had no divine service, by default of the said Sir Edward. *Item,* that William, son of John Phyppes, lately deceased, was buried without Mass and burial service, by default of the said chaplain. *Item,* William Webbe's son was buried without Mass and service, as above. *Item,* that Sir Edward refused to receive to her purification Maiota, wife to John Crowe [*corner of leaf torn off*] unless she would offer [a fee] at his will. *Item* the said Sir Edward is incontinent with Alice, daughter of Thomas Eynones, and even baptized his own son begotten on her, and afterwards knew her carnally and begat on her another child [*corner torn off*]. Byllyng obtained letters from the lord archbishop of Canterbury and the lord bishop of Hereford containing an indulgence for benefactors of the bridge of Parsloe, in virtue whereof he collected in [these] parts 20*s*., which he spendeth to his own uses, paying nought for the repair of the said bridge [*torn corner*] common usurer. [*Torn corner*] is a common usurer. *Item,* that the prior of Wenlock refuseth to have the cure of souls here, saying that this pertaineth to the vicar, wherefore he saith he himself hath no cure of souls there. *Item,* that the vicar is bound to find a deacon to serve in the Church, which he doth not. *Item,* that the rector [i.e. the prior and convent of Wenlock] is bound to find a set of vestments for ordinary days. *Item,* that the rector is bound to find an ordinal-book, and doth not. *Item,* that Richard Davys of Churton is a common worker on Sundays and holy-days [*added in another hand:* "He was dismissed."]. (B) *Selections from other parishes.* At Kilpeck (p. 287) "Sir John, their chaplain of the place, haunteth the taverns and chattereth indecently there, to the great scandal etc. [*sic*]. *Item,* he is incontinent with one Margaret, surname unknown." At the next village of Garwy "the sidesmen say that Sir Thomas Folyot haunteth taverns inordinately and excessively, to the great scandal of the clergy, and that he revealed publicly the confessions of Robert Scheppert his parishioner. . . . Richard, the chaplain, is unfit for cure of souls there, for he knoweth not the Welsh tongue, and many parishioners there know no English ". In another village, the priest had celebrated a clandestine marriage for 12*d.* (444) and the parishioners report two other clandestine marriages. The servant of another kept a tavern in the rectory (445). Of another it is reported " he merchandizeth, to wit, buyeth and selleth divers goods to get gain thereby " (446). Another " refused burial to Jane, daughter of Davy Godemon, without just cause, and left her body unburied " (447). At another parish " the rector resideth not, and they know not where he dwelleth; otherwise all is well there " (447). At another (448) the outgoing curate " carried off with him from the church two silk chasubles, one red and one white, with a new surplice, to the grievous damage of the parishioners ". Another had forged a will (449). Another " came, vested in his surplice, as is customary, with bell and lantern, to visit a certain Alice Clerke at the point of death, with an empty pyx, without the Body of Christ, to the great scandal [of the parish], causing the people to adore the Sacrament where it was not " (449). In that same parish " R. R. smote one J. S. violently with his fist in church, before the high altar. . . . Moreover noon was sometimes past before Mass was finished on Sundays and holy-days "; one priest had refused to purify a parishioner and the vicar " absenteth himself from his post, notwithstanding his oath " (449-50). Another (450) " is drunken and continually frequenteth the taverns, against clerical decency, nor doth he duly perform divine service ". At Dymock, " The rector is bound by ancient custom to distribute weekly to the poor two bushels of mixed rye and wheat, which hath now been withdrawn for 20 years and more. . . . Richard Stokke, lately promoted to Holy Orders, keepeth a certain Isabel Llarau, with whom he hath contracted (as he asserts) before such ordination, but the marriage was not yet celebrated between them " (453). Another priest extorted money from his parishioners for giving them Holy Communion (99). At Leominster, one priest is (99) " a common trader in beasts and sheep, buying and selling for profit, and partner in the gain accruing in the parish from baggers "; so also is another; a third is incontinent and a fourth haunts taverns " and other indecent [*inhonesta*] places ". Another " threatens those parishioners who are in the bishop's service for the reporting of the transgressions and defaults of delinquents [i.e. the sidesmen] because they reported his transgressions ". Another (445) receives 7 marks a year as chantry chaplain for the late vicar's soul, and breaks the oath which binds him to celebrate duly. At Staunton Lacy (432) the priest is " a common trader ". (6) *Reg. Stapeldon,* 107, 133; *Reg. Grandisson,* 570.

CHAPTER 15 (pp. 208-217)

(1) Wadding, *Annales Minorum,* an. 1242, § 17. (2) *Catholic Dictionary* (Addis and Arnold, 1885), 782a. (3) The story has

been told by the Bollandist Fr H. Delehaye with his usual exhaustive learning (Acad. Royale de Bruxelles, *Bulletin, Classe des Lettres* (1899), 171). A summary by Fr H. Thurston, S.J., with useful further information as to English conditions, may be found in *The Nineteenth Century* for July 1899. Fr Thurston writes concerning Innocent III's patronage of this epistle: "There is not the least foundation for such a statement, and as a matter of fact the fabrication was one of very ancient date, which may be traced back to the time of Licinianus, Bishop of Carthagena at the end of the sixth century." But Fr Delehaye, who has traced the letter in all its ramifications, permits himself no such scepticism: and, after all, Eustache's mission happened in the lifetime of both Wendover and Matthew Paris. The fact that nobody now believes Christ to have written this letter is no proof that Innocent did not believe it, as these two first-rate chroniclers apparently did. The astounding vogue of this almost incredible forgery for a thousand years, in spite of papal and conciliar repudiation in its earlier stages, is traced very fully by Fr Delehaye, but not sufficiently in *The Nineteenth Century*. (4) Blomefield's *Norfolk*, IX. 276. (5) *Provinciale*, 56-7. (6) *Depositions etc. of Durham* (S.S. 1845), 26ff. (7) *Dives and Pauper*, Com. IV, c. 11. (8) D. Hay Fleming, *Influence of the Reformation*, 28.

CHAPTER 16 (pp. 218-228)

(1) *The Knight of La Tour Landry* (E.E.T.S), 41-2. (2) *Dives and Pauper*, Com. I, c. 51 *ad fin.* (3) *Lay Folks' Mass-Book* (E.E.T.S. 1879), introd. xxvii. Compare p. 158, where the editor prints a conversation recorded from 1527 between the future Queen Mary of Scotland, then thirteen years old, and her chaplain (*aumônier*), Giles de Guez, who taught her French.

"M. I have good memory, maistre Amnere, how ye sayd one day that we ought not to pray at Masse, but rather onely to here and harken . . .

G. Ye, verely, madame . . .

M. In my God, I can not se what we shall do at the Masse, if we pray not.

G. Ye shall thynke to the mystery of the Masse and shall herken the wordes that the preest say.

M. Yee, and what shall do they which understande it not?

G. They shall beholde, and shall here, and thynke, and by that they shall understande."

Similarly we find, in the unusually enlightened and broad-minded *Dives and Pauper*: "every prayer that is made to the worship of God by way of charity and for a good end with purpose to please God, that prayer is made with devotion, though he that prayeth be distracte and thinketh not on his words, and peradventure understandeth them not, ne hath but little liking therein." *Charity* has here its frequent sense of "love towards God", which, in the later Middle Ages, practically became "Church orthodoxy". (4) In the new edition of Rashdall's *Universities of Europe,* the editor of vol. III has added a note which ignores essential qualifications in that great scholar's judgment on this point, and which throws doubt upon it without adequate rebutting evidence. (5) *Dives and Pauper,* Com. v, c. 10. (6) *Prediche Volgari,* I. 66. (7) De la Bigne, *Max. Bib. Patrum,* xxv, Lib. II, cc. 83 and 86. (8) *Preaching in Med. Eng.* 169, 173. (9) *Summa Major,* pars III, tit. 2, c. 4, § 13. (10) *Opera* (1745), I. 83; *Five Cent.* II. 595. (11) *Dives and Pauper,* Com. I, ch. 46. (12) *Exempla* (ed. Crane), 112. (13) Froissart (Globe ed.), 60, 209, 392ff., 439, 460.

CHAPTER 17 (pp. 229-239)

(1) Brit Mus. MS. Arundel 285, f. 165b. (2) I quote here from my translation into modern English (Methuen). (3) G. de Lagarde, *Naissance de l'esprit laïque,* II. 240, note. (4) *Med. Vill.* 262. (5) *Speculum* (July 1936).

CHAPTER 18 (pp. 240-256)

(1) On the whole, the best English essay on this subject is probably that of R. W. Church, which has been reprinted in more than one cheap edition. Very valuable also is Professor E. G. Gardner's little primer, *Dante* (Dent, 1900).

CHAPTER 19 (pp. 257-269)

(1) Radulfus Niger (ed. Anstruther), 169. (2) *Ep.* XIV (*Life in M.A.* III. 2).

CHAPTER 20 (pp. 270-283)

(1) This is printed in *Chivalry.* A series of studies to illustrate its historical significance and civilizing influence. By members of King's College, London. Edited by Professor Edgar Prestage (Kegan Paul, Trench, Trubner and Co. 1928). The most elaborate book from the conservative and sympathetic side is Léon Gautier, *La Chevalerie* (Nouvelle Édition, Dentu; 850 pp. n.d.). (2) Ed. 1846, pp. 31,

105. (3) A. Abram, *Eng. Life and Manners in the Later M.A.* 99. (4) Froissart (Globe ed.), 198. (5) *Blonde of Oxford* (Camden Soc.), 14. (6) *English Association Tract*, no. 51 (1892). (7) A. Abram, *l.c.* 1; cf. 162, 188, 204, 231-2, 284. (8) *Sir Gawayne and the Green Knight* (E.E.T.S.), ll. 915ff. (9) *English Association Tract*, no. 51, p. 14. (10) *Petri Blesensis Epistolae*, no. xciv. (11) A. Abram, *l.c.* 140. (12) A. S. Green, *Town Life in the Fifteenth Century*, I. 261. (13) Froissart (Globe ed.), 349; cf. 104, 126, 198, 380.

CHAPTER 21 (pp. 284-295)

(1) *Times Lit. Supp.* (Aug. 19th, 1926). (2) Froissart (Globe ed.), 201. (3) M. Arnold, *Discourses in America*, 141; J. H. Newman, *Par. and Plain Sermons*, VI. 25. (4) The best studies on Malory are those of E. Vinaver, *Malory*, and E. Hicks, *Sir Thomas Malory.*

CHAPTER 22 (pp. 296-308)

(1) Cf. A. Harnack, *Das Mönchtum* (Giessen, 1903). (2) L. Duchesne, *Hist. ancienne de l'Église*, II. 491. (3) *Ibid.* 493. Cf. Martène, *Comment. in Regulam S.B.* (1690), 816; *Hist. Lausiaca*, c. 7; More's *English Works*, 227. (4) *P.L.* XVI. 1168 (*Ep.* XLI, § 27); Duchesne, *Hist. ancienne de l'Église*, II. 521. (5) A. Savine, *English Monasteries on the Eve of the Dissolution*, 87. (6) *Ibid.* 266.

CHAPTER 23 (pp. 309-322)

(1) *Piers Plowman*, B, xx. 60; *Ten Medieval Studies*, 172, corrected by 179-80. (2) *Dives and Pauper*, Com. VII, c. 12. (3) *P.L.* CLXXVI. 949ff.; *St F. to D.* (2nd ed.), 65ff., 367-8.

CHAPTER 24 (pp. 323-341)

(1) In this connection we may note that the Lord Mayor of London was elected or sworn in on the Feast of Saints Simon and Jude, October 28th, and that the same feast was of similar significance at Paris. In 1262 St Louis ordained that all the "communes" of the Ile de France and Normandy should present their accounts on November 16th, but that the mayors should be sworn in on October 29th.

CHAPTER 25 (pp. 342-359)

(1) *Social Life*, 373. (2) E. L. Cutts, *Scenes and Characters of the M.A.* 508ff. (from *Rotuli Parliamentorum*, I. 228). (3) *Social Life*, 324. (4) *Epistolae* (ed. Allen), v. 613; *Letters and Papers*, IV, ii, 1090; compare P. S. Allen, *Age of Erasmus*, chap. xxv. (5) *Babees Book* (E.E.T.S.), introd. lxv. (6) *Ibid.* introd. lxiii. (7) *Social Life*, 314. (8) *Ibid.* 329. (9) *Babees Book*, introd. (10) E. L. Cutts, *Scenes etc.* 509. (11) *Art and Ref.* 116. (12) *Œuvres de Montaigne* (ed. Buchon), 646. (13) *Book of Husbandry* (ed. Skeat), 101. (14) *Social Life*, 383. (15) *Cal. Early Chancery Proc.* II (1903), 163. (16) A. Abram, *Engl. Life and Manners in the Later M.A.* 130ff. (17) *Ibid.* 132.

CHAPTER 26 (pp. 360-374)

(1) *Life of St Godric* (S.S. 1847). (2) R. Beazley, *Dawn of Med. Geography*, II. 460. (3) Eileen Power and M. M. Postan, *English Trade in the Fifteenth Century* (1933). (4) *Social Life*, 427. (5) *Ibid.* 420. (6) *Ibid.* 422. (7) Froissart (Globe ed.), 83. (8) For full text see *Social Life*, 427ff.

CHAPTER 27 (pp. 375-390)

(1) Much of this chapter is transcribed from a paper which I read before the Historical Association at Cambridge in 1921, and which evoked no contradiction of fact. It was printed in *History* for July of that year. (2) *History* (July 1921), 63. (3) *Summa Theol.* 2*a*, 2*ae*, LXXVII. 4. (4) On this point there is an extraordinary misstatement in Dr G. O'Brien's essay on *Medieval Economic Teaching* (p. 122). He writes: "In the fourteenth and fifteenth centuries there is little to be found [in the theorists] bearing on the subject [of the Fair Price]. . . . The reason for this paucity of authority upon a subject of so much importance is that . . . the proper remuneration of labour was so universally recognised as a duty, and so satisfactorily enforced, that it seems to have been taken for granted, and therefore passed over, by the writers of the period." It would be difficult to find a plainer instance of the danger of studying *theory* alone (for Dr O'Brien frankly confesses that limitation in his preface) and of deducing from such one-sided evidence all sorts of wider inferences as to actual *practice*. (5) Crump and Jacob, *Legacy of the M.A.* 343 (by Prof. Gabriel le Bras, Strasbourg). (6) *Chron. Major* (R.S.),

v. 465 (A.D. 1253). (7) *Ibid.* III. 188-9. (8) Oxenedes, *Chron.* (R.S.), 168, 197. (9) *Social Life*, 345. (10) *Chaucer and his England*, 194. (11) *Comentum* (ed. Lacaita), I. 579; *Social Life*, 342. (12) *Cal. Early Chancery Proc.* II (1903), 109. (13) *Rôle des monastères comme établissements de crédit* (1901), 56-69.

CHAPTER 28 (pp. 391-402)

(1) *Jewish Encyclopaedia*, V. 161ff. (2) *Hist. Eng. Law* (1895), I. 451. (3) *Jew. Encyc.* V. 164. (4) *Ibid.* 162. (5) *Ibid.* 166. (6) *Ibid.* 166. (7) Will. Malmesbury, *Chronicle*, Bk IV, c. I. (8) *Jew. Encyc.* V. 162. (9) *Summa Theol.* 2a, 2ae, q. x, art. x, conclusion. (10) *Hist. Eng. Law*, I. 456. (11) *Ibid.* II. 391. (12) Cooper, *Annals of Cambridge*, I. 27. (13) *Ibid.* I. 44. (14) *Jew. Encyc.* V. 165-6. (15) *Hist. Eng. Law*, I. 453.

CHAPTER 29 (pp. 403-412)

(1) Stubbs, *Select Charters*, 385. (2) *Chron. Major* (R.S.), III. 332. (3) L. F. A. Berliner, *Jewish Self-Government in the M.A.* 217. (4) *Chronicon* (ed. Hearne), II. 367. (5) Knighton (R.S.), I. 157. For the whole subject of chapters XXVIII and XXIX see a recent paper by Dr Cecil Roth, *The Challenge to Jewish History* (The Jewish Hist. Soc. of England, Univ. Coll. London, 1936-7).

CHAPTER 30 (pp. 413-433)

(1) *Feudal Monarchy in France and England*, 137. (2) *Hist. Eng. Law* (1895), I. 112. Since these words have been pressed into the theory that we owe our Common Law rather to the Church than to our kings, it is well to note how entirely Bishop Stubbs agrees with Petit-Dutaillis (and, it may be added, with medieval chroniclers themselves) in regarding Henry II as the main initiator, and giving similar credit to other sovereigns. Stubbs writes (*Lectures on Medieval and Modern History* (1886), 210): "We all know how enormous is the debt which English law owes to the great legislators of the twelfth, thirteenth, and fourteenth centuries; Henry II and Edward I are, both of them, conspicuous examples of both the tendencies which I have coupled under the term; in their better actions defenders of the law, in their worse actions captious defenders of their right. The same is approximately true in other countries; Lewis IX is not only the great legislator of France, but almost the single example of the period, in which the more powerful sovereign grants to his competitor, even in the hour of his

utmost weakness, the full extent of his legal right; the treatment of Henry III by S. Lewis is a very striking example of the respect for rights that do not happen to be your own. As to generalities, I need only remark that the names of Frederick II and Alfonso the Wise stand by those of Edward and Lewis as the founders of the non-Roman jurisprudence of Europe; and that in Germany in the fourteenth century the two great legislators are the two champions of the rival houses, Lewis of Bavaria on the one side, and Charles the IV on the other; the codification of Bavarian law and the issue of the Golden Bull were at all events attempts in the direction of civilisation in accordance with the highest existing ideal." (3) Hudson-Tingey, *Records of the City of Norwich,* I. 357. (4) *Ibid.* introd. cxxxviii. (5) *Ibid.* introd. cxxxix. (6) *Med. Vill.* 342. (7) *Chaucer and his England,* 235. (8) *Jeunesse de B. du Guesclin* (1882), 158. (9) *Chaucer and his England*, 284. (10) J. Fortescue, *De Laudibus* (1616), 46; *Social Life*, 518. (11) *Cal. Early Chancery Petitions,* I. 261; cf. 197.

INDEX

NOTE: *a complete index to both volumes will be found at the end of volume II.*